The Black Chicago Renaissance

The
Black Chicago

THE NEW BLACK STUDIES SERIES

Edited by Darlene Clark Hine
and Dwight A. McBride

*A list of books in the series appears
at the end of this book.*

Renaissance

Edited by **DARLENE CLARK HINE** and **JOHN McCLUSKEY JR.**

MARSHANDA A. SMITH, Managing Editor

UNIVERSITY OF ILLINOIS PRESS

Urbana, Chicago, and Springfield

Library of Congress Cataloging-in-Publication Data
The Black Chicago Renaissance / Edited by
Darlene Clark Hine and John McCluskey Jr.
pages cm—(The New Black Studies Series)
ISBN 978-0-252-03702-3 (hardback)
ISBN 978-0-252-07858-3 (paper)
1. African American arts—Illinois—Chicago—20th century.
2. African Americans—Illinois—Chicago—Intellectual life—
20th century. 3. Arts and society—Illinois—Chicago—History—
20th century. 4. Chicago (Ill.)—Intellectual life—20th century.
I. Hine, Darlene Clark, editor of compilation. II. McCluskey, John,
editor of compilation.
NX512.3.A35B595   2012
700.89'96073077311—dc23   2012014384

Contents

In Memory of Dr. Murry N. DePillars
(December 21, 1938–May 31, 2008)

Dedication

Murry N. DePillars made a unique contribution to
this volume. Dr. DePillars historicizes both artistic creations and the shapers of the Black Chicago
Renaissance in ways that differ from those of several
writers in the volume. Rejecting the more common 1932–50 period as defining the Black Chicago
Renaissance, DePillars identified two waves or cycles
that shaped the contributions of visual artists to the
Black Chicago Renaissance, 1914–41 and 1941–60.
The question of periodization will continue, especially the precise beginning and end points, as it will
in defining any "renaissance" anywhere. However,
Dr. DePillars supports his claims by introducing a
comprehensive roster of African American artists
who were born, lived, or studied in Chicago. In form
and intent, his essay approaches the encyclopedic.

Murry DePillars limits his theorizing about a
"Chicago School" of African American visual art.
Rather he introduces contemporary readers and
scholars to those artists who were recognized
nationally and internationally during the first half
of the twentieth century for their talent and commitment to representing black people as they lived
their specific realities. With equal verve and insight,
DePillars introduces those who have been dismissed,
neglected, or forgotten by art and cultural historians.
John McCluskey's several marathon-length conversations with DePillars demonstrate clearly DePillars's
capability of writing a distinguished book-length
work, or two, on this period had he chosen to do so.
DePillars's essay highlights the works of individual
artists and the political and social contexts of their
compositions. He was determined, as he often said,
to "shake the trees" for others to help gather the
fruit for closer individual examinations in the future.
And shake he did! We dedicate this anthology to the
memory of friend, collaborator, and inspiration Dr.
Murry N. DePillars.

Tucked away in the footnotes
of jazz history, [Lil] was an afterthought
to the life of her husband, Louis Armstrong
—JAMES DICKERSON

Let's Call It Love

J. M. MAHLUM[1]

I: *"Just for a thrill, you changed the sunshine to rain"*

The blue sounds of Memphis—

the bent chords and flattened
thirds, fifths, and sevenths;
the robust riffs that sway the night into
     night caps
     cigarettes &
     negligence

—ease past W. C. Handy's house,
     "Father of Blues" and "St. Louis Blues" too
and spill down the blocks of Beale Street

past pearl-draped girls with swept-high curls,
gentlemen with slurred words, and laughs
laced with absinthe and whiskey, where

classically-trained, nine-year-old Lil,
     (*never* Lillian),
waits to hear and pocket its rhythm

before Dempsey (her mother) can slam
the windows, muffle the devil, and pane the sin.

---

1. The title is taken from "Let's Call It Love," music and lyrics by
Lil Armstrong. All subsequent section titles are taken from "Just
for a Thrill," music and lyrics by Lil Armstrong (1936).

II: *"You made my heart stand still"*

Dempsey demands [music lessons]
     decides [Chicago's cold would
          dampen even the devil]
     and disowns [not yet]

Lil shelves sheets of
     Fare thee-honey Blues,
     Moonlight Echoes &
     Goodnight Angeline
scaling their melodies across
invisible ivories that tangle her thoughts
in clefs and chords, notes only she can hear—
     even the silence has cadence.

Rumors propagate like peat fire
beneath employee
     blatherings
     smoke breaks &
     solicitude

at State Street's Jones Music Store, south side:
     whisperings about
a new New Orleans Creole Jazz Band;
a meeting between Ms. Jones and Lawrence Duhé;

     and an audition.

The wind shuffles Lil's worries: swish
swoosh ah, swish swoosh ah;
optimism flits, severs free.

She sits at the black-buttoned bench
with feigned moxie—composing confidence
with each inhale like she composes
        harmonies in her hums—
and swivels her slender frame toward
the songless mantle: eighty-eight rectangles
polished and primed.

"What number are [we] playing
and what key is it in?"
"Key? What key?" Lawrence said.
"When you hear two knocks just start playin'"

III: *"To me, you were my pride and joy"*

Lil's fingers hover hungry above the
parallels of stacked black, sharp with flats,

and fall into attention
                with the shine of Dreamland's spotlight,

ripping keys into new octaves,
shredding sounds until they scream,
battering pedals to the floor
throttling chords until their lingering
breath fades into audience applause.

"From nine to before one, she became 'Hot Miss Lil,'"
a ninety-pound, high-heeled hybrid:

        her petal light fingers too quick to settle
                for more than a measure,
        her hard-pounding hands too strong to let
                any note escape its fated sound:

sanguine cheeks kissed once each
by fans she let close enough—
prohibition's attractive attraction,
                addiction;

        let stay, let stay,
                let in the crowds.

IV: *"Baby you, you made my heart stand still"*

Night stirs early as the sky puddles
into a haze of blackest-black.

Her band, his band.

His 21-year old smile.
Her 24-year old laugh.

Fall flakes the ground in scissored stems;
he offers his coat, she pulls it close,
                collar to nose.

Whistled riffs blend into swirling
        powder-sugared wind and dip the air in
        rhythm and rhyme—

she tosses her hair, he straightens his tie.

He's diffident, she advocates,
                advertises,
                arranges the Chicago Defender to
                announce him as *"The World's Greatest*
Trumpet Player."

He can't read music, she teaches.

Spring drizzles the ground a sheen reflection.[2]

        He asks, she answers.

Yes.

V: *"Although you're free and havin' your fun,*
to me you're still the only one"

Time bends toward its observer:
        like piano strings that vibrate 440 times
        per second, then loosen unnoticed

---

2. sliced Red
    Delicious crisp

    possibilities
    spoiled & tart

    wide red smiles
    start slow

    you first
    nape to nose

    tights heels slip
    buttons and lace

    hooped earrings
    heaped pillows

    coming coming
    coming, becoming

    slip, tights, heels,
    buttons over lace,

    Aphrodite's apple
    snapping sweet

The glass armoire stuffed with chipped wedding
china
        masks peeled wallpaper,
        its creaks squeaking with gibes;

        glistening eyes.

Gone the night and the picket fence:
broken the paisley teapot Lil always meant to return.

Shores of infidelities and marijuana use [abuse],
        of children never had;

rippled wrinkles,
forgiveness
                parched thin,

Shores of sighs and tries
            and jazz improvised,
        of codas [his] and hoped caesuras [hers]

a river fourteen-years wide[3]

VI: *"You're still the only one"*

The blue sounds of mourners—

the small sniffles and crumples
of tissues; the tiny hum of the camera
as it captures the night in live
        landscaped
        pans &
        zooms

—ease past *his* head-bowed admirers,
        bent heavy in echoed elegy,
spill down carpeted aisles, and over-
flow the masonite planked stage.

Lil's fingers hover brittle, hectored above the
parallels of stacked black, sharp with flats,

but fall into remembering
                with the shine that silhouettes
her shadow across the stage in spotlight's solo
glow.

Riffs of "St. Louis Blues" sway the audience
into hand-claps and foot-taps [tempered, slight]
while the light catching Lil's ring
           his promise, her yes,
           his remarriage, her retain
whorls across the piano's outer rim in flashing
flickers;

she squeezes the last chords, her lips parted in a wide
red smile, waiting for the lingering vibrations to
sojourn
and the notes to soothe themselves silent[4]

■ ■ ■

"[Lil] disappeared from the jazz scene
with barely a ripple"
—JAMES DICKERSON

---

3. The world hooked on a fraying cord
   lopping back and forth,
   like a blue-green pendulum;
   black-tipped arrowed hands pouring across a portrait of twelve.

   Like falling through the glow
   that breaks night from morning,
   mirth slips shallow, leaving muzzy imprints

---

4. Seconds later, Lil collapses, her fingers falling last.
   She is pronounced dead an hour later.

Acknowledgments

We are grateful for the support, encouragement, and wisdom of so many who sustained us during the long process of assembling the scholars who contributed to the production of this Black Chicago Renaissance anthology.

Joan Catapano, an amazing editor and treasured friend, deserves special words of appreciation for the fourteen years of interest in our project and for refusing to allow us to doubt whether it could be done. Without her commitment and belief in this project designed to locate the Black Chicago Renaissance at the center of the ongoing conversation about the deep and enduring significance of black culture, this anthology would not exist.

We owe an enormous debt of gratitude to Marshanda Smith, who facilitated the management of the project, tracked down elusive sources and visual images, and kept editors and contributors to their deadlines.

Many scholars read all or parts of the manuscript and made helpful suggestions and shared documents that not only improved the essays in the anthology but also reaffirmed our belief in the importance of the Black Chicago Renaissance in the aftermath of the highly acclaimed Harlem Renaissance. We offer profound thanks to William C. Hine (South Carolina State University), Adam Green (University of Chicago), Farah Jasmine Griffin (Columbia University), Thavolia Glymph (Duke University), Kathleen Thompson (independent scholar), Gerald Lombardi (writer), Anne Meis Knupfer (Purdue University), Aldon D. Morris (Northwestern University), and Michael Flug, archivist of the Vivian G. Harsh Collection at the Carter G. Woodson Library at Ninety-Fifth and Halsted Streets in Chicago. Early enthusiasm for our project came from James Grossman of the Newberry Library and from Kathleen Bethel, African American Studies librarian at Northwestern University.

Special thanks to all contributors to the volume and to the members of the Chicago Black History Forum: Christopher Robert Reed, Lerone Bennett Jr., Timuel D. Black (who was also a reader for this volume), Charles V. Hamilton, Robert T. Starks, Robert Howard, and Clovis Semmes.

At the outset of the project, editors and contributors made presentations about the Black Chicago Renaissance at historical conferences, including the Association for the Study of African American Life and History in 1996 and the Organization of American Historians in 1998.

John McCluskey Jr. gratefully acknowledges the intellectual engagement of the graduate students in his

Harlem Renaissance courses at Indiana University. Darlene Clark Hine relishes the enthusiasm and interest of the undergraduate students in the Black Chicago Renaissance course at Northwestern University, with a special shout out to Jennifer Mahlum, who wrote the poetic tribute to Lil Hardin Armstrong, included in this volume. Northwestern Provost Daniel Linzer and colleagues Tracy L. Vaughn-Manley, Richard Iton, Dwight D. McBride, and Mary Pattillo have been wonderfully supportive of this project. Our colleagues and students challenged us to sharpen conceptions of black renaissancism and its periodic necessity and to explore the diverse dimensions of the Black Chicago Renaissance and the black urban renaissances that occurred across this country during the twentieth century.

From the outset, visual artist Dr. Murry N. DePillars, former dean of the School of the Arts, Virginia Commonwealth University, believed passionately in this project and remained strongly engaged throughout the last decade of his life. His erudition and humor kept us going. We are deeply grateful to Murry's widow, Mary DePillars, for her sustained commitment to this project.

Audrey McCluskey, John's wife, likewise helped sustain us with strategic words of encouragement. She had faith that we could do this and an unflagging belief in the intrinsic significance of the Black Chicago Renaissance as an intellectual, artistic, and political project.

A special word of thanks is owed to Linda Werbish, who worked on this project while serving as Darlene's administrative assistant, and to Erik Hofstee, who served as her research assistant at Michigan State University.

We also offer heartfelt thanks to curators, librarians, archivists, and art directors and to relatives of the visual artists who assisted and granted permissions to include the visual images that enhance and distinguish this Black Chicago Renaissance anthology. The list includes: Heather Becker and Rebecca Gridley (Chicago Conservation Center), Patrick Albano (Aaron Galleries), Theresa Christopher and Charles Bethea (DuSable Museum of African American History), Darryl D. Pettway (Michigan State University), Jason Gray and Ella Rothgangel (Saint Louis Art Museum), Tina Dunkley, Sheena Earl, and Cynthia Ham (Clark Atlanta University Art Gallery), Eileen Johnston (Howard University Gallery of Art), William M. Farrow III, C. Ian White, Blake Kimbrough, Eleanor W. Traylor, Lester McKeever, Nancy McKeever, Daniel T. Parker, Dr. Walter O. Evans, Linda J. Evans, and Candi Williams (Savannah College of Art and Design), Joellen ElBashir (Moorland-Spingarn Research Center, Howard University), Annika Keller, Ann Handler, and Liz Kurtulik (Art Resource), Erin Tikovitsch (Chicago History Museum), Linda Sanns (Huntington Museum of Arts), Jacqueline Maman (Art Institute of Chicago), Vanessa Thaxton-Ward and Crystal Johnson (Hampton University Museum), Marjorie Van Cura (Michael Rosenfeld Gallery), Michael Tropea (Michael Tropea Photography), Sheila Pree (Sheila Pree Bright Photography), Elizabeth (Lisa) Petrulis and Jennifer Lanman (Swope Art Museum), and Melanie Zeck (Columbia College).

The editorial and production support and expertise provided by Larin McLaughlin, Dawn Durante, Daniel Nasset, and Jennifer L. Reichlin of the University of Illinois Press and freelance editor Mary Lou Kowaleski have been absolutely invaluable to the completion of this project.

We offer special thanks to presidents of two universities, President (Emeritus) Henry Bienen and President Lou Anna K. Simon of Michigan State and President Morton Schapiro of Northwestern, and to the John A. Hannah Distinguished Professorship (MSU) and the Board of Trustees Professorship (NU) for the invaluable resources across the decades that made it possible to do this project on the Black Chicago Renaissance.

If white people are pleased, we are glad.
If they are not, it doesn't matter. . . .
We stand on top of the mountain free within ourselves.
—LANGSTON HUGHES, "The Negro Artist and the
  Racial Mountain"

Introduction

DARLENE CLARK HINE

Beginning in the 1930s and lasting into the 1950s, black Chicago experienced a cultural renaissance that rivaled and, some argue, exceeded the cultural outpouring in Harlem. The Black Chicago Renaissance, however, has yet to receive its full due. This volume addresses that neglect. The Black Chicago Renaissance was unparalleled in many respects. Like Harlem, Chicago had become a major destination for black southern migrants. Unlike Harlem, it was also an urban industrial center. This fact gave a unique working-class and internationalist perspective to the cultural work that would take place there.

The contributors to this Black Chicago Renaissance anthology analyze a dynamically prolific period of African American creativity in music, performance art, social science scholarship, and visual and literary artistic expression. Each author implicitly discusses forces that both distinguish and link the Black Chicago Renaissance to the Harlem Renaissance.[1] New scholarship, to which this volume contributes, suggests that we are better served and our understanding of black culture significantly enriched by placing its modern development in a national and international context and by probing the histories of multiple (sequential and overlapping—Philadelphia, Cleveland, Detroit, Los Angeles, Memphis) black renaissances.[2]

The "New Negro" consciousness with its roots in the generation born in the last and opening decades of the nineteenth and twentieth centuries respectively, replenished and watered by migration, and solidified into the creative force, the Harlem Renaissance in the 1920s, was destined to reemerge significantly transformed in the 1930s as the Black Chicago Renaissance.[3] A younger generation built on the strengths of the previous generation of New Negroes and created a dynamic legacy distinctly Chicagoan. To be sure, there was considerable generational overlap, but it still begs an important question. Why was a Black Chicago Renaissance necessary or, for that matter, the cultural flowerings that arose in Indianapolis, Indiana, Memphis, Tennessee, and Los Angeles, California, to name only a few?

Speaking from a post–civil rights movement and a member of AfriCOBRA (1968 to the present) perspective, art historian Michael D. Harris suggests a starting point for considering the overarching question of why renaissances were important to African Americans in the first half of the twentieth century: "The momentum of over 150 years of derogatory images and characterizations flowed down on our heads with real consequences because white power enforced and depended on black racial identity. We reinvented ourselves repeatedly to resist and frustrate the oppressive systems and representations that circumscribed us collectively, acting on the belief that we either became coproducers or might change the worldview by our actions. We re-presented ourselves to counter the other form of representation." Black expressive cultural workers endeavored to produce "art that attempts to provide a double vision rather than a double consciousness," and, Harris maintains, that "art imbued with that double vision locates itself in the center of an African American epistemology rather than on the periphery where definitions and contentions of race are found."[4] An urgency radiated throughout the Black Chicago Renaissance, an urgency to create music, literature, paintings, radio programs, magazines, photography, comic strips, and films that expressed black humanity, beauty, self-possession, and black people's essential contributions to not only the local geographical community but also to the development of global communities. In the 1920s, black Chicago commercial and cultural activity centered around Thirty-Fifth and State Streets. By the early 1930s, the commercial and social heart had moved to Forty-Seventh Street, and its intellectual and political heat radiated far beyond the borders of Chicago and the United States.

Black Chicagoans, both old settlers and new migrants, energetically engaged in the challenging work of community building, economic development, political engagement, and the production of a new expressive culture giving voice and form to their New Negro, urban/cosmopolitan identities.[5] Moreover, black cultural artists in music and dance and in visual and literary arts demonstrated cognizance of the centrality of race and sex in the distribution of power, the ways in which the social construction of both interacted to determine social privileges and exclusions. The challenge was to deconstruct racial categories and rid "blackness" of its negative symbolism and upend beliefs that held whiteness and maleness as the only authentic markers of American identity and citizenship. The creative agents of the Black Chicago Renaissance had their work cut out, the pieces arrayed, waiting to be fashioned into a new garment.

It is important to underscore that African Americans had been in Chicago since its founding in 1833. Indeed, an enduring source of pride to black citizens of the Windy City is the fact that a black man, Jean Baptiste Point DuSable, was its first settler.[6] By the time of the Civil War, in 1861, the city's black population numbered 955. Within twenty years, the city boasted the nation's second-largest population, numbering 200,000 people, 6,480 of whom were African American.[7] World War I and southern economic decline combined with the rise in lynching violence to fuel the onset of the Great Migration and successive ebbs and flows of black southerners. The onset of the Great Depression for a brief period severely curtailed the flow of black migrants. The numbers began to increase after 1936.[8]

The two generations of Great Migration "New Negroes" who settled in Chicago gave added weight to the complex forces that spurred the rise of multiple artistic renaissances, or flowerings, of African American culture production. The influx of the migrants helped to fuel and shape the Black Chicago Renaissance of the 1930s through the first half of the 1950s. As southern migrants redefined themselves as urban and northern, they helped to propagate a dynamic, multifaceted, modern metropolitan culture.[9]

The Great Migration brought to Chicago a cadre of young black writers and artists. These include Richard Wright (1908–60), born near Roxie, Mississippi, moved to Chicago in 1927; Arna Bontemps(1902–73), a native of New Orleans, migrated to California before landing in Chicago; Margaret Walker (1915–98), born in Birmingham, Alabama, was a 1934 graduate of Northwestern University; and Mahalia Jackson (1911–72), a great gospel singer, collaborated with composer Thomas A. Dorsey (1899–1993), born in New Orleans, who arrived in Chicago in 1927. A serial resident in the cultural capital of the nation's heartland, poet Langston Hughes (1902–67), born in Joplin, Missouri, and a 1929 graduate of Lincoln University, used his literary talents, blues aesthetics, humor, and *Jesse B. Semple* comic strips published in the *Chicago Defender*, one of the nation's most influential black weekly newspapers, to capture and convey with humor the hope, weariness, and excitement of the migrants. These men and women joined native Chicago-born black expressive-culture creators like Katherine Dunham (1909–2008), who attended Joliet Township Junior College before entering the University of Chicago.

All who contributed to the literary, cinematic, intellectual, and dance and music performing arts community in Chicago were at once captives and yet purveyors of Great Migration fever. The shifting terrain of black bodies fostered new urban geographies and aspirations while molding self-affirming agency (or resistance) to white racial and political domination. Artists comprised the vanguard of the struggle to fashion new expressive sites for contesting racial, class, and gender hierarchies and reshaping public culture. They led the way in forcefully representing the humanity, work, and political agency of black citizens who moved from farms to factories and across regions better to seize greater freedom and equality of opportunity. In 1900, Chicago's black citizens numbered only 30,150 out of a population of 1,698,575, or 1.8 percent of the total. From 44,000 in 1910, the number of black residents reached over 250,000 by the mid-1930s. Langston Hughes's poem "One Way Ticket" bluntly but elegantly captures the motivations that had set the stage for early-twentieth-century black migration.

I am fed up
With Jim Crow Laws
People Who are Cruel
And Afraid
Who lynch and run,
Who are scared of me
And me of them.

I pick up my life
And take it away
On a one-way ticket—
Gone up North,
Gone West,
Gone![10]

Moving north, however, did not automatically translate into becoming northern. The development of a sense of becoming and belonging in the black urban and northern freedom spaces, especially on the South Side of Chicago, was an evolutionary process more complicated than even Hughes's poem suggests. The ticket to the so-called promised land was never just a one-way journey. Many of the "gone" often returned to rural homes, if only for intermittent visits, or after death to be buried in a graveyard near the family church. Black southerners who did not move north made short and extended trips to visit friends and family in the north. In other words, migrants zigzagged between southern rural home bases and urban ones in northern towns and big cities. This fluid migration contributed to the southernization of the north, just as black migrants affected southern black perspectives. At its most fundamental level, the

movement of black people south to north and back again fostered a resiliency and determination to break mental shackles of subordination in both regions.[11]

Transformations in black consciousness and identity were also affected by major national and international events ranging from the Scottsboro Boys' infamous "rape" trials (1931) to Italy's invasion of Ethiopia (1935) and the "Double V" national campaign of African Americans during World War II, reflecting a grim determination to fight not only for freedom from fascism, Nazism, and colonialism abroad but also against legal segregation and social injustice at home.[12] Hughes's 1935 black poem "Call of Ethiopia," for example, exemplifies the interconnectedness of the local and national with a global awareness:

Ethiopia's free
Be like me
All of Africa,
Arise and be free!
All you black peoples
Be free! Be free![13]

Black migration and socioeconomic mobility bracket the demographic shifts, identity and consciousness changes, and new urban community formations in the first half of the twentieth century. Black responses to white racial violence, ingrained negative representations, and constant stereotypical denigration provide one context for our collective interest in mounting explorations of the creative artistic fluorescence that occurred in the critical years, from 1930 to 1955, and the several interrelated themes that characterize and distinguish the Black Chicago Renaissance. Themes of class mobility and tensions within the black community, white violence and black resistance, hope and despair, and stirring debates over the purpose of black cultural creations form the backdrop connecting and framing the lives and deaths of two Chicago black males. Or queried another way, what do the *deaths* of two Chicago black boys and the responses provoked have in common? On July 27, 1919, the body of Eugene Williams was retrieved from the waters of Lake Michigan at the foot of Twenty-Ninth Street. A few days later, the deadliest race war in Chicago's history claimed the lives of thirty-eight men and women (twenty-three African Americans and fifteen white residents), with 537 injured. More black people would have died or suffered injuries had it not been for a strong mobilization of black people determined to fight to keep white mobs from invading their neighborhoods. Still, it was the bloodiest conflagration in what James Weldon Johnson termed the "Red Summer of 1919."

Thirty-five years after the killing of Eugene Williams on the banks of Lake Michigan, searchers retrieved the mutilated body of another black teenager, Emmett Louis Till (July 25, 1941–August 28, 1955), from the watery grave of Mississippi's Tallahatchie River. His mother, Mamie Till-Mobley, made the courageous decision to open his casket at the Chicago funeral in order to let the world see what had been done to her son. She declared, "Let the world see what I've seen," let the "whole nation . . . bear witness" to this crime.[14] The photographs of Till's brutalized body appeared in *Jet Magazine* with its impressive half-million circulation.[15] The publication of the Till photographs marked a formative moment in the consciousness development of a generation of youths who would, beginning with the 1960 sit-ins in Greensboro, North Carolina, destroy legal segregation and discrimination in the Jim Crow south.[16] Mamie recalled the warning she had given Emmett before he left Chicago to visit family in Mississippi: "I did warn him that he had a place down there that was a little bit different than Chicago. I told him that if anything happened, even though you think you're perfectly within your right, for goodness sake take low. If necessary, get on your knees and beg apologies. Don't cross anybody down there because Mississippi is not like Chicago. What you get away with here, you might not be able to do it there."[17] Mamie's warning to her son alludes to an array of important tangible realities and imaginative concerns that took hold in Chicago between Eugene Williams's death and the eve of the departure of her son.

To be sure, the Black Chicago Renaissance had deep antecedents in the pre–World War I decades. Unlike the dozens of riots that erupted in the aftermath of the Great War in cities across the country during the crimson summer of 1919, black observers heralded the Chicago race riot as the most graphic illustration of the determination and willingness of first-wave African American migrants and descendants of old settlers to resist white violence in kind. A prominent black clubwoman community activist and a stalwart crusader of antilynching renown, Ida B. Wells-Barnett, had penned a premonitory article in the July 7, 1919, issue of the Chicago *Daily Tribune*.

With one Negro dead as a result of a race riot last week, another one very badly injured in the county hospital; with a half dozen attacks upon Negro children, and one on the Thirty-fifth Street car Tuesday, in which four white men beat one colored man . . . the bombing of Negro homes and the indifference of the public to these outrages. It is just such a situation as this which led up to the East St. Louis riot.[18]

Less than three weeks after Wells-Barnett detailed the origins of the East St. Louis riot, Eugene Williams made the fatal error of swimming across an imaginary line onto the "white side" of Twenty-Fifth Street Beach in Chicago.[19] Williams died from injuries sustained in the attack of white ruffians. Black Chicagoans fought back, rejecting the mantle of a bewildered, defeated, and disillusioned people. In the ensuing decades, they worked to shape a new sense of black identity and to create and secure autonomous spaces from which they proudly proclaimed their humanity and claimed rights to full citizenship and protection from violence and called for an end to economic exploitation and discrimination.

The "Red Summer of 1919" witnessed not only race riots over spatial geography as black people defended their citizenship rights but also an upsurge in labor struggles as white and black workers, on occasion, joined forces to challenge industrial capitalists' refusal to pay them higher wages and make safer their working environments. In 1916, twelve thousand of the nearly fifty thousand workers in the Chicago stockyards were black people. The Great Steel Strike of 1919 involved approximately 365,000 workers in Gary, Indiana, and Pittsburgh, Pennsylvania, including 7,000 unskilled black steelworkers in Pittsburgh. In Seattle, Washington, the Central Labor Council took over the city as 35,000 shipyard workers rejected postwar wage cuts. Although many labor unions refused to accept black members, there were enough instances of cross race collaboration and examples of shared working-class consciousness in the labor movement to give the big business–big government alliance cause to panic in spite of the corporate penchant for using black workers as strikebreakers.[20] It was Jamaican-born poet Claude McKay's stirring poem "If We Must Die" that most poignantly captured the universalism inherent in the twin manifestations of labor radicalism and black insurgency.

> If we must die, let it not be like hogs
> Hunted and penned in an inglorious spot,

While round us bark the mad and hungry dogs,
Making their mock of our accursed lot,
If we must die, O let us nobly die,
So that our precious blood may not be shed
In vain, then even the monsters we defy
Shall be constrained to honor us though dead!

O Kinsmen! We must meet the common foe!
Though far outnumbered let us show us brave,
And for their thousand blows deal one death blow!
What though before us lies the open grave?
Like men we'll face the murderous, cowardly pack,
Pressed to the wall, dying, but fighting back.

The poem does not explicitly refer to race or labor. Nevertheless, African Americans claimed it as the encapsulation, or representation, of their ideological and on-the-ground struggles against racial oppression and economic exploitation. Many black Chicago intellectuals and cultural workers seamlessly conjoined involvement in radical leftist politics, membership in the Communist Party, and Marxist critiques of capitalism and imperialism with expressive cultural production. Horace Cayton, who had arrived in Chicago in 1931 to begin graduate study at the University of Chicago, declared that McKay's poem satisfied "a deep hunger in the hearts of more than a million Negroes in the postwar period."[21] In short, McKay's poem harnessed a complicated New Negro consciousness in Chicago that was as equally determined to secure economic opportunities as it was to create new cultural and aesthetic forms and to join artistic expression and radical political ideologies. According to historian Nikki Brown, in the 1920s a "wide array of black politics in the New Negro Movement focused on a few unifying objectives—ending segregation, securing voting rights, abolishing lynching and mob violence, reaffirming the legitimacy of black culture."[22] Black intellectuals engaged in sociological study under the tutelage of Robert Parks at the University of Chicago were embracing theories of race that abandoned assumptions of black inferiority. Scholars such as Charles Johnson and E. Franklin Frazier also focused on the significance of black migration and the consequences of social cultural changes, not only in the formation of theories of race relations and hierarchies but also in transformations in northern metropolises.[23]

In reaction to labor and racial upheavals, U.S. Attorney General A. Mitchell Palmer and soon-to-be director of the Federal Bureau of Investigation J. Edgar Hoover compiled a list of 450,000 "subversives," paying particular attention to prominent black activists. Chicago's Wells-Barnett was labeled dangerous. The condemnation of A. Philip Randolph was even more ominous. In 1917, Randolph and his friend Chandler Owen cofounded the Messenger, which they described as "the only magazine of scientific radicalism in the world published by Negroes" (my emphasis). The best-known labor leader of his generation, the radical New Negro Randolph was arrested briefly in 1919 for his activism. Already well known to justice department officials for his opposition to America's involvement in World War I, he was branded "the most dangerous Negro in America."[24]

A socialist and labor organizer, Randolph successfully spearheaded the formation of a black union of Pullman porters. In many urban, black communities, the porter, as one writer puts it, was "among the most revered and successful members of the community, he was a homeowner and civic leader who symbolized black success."[25] The single-largest employer of black people in the United States, the Pullman Company, during the 1920s employed more than twelve thousand black men as porters on Pullman railroad cars. According to historian Susan Hirsh, Pullman management forced black porters to rely on tips to support their families instead of paying them a decent wage. Thus "low base pay, extremely long hours, and lack of opportunities for advancement" frustrated their expectations for a better life for themselves and their families.[26] In 1925, a group of Chicago's Pullman Car Company workers met with Randolph in Harlem to organize the Brotherhood of Sleeping Car Porters (BSCP). They met there, instead of in Chicago, in order to protect themselves from repercussions of the Pullman Car Company. Randolph served as president, with Milton Webster as vice president. The BSCP's slogan, "Service not servitude," emphasized self-respect.[27] Thus, a decade before the burgeoning of the Black Chicago Renaissance, workers and activists, operating under a relentless white corporate gaze, moved strategically to create in private community spaces a means by which to protect their bodies and livelihoods while cultivating an independent race consciousness. Like Pullman porters, other members of the black working class were determined to distinguish service from servitude, to provide the former while fighting the latter. Unionization, albeit ambivalent, was an important aspect of the migrants' experience and adjustment and in their efforts to survive and thrive in the destination cities of the Northeast and Midwest.[28]

The organization of the BSCP in 1925 came in the wake of the fierce determination of the U.S. Justice Department, backed by the resolve of corporate leaders in 1922, to crush black radicalism in the New Negro movement. The justice department's most notable success was the conviction, subsequent imprisonment, and eventual deportation of Marcus Garvey for fraudulent use of the mail to sell stock in the Universal Negro Improvement Association's (UNIA) Black Star Line. Clearly, Garvey's imprisonment and deportation dampened overt black radical nationalism. Nevertheless, a branch with approximately a thousand members continued to thrive in Chicago, where, due to the organizational activism of black women, impressive gains were made in electoral politics. In 1928, as a consequence of Wells-Barnett's successful mobilization of African American women members of the Alpha Suffrage Club, a Chicago politician, Oscar Stanton DePriest, won election to the U.S. House of Representatives, becoming the first black man from the north to serve in the Congress.[29] DePriest's election to a national office launched a striking and portentous resurgence of political engagement that would become even more pronounced during the era of President Franklin D. Roosevelt's New Deal as African Americans in Chicago and across the nation became increasingly adept in the use of the ballot to battle for their citizenship rights. In 1934, former Republican Arthur W. Mitchell joined the Democratic Party and succeeded DePriest in the House of Representatives.

The years between 1930 and 1955 comprised the most productive and intense phase of the Black Chicago Renaissance. A desire to live freely in "the metropolis" continued to characterize the aspirations of migrants as second-wave Chicago migrants arrived during the depths of the Great Depression, the World War II emergency, the most repressive years of the Cold War, and at the advent of the modern civil rights movement. Against the backdrop of the economic devastation and the dire urgency of the depression, the 1930s and the 1940s witnessed a resurgence of black working-class political radicalism that was captured and reflected in the expressive visual and literary productions of Chicago Black Renaissance artists. Here, historian Adam Green's injunction is worth underscoring. Studying African American life and development of cultural institutions in Chicago,

Green emphasizes, "compels us to acknowledge that blacks did more than survive the twentieth-century city; they initiated and appropriated its core conventions, thereby revising their terms of engagement with American society."[30]

Interrelated themes of wholeness and mobility, poverty and despair, struggle and resistance, hope and joy radiated from canvasses, the stage and screen, and in the literary voices of Black Chicago Renaissance social realists who shared the radical race and class consciousness of the Popular Fronts of the U.S. Communist Party, with whom they worked closely when interests converged.[31] The artistic work of Langston Hughes, Charles White, Margaret T. Burroughs, Gwendolyn Brooks, Katherine Dunham, and others was inextricably linked to the basic fabric of everyday life of black citizens. It was but a thin line that separated the black cultural workers from politically engaged steel, meatpacking, industrial, and service workers, and even that line was porous. The first meeting of the National Negro Congress hosted by Chicago in February 1936 was exemplary in this regard. The congress brought together 817 delegates representing hundreds of organizations and labor unions. The opening session attracted 5,000 people who listened to keynote speakers address the goal of fighting against the "cultural retardation of the cultural life" of black people and pledge to advance black culture and support cultural workers, particularly those determined to destroy "demeaning and stereotypical images in the public arts."[32] The unique labor struggles and organizing in Chicago compelled a unique cultural renaissance. In his contribution to this volume, Erik Gellman shows, for example, how Charles White's early drawings and sketches capture the fusion of radical politics and the cultural imperative that effectively distinguish the Black Chicago Renaissance from its Harlem predecessor.

On February 13, 1943, Hughes introduced his fictional character Jesse B. Semple, who in many respects was the comic embodiment of the southern-rural and northern-urban fusion. As one biographer observes, Semple "came to represent Hughes own close identification with the worries, fears, and frustrations of the working-class black community." Hughes called Chicago "a Joe Louis town with a knockout punch in its steel mills and stockyards" and "a Katherine Dunham town, seductive, determined, theatrical and clever."[33] In his columns and in the *Jesse B. Semple* comic strip, Hughes took the Black Chicago

Renaissance to the everyday working people, and although his humor and insights may not have raised wages, they did raise black self-consciousness.[34] It is also important to note that the long-lasting comic strip *Bungleton Green*, created by photographer William A. Woodward and *Chicago Defender* cartoonist Leslie Rogers, was published in the newspaper from 1920 to 1968.

The Black Chicago Renaissance: Arts, Intuitions, Consciousness

This anthology advances the larger project by focusing sustained attention to the myriad dimensions of black Chicago's cultural fluorescence from the eve of the Great Depression in the 1930s through the beginnings of the Cold War following World War II and into the emergent modern civil rights movement era of the mid-1950s.[35] By the mid-1930s, Chicago's black population numbered over a quarter of a million, making it the second-largest outside of Harlem. As geographer James Tyner writes, institutional neglect, legal restrictions, violence, and intimidation all contributed to "the concentration of African Americans in impoverished spaces."[36] In the pre–Chicago renaissance decades, the consignment of African Americans into intensely overcrowded, clearly demarcated, and/or de facto segregated spaces proved critical to the emergence of black entrepreneurial leaders who in turn became patrons of (high and vernacular) black expressive culture as well as important employers of black residents, and important political forces. Uniquely urban entrepreneurial developments such as the black beauty culture industry launched by women like Annie Malone and Madame C. J. Walker represented one facet of these interwoven strands. The beauty culture created economic opportunities for black women to own their own shops and to hire other women who otherwise would have been restricted to domestic service in white homes. As historian Tiffany Gill suggests, these new "beauty salon" urban sites became "one of the few places where black women felt safe to deal with intimate issues . . . and have their dignity restored, a political act in and of itself." Beauticians were considered "trustworthy . . . respected enough to help them make important political decisions."[37] Migrants treasured their increased leisure time and disposable incomes derived from working in a thriving internal service economy as well as in the city's industrial and manufacturing

sectors.[38] Over time, first- and second-wave black migrants shaped their communal public spaces into sites that supported new strategies and claims for social justice.

Chicago's black elites, artists, and workers, men and women and their families, all became cultural consumers, patrons, and agents in the conveyance, if not commoditization, of racial pride. They collectively invested themselves in the quest for self-affirmation and imbued each other and their communities with a sense of belonging, the determination to struggle, to stay, and to celebrate achievement in spite of racial discrimination. Indeed, overcrowded housing, restrictive covenants, few opportunities for economic advancement, low wages, inadequate health care, and limited access to higher education and professional training, the products of entrenched white supremacy, were eerie reminders of conscripted raced and classed spaces and hierarchies in Mississippi. Black Chicagoans, at least, had room for hope, for intellectual growth, freedom to engage in social activism and to espouse liberation politics. Moreover, the circumscribed or segregated housing and public spaces that fueled black entrepreneurialism simultaneously facilitated the creation and maintenance of black-controlled and black-managed social institutions ranging from Provident Hospital and Nurse Training School, the George Cleveland Hall Public Library, and the Regal Theater (1928–73) to the South Center Department Store and the Savoy Ballroom. Black Chicagoans found an impressive array of artistic, leisure, and social and religious institutions, and legitimate economic enterprises existed alongside well-organized underworld policy numbers (lotteries) rings.[39]

Whether transparent or opaque, all of the structures and institutions that black Chicagoans created and mobilized to engender autonomy and agency were grounded in the understanding that existing racial hierarchies were neither permanent nor unassailable and black complacency was unacceptable.[40] In sum, everyday black residents continually improvised a fluid, resistant urbanity. Within the circumscribed communal spaces of Chicago, the work of visual artists, dance choreographers, literary creators, and musicians helped to mold both recognition of the right to freedom and of the license to perform and elaborate its myriad meanings. From the wombs of this space emerged visual artists White and Burroughs; literary artists Hughes, Bontemps, Wright, and Brooks; and musicians, composers, singers and dance performers ranging from Dorsey and Dunham to Jackson and Muddy Waters. These artists countered the stereotypical negative images and estimation that prevailed outside of the "Black Metropolis." In synchronic ways, the artistic community provided new representations of black humanity and articulated the pride, hope, humor, dreams, desires, frustrations, anger, and beauty in the lives of everyday black people.

The rich cultural productions of the Black Chicago Renaissance reflected the critical perspective essential to empowerment, hope, and change. It breached the Du Boisian "double consciousness" that echoed a lingering sense or feeling of not belonging or measuring up in the eyes of white America. Chicago native, dramatist Lorraine Hansberry, brilliantly captured these complexities. Her acclaimed award-winning play, *A Raisin in the Sun*, written in 1956, premiered on March 11, 1959, on Broadway (New York) and launched the modern era in black theater. Hansberry assessed and analyzed the reality of hegemonic racism, of black resistance to segregated housing covenants that circumscribed black mobility. She created, as Amiri Baraka observes, "an aesthetically powerful and politically advanced work of art . . . [and characters who were] crafted meticulously from living social material."[41] About her play, Hansberry explained, "Not only is this a Negro family, specifically, definitely, and culturally, but it's not even a New York family or a Southern Negro family. It is specifically a South Side Chicago family." She insisted that "to create the universal, you must pay very great attention to the specific."[42]

Still, three points about the processes of innovation and evolution of black cultural hybridism require elaboration fully to appreciate the complexity of the Black Chicago Renaissance. The decades-long, multiphased Great Migration, a process and ideology that kept black bodies in motion, also inhibited or thwarted impulses that would have contained black cultural expressions and formations. The migration of rural or "folkloric" southerners to the urban northern metropolises was complicated by the fact that the migrants and their children often engaged in reverse migration. To wit, in their frequent visitations or commutes back and forth between the old and the new locations, serial migrants infused respective sites with cultural accoutrements of the other. In short, Chicago received continu-

ous replenishment of black, southern folkways, idiomatic expressions, musical sounds, religiosity, desires, gestures, and, of course, food, all things that cross-pollinated sites of origin and destination. Indeed, the cultivation of a blended or hybrid culture was at once uniquely urban north and fundamentally fettered to the black rural-urban south.[43] Black Chicago Renaissance musical, dance, theater, visual, and literary artists and intellectuals and social activists looked backward not only to Africa and Caribbean inflections for ingredients with which to construct cosmopolitan imaginings and goals to fuel new black consciousness journeys and resistance to racial oppression and dehumanization but also to the south. The migrants had to, as did Wright, Bontemps, Dunham, and others, return and leave and return, again, back home in order to make life in Chicago seem and feel closer to freedom. As historian Davarian Baldwin argues, "the black metropolis [w]as both a built environment and . . . an ideal."[44]

Second, when returning to origination sites, reverse migrants carried back a range of accoutrements both real and imagined. They carried consumer items that hinted of a more expansive freedom and the possibility of escape from white oppression, segregation, and violence. Urban New Negroes shared lexical inventions (new words), fresh tastes, stylish clothing, and a mixture of musical innovations and popular dance moves with southern relatives and friends. As impossible as it no doubt was for serial two-way migrants to divest their bodies and minds of every politically progressive idea or desire before they arrived back home, it was equally as difficult for Chicago's black citizens to ignore or remain oblivious to world affairs. It was, however, their fresh boldness in challenging notions of white supremacy and black inferiority that proved the fault line or, as Mamie Till had warned, that enabled black people to do and say and get away with in Chicago what when practiced in Mississippi "got you killed."

Third, renaissances were promoted. In the *Chicago Defender*, as sociologist E. Franklin Frazier points out, Chicago had "the largest Negro newspaper in the country."[45] The paper became the primary publishing vehicle for the cultivation and promotion of the Black Chicago Renaissance as well as a source for international news and perspective. Even in the midst of the Great Depression when most black Americans were struggling to survive, the *Chicago Defender* provided coverage of national and international events, including travelogues by black Chicagoans. One of the most riveting was the travelogue of attorney Patrick B. Prescott Jr. and his educator wife, Annabel Carey (daughter of Bishop Archibald J. Carey of the Woodlawn AME Church), to select western European capitals in 1934. The *Defender* published the fifteen articles and, as independent scholar Hilary Mac Austin points out, exulted over its coverage of the "Grand Tour," claiming that it did so "for the benefit of those readers of the *Chicago Defender* who desire a glimpse of Europe as it is today. It is in keeping with this paper's policy to give its readers the best." The Prescotts joined poet Hughes in sharing their impressions and travel experiences with readers of the *Chicago Defender*.[46] Hughes spent 1932 in the Soviet Union. On November 21, 1942, Hughes's column, "Here to Yonder," appeared. The column explored topics of significance and interest not only to the local black Chicagoans but also to the broader national black community.

It is important to note that from the outset, refined, learned, and economically established members of the Chicago black professional and entrepreneurial class supported black visual artists. Thus, in myriad ways, in addition to the grants received from white philanthropist Julian Rosenwald, who also supported black artists and intellectuals, the black community was heavily invested in cultural production more so than evident at first blush. In 1923, William Farrow and Charles Dawson founded the Chicago Art League at the YMCA on Wabash Avenue. The Chicago Art League and the South Side Community Art Center, founded by Burroughs, provided exhibition space and opportunities to showcase and distribute black art and their creations. Material support came from black workers, "old settlers," and leaders in the black enclave economy, that is, heads of the "policy" or "numbers" syndicate. The politically protected black "policy kings" acquired a measure of respectability by contributing substantial sums to community charities as well as to cultural institutions. In other words, patrons of the Black Chicago Renaissance ranged from Jesse Binga, founder of the Binga Bank, to number runners.[47] To be sure, funds from the New Deal's Work Progress Administration (WPA) significantly assisted creative literary and performance artists, and the WPA provided relief to thousands of unemployed workers.[48] Still, black Chicago visual arts that appealed across class lines reflected positive constructions of the black people

and simultaneously underscored the imperative of community to fight oppressive hegemonic paradigms that alleged black social, intellectual, commercial, and cultural incapacity.

These then are some of the themes, individuals, and creative productions that characterize the Black Chicago Renaissance. To be sure, for many black migrants, the dream of reaching a promised land in the urban north was not only deferred but also never achieved. For some, the changes required proved too daunting and the excesses of urban life too destructive. The emergence of social science scholarship, especially with the 1945 publication of *Black Metropolis*, a sociological classic written by St. Clair Drake and Horace Cayton, brought a new level of sophistication to the study of the class stratifications evident within the racially segregated neighborhoods.[49] This scholarship makes clear that a sense of belonging and the creation of black urban identities took time to develop for residents of Chicago's South Side. The arts in all their representations proved invaluable to the process by providing neutral ground for bridging class divisions. Importantly, the passionate engagement in radical politics by visual and literary artists, the rising tide of black working-class radical racial consciousness, and the institution-building activism of community black women and men also shaped the content and reach of the Black Chicago Renaissance.

Artists such as Archibald J. Motley, White, Burroughs, and Elizabeth Catlett exemplified this meeting of purpose. Motley (1891–1981) was born in New Orleans, Louisiana, and attended the Chicago Art Institute from 1914 to 1919. In 1926, he received a Guggenheim Fellowship to study and paint in Paris and in 1928 won the Harmon Foundation's Gold Medal for his portrait *Octoroon Girl* (1925). While serving as a visiting faculty member at Howard University, Motley executed one of his best-known paintings, *Saturday Night* (1935). Motley was arguably one of the more celebrated visual artists in Chicago in the first half of the twentieth century.[50] His career spanned the decades preceding and following the Chicago renaissance. His biographer, Wendy Greenhouse, describes him as an artist who "matured during the Jazz Age, in contrast to the next generation of artists, social realists who emerged in the era of the Great Depression to tackle in their art weighty themes of social injustice and individual despair."[51] At the end of his life, Motley reflected on his objectives as an artist: "The thing I was trying to do was trying to get their [African Americans] interest in culture, in art. I planned that by putting them in the paintings themselves, making them part of my own work so that they could see themselves as they were. . . . I've always wanted to paint my people just the way they are."[52]

Chicago's "native son," visual artist Charles White (1918–79), also played a key role in the dialogue concerning the usefulness of black art and scholarship in the struggle to forge strong relationships between liberation politics and cultural production. Historian Erik S. Gellman offers a detailed portrait of the ways in which White conveyed his solidarity with the black working class and other politically radical groups during his years in Chicago. Both White and Horace Cayton in his work as a WPA Illinois administrator created art and produced scholarship that reflected their understandings of the complex lives of working-class black people and communicated their own political beliefs as advocates of transformational social activism.[53]

In 1940, White completed a mural for the Chicago Public Library, Five Great American Negroes, and later provided illustrations and graphics to New Masses, the Worker, and Masses and Mainstream. According to James Porter, White's "vivid pictorial symbols" were "altogether free of false or distorted ideas or shallow and dubious emotion."[54] White was motivated by a desire, as he wrote, "to get my work before common, ordinary people . . . for my work to portray them better, and to be rich and meaningful to them. . . . Art should take its place as one of the necessities of life, like good clothing and shelter."[55] For a brief time, White shared his art and politics with his wife, the talented sculptor and printmaker Elizabeth Catlett. She was born in 1915 in Washington, D.C., studied at Howard University (1931–35), and taught briefly in the public schools in Durham, North Carolina, before entering the University of Iowa to earn a master of fine arts degree. Catlett joined friend and fellow artist Burroughs to study sculpture at the Art Institute of Chicago and lithography at the South Side Community Art Center that Burroughs founded and maintained with support from the WPA.[56]

Burroughs remained in Chicago and beginning in the 1930s developed and sustained numerous creative arts and educational institutions, one of which is now the DuSable Museum of African American History. The desire to connect art to the lives of ordinary people propelled the establishment of an array of critical social spaces and institutions ranging from the South Side Community Art Center, the Cleveland Hall Library, the South Side Writers' Group, formed in 1936 by Wright, to art galleries, union halls, theaters, journals, newspapers, publishing houses, and radio programs that nurtured and expanded the reach of the Black Chicago Renaissance. As John McCluskey Jr. indicates, it was out of the South Side Writers' Group that Wright's powerful 1937 manifesto, "Blueprint for Negro Writing," emerged.[57]

Like Burroughs, and White, Catlett possessed a passionate commitment to creating art that countered derogatory stereotypes of African Americans. She worked to substitute positive and more meaningful representations that would raise black consciousness, nurture pride and self-affirmation, and yet fan desires for greater freedom and social justice. Catlett's work was included in the 1940 Chicago American Negro Exposition, where she won first prize for her limestone sculpture Negro Mother and Child, which had been her master's thesis. In 1942, White and Catlett moved to New York City. Their marriage did not survive. Catlett, who later relocated permanently in Mexico, described her reasons for creating art: "I have always wanted my art to service my people—to reflect us, to relate to us, to stimulate us, to make us aware of our potential. . . . You can't make a statement if you don't speak the language. . . . We have to create an art for liberation and for life."[58] In the 1960s, Catlett became an outspoken supporter of the Black-Power movement and its visual arts equivalent, the Black Arts movement. She repeated her injunction that art should express "racial identity, communicate with the black community, and participate in struggles for social, political, and economic equality."[59]

A few migrant writers, of course, were already accomplished by the time they settled in Chicago. They were determined and eager to embrace the city, none more so than Arna Bontemps (1902–73). Bontemps was an outspoken critic of the charge that Chicago's Black Renaissance was a pallid imitation of the Harlem Renaissance, boldly asserting, "The Depression put an end to the dream world of renaissance Harlem and scattered the band of poets and painters, sculptors, scholars and singers who had in six exciting years made a generation of Americans aware of unnoticed and hitherto undervalued creative talent among Negroes." Chicago, he insisted, was not only the successor to the Harlem Renaissance but also could claim its own unique lineage, power, and purpose. The emergence of Chicago's Black Renaissance represented "a second awakening, less gaudy but closer to realities" that was "already in prospect. . . . One way or the other, Harlem got its renaissance in the middle twenties, centering around the *Opportunity* contests and the Fifth Avenue Awards Dinners. . . . Ten years later Chicago reenacted it on WPA without finger bowls but with increased power."[60]

Born in Louisiana to Paul Bismark Bontemps, a bricklayer, and Maria Carolina Pembroke, a schoolteacher, Bontemps completed college and began his adult migration from Los Angeles, California, to Harlem, where he became friends with and a collaborator of Hughes. He also knew Claude McKay, W. E. B. Du Bois, and James Weldon Johnson. As the Depression woes worsened, Bontemps, with his wife and six children, left Harlem to teach at a junior college in Huntsville, Alabama. In 1931, he published his first novel, *God Sends Sunday*. The following year, he collaborated with Hughes to publish the first of his numerous children's books, *Popo and Fifina*, a travel book that featured the lives of a brother and sister in Haiti. By this time, the Scottsboro trials were underway, and Bontemps pulled up stakes and returned home to California. He continued writing, and shortly before the publication of his best-known work in 1936, *Black Thunder*, a story of Gabriel Prosser's 1800 slave rebellion near Richmond, Virginia, he moved to Chicago where he found employment with the WPA's Illinois Writers' Project.

In Chicago, Bontemps met Wright and joined the South Side Writers' Group, which Wright founded in 1936 to offer critical and moral support to black writers. The group included poet Margaret Walker, playwright Theodore Ward, and many younger poets who would perfect their talents as they learned from the pioneers of black Chicago poets. Bontemps's own writing was influenced by his association with this cadre of fledgling writers. After 1935, his novels and short stories reflected a more militant restlessness and a revolutionary spirit. Evident in *Black Thunder*, this sensibility became even more pronounced in his last novel, *Drums at Dusk* (1939), a treatment of the Haitian revolution and its leader, Toussaint L'Ouverture (1746–1803), which he completed with support from a Rosenwald Fellowship. After earning a master's degree in library science from the University of Chicago in 1943, Bontemps accepted a position as head librarian at Fisk University, a post he relinquished in 1964. His writings from the 1940s

onward focus on children's books, poetry, and biographies for teenage readers.[61]

Revolutionary work in radio and music also occurred in Chicago, which early on had become a center both for recording and performing music. On November 3, 1929, *The All Negro Hour* debuted on Chicago radio station WSBC, marking the launch of the black radio industry. Founder Jack L. Cooper created the program to display the variety of talents and religious convictions within the black community and thus undermine the negative mainstream radio stereotypical treatments of black life and culture. Unable to thrive in a Depression economy, Cooper sought and received support from two prominent Bronzeville or South Side black-community businessmen, Robert A. Cole and Fred W. Lewing, owners of the Metropolitan Funeral Systems Association.[62] In 1931, Cooper added an innovative new program, *The All Negro Children's Hour*, promoting self-esteem among the youngest residents of Bronzeville. As black music became a profitable commodity, influential black disc jockeys like Al Benson (Arthur B. Leaner) appeared on the radio in Chicago. A migrant from Mississippi, by the end of the 1940s Benson was hosting shows on three radio stations. He became such a celebrity that readers of the *Chicago Defender* voted him the "mayor of Bronzeville." Diverse artists from gospel singer Mahalia Jackson to bluesman Muddy Waters attracted loyal fans who listened to them on Benson's programs.[63]

Inarguably, Chicago was most noted for being the home of one of radio's most popular programs during the 1930s, *The Amos 'n' Andy Show*. Although two white performers (Charles Correll and Freeman Gosden) played the leading roles, they carefully ingratiated themselves into Chicago's black community, making regular appearances at Bud Billiken parades and at the Regal Theater. By the 1940s, black audiences had become less enthralled with the show; the National Association for the Advancement of Colored People (NAACP), Robert L. Vann, editor of the Pittsburgh *Courier*, and others protested the show's minstrel ambience of mispronounced words, garbled grammar, and characterizations of black women as bossy and black men as clownish. A subsequent television version of the broadcast would feature black actors in the title roles. Alvin Childress became Amos, and Spencer Williams Jr. played Andy. Tim Moore assumed the role of the Kingfish of the Mystic Knights of the Sea Lodge, and Johnny Lee portrayed the lawyer Algonquin J. Calhoun.

A much more progressive-thinking Chicago scriptwriter and producer developed projects and a series of positive programs that engendered pride and educated African Americans about their history and contributions to the struggles for freedom and justice. Between 1948 and 1950, Richard Durham's *Destination Freedom* hit the airwaves. It was a serious radio program that marked a radical departure from *The Amos 'n' Andy Show*. *Destination Freedom* broadcast a black perspective on politics, culture, and history, one that was uniquely suited for a northern urban audience. Chicago was a destination. *Destination Freedom* provided the historical facts and context that black Chicagoans needed to continue forging a more empowering and assertive modern identity. Innovative programs of this nature facilitated local radio's ability to open lines of communication between white and black citizens and to initiate conversations about race within the black community. Durham helped in the fashioning of oppositional consciousness by reminding black Chicagoans of the exploits of black freedom fighters across the long decades of slavery, emancipation, and reconstruction. In one show, Durham used the powerful words of Wells-Barnett to demonstrate the intertwined nature of racial violence and economic oppression. "The real motive behind all lynching was not the 'moral' issue pretended—but underneath it was a matter of murder for money and jobs," Wells had declared.[64]

A multitude of individuals and key structures institutionalized the Black Chicago Renaissance. Cultural centers and museums, libraries and schools, parades and paintings, murals and sculptures, and music and radio along with film and dance ensured Chicago's long reign as an important site, incubator, and exporter of a modern black culture across the nation and globally. Performance theatricals and silent films, especially the creative filmmaking of Oscar Devereau Micheaux (1884–1951), and the establishment of theatrical palaces and movie houses comprised critical components of the renaissance. Born in Metropolis, Illinois, Micheaux worked as a Pullman Car porter and a ranch operator in the west before settling in Chicago. In 1918, he launched what would become a remarkable career as the nation's premier black filmmaker. The following year, he completed the film *Within Our Gates*, exploring themes of lynching, sex, and race. It opened in 1920 at Chicago's Vendome Theater. In 1925, Micheaux cast Paul Robeson in his first film appearance, *Body*

and Soul. Between 1919 and 1948, the prolific Micheaux produced over forty feature-length films. The race films expanded the range of representations of black men and women, while boldly exploring semi-private topics of interest to modern black urbanites. He probed deeply into black inner life and dissected the tensions in interracial relationships from a New Negro prospective. To attract more black theatergoers, he adroitly deployed the frequent controversy that erupted over his graphic treatment of lynching, rape, corruption in the church, and passing. His films facilitated the commercial survival of an independent network of black owned-and-operated movie houses across the country. Micheaux exported his New Negro metropolitan identity and the modern representations of the race directly to his people.[65]

Along with making movies, innovative Chicagoans also helped to create modern black dance. To be sure, dance has always been an integral part of African American life and culture. In 1931, the New Negro Art Theater Dance Company, cofounded by Edna Buy and Hemsley Winfield, performed the first "Negro Dance Recital in America." In that same year, Katherine Dunham (1909–2006) founded the Negro Dance Group in Chicago, which garnered financial support from the WPA. As Dunham recalled, "Black Dancers were not allowed to take classes in studios in the '30s. I started a school because there was no place for blacks to study dance. I was the first to open the way for black dancers and I was the first to form a black dance company." Trained in anthropology, Dunham studied African-based ritual dance in the Caribbean. In 1940, following her relocation to New York, she renamed the company the Katherine Dunham Dance Company. Dunham was also motivated by the desire to create unique dance performances: "I felt a new form was needed for black people to be able to appear in any theater in the world and be accepted and exciting. One of the prerequisites of art is uniqueness."[66]

Dunham was never one to hold her tongue or to acquiesce in the face of injustice. Her art ushered in a new way for black people to express their talent and desires for freedom, but she was equally adept in speaking and acting her protest politics. In the early 1940s, Dunham denounced discrimination following a dance performance in Louisville, Kentucky. "We are glad we have made you happy," she announced to the audience. "We hope you have enjoyed us. This is the last time I shall play Louisville because the management refuses to let people like us sit by people like you. Maybe after the war we shall have democracy and I can return." Not only was Dunham a gifted pioneer in dance who laid a firm choreographic foundation for future generations but she also simultaneously underscored the responsibility and obligation to the community that the black artist had to combat racism.[67]

Dunham's position was in keeping with that of Hughes, who, at the end of the Black Chicago Renaissance, penned a propitious mobility poem, "Brotherly Love: A Little Letter to the White Citizens Councils of the South." "Brotherly Love" anticipated and illuminated radical changes occurring in black oppositional consciousness, from the start of the Great Migration to the beginnings of the modern civil rights movement:

> So long, *so long* a time you've been calling
> Me *all* kinds of names, pushing me down—
> I been swimming with my head deep under water,
> And you wished I would stay under till I drown.
> But I didn't! I'm still swimming! Now you're mad
> Because I won't ride in the back end of your bus.[68]

III: The Essays: Brief Description

Part I. Black Chicago: History, Culture, and Community

Christopher Robert Reed in "African American Cultural Expression in Chicago before the Renaissance: The Performing, Visual and Literary Arts, 1893–1933" examines the local historical context of the Black Chicago Renaissance. He delineates the existence of a layered class structure within the black community and underscores the importance and the complicated tradition of support of the arts by elite black and later members of the black entrepreneurial and professional middle class. Black patronage, for both aesthetic and exploitative reasons, served an important function in providing space for creative expression and means for its distribution and commoditization. Further, Reed's essay is a response to the claims made by social scientists Charles S. Johnson and E. Franklin Frazier. In 1923, Johnson declared that Chicago's "intellectual life has numerous excuses for not existing." In 1929, Fraser echoed Johnson's assertion, insisting, "Chicago has no intelligentsia." Reed documents the existence and work of a black intelligentsia in Chicago from the 1920s throughout

the era of the Black Chicago Renaissance as a critical, though often ignored, intervention.

In "The Negro Renaissance: Harlem and Chicago Flowerings," Samuel A. Floyd Jr., citing Tony Martin, argues that the "Negro Renaissance" in Harlem (1917–35) and Chicago (1935–50) was "spawned by Pan-Africanism, which posits the belief that black people all over the world share an origin and a heritage, that the welfare of black people everywhere is inexorably linked, and that the cultural products of blacks everywhere should express their particular fundamental beliefs." Floyd describes the quandary of renaissance artists, intellectuals, and entertainers who drew inspiration from the vernacular yet professed allegiance to the styles and tone of high or modern culture. Poet Hughes was a figurative link connecting the two renaissances. Floyd notes that the black arts manifesto of Hughes's generational cohort exemplifies the refusal of these artists and intellectuals to accept the hierarchical oppositional distinction between high (middle class, northern, urban) and low (folk, spiritual, rural). Hughes and the creative artists in Chicago carved a bold new position of cultural hybridism and individual agency that reflected the ideology of an emergent generation of New Negroes determined, as Hughes wrote, to "build temples for tomorrow, strong as we know how. We stand on top of the mountain, free within ourselves."

Clovis E. Semmes's essay describes the literal "temples" built in Chicago for the performance, display, and consumption of popular culture, examining their significance to the development and dissemination of black culture. In "The Problem of Race and Chicago's Great Tivoli Theater," Semmes historicizes the building of "the great palace theaters" of the early twentieth century, paying particular attention to real-life racial politics. Inspired by the architectural designs of the Chateau de Versailles, the Tivoli Theater was located in Washington Park with its 85 percent white population. The theater, originally built in 1921 for white neighborhood residents, employed a number of black men and women in service capacities. Due to gradual demographic shifts, Tivoli Theater management pursued a policy of separate seating for audiences for the live performances (stage shows in black parlance) and film exhibitions. Semmes notes that the large, elaborate, ornate theaters, including the Regal Theater, which was the black counterpart to the Tivoli Theater, "sought to sell the feel of being upper class while giving access to all classes."

In 1928, the owners of the Tivoli opened in Bronzeville a vast entertainment complex that included the Regal Theater (which predated New York's Apollo Theater), the Savoy Ballroom, and the South Center Department Store. Semmes, in tracing the history of these "theatrical palaces," shows how middle-class black Chicagoans fought segregation imposed by cultural entrepreneurs and the transition of Tivoli across the decades until the Regal closed in the late 1960s. The Regal Theater, Semmes has argued, was for forty years "the most prominent Black-oriented theater in Chicago and, arguably, at various times, the most significant black-oriented theater in the country." The "Tivoli Theater, born to service a white market while maintaining white racial hegemony, died in the service of a black community while catering to the sensibilities of black entertainment culture in the civil rights era."[69]

Hilary Mac Austin, in "The *Defender* Brings You the World: The Grand European Tour of Patrick B. Prescott Jr.," follows the European journey of Prescott and his wife as chronicled in the pages of the *Chicago Defender* in 1934, showing simultaneously how the paper facilitated the nationalization of African Americans in the United States and opened windows onto international experiences and events. Identities are relational, and the process of becoming metropolitan required not only local consciousness but international awareness. The prominent black Chicago couple wrote the last series of travel reports published in the *Chicago Defender*. In terms of identity formation, the trek of black southerners to Chicago during the 1920s was as complicated a process and practice as it must have been to leave the known confines of the United States to find meaning and fresh experiences in European capitals during the 1930s. Following the European journey of the Prescotts, Mac Austin points out what they saw and what escaped their notice at a time of momentous political changes in Germany, France, and England.

Part II. Black Chicago's Renaissance: Culture, Consciousness, Politics, and Place

Richard Wright and Gwendolyn Brooks, perhaps the two most famous literary figures of the Black Chicago Renaissance, shared a common struggle to discern a new black consciousness in the physical and metaphoric spaces of Chicago's South Side streets. Elizabeth Schlabach examines the poetic and pho-

tographic 12 *Million Black Voices* of Wright and Edwin Rosskam as well as Wright's last novel, *The Outsider*, to show how he depicted the confining realities of the kitchenette apartment as well as the segregated, overcrowded city pavement of black neighborhoods. Schlabach then compares Wright's attempt to define and defy these urban realities to poet Gwendolyn Brooks's *Street in Bronzeville* and *Maud Martha* that similarly elucidated the boundaries of racial proscription as well as the intense material deprivation of African Americans. Both authors wanted to portray how black people transcended their environment through dignified resilience, but, as Schlabach concludes, Brooks found a less destructive way out of the suspension "between two planes of existence." While Wright saw "death" or the need for rebirth as the route to what he termed "an honest and frontal vision," Brooks's female characters resisted "racial exile through the triumph of simplicity."

John McCluskey Jr. examines the significance of the timing of Richard Wright's "Blueprint for Writing" and its applications to his nonfiction work, specifically his early journalism and work as a journal editor. The essay places Wright's piece among the earliest in an international flurry of black diaspora manifestoes articulating generational and language disruptions. This is especially the case for Haitian and other francophone writers whom Wright would join in Paris by 1947. In their attempt to resist American oppression and French colonialism, nearly all called upon a return to embrace folklore, traditional expressive culture, and the complexity of their own history. Thus, Wright internalizes the Chicago impulses coursing through the literary thought of his generation throughout the African diaspora.

David T. Bailey places the black intellectual Horace Cayton into the vibrant community of Chicago's South Side during the Depression and World War II era. This chapter details the myriad of research projects undertaken by Cayton in Chicago, including his labor scholarship and journalism, Cayton-Warner and WPA projects, and ultimately his crowning achievement: the coauthored 1945 *Black Metropolis*. In charting this flurry of activity, Bailey shows how Cayton never felt satisfied with his position in the black elite and the Chicago School of Sociology. To broaden his activities among working people and artists, Cayton managed the Parkway Community House that he fashioned into a central hub for the black arts movement. The programs, protest meetings, and cultural events at the Parkway House—as well as the lavish parties there where artists, intellectuals, and "shadies" mingled—reflected the gregarious personality of Cayton, who crossed boundaries of class, race, and respectability. But Cayton's desire to broadly and deeply engage the world, Bailey concludes, ultimately led to his inability to survive in any of these social and cultural communities.

Jeffrey Helgeson reexamines the 1940 American Negro Exposition in Chicago, the first black-organized world's fair that sought to showcase these African American artists on a national stage. In so doing, he delineates the diversity of voices and competing visions of racial progress that defined the character of the Black Chicago Renaissance. Historians have described the exposition as a failure; the event did not attract mass audiences, and it did not create a broader public debate about the meanings of black identity, legacies of slavery, or contemporary discrimination in the United States. Yet, by examining the exposition as presented, rather than what it failed to be, Helgeson uncovers important and sometimes surprising influences on the fair's messages. This chapter concludes that the local black elite and New Deal officials unintentionally opened public space for critical assessments of the persistence of racial exclusion in the paintings of artists like Charles White and in the poems of Margaret Walker. The official organizers of the exposition may have marginalized black artists' role in the exhibition, but these artists nonetheless articulated a class-based critique of U.S. racial politics that emphasized the injustices of racism and the contributions of black Americans to American history.

By exploring the early career of Chicago-born painter Charles White, Erik S. Gellman argues that the artistic production of a cadre of young black artists became intricately intertwined with protest politics during the 1930s. As a young man, White educated himself in the history of African Americans by discovering books like *The New Negro*, the definitive collection of the Harlem Renaissance, and by joining the Arts Craft Guild, where White and his cohort taught each other new painting techniques and held their own exhibitions. These painters developed as artists by identifying with and existing among the laboring people of Chicago and by pushing to expand the boundaries of American democracy. They embraced interracial labor unions, not just for other

workers but also for them to powerfully demand inclusion in the government's Illinois Arts Project of the WPA as well as to create and run the South Side Community Arts Center, which became the central space of black community engagement with art and culture after its 1940 opening. All the while, White's paintings and murals "for the people" emphasized the dignity of black workers as well as the previously obscured history of African Americans who had militantly resisted slavery and other forms of oppression. Thus, Gellman contends, rather than becoming junior partners in art as well as politics to their white, working-class colleagues, African American artists like White came to represent the vanguard of the cultural movement among workers in the 1930s, making Chicago's South Side the center of the black arts movement as well as a cultural magnet for all American artists.

Part III. Visual Art and Artists in the Black Chicago Renaissance

In the closing section of this anthology, Chicago artist and scholar Murry N. DePillars explores the history of black visual arts in Chicago and highlights the distinctive influence of the Art Institute of Chicago, formed in 1879 (relocated in 1893 to its present site, Michigan Avenue and Adams Street), in the emergence of a black visual artistic tradition. In the opening decades of the twentieth century, the Art Institute of Chicago was one of a handful of arts schools that admitted black Americans. Among the earliest black students to attend the school was figurative painter Lottie E. Wilson (née Moss) of Niles, Michigan, who created the famous picture of Abraham Lincoln and Sojourner Truth that appeared on the cover of the NAACP's *Crisis* in August 1915. William Edouard Scott (1884–1964), born in Indianapolis, Indiana, attended the Art Institute from 1904 to 1907 and won acclaim from 1912 to 1914 in Paris, where Henry Ossawa Tanner served as his mentor. In 1927, Scott received the Harmon Foundation's gold medal for his work as a muralist. He was commissioned to paint more than seventy murals, thirty for the Chicago Park District and approximately forty for Chicago churches, including one in 1943 for Pilgrim Baptist Church. According to DePillars, Scott was the "dean of African American Art" in Chicago.

Notes

1. For notable examples of their scholarship, see St. Clair Drake and Horace R. Cayton, *Black Metropolis: A Study of Negro Life in a Northern City* (New York: Harcourt, Brace, 1945); Abram Harris, *The Negro as Capitalist: A Study of Banking and Business* (Glouster, Mass.: Peter Smith, 1936).

2. R. J. Smith, *The Great Black Way: L.A. in the 1940s and the Lost African American Renaissance* (Cambridge, Mass.: Public Affairs, 2006).

3. Anthony M. Platt, *E. Franklin Frazier Reconsidered* (New Brunswick: Rutgers University Press, 1991), 11. Platt reminds us that the generation of New Negroes born in the last decade of the nineteenth and first decade of the twentieth centuries included the following prominent men: E. Franklin Frazier (b. 1894), Charles Johnson (b. 1893), A. Philip Randolph (b. 1889), Elijah Muhammad (b. 1897), Marcus Garvey (b. 1887), Claude McKay (b. 1890), Paul Robeson (b. 1898), Arna Bontemps (b. 1902), Langston Hughes (b. 1902), and Richard Wright (b. 1908).

4. Michael D. Harris, *Colored Pictures: Race and Visual Representation* (Chapel Hill: University of North Carolina Press, 2003), 9. AfriCOBRA stands for African Commune of Bad Relevant Artists.

5. Robert E. Weems Jr., *Black Business in the Black Metropolis: The Chicago Metropolitan Assurance Company, 1925–1985* (Bloomington: Indiana University Press, 1996), 8. Carole Marks, *Farewell—We're Good and Gone: The Great Black Migration* (Bloomington: Indiana University Press, 1989), 1–19. Carole Marks persuasively argues that the early waves of black southern migrants into the urban north were more often than not skilled workers, landed people who had sold their farms, or entrepreneurs who sought greater economic opportunity.

6. Christopher Robert Reed, *Black Chicago's First Century, Vol. I, 1833–1900* (Columbia: University of Missouri Press, 2005), 4. Reed points out that DuSable settled in what would become Chicago in the 1770s. The continuous flow of migrants across the generations into Illinois and specifically Chicago led sociologist Charles S. Johnson to describe it as the "Mecca of the Migrant Mob." Quoted in Reed, *Black Chicago's First Century*, 40.

7. Reed, *Black Chicago's First Century*, 111, 229–30. Historian Kevin J. Mumford reminds us that the actual number of black migrants represented a small percentage of the total northern metropolitan populations but that it was "the sudden surge in their numbers" that caused alarm in non-black groups. Kevin J. Mumford, *Interzones: Black/White Sex Districts in Chicago and New York in the Early Twentieth Century* (New York: Columbia University Press, 1996), xviii, 180. Thus, by the 1930s and 1940s, at the height of the Black Chicago Renaissance, "the nightly parade of wealthy and various whites traveling to Harlem" was not replicated in South Side Chicago. Mumford, *Interzones*, 180.

8. Adam Green, *Selling the Race: Culture, Community, and Black Chicago, 1940–1955* (Chicago: University of Chicago Press, 2007), 10. In his important contribution to the history of the Black Chicago Renaissance, Green reorients attention away from the traditional approach to the study of black Chicago that focuses on examining the processes African Americans employed to facilitate adjustment to the urban centers to which they migrated. Rather, Green asks, how did African Americans transform the modern city upon arrival? The essays produced for this anthology approach both questions but with the primary objective being to explain how African Americans through their expressive cultural production and political agency defined themselves and resisted imposed representations of their humanity. Creative artists, intellectuals, political organizers, and members of the working poor and aspiring middle class struggled in the new political economy of the Windy City to secure living and breathing transformative space in spite of an often hostile and deadly environment.

9. Richard Wright injects a caveat in the migration saga by noting that the numbers of black migrants into Chicago actually declined during the early 1930s. In a December 11, 1935, report, Wright notes that the rate of in-migration increased between 1927 and 1930 from 163,800 to 233,930; however, between 1930 and 1935, the number grew by less than 3,000, from 233,903 to 235,000 African Americans in Chicago. Wright, "Ethnographical Aspect of Chicago's Black Belt," folder 1, box 53, Illinois Writers Project, Vivian Harsh Manuscript Archive, Carter G. Woodson Library, Chicago, Illinois. Wright does not explain the reasons for the decline in black migration but notes, significantly, that because "the Negro has ceased to invade Chicago in great numbers, . . . a measure of relative stability has been attained. The decline of migration has tempered the anxiety of the whites." Wright, "Ethnological Aspect," 9. See also documents included in Malaika Adero, ed., *Up South: Stories, Studies, and Letters of This Century's Black Migrations* (New York: New Press, 1993), xiii. Historian Ira Berlin observes, "Whatever their liabilities, ghettos became the destinations of thousands of black Southerners, many of whom knew little of Chicago, Detroit, Pittsburgh, or New York but knew all about the South Side, Paradise Valley, Little Africa, or Harlem." Ira Berlin, *The Making of African America: The Four Great Migrations* (New York: Viking, 2010), 183–84. Clearly, due to the demographic concentrations, by the time of the Black Chicago Renaissance, the South Side had become a site of emerging black political power.

10. Langston Hughes, "One-Way Ticket," in *Selected Poems by Langston Hughes* (New York: Knopf, 1948); Farah Jasmine Griffin, *"Who Set You Flowin'?": The African-Migration Narrative* (New York: Oxford University Press, 1995), 45. Griffin writes, "In the creative imagination of black literary and visual artists, the systematic forms of violence enacted upon black bodies is a primary cause for their choosing to leave the South." See etching, Albert A. Smith, "The Reason," *Crisis*, May 1921, included in Griffin, "Who Set You Flowin'?" 17; Barbara Foley, *Spectres of 1919: Class and Nation in the Making of the New Negro* (Urbana: University of Illinois Press, 2003), 28. According to historian Crystal Feimster, between 1880 and 1930, approximately 130 black women lost their lives to lynch mobs in the south. *Southern Horrors: Women and the Politics of Rape and Lynching* (Cambridge: Harvard University Press, 2009), 159–61.

11. Laurie B. Green, *Battling the Plantation Mentality: Memphis and the Black Freedom Struggle* (Chapel Hill: University of North Carolina Press, 2007), 5. Green describes the "plantation mentality" as a framing concept for a narrative of resistance and the construction of a "counter-hegemony" political discourse about democracy, justice, equality, and freedom.

12. Dan Carter, *Scottsboro: A Tragedy of the American South* (Baton Rouge: Louisiana State University, 1970, with new introduction, 2007); William R. Scott, *The Sons of Sheba's Race: African Americans and the Italo-Ethiopian War, 1935–1941* (Bloomington: Indiana University Press, 1993). See discussion of Chicago-based aviator John C. Robinson, "The Brown Condor," in Scott, *Sons of Sheba's Race*, 69–80; William H. Harris, *Keeping the Faith: A. Philip Randolph, Milton P. Webster, and the Brotherhood of Sleeping Car Porters, 1925–1937* (Urbana: University of Illinois Press, 1977); Beth Tompkins Bates, *Pullman Porters and the Rise of Protest Politics in Black America, 1925–1945* (Chapel Hill: University of North Carolina Press, 2001).

13. Langston Hughes, "Call of Ethiopia," *Opportunity: Journal of Negro Life* 13, no. 9 (September 1935): 276, in Scott, *Sons of Sheba's Race*, 1.

14. Mamie Till-Mobley and Christopher Benson, *Death of Innocence: The Story of the Hate Crime That Changed America* (New York: Random, 2003), 139.

15. A. Green, *Selling the Race*, 16, 179–82. Green moves beyond interpreting Till's lynching and the publication of the photographs of his mutilated body as an iconic episode in black pain. He argues that the response to the Till lynching in Chicago "offered an agonized statement of collective racial will, one illuminating an African American sense of self as comradeship that occupied a shared place and time." *Selling the Race*, 182. Twenty-five years later, in 1969, black Chicago would once again mourn the wrongful death of a young black man, the assassination of Fred Hampton. Jeffrey Haas, *The Assassination of Fred Hampton: How the FBI and the Chicago Police Murdered a Black Panther* (Chicago: Lawrence Hill Books, 2010).

16. Clenora Hudson-Weems, *Emmett Till: The Sacrificial Lamb of the Civil Rights Movement* (Troy, Mich.: Bedford, 1994), 29–30. For a discussion of culture and black identity formations, see Roy Eyerman, "Cultural Trauma: Slavery and the Formation of African American Identity," in *Cultural Trauma and Collective Identity*, ed. Jeffrey C. Alexander, Ron Eyerman, Neil J. Smelser, and Piotr Sztompka (Berkeley: University of California Press, 2004), 60–111.

17. Mamie Till-Mobley, quoted in Hudson-Weems, *Emmett Till*, 335.

18. Wanda A. Hendricks, *Gender, Race, and Politics in the Midwest: Black Club Women in Illinois* (Bloomington: Indiana University Press, 1998), 340.

19. William Tuttle, *Race Riot: Chicago in the Red Summer of 1919* (New York: Atheneum, 1974), 3–8.

20. Foley, *Spectres of 1919*, 9.

21. Horace Cayton, "Ideological Forces in the Work of Negro Writers," in *Anger and Beyond: The Negro Writer in the United States*, ed. Herbert Hill (New York: Harper and Row, 1966), 43.

22. Nikki Brown, *Private Politics and Public Voices: Black Women's Activism from World War I to the New Deal* (Bloomington: Indiana University Press, 2006), 115; Foley, *Spectres of 1919*, 13.

23. Vernon J. Williams Jr., *The Social Sciences and Theories of Race* (Urbana: University of Illinois Press, 2006), 63–66; Timuel D. Black, *Bridges of Memory. Chicago's Second Generation of Black Migration* (Evanston: Northwestern University Press, 2007). Williams argues, "Confronted with the evidence of black progress [in the wake of the Great Migration to urban areas] the leading sociologists found it exceedingly difficult to reconcile that empirically verifiable evidence with theories of black inferiority." *Social Sciences*, 66.

24. *Encyclopedia of the Harlem Renaissance*, ed. Cary D. Wintz and Paul Finkelman (New York: Routledge, 2004), 1026.

25. R. J. Smith, *Great Black Way*, 5.

26. Susan Eleanor Hirsch, *After the Strike: A Century of Labor Struggle at Pullman* (Urbana: University of Illinois Press, 2003), 121.

27. Ibid., 121–24.

28. James R. Grossman, "The White Man's Union: Great Migration and the Resonance of Race and Class in Chicago, 1916–1922," in *The Great Migration in Historical Perspective: New Dimensions of Race, Class, and Gender*, ed. Joe W. Trotter (Bloomington: Indiana University Press, 1991), 83–105; James R. Grossman, *Land of Hope: Chicago, Black Southerners, and the Great Migration* (Chicago: University of Chicago Press, 1989).

29. Dianne M. Pinderhughes, *Race and Ethnicity in Chicago Politics: A Reexamination of Pluralist Theory* (Urbana: University of Illinois Press, 1987), 95–96; Hendricks, *Gender, Race, and Politics in the Midwest*, 111.

30. A. Green, *Selling the Race*, 6–7.

31. Steven A. Reich, "The Great Migration and the Literary Imagination," *Journal of the Historical Society* 19, no. 1 (March 2009): 87–128.

32. Bill V. Mullen, *Popular Fronts: Chicago and African-American Cultural Politics, 1935–46* (Urbana: University of Illinois Press, 1999), 3.

33. Hughes quoted in *Langston Hughes and the Chicago Defender*, ed. Christopher C. DeSantis (Chicago: University of Chicago, 1995), 238–40. Langston Hughes, June 11, 1949, "From the International House, Bronzeville Seems Far Far Away."

34. DeSantis, *Langston Hughes and the Chicago Defender*, 14–15.

35. A. Green, *Selling the Race*. Green notes that due to the ubiquity of the Harlem Renaissance, "previous attempts to account for cultural innovation in Black Chicago have often transplanted the [Harlem] Renaissance template there, down to matching lists of awards cycles, patronage structures, and parlor festivities. This sense of historical derivation helps explain why . . . arguments that Chicago provides a landmark seat of black creativity have yet to take root in recent African-American cultural history." 4.

36. James A. Tyner, "Urban Revolutions and the Spaces of Black Radicalism," in *Black Geographies and the Politics of Place*, ed. Katherine McKittrick and Clyde Woods (Cambridge, Mass.: South End Press, 2007), 220, 218–32.

37. Tiffany M. Gill, *Beauty Shop Politics: African American Women's Activism in the Beauty Industry* (Urbana: University of Illinois Press, 2010), 136.

38. A. Green, *Selling the Race.* See R. J. Smith on Los Angeles's Bronzeville, "a black space carved out in the heart of the city, and it was created not from segregation but from black entrepreneurialism" following the internment of American Japanese citizens. *Great White Way*, 140–53.

39. Clovis E. Semmes, *The Regal Theater and Black Culture* (New York: Palgrave, 2006), 1–14. For a probing and illuminating study of African American religious practices and institutions in Chicago, see Wallace Best, *Passionately Human, No Less Divine: Religion in Culture in Black Chicago, 1915–1952* (Princeton: Princeton University Press, 2005); Wallace Best, "The South and the City: Black Southern Migrants, Storefront Churches, and the Rise of an African American Diaspora," in *Repositioning North American Migration: New Positions in Modern Continental Migration* (Rochester, N.Y.: University of Rochester Press, 2005), 302–25. Best argues that the upheaval, dislocation, and relocation that defined the Great Migration encouraged black religious people (especially women) to restructure the content and contour of their programmatic initiatives, worship patterns, cultural innovations, and liturgical practices in Chicago. Best, importantly, underscores the point that while the overwhelming majority of members of the black churches were women, gender conventions dictated that few would acquire ministerial authority.

40. Anne Meis Knupfer, *The Chicago Black Renaissance and Women's Activism* (Urbana: University of Illinois Press, 2006), 2–6. Knupfer reminds us of the expansive meanings and manifestations of culture: "Culture also refers to how people make meaning from their lives and create identities for themselves and future generations." 2.

41. Amiri Baraka, "A Critical Reevaluation: *A Raisin in the Sun*'s Enduring Passion," in Lorraine Hansberry, *A Raisin in the Sun*, ed. Robert Nemiroff, expanded twenty-fifth anniversary ed. (New York: New American Library, 1987), 10, 9–20; Richard Iton, *In Search of the Black Fantastic: Politics and Popular Culture in the Post-Civil Rights Era* (Oxford: Oxford University Press, 2008), 63–68.

42. Robert J. Blakley with Marcus Shepard, *Earl B. Dickinson: A Voice for Freedom and Equality* (Evanston: Northwestern University Press, 2006), 101–2. See chapter 5, "The Fight against Racially Restrictive Covenants," for coverage of the case *Hansberry v. Lee* (1940) that laid the groundwork for *Shelley v. Kramer* (1948), in which the U. S. Supreme Court outlawed restrictive covenants. 91–110.

43. Marks, *Farewell*, 158–62. Marks offers an insightful critique of the positive and negative benefits of return migration.

44. Davarian L. Baldwin, *Chicago's New Negroes: Modernity, the Great Migration, and Black Urban Life* (Chapel Hill: University of North Carolina Press, 2007), 51.

45. E. Franklin Frazier, "Chicago: A Cross-Section of Negro Life," *Opportunity: Journal of Negro Life* 7, March 1929, 73.

46. DeSantis, *Langston Hughes and the* Chicago Defender. In 1942 Langston Hughes wrote a weekly column for the *Chicago Defender.*

47. Christopher Robert Reed, *The Chicago NAACP and the Rise of Black Professional Leadership, 1910–1966* (Bloomington: Indiana University Press, 1997), 59–62.

48. Arvarh E. Strickland, *History of the Chicago Urban League* (Columbia: University of Missouri Press, 2001), 109–10.

49. Vernon J. Williams Jr., *The Social Sciences and Theories of Race* (Urbana: University of Illinois Press, 2006), 95. See Williams for a detailed discussion of the life and career of one of Chicago's earliest black social scientists, Monroe Nathan Work. 93–119.

50. Michael D. Harris, *Colored Pictures*, 152–78. Motley explained himself, "In my paintings, I have tried to paint the Negro as I have seen him and as I feel him, in myself without adding or detracting, just being frankly honest." Harris, *Colored Pictures*, 169.

51. Wendy Greenhouse, "Motley's Chicago Context, 1890–1940," in *The Art of Archibald J. Motley, Jr.* (Chicago: Chicago Historical Society, 1991), 34, 33–63.

52. Archibald Motley, quoted in Jontyle Theresa Robinson and Wendy Greenhouse, *The Art of Archibald J. Motley, Jr.* (Chicago: Chicago Historical Society, 1991), 34.

53. Bill V. Mullen, *Popular Fronts: Chicago and African American Cultural Politics, 1935–46* (Urbana: University of Illinois Press, 1999). Mullen provides a detailed examination of the evolution of the American Negro Labor Congress, founded in 1925, to the opening session in 1936 of the newly established Nation Negro Congress. 3–6.

54. James Porter, quoted in Samella Lewis, *African American Art and Artists* (Berkeley: University of California Press, 1990), 132.

55. Charles White, quoted in Mullen, *Popular Fronts*, 192.

56. Lisa E. Farrington, *Creating Their Own Image: The History of African-American Women Artists* (New York: Oxford University Press, 2005), 118–25.

57. Mullen, *Popular Fronts*, 27; Richard Wright, "Blueprint for Negro Writing," *New Challenge*, Fall 1934, 53–62.

58. Elizabeth Catlett, quoted in Lewis, *African American Art and Artists*, 134–35.

59. Catlett, quoted in Farrington, *Creating Their Own Image*, 126.

60. Arna Bontemps, "Famous WPA Authors," *Negro Digest* (June 1950): 46–47; Darlene Clark Hine, William C. Hine, and Stanley Harrold, *The African-American Odyssey*, 4th ed. (Upper Saddle River, N.J.: Pearson, 2009), 518.

61. Robert E. Fleming, "Arna Wendell Bontemps," in *African American National Biography*, ed. Henry Louis Gates Jr. and Evelyn Brooks Higginbotham (New York: Oxford University Press, 2008), 1:480–82.

62. Weems, *Black Business in the Black Metropolis*, 57.

63. A. Green, *Selling the Race*, 86; Michael W. Harris, *The Rise of Gospel Blues: The Music of Thomas Andrew Dorsey in the Urban Church* (New York: Oxford University Press, 1992).

64. Barbara Dianne Savage, *Broadcasting Freedom: Radio, War,*

and the Politics of Race, 1938–1948 (Chapel Hill: University of North Carolina Press, 1999), 264–70.

65. Pearl Bowser, Jane Gaines, and Charles Musser, *Oscar Micheaux and His Circle: African-American Filmmaking and Race Cinema of the Silent Era* (Bloomington: Indiana University Press, 2001); Jacqueline Najuma Stewart, *Migrating to the Movies: Cinema and Black Urban Modernity* (Berkeley: University of California Press, 2005).

66. "Katherine Dunham: A Talk with the Matriarch of Black Dance in America," interview by Cheryl Jarvis, in *'Ain't But a Place': An Anthology of African American Writings about St. Louis*, ed. Gerald Early (St. Louis: Missouri Historical Society Press, 1998), 351.

67. Susan Manning, *Modern Dance, Negro Dance: Race in Motion* (Minneapolis: University of Minnesota Press, 2004); Katherine Dunham, *A Touch of Innocence* (London: Cassell, 1960); Darlene Clark Hine, William C. Hine, and Stanley Harrold, *The African-American Odyssey: Combined Volume* (2009), 524.

68. Langston Hughes, "Brother Love: A Little Letter to the White Citizens Councils of the South," in *Burning All Illusions: Writings from The Nation on Race*, ed. Paula J. Giddings (New York: Thunder Mouth Press, 2002), 83.

69. Clovis E. Semmes, *The Regal Theater and Black Culture* (New York: Palgrave, 2006), 2–3. The Regal complex included the Savoy Ballroom and the South Center Department Store.

Part I

Black Chicago

History, Culture,
and Community

Chapter 1

African American Cultural Expression in Chicago before the Renaissance

The Performing, Visual, and Literary Arts, 1893–1933

CHRISTOPHER ROBERT REED

Chicago historically was a proven incubator from which cultural creativity arose from various sources, institutionally, organizationally, and individually. The city also had established itself as magnet, locus, wellspring, and actualization of cultural expression, appearing as an especially nurturing hostess.[1] Ignored from widespread historical recognition until the late twentieth century, then, was the saga of black Chicago's civic and cultural elite as an aesthetic trendsetter, the emergence of a clearly defined class structure based on discernible lines of accumulating and celebrating wealth, and the rise of entrepreneurial and business classes both supportive and exploitative of the arts. Several major factors contributed to these phenomena. First, demographic transformation propelled a minuscule minority population into a burgeoning audience for the arts, with a range of interests that stretched from the cosmopolitan to the parochial. Second, class evolution paralleled twentieth-century business growth

and professional development, both wellsprings from which socioeconomic differentiation and class structure naturally derived. Third, the appreciation of aesthetics for its own sake, the individual's limits of enjoyment, and racial affirmation all existed simultaneously and bestowed their own peculiarities to the linkage of spirit, mind, and heart to artistic taste. The most cogent example of this was the influence of the sojourners of the Great Migration that further strengthened the black Chicago artist's search for independence from external directives affecting his or her aesthetic creativity. With the advent of the Jazz Age in the 1920s, black Chicago's literary production unfortunately drifted into a penumbra of relative unimportance in contrast to the rising interest and support given to the performing arts. Contemporaneously, an upsurge of creativity manifested itself in the performing arts and, to a lesser extent, was complemented in the visual arts. When economic depression and reform dominated life during the succeeding decade, literary revitalization matched growing musical versatility and visual production, producing a Black Chicago Renaissance.[2] Changes in the socioeconomic class structure found elite, middling, and proletarian interests often coinciding around several aspects of the arts but still most often dividing.

During the 1920s, a contrarian view emerged, disquieting the artists who had built on several generations of creative activities within the city. With canonical preciseness, the usually perceptive and accurate social analysts Charles S. Johnson and E. Franklin Frazier depicted black Chicago as devoid of an intelligentsia and a creative, supportive, cultural milieu. According to Johnson in 1923:

> The intellectual life has numerous excuses for not existing. The frontier mind is too suspiciously sentimental about the virtues of mother wit and too brutally contemptuous of culture. . . . [L]ittle literature comes out of the city. No, the kingdom of the second ward has no self-sustaining intelligentsia, and a miserably poor acquaintance with that of the world surrounding it. But it leads these colored United States in its musical aspirations with, perhaps, the best musical school in the race, as these go. The city has developed many accomplished artists who incidentally have been forced to seek recognition in the "Loop."[3]

His fellow researcher at the University of Chicago concurred later in the decade:

> Chicago has no intelligentsia. It is true she has the largest Negro newspaper in the country . . . [but] the direction of her energies [gravitate] towards practical accomplishments. . . . At the recital given by George Garner, who returned from triumphs abroad to entertain the home folks in Chicago, many an old woman struggled up the stairs of Orchestra hall after the day's work to hear him sing. Some of them were uncouth and greasy and thought he was singing an English number on the program when he was singing Schubert's *Der Linderbaum*. But they were happy to hear one of their own.[4]

For reasons lost to posterity, the conclusive bases for their combined lack of awareness of what historical evidence has revealed about the previous decades— creativity, innovation, independence—are unknown. A priori assumptions, personal inclinations, and perhaps a preoccupation with the celebrity of Harlem during the 1920s provide answers.[5]

Examination of the historical record proved them thoroughly misinformed. As early as the World's Columbian Exposition, black Chicago's population was introduced to aesthetic expression's most dynamic element, that of external contact and interaction. Scott Joplin brought ragtime; Henry Ossawa Tanner and George Washington Carver took to canvas and produced genre and natural productions; Paul Laurence Dunbar, along with Hallie Q. Brown and Harry Burleigh, contributed from the beaux arts, in poetry, elocution, and music. The Fon people of Dahomey, more than one hundred strong, broadened America's appreciation of syncopated music through drumming and other instrumental playing.[6] At the Haytian Pavilion, Frederick Douglass barred Fon drumming, heard nightly at home in Haiti as the music of Vodun, but encouraged the beaux arts. The Great Sage threw his lot in completely with a European-based mode of cultural expression and thereby continued to demonstrate his classism through his disdain for any part of African-based, popular culture.[7]

The arts as defined extend beyond grand culture, or the beaux arts, which encompass classical music, dance, painting, sculpture, and theater, all European grounded. The arts in their totality include African-based popular forms in music, dance, painting, sculpture, theater, and other expressive modes. Specifically in music, the genres included ragtime, "coon songs," spirituals, gospel, swing, progressive jazz, or bop, and the first phase of the blues, now known as classical, and after World War II, modern blues. Literary production among the expanding refined element of society advanced slowly from biography and political history to poetry, drama, fiction, and criticism, all destined to flower during the New Deal period and afterwards. Sculpture and painting blossomed and then flowered at their own pace. Lastly, even technology advanced to become a major influence in the creative process.

Among the foundations of culture in black Chicago were the various, mixed-class, weekly church forums, along with the elite-oriented Prudence Crandall Club and the Frederick Douglass Center, established in 1905 by Reverend Celia Parker Woolley, with assistance from Fannie Barrier Williams, Ida B. Wells-Barnett, and others.[8] As Chicago's first interracial center attracting both the white middle class and the black middling class, it contributed to better racial understanding. As an intellectual fulcrum, it stimulated thought in a variety of areas beyond race and informed the foundations of a literati. This organization contributed mightily to the establishment of artistic-support groups among African Americans in the city, with one of its primary reasons for being the establishment of a meeting place for the learned among the African American elite to interact with their counterparts across the racial divide and to elevate the appreciation of beaux arts culture among African Americans. Housed in a three-story, attractive, white-stone building with twelve rooms, it contained "a beautiful assembly room filled with books . . . [and featured] a fiction class in literature, now studying George Eliot."[9] The members of the Prudence Crandall Club belonged as did other college-trained blacks. Fannie and S. Laing Williams, Ferdinand and Ida Barnett, George Cleveland and Fannie Hall, and Edwin and Florence Bentley all belonged.[10]

Fannie Barrier Williams continued to write critically for various black and white publications and continued to garner recognition based on her erudite oratory on "The Intellectual Progress of the Colored Women of the United States since the Emancipation Proclamation" at the World's Columbian Exposition of 1893.[11] That Williams had ventured to link intellectual development and not mere intelligence with African American progress was revealing in itself. Careful in her thought and lectures, she challenged prophetically the assessments of black Chicagoans from scholars far ahead in time. For example, Louis R. Harlan's short description of these folk as belonging to a population composed "mostly of the inarticulate, the unskilled working and servant class" told only a part of their collective socioeconomic character as well as the saga to improve their lives.[12] If they were inarticulate, Williams found that their activities belied any ignorance associated with this trait. She reported that hundreds of young men availed themselves of church-sponsored literary-club and other social activities in efforts to improve themselves. When Johnson and Frazier condemned black Chicago because of, as they claimed, its lack of high intelligence, yet alone intellectual interests and abilities, neither provided evidence of any sort nor compelling arguments on the subject, only assertions.

The formation of the Washington Intercollegiate Club in 1909 brought together young adults who attended area colleges in proximity. The Wabash YMCA opened in 1913 and also served as meeting place of the inquisitive as well as the dilettante to higher learning and various forms of cultural expression. During his summer visits to Chicago after receiving his doctorate in history at Harvard University, Carter G. Woodson resided at the Y. There, he engaged

in discussion and strategic planning with fellow Harvard graduate, A. L. Jackson, the Y's administrative leader, who held the position of secretary. Woodson, along with Jackson, James Stamps, H. B. Hargrove, and Dr. George Cleveland Hall, organized the first modern body to scientifically study the life and culture of people of African descent. It was aptly named the Association for the Study of Negro Life and History. Impressive in its own right, it was not the case of a new idea bearing fruit. Reverend Richard R. Wright Jr. (who was trained at the University of Chicago in religion and sociology) organized his own Negro history club at Trinity Mission Church, and Wells-Barnett, assisted by Harvard-trained Richard T. Greener, organized a history club at Grace Presbyterian Church as early as 1908.[13]

One critical point in black Chicago's interest in critical thinking occurred in 1903 after Harvard-trained Du Bois's destined classic, *Souls of Black Folk*, appeared in print. Its raising of substantive issues informed dialogue at Reverend Woolley's home as well as the intellectual coterie formed at the competing Men's Sunday Forums at the local AME churches—Bethel, Quinn Chapel, and Institutional. Reverend Wright participated in the discussions firsthand at the Institutional AME Men's Sunday Club and in the split developing between the two intellectual currents and among fence straddlers. While half agreed with Du Bois's assessment of higher education as well as black life and its leadership needs, only one quarter sympathized with Booker T. Washington's position, which ranked as anathema to assertive northern blacks.[14]

Paralleling an interest in learning and the promotion of education that had proceeded steadily forward since antebellum days, a close-knit circle of African Americans within the ranks of the elite was slowly building a literary tradition. True, by this early date, black Chicago had not produced a formal literati, but, nonetheless, a foreshadowing of the potential held in the literary arts appeared. Notable for their intellectual and musical appreciation were the Bentleys, who "were engaged in a highly active social life which included on Sunday afternoons, fashionable assemblages of artists, literary figures, [and] musicians. . . . Bentley's [concert] vocal renditions were part of the entertainment of these salons. . . . Many black and white personages, who at the turn of the century were students in the Chicago area, held fond memories of the Bentley's sociability and hospitality."[15]

Journalists such as Fannie Barrier Williams, Ida B. Wells-Barnett, Ferdinand L. Barnett, and Robert S. Abbott among others exchanged ideas and on occasion transferred them into prose beyond the pages of newspapers. Moreover, an intelligentsia had been forming since the late nineteenth century that produced intellectual and creative pieces, some semblance of scholarship in critical essays and autobiographical narratives.

At critical junctures in the settling of Chicago, black intellectual progression, literary interest, critical appreciation, and educational advancement for both children and adult learners achieved incremental movement forward. It was not monumental to be sure, but progress was evident. Importantly, in some aspects it anticipated the interest some of the writers of the postwar Harlem renaissance had in examining the inner dynamics of black life. African American interaction within a communal setting overshadowed aesthetic curiosity in racial reaction and relationships. According to the 1910 census, their numbers included ten editors and reporters to be added to scholarly and critically minded individuals such as Major John R. Lynch, Fannie Barrier Williams, and Ida B. Wells-Barnett. The census cited fifteen persons who were identified as artists of one variety or another with a visual artist such as William Edouard Scott moving to perfect his techniques in genre (locally focused or indigenous) art. This approach concentrated on the everyday goings of rank-and-file African Americans that brought so much pride, joy, and excitement into the black world. In the area of the literary arts, the same development proceeded forward. The performing arts included 54 actresses and 136 musicians.[16]

By the 1910s, conditions appeared ripe for building a serious literary tradition. A local committee of writers and authors coalesced into a formal body affiliated with an even-larger national grouping, the National Association of Negro Authors and Writers. Physician M. A. Majors and others took the lead in seeking a greater appreciation in writing, reading, and critical thinking. Their one major aim was to elevate their group to a level at which independent, indigenous thinking emerges, less dependent than ever before on friendly whites for support and less vulnerable to harmful, racist-based, white criticism. In seeking racial self-definition and hoping to capture the popular imagination, they eschewed mimicry of whites while promoting an earnest interest in the group's essence, sometimes in the dynamics of everyday, working-class life. Further, they sought to stimulate a racial consciousness that would withstand all abuse and engender a higher sense of unity. In this endeavor, their efforts would parallel advancements in politics, business, and fraternal life.

Majors assumed the presidency sometime during this period and was in office in 1915 when the Chicago committee hosted the national conclave. Majors's educational background extended beyond his medical training at Meharry Medical College. Majors was a Texan by birth, physician by training, an organizer of the 1893 Columbia Exposition offering by African Americans, and a writer through avocation. He embarked on his second career in the arts by heading the Department of Penmanship at Meharry Medical College in Nashville. Next he edited the *Western News* in California and returned to Texas by 1890, where he began compiling *Noted Negro Women, Their Triumphs and Activities*. This effort afforded him the opportunity to commit himself to elevating his race's perception of itself by honoring African American women.[17] His earliest vehicle of expression, after his commitment to medicine at Meharry College, was literary, demonstrated through his compilation of data for this book. Once in Chicago by the world's fair year of 1893, he found a publisher for his work and laid the foundation for a writing tradition that would bloom within two generations.

Over a two-day span in mid-August, Majors and his committee of Professor Greener, George W. Ellis, Major Lynch, W. H. A. Moore, Hiram Holland, and Henry David Middleton played host to one hundred writers. Their purpose was clear-cut and indicative of the times when an aroused sense of racial destiny was evident: "impress the rest of mankind with his literary prowess . . . while with poetic and literary grace he tells his story—a wonderful story; one that will carry the listener wherever human thought has evolved an idea."[18]

Greener, who holds distinction as the first African American graduate of Harvard University, in 1870, arrived in Chicago in 1906 upon his retirement from public service with the U.S. Department of State. Overseas, he served at diplomatic posts in Bombay, India, and Vladivostok, Russia. Earlier, Greener had built a successful career in education and law. He earned a law degree at the University of South Carolina, practiced in Washington, D.C., and served as a librarian and professor of Greek, mathematics, and constitutional law. In addition, he assumed an associate editorship with the *Encyclopedia of American Biography*. Once in Chicago, Greener joined the prestigious Harvard Club and devoted himself to civic matters. No doubt, he met Woodson on Woodson's summer sojourns to the University of Chicago before he finished his work toward a doctorate at Harvard in 1912. Jackson was to be found at the Wabash YMCA, and W. E. B. Du Bois was a regular visitor to Chicago, speaking at Jane Addams's Hull House, the black Wendell Phillips Center on the West Side, and numerous religious and secular venues on the South Side.

Rivaling Greener's credentials were those of George Washington Ellis, an attorney, author, and diplomat, who served for eight years as secretary to the U.S. legation to Liberia. Born in Missouri, "at an early age he evidenced unusual studious application to his books, showing a strong desire for knowledge." During his adult years, he acquired an education at Howard University and New York City's Gunton Institute of Economics and Social Science. As part of an emerging intelligentsia, he displayed a "cultured mind and philosophical viewpoint [that] made him acceptable in the company of the most critical minds." His scholarship included *Negro Culture in West Africa: A Social Study of the Negro Group of Vai-Speaking People, with Its Own Alphabet and Written Language, Islam as a Factor in West Africa, Liberia in the Political Psychology of West Africa,* and *The Psychology of American Race Prejudice*.[19]

Critically, as an author on African peoples, recently he has been labeled as a "racial romanticist," his writing being too sympathetic to the humanity of his black subjects. However, the University of Chicago anthropologist writing his introduction assessed *Negro Culture in West Africa* thus: "As a scientific investigation, as a contribution to social problems, as a basis for political action, it has a definite mission." Further, to a contemporary, his writing evinced a "clarity of vision" and "that sympathizing interest which is always calculated to do justice to the cause under consideration." In contrast, his only novel, *The Leopold's Claw* (1917), was uncharacteristically patronizing to Africans and focused on love and adventure. Ellis's early and unexpected death in 1919 dealt a blow to black Chicago's evolving intellectual climate.[20]

Yet, another contributor to this incipient literary tradition and circle appeared when former Mississippi Reconstruction congressman and now Chicago resident (since 1912) John R. Lynch published his perspective on that turbulent time in U.S. political history. As an introspective view of American politics from the freedman's viewpoint, Lynch's *Facts of Reconstruction*, published in Chicago in 1913, was a turning point in African American literary production. He acquired a taste for learning early as a slave but lacked formal educational training. By chance, a friendly slave master allowed him to learn the rudiments of reading and writing despite a Louisiana law prohibiting the practice. Further efforts at self-education followed, and in adulthood he became an insatiable reader of ancient and modern Western literature. The *New York Times* even took note of this freedman who demonstrated "an unquenchable thirst for knowledge." He soon transformed himself into a master of parliamentary procedure and an effective Republican party leader in Mississippi. By 1872, ambition and rigorous discipline and self-training allowed him to pass the Mississippi bar. After success in southern politics, in his later years in Chicago he would make up for his nearly invisible role in local politics with his pen and interest in writing his race's version of its role in the Reconstruction.[21] With a sense of purpose, Lynch assumed a role as *the* black voice on what transpired and why during that pivotal epoch in a way no other contemporary, black written works did. Repeatedly in the twentieth century, he would challenge academicians who posed as serious a threat to black advancement as Reconstruction-era racists did in his young adult years. In at least three instances, he produced written refutations to the racist Dunning-Burgess-Rhodes schools of race prejudice that tainted scholarship for decades. Using the academic framework his friend Woodson's journal, the *Journal of Negro History*, provided, he constructed a formidable point of challenge. As to his critical skills, one of William A. Dunning's students, J. W. Garner, assessed Lynch's work as balanced in the *Mississippi Valley Historical Review*: "On the whole, the book is a fair and temperate presentation of the case of the reconstructionists." Garner, despite his support for the prevailing negativism toward Reconstruction-era interpretation, wrote that Lynch's piece was objectively presented, being devoid of emotionalism: "There is no evidence of bitterness or vindictiveness."[22] New York publisher Walter Neale, who saw something quite positive on the horizon for black writing and American race relations, wrote to Lynch, "Once give your race in this country a literature of its own—an adequate literature—and the problem of the races will have been solved. And, I am glad to say, there seems to me to have been greater activity among Negro writers in America during the past five years than during the 200 preceding years. Why, I now have before me, recently submitted to our house, the manuscript of a superb work by a member of your race, George W. Ellis [of Chicago]."[23] When Woodson evaluated Lynch's integrity and contribution to letters upon his death in 1940, he noted, "Lynch emerged as a clean man whose enemies eloquently testify as to his honesty and sincerity of purpose. Although denied the opportunity for education which many of his contemporaries enjoyed, no man of his time had a better grasp of the meaning of the political drama in which he participated or the ability to express his thought in more forceful and convincing language." Perhaps, Woodson's declaration that "he [Lynch] must take his place in History as a statesman to whom historians will inevitably direct attention" bore fruit most productively in the works of Du Bois's *Black Reconstruction* (1935) and John Hope Franklin's *Reconstruction* (1963), who both built upon Lynch's clear-cut work to provide another scholarly position from which to assault racism in the American academy as well as the national mind.[24]

While Henry David Middleton was being acclaimed as another Dunbar with a style so similar that "many of his stray gems are mistaken for Dunbar," and James D. Corrothers was rising to fame, the youthful Fenton Johnson deserved recognition as another of black Chicago's earliest exponents of genre poetry.[25] His exploration of the black lifestyle in dialect also made his name reflective locally of Dunbar's works, but a major difference was Johnson's being credited with employing the medium of free verse. He was born in Chicago in 1888 to a Pullman porter and homemaker who owned their home. But the network of patronage support for his fledgling artistic ambitions encompassed his entire family, including his wealthy uncle, the infamous gambling czar John "Mushmouth" Johnson. Even before his matriculation at the University of Chicago in 1910, the younger, talented Johnson had published in the *Broad-Ax* newspaper in 1900 and written dramas that were presented at the Pekin Theater. He later taught English at the State University at Louisville in 1910–11 and by 1913 had his first collection of poems, *A Little Dreaming*, published. The theme was consistent with black Chicagoans' interest in the dynamics of their lives, and

so it celebrated elements of African American and African life.[26] In 1915, his *Visions of the Dusk* explored in dialect the horrors of the slavery experience. The next year, he published the first of two magazines devoted solely to poetry, *The Champion Magazine* followed by *The Favorite Magazine*. These early years of his literary production became more limited after 1920.

Chicago businessman Anthony Overton contributed to the advancement of literary interests through his sponsorship of *Half-Century Magazine*, which began publication in 1916. While *Half-Century* began primarily as a business organ promoting the emerging Overton financial empire as well as across-the-board South Side entrepreneurial and business operations, it also presented the literary strivings of unknown Chicagoans. It further challenged any publication that relegated its pages only to the literary renderings of high brows, indicating that it was willing to compete with Du Bois's *Crisis* with its New York leanings. During the 1920s, *Half-Century Magazine* focused heavily on publishing local writers of short stories and poetry. Majors soon assumed the helm as an associate editor and contributed articles, and Middleton produced several interesting short stories. Significantly, James Weldon Johnson's *Autobiography of an Ex-Colored Man* was serialized during this period. For his part, Greener added his support through these encouraging words: "*Half-Century Magazine* outstrips anything published by the race, and it ought to." The editors blushed and further reacted, "Words of gold falling from a philosopher's lips, almost stunned us."[27] Fellow Harvardite Du Bois's comments from the *Crisis*, if available, would have been equally interesting to report. At this time, it was reported that "contributions to the *Crisis* and other magazines, give evidence of a remarkable ability for writing."[28]

Beyond the ranks of Majors's writers' committee, publisher Abbott introduced a new style of journalism to the city in May 1905 when he first produced his *Chicago Defender*. Beyond the sensationalism that allowed him to build his national readership steadily over the years, he contributed to aesthetics through his innovative ideas and broad cultural appreciation. Perhaps the city's sixth black newspaper since the founding of the *Conservator* in 1878, the *Chicago Defender* promoted protest for civil rights as well as race pride through various forms of black culture. Abbott's fullest interest in the literary arts personally would be realized in the next decade when he published *Abbott's Monthly*.

Contemporarily, Abbott demonstrated his evolving critical skills in analysis on his editorial page. He also unfortunately showed his tendency to engage in hyperbole and outright propaganda. The *Defender*'s mainstay in the early years was, of course, its sensationalistic and deliberately lurid articles that appealed to the masses. Overall, the assessments of Charles S. Johnson and Carter G. Woodson of Abbott were most telling as they agreed that he had succeeded in making good on his pledge to make the *Defender* the world's greatest weekly, at least for African Americans. Johnson wrote, "My personal judgment at the time was that the progress of the racial movement, supported by the *Defender*, exceeded the *Defender*'s own calculated designs; that paradoxically, if Mr. Abbott had had more of the discipline of formal education, he would have achieved less, because he would have been restrained by history and precedent."[29] In concurrence, Woodson analyzed, "Abbott deserves credit especially for what he did for the Negro press. Prior to the success of *The Chicago Defender* Negro newspapers were ordinary sheets which had little influence upon the locality in which they printed. Not a single one had a circulation exceeding 25,000 and most of them considered themselves doing well if the circulation ran as high as 5,000. When Abbott demonstrated, however, the possibility of the newspaper that would cater to the wants of the Negro people in publishing news concerning them and in a way that they could understand and appreciate it, the publications changed their methods and imitated Abbott."[30]

From outside the city, an impressive array of talented, lecturers visited constantly, sharing their thoughts with receptive minds. Du Bois and William Monroe Trotter were frequent visitors. Peripatetic Du Bois spoke on numerous occasions, such as at Hull House on Lincoln's birthday in 1907 and at the 1912 NAACP convention session, and in 1913 at an Emancipation Half Century celebration at Orchestra Hall.[31] Trotter, editor of the *Boston Guardian* and president of the National Equal Rights League, to which novelist Charles Chestnutt and journalist editor Ida B. Wells-Barnett belonged, also spoke on numerous occasions.[32] Aspiring novelist J. A. Rogers wrote *From Superman to Man* (1917) while on one of many extended stays in Chicago.[33]

If the elite and the middling classes appreciated the need for a literati, the arts—performing, visual, and literary, and especially aspects related to musical presentation—fully captured a greater segment of the general population's fancy. All classes enjoyed music's variety and entertainment value. Before jazz or blues rose to prominence, choral music and individual song performance dominated. Whether appearing in public venues, churches, or private venues (including as far north as on the exclusive, white Gold Coast), the professional voices of choral groups seemed to dominate the musical horizon. Musical pioneer Pedro T. Tinsley formed the Choral Study Group, which was accompanied on occasion by the Chicago Symphony Orchestra. When newcomer Abbott sought acceptance into Chicago's socially active musical elite, he joined Grace Presbyterian Church and the Choral Study Group.[34] Yet, perhaps the most notable musical group was the Chicago Umbrian Glee Club, seen by some as the premier choral group of the early twentieth century as well as a group from S. I. Lee's Coleridge-Taylor School of Music.[35]

Venues in which creative activities found encouragement along with nourishment included both the sacred and the profane. Churches such as Bethel AME Church led the way with Professor James A. Mundy at the rostrum. Quinn Chapel, Olivet Baptist, and Grace Presbyterian also formed impressive choirs. Organizing a chorus of six hundred voices from these churches, Mundy led the group at the Lincoln Jubilee of 1915. Two years earlier, Mundy successfully directed the first black choir to sing at famed Orchestra Hall, home of the Chicago Symphony Orchestra. The director followed these triumphs with a presentation by a mass choir of five hundred at the Auditorium Theater, another first.[36]

Secular spaces, such as theaters, saloons, cabarets, and conference sites as well as crowded apartments, hosted other forms of musical expression. The Pekin Theater, opened in 1905 as the nation's first black-owned theater, was credited with giving "the start to most of the theatrical performers of the race on the stage to-day," according to a local newspaper reporter.[37] Its owner was Robert "Bob" Motts, who was described within theatrical ranks as "a man of broad vision and a big heart [who] opened an extended hand of welcome to all Negroes on the stage and as the spot on the bank of the Chicago river where . . . De Saible built his humble cabin bears mute evidence of a history-making shrine to members of the race, so does the old Pekin Theater building."[38] The Pekin Theater's troupe carried an executive staff numbering eighteen that "included everything from manager to house physician . . . [and was] manned on both sides of the footlights by men and women of his race, [while] presenting the product of colored composers and librettists."[39] The Pekin's stock company also boasted of a house comedian, dramatists, and composers.

In the various smaller venues, several musicians made a mark in composition, most of the time without widespread public recognition. Notable were Tony Jackson, Clarence M. Jones, Spencer W. Williams, Shelton Brooks, and Alfred Anderson. Even without professional training, cabaret pianist Jackson produced the hit "Pretty Baby," which was featured in Ziegfeld's Follies of 1916. Innovator Ferdinand "Jelly Roll" Morton considered Jackson "maybe the best entertainer the world has ever seen."[40] In contrast to Jackson, Jones had received technical training in musical composition. This background afforded him the opportunity to stretch his talents to the limit as he played piano in a theater at nightly film presentations and worked daily at writing music at one company and making piano rolls at another. Contemporarily, he was described as having the ability of "tak[ing] down by shorthand a whistled or hummed melody and play[ing] it from the notes as a stenographer would write a letter. He [could] run through the score of an opera once and after that play it by ear. [And he could] call any note as it sounded on a musical instrument."[41] Jones composed such notable selections as "One Wonderful Night," "Just Because You Won My Heart," and "La Danza Appassionata." Williams, who worked as a full-time Pullman porter, had aspirations beyond rail service. He doubled as a composer, being credited with writing the popular "I Ain't Got Nobody" and "Chemise Chihuahua." Brooks could claim credit for the compositions "Walkin the Dog," "All Night Long," and "Some of These Days." Last, Alfred Anderson collaborated with DeKoven Thompson in writing the lyrics and arranging the music, respectively, to "If I Forget." Thompson also wrote "Dear Lord, Remember Me" and "My Twilight Dream of You" along with lesser-known musical creations. Later, he would try his hand at filmmaking with some success.

Outside of the confines of the black belt, farther north in and near the Loop, Orchestra Hall, the Auditorium Theater, Kimball Hall and the Coliseum provided stage exposure. Correspondingly, the number of musicians continued to increase as the market for black cultural production expanded. As early as the turn of the century, black musicians considered the advantages to be accrued through formal orga-nization as an independent union and so sought affiliation with the newly formed Chicago Federation of Musicians. Led by members of the Eighth Infantry Regiment's band, the musicians carried through on their plans. On July 4, 1902, after being rejected by the general body of white musicians in what the African Americans considered a disingenuous offer in the first place with their talent level, the black performers moved forward as Musicians Protective Union, Local 208, a part of the national body within the American Federation of Musicians.[42] Their creativity was expressed first in minstrel productions, where songs of all variety flourished.

These innovative musicians were proud of their creative productions and, no doubt, were equally impressed with their influence over both white musicians and patrons. True to the spirit and skills they possessed, they played original music to their satisfaction and mesmerized their audiences to their will.[43] The number of musicians continued to increase as the market for black cultural production expanded. Certain names appear as instrumental in promoting black artistic expression. Notable among this group was Oklahoma native Major N. C. Smith, who in 1905 created his famous Ladies Orchestra.[44] As part of a wave of immensely talented migrants from the Plains and Midwest states of Oklahoma, Kansas, Nebraska, and Missouri, Smith injected into the Chicago musical scene a vibrancy that built upon itself to reach impressive levels of proficiency and creativity. Beulah Mitchell Hill, a talented musician of the period, wrote that "the passing of the years has drawn a veil of glamour and illusion over the events of the past and we are wont to think only of the achievements and to forget the hard work and trouble which made those achievements possible. It was a decade of high things, a time when our musicians banded together and did great things for the sake of art, rather than individual achievements for individual glory."[45]

In the midst of this second decade of creativity, 1915 proved to be another year of musical excitement. The second annual All Colored Composers' Concert was held at Orchestra Hall on Friday, April 23, 1915, where the popular Umbrian Glee Club performed.[46] By the summer of 1915, on the fiftieth anniversary of the end of slavery by law, the Lincoln Jubilee and Exposition was held at the Coliseum outside the Loop.

New technology entered the sphere of the performing arts as the enterprising William Foster embraced a new medium—motion pictures—in 1913. As a press agent for local vaudevillians, he knew the scope and abundance of talent available to capture the vibrancy of black performance on celluloid. Foster was also aware of the New Negro's assessment of himself [and herself], writing that "nothing has done so much to waken race consciousness . . . as the motion picture. It has made him [the African American] hungry to see himself as he has come to be." The next step was for Foster to begin his own business, Foster Photoplay Company, making him owner and operator of the first African American film production company in America. Committed to turning out "nondegrading comedies about black urban life," his efforts resulted in his being lauded by the African American press. Foster produced a dozen films, including *The Railroad Porter* (1913).[47] Politician Louis B. Anderson joined with a dentist, W. F. Watkins of Montgomery, Alabama, to form the Anderson-Watkins Film Company. By February 1913, they had produced and were ready to distribute a three-reel, thirty-three-hundred-foot film entitled *A Day at Tuskegee*. The first showing was scheduled for the Washington Moving Picture Theater on State Street.[48] Additional filmmakers joined the business including the Unique Film Company (1916), Peter P. Jones Film Company (1916), Birth of a Race Photoplay Company (1917), and the Micheaux Film and Book Company (1918). Black America's response to the distribution of the infamous *Birth of a Nation* was the formation of the Birth of a Race Photoplay Company.

Painting and sculpture remained popular among the visual arts. Art trendsetter and city founder Jean Baptiste Point DuSable covered the walls of his homestead at the mouth of the Chicago River over a century before.[49] In subsequent generations, wealthy matron Mary Richardson Jones and rising maven Fannie Barrier Williams displayed their taste in artistic creations in their homes. By the twentieth century, aesthetically inclined African Americans could purchase works and adorn their homes with the works of their fellow African Americans. The most well-recognized figures of the day were William Edouard Scott and Archibald Motley Jr.

Scott arrived in Chicago in 1904 from Indianapolis and engaged in five years of training at the School of the Art Institute of Chicago, followed by a stint at independent production. He then ventured to Paris to study with Henry Ossawa Tanner and other artistic masters at several French institutes, including the École des Beaux-Arts.[50] He returned to Chicago in 1913 (but only for two years), at which time he initiated a decades-long journey in which the production of portraits, murals, and genre (everyday folk life) dominated his works. Back in Chicago and free from the artistic constraints imposed with training in America, Scott painted black America as he perceived it in all its poignancy, flavors, and vibrancy. Consistent with the spirit of the city and the tradition that black Chicagoan artists would develop and engender, Scott followed an independent course in that he painted his subjects as he saw them and not as mainstream America imagined them to be. Moreover, these emboldened, if sometimes impoverished, African Americans assumed an awareness of their conditions but never a resignation to fate. Sensitive always to their humanity, Scott's subjects exude an optimism born of inner strength and rooted in the indomitability of the human spirit.[51] In his pursuit of artistic authenticity, he importantly achieved historical accuracy.

The demographic onslaught known as the Great Migration (1916–18) brought fifty thousand newcomers who represented an expanded talent pool as well as eager consumers of popular, African-based culture. Beyond what polite society enjoyed in choral production, ragtime provided the entre of a new type of music into the public's heart, and feet. Morton, the self-proclaimed inventor of jazz, thrilled audiences throughout the city during this transitional period. When the end of the war ended employment opportunities, it fortunately did not end migration as numerous musically talented individuals from New Orleans, the Mississippi Delta, St. Louis, and Kansas City headed to Chicago. Not to be overlooked within this wartime migration were the professionals and educated persons who supported the arts in their totality, producing even more aesthetically interested black consumers, customers, and enthusiasts. As to their tastes, they leaned more toward their own cultural productions, for example, the first phase of blues from the Delta to join with vaudeville and song. For film, they looked to producer and director Oscar Devereau Micheaux, pronounced by John Hope Franklin to be "the most important and prolific producer of black film during the 1920s."[52] Micheaux filmed on the streets of the South Side and chose his characters from passersby, from millionaire Abbott to the average pedestrian.

An African American business directory, Black's *Blue Book* (1918), affirmed the economic growth. So not only was a business base extant but it also appeared to thrive and provide the foundation for the unbridled success of black businesses in the following decade. Important for the arts, African American businesses lent essential support for the arts by building venues for the performance and enjoyment of the arts, maintaining a workforce with money to spend on entertainments, donating directly to artistic enterprises, and providing a class of persons who felt they elevated themselves through their rising sense of appreciation of the arts, primarily of the indigenous, or popular varieties.

Nonetheless, the artistic production from such painters as Scott and Motley found only a limited market among African Americans. Scott resorted to selling his services wherever his paintings were accepted, in public buildings, churches, and schools. Although he originally focused on French-genre scenes, back home in his adopted Chicago, he pioneered "a school of racial art" a decade before Alain Locke's call for such an endeavor.[53]

These developments and events contributed immediately to the making of the Jazz Age of the 1920s. Various new forms of aesthetic expression bloomed, and significantly, a distinct "Chicago style" of this mesmerizing music appeared. Jazz, which had entered the musical sphere in the form of ragtime, was now transformed into the most influential musical form of the times. It was so dominant a cultural phenomenon that it lent its name to the decade. Individualistic, syncopated, invigorating—it was prone to leave the listener moving expressively and dancing in wild abandonment. Originally centered around the piano, string bass, and drums, now the cornet (or trumpet) and saxophone evolved as lead solo instruments. Structurally, the attention given the individual performer now rivaled that previously accorded the ensemble.

Fueling the spirit of independence in creativity was the mindset of the period described aptly by African American intellectual Alain Locke, both a Harvard graduate and a Rhodes Scholar. It was one that demanded equitable treatment in enjoying one's own artistic production. It appeared under the sobriquet of the "New Negro" and had its locus in

the younger generation [which] is vibrant with a new psychology; the new spirit is awake[ning] in the masses [too as both

transform] what has been a perennial problem into the progressive phases of contemporary life. . . . For generations in the mind of America, the Negro has been more of a formula than a human being—a something to be argued about, condemned, or defended. . . . With this renewed self-respect and self-dependence, the life of the Negro community is bound to enter a new dynamic phase, the buoyancy from within compensating for whatever pressure there may be of conditions from without . . . [even] the migrant masses, shifting from countryside to city, hurdle[d] several generations of experience at a leap.[54]

Locally, Abbott's *Defender* offered its analysis in 1920 of this transformed personality with its indomitable resolve and titanic abilities. "Much is said of the 'New Negro,' we haven't seen such a critter, just the same old tinted individual, roused into self-consciousness, awakened to his own possibilities, with stiffened backbone, and new ambitions, new desires, new hopes for the future."[55] At Northwestern University, Frederick H. H. Robb, a law student, wrote: "He is a new type of Homo sapiens psychologically. . . . He has no narrow religious creed, supports human principles instead of race prejudice, ignores the unfounded flattery heaped upon the Negro, does not boast, but achieves [and] has a scientific mind. . . . He does not seek philanthropy but an opportunity."[56] As to aesthetic preferences, he or she was working class, middle class, or "dicty" (snobbish) and determined to enjoy the black aesthetic to the fullest, and whenever he or she desired, the beaux arts, also.

Well-defined territorial boundaries defined the Black Metropolis (an African American "city within a city") that existed as a physical affirmation of the African American tendency toward gregariousness as well as a confirmation of white hostility.[57] Within the South Side black community, a new sentiment affecting artistic appreciation and enjoyment among the masses, the petit bourgeoisie, and elite prevailed. In jazz clubs throughout the South Side, indigenous music reigned free from the cultural compromises dictated in Harlem. Racially, whites and blacks mingled as well in "black and tan clubs." In the latter venues, "sophisticates, street mongrels, businessmen, and chimney sweeps alike were in love with [jazz]. It transcended race and class like few other art forms."[58]

Positioned along major half-mile thoroughfares such as Thirty-First Street were pugilist Jack Johnson's stamping ground, the Club du Champion's Cabaret, and the Lincoln Gardens Café. On Thirty-

Fifth Street, the Grand Terrace, the Sunset, and the Plantation held sway; on State Street with its famous "Stroll" that millionaire publisher Abbott deigned to walk, [59] the Vendome, the Dreamland Café, the Elite Café, and the Deluxe Café stood supreme. With droves of multicultural, mixed-race, and cross-class patrons always at the doors, the major drawback found in Harlem had been overcome for the most part in Chicago as black patrons had as much direct access to black entertainers as others. [60]

Significantly, Harlem historian David Levering Lewis found that artists in Chicago performed in a manner suitable to them rather than to meet the desires of their patrons, white or otherwise. [61] Aesthetic compromise was avoidable, thereby eliminating the restrictions imposed by a white racial protocol over black creative production. In music, whites, in fact, became imitators of blacks. Tenor saxophonist Bud Freeman remembered, "I feel I owe a great debt to black people because it was through the music of Louis Armstrong and King Oliver that I got my best inspiration and direction. I didn't learn anything from just ordinary black musicians. It was the geniuses of jazz music who really gave me my lessons . . . King Oliver, Louis Armstrong, Earl Hines and Bessie Smith. When you heard Bessie Smith sing, you heard a whole symphony of jazz in one song." [62]

While true independence in performance might have reigned in Chicago, production was another story. As the number of homes owning phonographs grew, so did recordings of African American performers. Joseph "King" Oliver earned the credit for making the first black recording on April 6, 1923, which was in reality the *second* jazz recording produced. The actual manufacture of records was in the hands of outsiders at studios such as Okeh, Paramount, and Vocalion. [63] Nonetheless, the tastes of the masses were being satisfied along with that of other groups.

Musical giants such as Oliver leading his Creole Jazz Band, Jimmie Raglund, famed clarinetist Jimmie Noone, and Louis "Pops" Armstrong and his talented wife, Lillian "Lil" Hardin, among others, perfected and then re-created over and over again America's only indigenous musical genre. On block after block, male and female musicians contributed to the musical vitality of the Jazz Age, while sharing the black belt's landscape with the intellectually inclined New Negro. King Oliver's Creole Jazz Band performed at the Royal Gardens Café (renamed the Lincoln Gardens Café), which accommodated eight

hundred music listeners, and then the Dreamland Café between 1917 and 1922 to be followed by pianist Earl "Fatha" Hines at the Grand Terrace.

In 1917, Hardin preceded her later husband of choice, Armstrong, to Chicago. An accomplished pianist and composer, she played with Freddie Keppard's Original Creole Orchestra and then King Oliver's Creole Jazz Band. Later in life, she led an all-female orchestra. When Armstrong arrived in Chicago, she encouraged and molded him socially while encouraging him professionally to reach his full potential free of his mentor Oliver's influence. He grew restless and headed to New York to seek his fuller recognition playing with the renowned Fletcher Henderson. Instead, he found disappointment because of the comparatively stagnant (in relation to Chicago) music scene. Hardin convinced him to return, and when he did, he took the city by storm, becoming the city's and globe's preeminent jazz cornetist. Wherever he played, the crowds flocked to hear this premier soloist's brash, loose, and propulsive rhythms. Together again, Hardin and Armstrong recorded as part of his Hot Five, later expanded to become the Hot Seven. Yet for total creativity found beyond the latter two artists, the name of Wilbur Sweatman reigned supreme.

Farther south, in what had been a white residential domain for decades, the Savoy Ballroom (1927), the Regal Theater (1928), and the Metropolitan Theater emerged on elegant South Parkway near Forty-Seventh Street as magnets for black consumers of culture. The scope of the Regal's musical fare was exemplified by the opening year's regular lineup. Fess Williams led the jazz component on stage, while Dave Peyton led the musicians in their complementary responsibilities as they returned to the pit to play European-style symphonic music in the commodious theater. Diagonally and across the thoroughfare, Erskine Tate's orchestra handled pit duties at the Met.

The clamor for jazz had to share its enthusiasm with the blues, which rose to musical prominence during this period, also. Migrants from the south were often reluctant to totally discard their musical heritage, so they more often than not promoted a musical tradition beloved to them. At times, older settlers with a class bent toward high culture disparaged the newcomers' love of "plantation melodies," southern revival music, work songs, and boogie-woogie—the ingredients that made the blues that Ma Rainey and Bessie Smith sang so popular. Of this cultural-class clash, the newspaper *Chicago Whip* observed, "It's no difficult task to get people out of the South, but you have a job on your hands when you attempt to get the South out of them."[64]

Before the days of commercial radio broadcasts, remote productions from hotels and nightclubs were common. Significantly, African Americans enjoyed great exposure. As early as 1922, Clarence Jones and his Wonder Orchestra appeared on Westinghouse station KYW. It was radio station WBBM radio that led the way in broadcasting of African American bands, but it was to white audiences.[65] Then, Earl "Fatha" Hines could be heard live from the Grand Terrace Hotel in the mid-1920s.

With a burgeoning Jazz Age population of 109,458 persons, who accounted for 4.1 percent of the city's population of 2,701,705 persons, variety in aesthetic preferences could be anticipated. More and more working-class persons expressed their predilections for African-based music and dance, while a smaller number saw fit to visit the activities at Orchestra Hall as Frazier has described. When Frazier criticized a local washerwoman who attended the Orchestra Hall recital of a black man, the academician failed to appreciate the meaning of her attendance. The scholar misinterpreted an act of racial vindication—in that one of their own had achieved great musical heights recognizable by high-status whites—and she wished merely to give him her racial support. Frazier assumed that she (and others of this occupational grouping) lacked a background of musical appreciation individually or collectively to appreciate the performance because of presumed aesthetic deficiencies related to class and a background of southern or urban cultural and educational impoverishment. Given the exposure of laboring-class persons to high culture even throughout the previous century, the scholar's view was most likely inaccurate.[66] Whether motivated by group recognition of a member's achievement in the highest rungs of white society or full appreciation of mastery over high culture's musical forms, the case is intriguing. Probably unknown to Johnson and Frazier, black Chicagoans would even organize the Imperial Opera Company in 1930 and present *Bohemian Girl* in the Loop's Kimball Hall. To these accomplished classical singers and musicians seeking recognition in the Loop at Orchestra Hall and the Auditorium, this opportunity to perform seemed simply a case of receiving acknowledgment from the most prestigious arbiters of culture within the artistic sphere.

Financially undergirding the various forms of the arts in Chicago was a small group of African American patrons of the arts who provided a level of financial support that stimulated independence and eliminated the need to compromise. Incomparable to Harlem's patronage network, Chicagoans, nonetheless, through the likes of Abbott, Jesse Binga, Overton, Dr. Charles E. Bentley, and others, financially supported the arts. Several merited recognition as part of Chicago's who's who. From their ranks and from various strata—entrepreneurs, businesspersons, and professionals—a discernible elite grew with money to satisfy the aesthetic tastes that matched their growing wealth. Carroll Binder reported on this aesthetically supportive arrangement, when in 1927 he wrote, "Well-to-do Negroes patronize the arts and letters and have country estates and country clubs like those of white people of the same economic and cultural status."[67]

Overton, cosmetics magnate, banker, and publisher, had already proven himself supportive of black Chicago's literary strivings by publishing *Half Century Magazine*, which promoted the arts as an indispensable part of urbanity and refined living. By 1925, he had transformed the monthly *Half Century Magazine* into the Sunday weekly *Chicago Bee* newspaper, which was geared toward the more refined elements of African American society. He left an example for his family to emulate. The actions of his granddaughter (and a daughter of prominent patrons of the arts, Dr. and Mrs. Julian Lewis), Gloria Lewis Evans—in promoting popularly based African American music forms while also sharing an interest in the fine arts, supporting the Chicago Symphony Orchestra, the Goodman Theater, and the Lyric Opera of Chicago—speak to exposure to this model of familial benevolence.[68]

For the Bentleys, their interest in and support for the beaux arts remained strong even as the doctor's health began to fail.[69] Bentley's library dealing with African American history and literature grew, and in his will, he bequeathed the three-hundred-book collection to a proposed community repository in order to establish a Special Negro Collection in the Black Metropolis. Following his death in 1931, his widow donated the collection over to the newly constructed George Cleveland Hall Library as the core of its future Vivian G. Harsh Research Collection of Afro-American History and Literature.[70] Others, such as Drs. A. Wilberforce Williams and Ulysses G. Dailey, identified closely with and supported the beaux arts with the former holding life membership in the Chicago Fine Arts Association.

Banker Binga's Christmas Ball was a "cultured person's" delight to attend, if one were fortunate enough to get an invitation. Noted muralist Scott was commissioned to produce a mural for the Binga State Bank at the newly built arcade on the corner of State and Thirty-Fifth Streets.[71] The Bingas' taste for the beaux arts had risen to a level where they commissioned professional artists to complete portraitures, and Binga initiated a prize in his name for outstanding painters.

As exhilarating as the Jazz Age was in stimulating creative production in the performing arts, development of a literary foundation continued its slow growth. Poet Fenton Johnson began with *For the Highest Good* in 1920 and ended with *Tales of Darkest America* in 1929 or 1930. Locally, black Chicagoans promoted their own young literary aspirants who specialized in poetry and short stories.[72] Outlets existed aplenty: It was reported that by 1927, black Chicago supported a field of twenty printers, four magazines, and six newspapers.[73] Nationally, the major African American outlets for literature, *The Crisis* and *Opportunity*, edited by Du Bois and Charles S. Johnson, respectively, contained almost no Chicago contributions. Seeking, ironically, to credit black Chicago with a critical, scholarly breakthrough, some twenty-first-century scholars have included the writings of Charles S. Johnson and E. Franklin Frazier, who during the decade were visiting scholars at the University of Chicago, as examples of African American productivity. Johnson is now acknowledged to have authored the tome *The Negro in Chicago* in 1922 (credited officially to the Chicago Commission on Race Relations in accordance with racial protocol); and Frazier's 1929 dissertation was later turned into a book, *The Negro Family in Chicago*.

Abbott, as would be expected for his part, continued his interest in letters. He invited the city's young literati—black and white Americans, Haitian, Chinese, and African—into his two homes to stimulate thought and write (the second of these homes being a mansion on elegant, patronage-rich Grand Boulevard, now Dr. Martin Luther King Jr. Drive). The nouveau patron then started *Abbott's Monthly* in 1927 (which did not survive the depression years) and contemplated publishing *ReflexUs* ("Reflects us"). He wrote a ten-part series on his 1923 sojourn

to Brazil that informally gained support for but did not merit Spingarn Award recognition. Evaluation of the former was that it was too "observant and not critical" enough for formal consideration, failing to reach a level of acceptable, high-quality nonfiction. In order to establish his credentials as a person appreciative of the arts, he maintained memberships in the Art Institute of Chicago, the Chicago Historical Society, and the Association for the Study of Negro Life and History. One especially positive result of his journey to Paris was his induction into L'Institut Litteraire et Artistique de France.[74] Meanwhile, Abbott's pea-green Rolls Royce quite frequently carried his wife and him to the doors of the Chicago Civic Opera building, where he pretended to enjoy the music.

With such attention being given the other spheres, the visual arts were not ignored. In fact, Frazier acknowledged, "Art has become the proper subject of conversation among a certain class who condemn the idle women who spend their time over bridge. . . . Chicago's artists are making significant contributions; among them are Scott, Farrow, Dawson, Barthé, and Motley, who brought the latest Harmon Award to Chicago. The recognition that was given to Negro art during the Negro in Art Week has created a new appreciation of racial contributions in this field and is gradually being reflected in the homes of the Negro community."[75] Encouraged by rising black interest and the suggestion of Locke, the Chicago Woman's Club (virtually all-white with the exception of art patroness Fannie Barrier Williams) sponsored a "Negro in Art Week" between November 16 and 23, 1927, and extended it to December 4, 1927. Another goal of the event was to expand "knowledge of the accomplishments of the Negro in the various fields of arts [which] would improve the relationship between the two races."[76] Importantly, a penniless and near-starving Richmond Barthé made his debut at the event.[77] Emerging architect William T. Bailey, who did not exhibit, helped in the organizing and welcoming eight thousand people to the Art Institute. For his part, William A. Farrow won major awards in 1928 and 1929 for his etchings that were on display at the Art Institute.[78]

Muralist Scott's star continued to rise for he was now considered the dean of African American painters. His reputation soared, and his repertoire broadened during the 1920s. Of his talent, it is written, "Although Scott had a special interest in genre scenes portraying the black experience, portraiture and mural painting were his principal livelihood."[79] He virtually painted the town as his works were seen from the far North Side to the South and West Sides in public buildings, art galleries, and churches. In recognition of his high level of artistic production, Scott was awarded the Binga Prize in 1931.[80]

Public art became another sphere used as a channel of expression in which the creativity of the individual reflected an entire community's consciousness and appreciation of art. In 1926, a movement began and gained impetus to honor the fallen dead and service of members of armed services during World War I. The proposed monument was eventually built at Thirty-Fifth Street and South Park Way. Concerted black legislative pressure both at the city and state levels succeeded in bringing completion to the Black Metropolis's famed Victory Monument.

The era of the Great Depression produced both economic and technological disruptions that counterbalanced artistic promise. The dream of the Black Metropolis foundered, unfortunately, on the rocks of the Great Depression, which began in earnest in 1930. The two black banking giants failed as did one of the three community insurance giants with so many smaller businesses. The consumer base for entertainment was adversely affected. At theaters such as the Regal, talking movies also eliminated the need for massive amounts of live music.[81] The African American population had reached 233,903 persons, representing 6.9 percent of the city's 3,376,438 citizens.

Jazz was transforming to meet popular interests as swing music became dominant. Aesthetic bright spots continued, nonetheless, illustrating that the link between any art form and economics was tenuous at best. Armstrong advised trumpeter and band leader Floyd Campbell that if he wanted work, there was only one place to go. Campbell recalled,

> When I finally came to Chicago on May 9, 1930, there was plenty of work for musicians. . . . I used to say that there were at least one hundred and ten full-time musicians working on salaries of up to seventy-five dollars a week within a one block radius of 47th Street and South Parkway. There were two bands at the Regal Theater and three large orchestras working at the Savoy Ballroom. Bud Byron's ten-piece band was working at Chin Chow's Restaurant on the second floor at 4709 South Parkway, and across the boulevard at the Metropolitan Theater

there was Erskine Tate's large pit symphony orchestra. Chicago was a musician's town."[82]

Duke Ellington lived through these same times in the city. He reminisced, "Chicago always sounded like the most glamorous place in the world. . . . By the time I got there in 1930, it glittered even more . . . the Loop, the cabarets . . . city life, suburban life, luxurious neighborhoods—and apparently broken-down neighborhoods where there were more good times than any place in the city."[83]

So, at least the music continued.

In 1929, Frazier editorially challenged Chicago literati to reach Harlem's heights: "Song and story and poesy have spread the fame of Harlem beyond the seven seas, but the story of the South Side of Chicago still awaits its Van Vechten or McKay or Fisher to give it expression through the medium of literary art."[84] Unknown to Frazier at the time was the emergence of a writing club, among whose ranks was Richard Wright, who had arrived in the city in 1927 with a thirst for writing. The intermittent Chicagoan, Langston Hughes, met this challenge by being the first writer to examine the effect of the Great Migration on the newcomers' lifestyles and adjustment to big city life in his *Not without Laughter* (1930), based on his 1917 stint in Chicago.[85] The opening of the George Cleveland Hall Library in 1932 brought good times and a salutary venue for the African American literati. Its guiding force was the first African American librarian in the city, Vivian G. Harsh, who distinguished herself as a bibliophile, early and constant supporter of Carter G. Woodson's Association for the Study of Negro Life and History, preserver of African American literature, and inspiration to a renaissance on the horizon. Totally unlike the "Niggerati manor" described in Wallace Thurmond's *Infants of the Spring*, the Hall Library would accommodate the likes of Hughes, Wright, and Arna Bontemps, who researched the subjects of their writings at the facility and drew inspiration to fully explore all dimensions of the African American experience.

Finally, an external boost came from the public sector and at the national level. With the federal largesse opened to promote artistic production, the South Side Community Arts Center, at Thirty-Ninth Street and Michigan Avenue, emerged at the end of the depression decade as a center dedicated to the perpetuation of the arts. Dancers, painters, and writers, such as Katherine Dunham, Bontemps, Wright, Margaret Burroughs, Motley, and others, benefitted from their associations and encouragement to remain productive from the WPA-sponsored center. Wright would lead the "Chicago Renaissance." Meanwhile, Chicago's dean of painting, Scott, "completed thirty murals for the field houses in the Chicago park district and forty murals for Chicago churches."[86] Middle-class artists had arrived as an artistic element in their own right.

In commercial undertakings that promoted African American aesthetic interests, Jack L. Cooper hosted on white radio station WSBC on Sunday evenings with his own radio program, *The All-Negro Hour*. He was followed into radio by Samuel J. Evans, who, aided by his wife, Gloria Lewis Evans, promoted all varieties of black music and artists including up-and-coming blues greats Muddy Waters and Bo Diddley. While the Evanses promoted popularly based African American music forms, they also shared an interest in and supported the fine arts. In their dual interests, they represented the latest phase in the variegated linkage between class and the arts.

Despite the period's economic dismalness and political paralysis of various levels of government, a Black Chicago Renaissance was clearly in the offing. With the advent of the New Deal in 1933, government agencies such as the WPA and Farm Security Agency encouraged aesthetic efforts. Private patronage continued as well, inspiring artistic production, although it was limited in scope. Moreover, ideological influences, such as those exerted by the Communist Party, served to generate interest in the arts if only intended toward political goals. With the aesthetic juices and nascent talents of Richard Wright, Gwendolyn Brooks, Arna Bontemps, Langston Hughes, Margaret Walker, Katherine Durham, and many others emerging, the South Side's aesthetic horizon loomed ever so bright.

Notes

1. Carroll Binder, who describes the city's landscape and the status and activities of African Americans, wrote in countervailing fashion to Johnson and Frazier: "Chicago's Negro community includes a number of men and women of high professional and intellectual distinction. It shelters writers and artists whose work is favorably known among both whites and Negroes, but from both a literary and artistic standpoint there is no group in Chicago comparable to the Harlem Negro literati." *Chicago and the New Negro* (Chicago: Chicago Daily News, 1927), 22.

Jack Conroy discusses the historical dimensions to this claim of a budding literary tradition in three successive drafts in "African American Literature in Illinois, 1861–1941," folders 1, 2, 3, box 46, Illinois Writers Project, WPA, 1941, Vivian G. Harsh Collection of Afro-American History and Literature, Carter G. Woodson Regional Library, Chicago. The current chapter is indebted to the monumental and comprehensive *Call and Response: The Riverside Anthology of the African American Literary Tradition*, edited by Patricia A. L. Hill and Bernard W. Bell (Boston: Houghton Mifflin, 1998), which posits the influence of a black aesthetic as the centerpiece of any dialogue on African American art. Chicago's early pre-jazz and pre-blues development is explored contemporaneously in volume 2 of Frederick H. H. Robb, ed., *The Negro in Chicago*, 2 vols. (Chicago: Washington Intercollegiate Club Books, 1927).

2. Arna Bontemps, "Famous WPA Authors," *Negro Digest*, June 1950, 47. English professor Richard Courage collaborated with Robert A. Bone (author of the renowned *The Negro Novel in America*) before the latter's death in completing a comprehensive view of the Black Chicago Renaissance. Their joint publication has now appeared as *The Muse in Bronzeville: African American Creative Expression in Chicago, 1932–1950* (New Brunswick: Rutgers University Press, 2011).

3. Charles S. Johnson, "'These *Colored* United States,' VII—Illinois: Mecca of the Migrant Mob," *Messenger*, December 1923, 926. The *Messenger* was a noted magazine of the 1920s with high name recognition. Countervailing evidence to this scholar's condescending impressions appeared a decade later, when the circumstances of economic depression and subsequent recovery in various areas, including the arts, brought forth the Illinois Writers Project (IWP), a component of the Federal Writers Project during the late 1930s and 1940s. The existence of this voluminous archive, compiled by scholars and rising literary figures and known as the "Negro in Illinois Papers," along with contemporary documents, lay bare many of Johnson's observations as to the superficiality of African American life and culture during the period in which he wrote. Displaying classism, Johnson could write disparagingly of the "peripatetic Knights of the Whisk-broom," when, in fact, from the ranks of these intrepid workers the likes of writer-historian J. A. Rogers and banker–arts patron Jesse Binga would emerge. "'These *Colored* United States,'" 928. And for that segment of other Chicago-bound Pullman porters who demanded more out of life than their racially prescribed occupational status accorded, their cultural pursuits knew no limits.

4. E. Franklin Frazier, "Chicago: A Cross-Section of Negro Life," *Opportunity: Journal of Negro Life* 7 (March 1929): 73. Based on the experiences with high culture in black Chicago's history, quite possibly some of these women were accustomed to both attending the Orchestra Hall and listening to opera. See Christopher Robert Reed, *"All the World Is Here!": The Black Presence at White City* (Bloomington: Indiana University Press, 2000),107–10, and *Black Chicago's First Century, Vol. 1, 1833–1900* (Columbia: University of Missouri Press, 2005), 396–400.

5. See Kevin K. Gaines, *Uplifting the Race: Black Leadership, Politics, and Culture in the Twentieth Century* (Chapel Hill: University

of North Carolina Press, 1996). Perhaps Gaines's chapter 6, entitled "Urban Pathology and the Limits of Social Research," holds the answer to how eager, young researchers (in the mold of a young Du Bois) could so easily reach the unfavorable conclusions they did about any particular African American population they were observing. Perhaps they conform to some academically rooted racial personality overlooked in [Charles S. Johnson], "Some Racial Types," *Opportunity: Journal of Negro Life* 5 (January 1927): 4, or acutely overanalyzed in E. Franklin Frazier, "The Mind of the American Negro," *Opportunity: Journal of Negro Life* 6 (September 1928): 264–66, 284.

6. See Henry Edward Krehbiel, *Afro-American Folksongs* (1913; rpt., New York: Frederick Ungar, 1967), 60, 64–66. See also Howard Reich, "Hotter near the Lake: From King Oliver to Nat 'King' Cole and Beyond, Chicago Has Been a Wellspring of Great Jazz," *Chicago Tribune Magazine*, September 5, 1993, 14.

7. Christopher Robert Reed, *"All the World Is Here!"*, 144, 150–51, 157, 168, 194.

8. Depending on the source, either Fannie Barrier Williams or Ida B. Wells-Barnett was instrumental in helping Celia Parker Woolley establish the center. See Koby K. Lee-Forman, "The Simple Love of Truth: The Racial Justice Activism of Celia Parker Woolley" (PhD dissertation, Northwestern University, June 1995). See Alfreda M. Duster, ed., *Crusade for Justice: The Autobiography of Ida B. Wells* (Chicago: University of Chicago Press, 1972), 280–81, and June O. Patton, "Fannie Barrier Williams," in *Women Building Chicago, 1790–1990: A Biographical Dictionary*, ed. Ruma Lunin Schultz and Adele Hast (Bloomington: Indiana University Press, 2001), 978. See also St. Clair Drake, *Churches and Voluntary Associations in the Chicago Negro Community* (Chicago: WPA, 1940), 145 (asterisked note).

9. Fannie Barrier Williams, "The Frederick Douglass Center," *Southern Workman*, 35, June 1906, 335–36.

10. Benjamin Brawley, *The Negro Genius: A New Appraisal of the Achievement of the American Negro in Literature and the Fine Arts* (New York: Apollo, 1937; repr., New York: Biblo and Tannen, 1972), 180. These club members could have been expected to have been aware of and visited the Art Institute in 1906 to view a $500 prize-winning painting by Henry Ossawa Tanner.

11. An example of her scholar-like production is Fannie Barrier Williams, "Social Bonds in the 'Black Belt' of Chicago," *Charities* 15, October 7, 1905, 40–44. Reflective of her detached self-analysis is "A Northern Negro's Autobiography," *Independent*, July 14, 1904, 91–96. On Williams's cerebral qualities and position as a female pragmatist, see Mary Jo Deegan, ed., *The New Woman of Color: The Collected Writings of Fannie Barrier Williams, 1893–1918* (DeKalb: Northern Illinois University, 2002), xvi, xxxiii. For her communication skills, see N. F. (Mrs. Gertrude) Mossell, *The Work of the Afro-American Woman* (1894; rpt., Freeport, N.Y.: Books for Libraries, 1971), 110–11.

12. Louis R. Harlan, *Booker T. Washington: The Wizard Of Tuskegee* (New York: Oxford University Press, 1983), 98, and Williams, "Social Bonds in the 'Black Belt' of Chicago," 40–44.

13. Richard R. Wright Jr., *87 Years behind the Black Curtain: An Autobiography* (Philadelphia: Rare Book, 1965), 107, and Drake, *Churches and Voluntary Associations*, 129.

14. Wright, *87 Years behind the Black Curtain*, 96.

15. Clifton O. Dummett, *Charles Edwin Bentley: A Model for All Times* (St. Paul, Minn.: North Central, 1982), 41.

16. "Colored Chicago," *Crisis*, September 1915, 236.

17. Monroe A. Majors, *Noted Negro Women, Their Triumphs and Activities* (Chicago: Donohue and Henneberry, 1893), v–x.

18. "America's Noted Authors to Meet Here in August," *Chicago Defender*, March 13, 1915, 4. Several years later, Majors expressed his lingering concerns: "We need books, and we need a deal of race pride to go with them. We need elevation of minds to go along with our better pride. . . . Initiative is lacking both as to spirit to write and to read what we write. . . . Let us read our own authors!" "Why We Should Read Books Written by the Negro," *Half-Century Magazine*, June 1918, 13.

19. A. N. Fields, "Early Chicagoan in U.S. Legation: G. W. Ellis, Author, Lawyer and Diplomat, Climbs Ladder of Success from Humble Beginning," *Chicago Defender*, April 1, 1933, 17.

20. Ibid.; Vernon J. Williams, "A Gifted Amateur: The Case of George Washington Ellis," *American Anthropologist* 104 (June 2002): 544–50; Frederick Starr, introduction, *Negro Culture in West Africa* (New York: Neale, 1917), 15.

21. *New York Times*, March 4, 1872; William C. Harris, introduction, *The Facts of Reconstruction*, by John R. Lynch (Chicago: Neale, 1913), xiv–xx.

22. Review by J. W. Garner, "The Facts of Reconstruction," *Mississippi Valley Historical Review* 3 (June 1916): 112.

23. Walter Neale to Major John R. Lynch, January 13, 1913, George W. Ellis Papers, Chicago History Museum (formerly the Chicago Historical Society).

24. Carter G. Woodson, "Personal [Remarks]," *Journal of Negro History* 25 (January 1940): 137.

25. [Jack Conroy], "African American Literature in Illinois," folder 3 (Lit II), box 46, 4, Illinois Writers Project; and "America's Noted Authors to Meet Here in August," *Chicago Defender*, March 13, 1915, 4.

26. Fenton Johnson, in Hill and Bell, *Call and Response*, 621–24.

27. Editorial, *Half-Century Magazine*, August 1916, 3, and "The Making of A Great Magazine," *Half-Century Magazine*, June 1918, 3.

28. Louise DeKoven Bowen, *The Colored People of Chicago* (Chicago: Juvenile Protective Association, 1913), n.p. [20].

29. Roi Ottley, *The Lonely Warrior: The Life and Times of Robert S. Abbott* (Chicago: Henry Regnery, 1955), 2.

30. Carter G. Woodson, "Personal [Remarks]," *Journal of Negro History* 25 (January 1940): 262.

31. Jane Addams to [W. E. B.] Du Bois, January 26, 1907, W. E. B. Du Bois Papers, Amherst Library, University of Massachusetts (Amherst); "NAACP Conference at Hull House," *Crisis*, May 1912, 80; "NAACP Conference at Hull House," *Crisis*, February 1913, 244.

32. Ida B. Wells-Barnett to Charles W. Chestnutt, May 15, 1915,

folder 1, box 5, Ida B. Wells Papers, Regenstein/University of Chicago Library; *Chicago Tribune*, January 4, 1915, 4; *Chicago Defender*, January 9, 1915, 8.

33. [Jack Conroy], "African American Literature in Illinois," folder 1, box 46, 22, Illinois Writers Project, Vivian G. Harsh Collection of Afro-American History and Literature, Carter G. Woodson Regional Library, Chicago. Conroy considered its impact on literature minimal as he described it as more of a pamphlet reciting facts than a novel.

34. Drake, *Churches and Negro Voluntary Associations*, 108. See also "Music Schools and Teachers," folder 10, box 48, Illinois Writers Project, Vivian G. Harsh Collection of Afro-American History and Literature, Carter G. Woodson Regional Library, Chicago.

35. Beulah Mitchell Hill, "The History Negro Music and Musicians of Chicago" in Robb, *Negro in Chicago*, 2:45.

36. "Chorus Leader of 500 Voices," in Robb, *Negro in Chicago*, 2:118. It is possible that one of the old women Frazier described on page 1 of this essay belonged to this assemblage, indicating a familiarity with both the venue and music.

37. Junius B. Wood, "Musicians, Artists, Writers and the Stray Genius," in Robb, *Negro in Chicago*, 1:15.

38. Robb, *Negro in Chicago*, 2:234.

39. "Colored People's Theater, Only One in World, Proves a Success," unidentified article, n.d., n.p., in author's possession.

40. Reich, "Hotter near the Lake," 14.

41. Wood, "Musicians, Artists," 1:15.

42. William Everett Samuels, *Union and the Black Musician: The Narrative of William Everett Samuels and Chicago Local 208* (Lanham, Md.: United Press of America, 1984), 10 (recorded by Donald Spivey).

43. Samuels, *Union and the Black Musician*, 39. The artistically satisfying, infectious atmosphere of the black theater, filled with responsive and interactive patrons, is captured in novel form in Langston Hughes, *Not without Laughter* (1930; repr., New York: Knopf, 1968), 315–20.

44. "Music and Musicians of Chicago, 1878 to 1910," in Robb, *Negro in Chicago*, 2:42.

45. Hill, "The History Negro Music and Musicians of Chicago," in Robb, *Negro in Chicago*, 2:45.

46. *Chicago Defender*, April 17, 1915, 4.

47. Arnie Bernstein, *Hollywood on the Lake* (Chicago: Lake Claremont, 1998), 46–60; Jacqueline Najuma Stewart, *Migration to the Movies: Cinema and Black Urban Modernity* (Berkeley: University of California Press, 2005), 194–96.

48. Louis B. Anderson to Emmett Jay Scott, February 25, 1913, vol. 12, Booker T. Washington Papers, ed. Louis R. Harlan and Raymond Smock.

49. "Development of Negro Culture in Chicago," folder 1, box 47, 7, Illinois Writers Project, Vivian G. Harsh Collection of Afro-American History and Literature, Carter G. Woodson Regional Library, Chicago.

50. Margaret Burroughs, "The Four Artists," in *A Shared Heritage: Art by Four African Americans*, ed. William E. Taylor and Harriet G. Warkel (Indianapolis, Ind.: Indianapolis Museum of Art, 1996), 13.

51. Harriet G. Warkel, "Image and Identity: The Art of William E. Scott, John W Hardrick, and Hale Woodruff," in Taylor and Warkel, *Shared Heritage*, 18–39; Edmund Barry Gaither, "The Mural Tradition," in Taylor and Warkel, *Shared Heritage*, 124–31.

52. John Hope Franklin and Alfred Moss Jr., *From Slavery to Freedom: A History of African Americans*, 7th ed. (New York: McGraw-Hill, 1998), 376.

53. Warkel, "Image and Identity," in Taylor and Warkel, *Shared Heritage*, 18.

54. Alain Locke, "The New Negro," in *The New Negro*, ed. Locke (1925; rpt., New York: Atheneum, 1992), 2, 3.

55. *Chicago Defender*, January 3, 1920, 15. One result of this new self-consciousness led to the building of a civic infrastructure at a time when it supposedly didn't exist. See Christopher R. Reed, "Black Chicago Civic Organization before 1935," *Journal of Ethnic Studies* 14 (Winter 1987): 65–77.

56. Robb, *Negro in Chicago*, 1:16.

57. Allen F. Spear, *Black Chicago: The Making of a Negro Ghetto, 1890–1920* (Chicago: University of Chicago Press, 1967), 26. See Christopher Robert Reed, *The Rise of Chicago's Black Metropolis, 1920–1929* (Urbana: University of Illinois Press, 2011), for a complete exploration of this attempted transformation of a dependent community into a self-sustaining racial enclave.

58. Harry Schuchmacher, "Best of the Best of American Music: Louis Armstrong, Changing the World," *American Mix*, May–June, 2001, 4 and Reich, "Hotter near the Lake," 14. Reich wrote that the economic diversity was such that "mobsters, musicians, socialites and working people danced past dawn to rhythms of America's only original art form." "Hotter near the Lake," 14.

59. Ottley, *Lonely Warrior*, 224. Abbott bridged the two worlds of culture. His stroll along his thoroughfare was an affirmation that he had not lost touch with the common person, upon whom he depended for both business and ego support.

60. For the jazz landscape, see "Alphabetical Listing of Chicago Jazz Clubs, ca. 1915–30," *Chicago Jazz Archives*, 1999–2003, http://www.lib.uchicago.edu/e/su/cja/jazzmaps/listalph.htm. For a description and analysis of the activities and changes at the Regal Theater, see Clovis E. Semmes, *The Regal Theater and Black Culture* (New York: Palgrave MacMillan, 2006); see also "Cab Calloway," in Dempsey J. Travis, *An Autobiography of Black Jazz* (Chicago: Urban Research Press, 1983), 230, 231.

61. David Levering Lewis, *When Harlem Was in Vogue* (New York: Oxford University Press, 1981), 171, 172. See also William Howland Kenney, *Chicago Jazz: A Cultural History, 1904–1930* (New York: Oxford University Press, 1993), 53, 54; Gaines, *Uplifting the Race*, 184. Moreover, the pressure to please white audiences, whether patrons, publishers, or readers, is well accepted as fact. See its exposition in both novel and scholarly forms in Wallace Thurmond, *Infants of the Spring* (1932; rpt., Carbondale: Southern Illinois University Press, 1979), and Gaines, *Uplifting the Race*, 184.

62. "Bud Freeman," in Travis, *Autobiography of Black Jazz*, 324. Likewise, the great clarinetist Jimmy Noone is credited with teaching Benny Goodman his level of proficiency. See Reich, "Hotter near the Lake," 18.

63. Kenney, *Chicago Jazz*, 120–46.

64. Quoted in James R. Grossman, *Land of Hope: Chicago, Black Southerners, and the Great Migration* (Chicago: University of Chicago Press, 1979), 154.

65. William Barlow, "Black Music on Radio during the Jazz Age," *North American Review* (Summer 1995), http://findarticles.com/p/articles/mi_m2838/is_n2_v29/ai_17534809/pg_3/.

66. Lawrence W. Levine, *Highbrow/Lowbrow: The Emergence of Cultural Hierarchy in America* (Cambridge: Harvard University Press, 1988), 30–32, 96–100. See also Christopher Robert Reed, *Black Chicago's First Century, Volume I, 1833–1900* (Columbia: University of Missouri Press, 2005), 396–401.

67. Binder, *Chicago and the Negro*, 4. In contrast, Langston Hughes said of Harlem, "Harlem nights became show nights for the Nordics." Certain writers were also affected and wrote to amuse white people. See Langston Hughes, *The Big Sea: An Autobiography* (1940: repr., New York: Hill and Wang, 1963), 226–28.

68. Obituary for Gloria Lewis Evans, "Roots in Bronzeville," *Chicago Sun-Times*, November 12, 1998, 62.

69. Dummett, *Charles Edwin Bentley*, 190, 201–2.

70. Doris Saunders, remarks on January 20, 2007, seventy-fifth anniversary of the opening of the George Cleveland Hall Library (author's notes); interview with Michael L. Flug, November 24, 2006, in Chicago; Michael L. Flug, "Vivian Gordon Harsh, "in *Women Building Chicago, 1790–1990: A Biographical Dictionary*, ed. Ruma Lunin Schultz and Adele Hast (Bloomington: Indiana University Press, 2001) 359; and Dummett, *Charles Edwin Bentley*, 190, 201–2. Saunders was a former student assistant to Vivian Gordon Harsh during the 1940s and founder of the Special Negro Literature Collection at the Johnson Publishing Company of Chicago.

71. Theresa Dickason Cederholm, comp., *Afro-American Artists: A Bio-Bibliographical Directory* (Boston: Boston Public Library, 1973), 249–50.

72. See "Greater Poets in Chicago," in Robb, *Negro in Chicago*, 1:86, 87.

73. Carroll Binder, "The New Negro In Chicago," in *Chicago and the New Negro*, 11. See also Robb, "Race Publications in Chicago," in Robb, *Negro in Chicago*, 1:124.

74. Ottley, *Lonely Warrior*, 224, 328.

75. Frazier, "Chicago," 73, and Robb, *Negro in Chicago*, 1:223.

76. Charles Dawson, "Celebrated Negro Artists," in Robb, *Negro in Chicago*, 2:27.

77. Roy Wilkins, *Standing Fast: The Autobiography of Roy Wilkins* (New York: Viking, 1982), 157.

78. "William A. Farrow-Etcher," *Opportunity: Journal of Negro Life* 7 (June 1929): 188.

79. Warkel, "Image and Identity," in Taylor and Warkel, *Shared Heritage*, 27.

80. Alain Locke, *The Negro in Art* (1940; repr., New York: Hacker Art Books, 1979), 135; "Artist Paints Way to Fame via Landscapes," *Chicago Tribune*, March 27, 1949, S4.

81. Semmes, *Regal Theater*, 39–41, and Reich, "Hotter near the Lake," 18.

82. "Floyd Campbell," in Travis, *Autobiography of Black Jazz*, 240.

83. Quoted in Reich, "Hotter near the Lake," 12.

84. E. Franklin Frazier, editorial, *Opportunity: Journal of Negro Life* 7 (March 1929): 69.

85. Hughes, *Not without Laughter*, chapters 18–30, and [Conroy], "African American Literature in Illinois," folder 1, 23, box 46, Illinois Writers Project, Vivian G. Harsh Collection of Afro-American History and Literature, Carter G. Woodson Regional Library, Chicago. See Hughes, *Big Sea*, 304.

86. Warkel, "Image and Identity," in Taylor and Warkel, *Shared Heritage*, 37.

I am a Negro:
Black as the night is black,
Black like the depths of my Africa.
—LANGSTON HUGHES

Would ye both have your cake and eat your cake?
The cat would eat fish, and would not wet her feet.
—JOHN HEYWOOD

Chapter 2

The Negro Renaissance

Harlem and Chicago Flowerings

SAMUEL A. FLOYD JR.

The flowerings of the Negro renaissance in Harlem (1917–35) and Chicago (1935–50) were spawned by Pan-Africanism, which posits the belief that black people all over the world share an origin and a heritage, that the welfare of black people everywhere is inexorably linked, and that the cultural products of blacks everywhere should express their particular fundamental beliefs.[1] According to Peter Olisanwuche Esedebe, Pan-African thought seeks to glorify the African past, inculcate pride in African values, and promote unity among all people of African descent.[2] Pan-African thinking was set off in part by the transatlantic slave trade and was intensified by the Haitian revolution of 1804 and the onset of nineteenth-century colonialism in Africa. Pan-Africanism flourished among persons of color in Europe in the late nineteenth century when, according to Rainer Lotz, "black entertainers roamed Europe from Scotland to Russia, from the Mediterranean to the polar circle. . . . Blacks—whether Africans, Afro-Americans, West Indians, European-born, etc.—were in close touch with one another, even across barriers of language, profession, or social status."[3]

It was in this European environment that Marcus Garvey, a West Indian who moved to England in 1912, began his development as the individual who, more than any other, "introduced the ideas of an African Nationalist and the African personality . . . to the uninformed masses in the villages and streets of the African world," developing a plan for the liberation of Africans in the diaspora.[4] Late in 1916, Garvey left England for New York. There he became the self-appointed leader of Africans and their dispersed descendants by founding the Universal Negro Improvement Association (UNIA), which, by 1919, could be found established in countries in all parts of the world.[5] The UNIA's official publication, *Black World*, first published in 1918, was the organization's news-and-propaganda organ. The organization's tricolor flag of red, black, and green was complemented by its "African National Anthem"—the first militant Pan-African musical product, referring as it does to

Ethiopia as "the land of our fathers," admonishing the oppressors to "let Africa be free," and proclaiming that "Ethiopia shall stretch forth her hand" to freedom.[6] Garvey's primary messages were direct and forceful: salvation for blacks existed only in the African homeland, to which they should return, and blacks in the United States should purchase only from black merchants, particularly from the UNIA's businesses.[7] In 1919, the year after Garvey's launching of *Black World*, W. E. B. Du Bois called a Pan-African meeting in Paris that was attended by fifty-seven delegates from fifteen territories, including, among others, "Abyssinia, Liberia, Haiti, the United States, San Domingo (Dominican Republic), French Caribbean, British Africa, French Africa, Egypt, and the Belgian Congo."[8] Between this gathering and 1927, Du Bois sponsored annual meetings, four of which were held in the United States, that helped keep alive Pan-African ideals.[9]

In England, black physician John Alcindor's African Progress Union Committee "included blacks born in Trinidad, Guyana, Barbados, Liberia, Sierra Leone, Ghana, and South Carolina, and was able to take a global view of the black world."[10] This was only one of several such groups, and musicians were comfortably among them:

> In August 1919 members of the Southern Syncopated Orchestra of Will Marion Cook were present with their leader and business manager George William Lattimore at a function in honor of several groups of blacks in London that had been organized by the Coterie of Friends, a student group of Caribbeans (and one Ghanaian) led by South Carolina–born Edmund Thornton Jenkins. Jenkins had been a student at London's Royal Academy of Music since 1914 and was currently teaching the clarinet there. [John Richard] Archer and Afro-American lawyer Thomas McCants Stewart mixed with South Africans and Guyanese in a room decorated with the flags of Haiti and Liberia. Jenkins, with two ladies from Cook's orchestra and vocalist Evelyn Dove, played works by Weber, Coleridge-Taylor, and himself. Dove, whose father was Francis Thomas Dove, a lawyer from Sierra Leone, was likened to Josephine Baker by Henry Champley.[11]

With Pan-Africanism widespread among blacks in England and with study opportunities widely available there, it is not surprising that black composers would emerge. The most notable, Samuel Coleridge-Taylor (1875–1912), was famous around the world in the 1890s. Coleridge-Taylor is marked as a Pan-Africanist by his contributions to the musical literature of the diaspora and by his interactions with other Pan-Africanists.[12] His Pan-Africanist orientation is demonstrated by his work, for example, with African American poet Paul Laurence Dunbar, whose poetry he set to music and with whom he collaborated on the opera *Dream Lovers* (1898). His African and African American–oriented compositions include *Symphonic Variations on an African Air* (1906), *The Bamboula* (1910), and *Twenty-Four Negro Melodies, Transcribed for the Piano* (1905).

Through his music and by his example, Coleridge-Taylor influenced African American composers and musicians, and societies bearing his name sprang up in cities across the United States in the early years of the twentieth century.[13] Coleridge-Taylor's friendships and professional relationships with African American artists, such as Dunbar, Harry T. Burleigh, John Turner Layton, Clarence Cameron White, Felix Weir, and Gerald Tyler, were developed through transatlantic visits and written correspondence. As a composer and conductor, Coleridge-Taylor became "the prototype for a renaissance of black culture," probably serving as a model for composers such as Robert Nathaniel Dett, William Grant Still, and Florence Price.[14] These composers would succeed in the years after Coleridge-Taylor's death with extended works of both significant and modest musical merit—for example, Dett in 1921 with *The Chariot Jubilee* and in 1932 with *The Ordering of Moses*; Still with the three-movement suite *Levee Land* and *From the Black Belt* in 1926 and *Africa* and *Afro-American Symphony* in 1930; and Price in 1932 with the *Symphony in E Minor* and in 1934 with the *Piano Concerto in One Movement*.

The American composers whom Coleridge-Taylor influenced were all nationalists, as their works attest. In America, black nationalism—an aspect of Pan-Africanism—had been developed, debated, and written about by free blacks as early as the first decade of the nineteenth century.[15] It was publicly elaborated by David Walker and Henry Highland Garnet in the early nineteenth century and around the turn of the century by Carter G. Woodson, Du Bois, and others.[16] But of all the major black-nationalist theorists, Du Bois was the only one who recognized—or at least wrote about—the importance of black music to nationalist thought. This importance is underscored in his book *The Souls of Black Folk* (1903) by the snippets of spiritual melodies and texts that appear at the beginning of each chapter, by his liberal quotations from the spirituals throughout his narrative, and by his essay "Of the Sorrow Songs." In this essay he discusses, perceptively and sensitively, the aesthetic and social value of the spiritual, focusing on the music itself, on the cultural and political contributions of the original Fisk Jubilee Singers, and on the spiritual singing of the South Carolina and Georgia Sea Islanders. Du Bois had seen and studied the ring and had heard the spirituals during his college and teaching days at Fisk University in Nashville, and he wrote about the shout, specifically, in The Souls of Black Folk.[17]

Another influential individual who recognized the importance of black music to nationalist thought was American journalist James Monroe Trotter, who, nearly thirty years before the publication of Souls, had documented the secular activities of black musicians in various locations in the United States. His Music and Some Highly Musical People (1878) was the first comprehensive survey on this aspect of American music history. Although Trotter was not a major theorist of the movement, his book is in the tradition of the "collective elevation" thrust of nationalist thought; in it, he was determined to put the race's best foot forward by treating only the accomplishments of those who could read music. Trotter's work covers aesthetics, music history, and the social contexts of more than forty-one black musical groups and figures who were then or had been active in the United States, including Frank Johnson, Justin Holland, Elizabeth Taylor Greenfield, Sam Lucas, Samuel Snaer, and others, in more than twenty American cities.[18]

Musically, the spirit of the Negro renaissance had begun to manifest itself, in the late 1890s and in the first and second decades of the twentieth century, in the work of Scott Joplin, Will Marion Cook, Harry T. Burleigh, John Turner Layton, Robert Cole, the brothers J. Rosamond Johnson and James Weldon Johnson, Alex Rogers, Ford Dabney, Will Vodery, Will Tyers, and others. Of these composers, Cook and Burleigh were perhaps the most important and revered. Cook, a kind of dean of black musicians, served as musical director, composer, and producer for a number of black shows on Broadway between 1898 and 1914, including A Trip to Coontown (1898), Clorindy: Or the Origin of the Cakewalk (1889), In Dahomey (1902), and In Bandanna Land (1907).[19] His Three Negro Songs—"Exhortation," "Rain-Song," and "Swing Along"—reveals his strong devotion to the African American cultural tradition as well as his training in the European concert tradition. "Exhortation" is the best example of this fusion, manifesting elements of black preaching within the context of a kind of recita-

tive-and-aria that comprises a declamatory setting of the text in the first part of the song and a lyrical treatment of the second part. The text of "Exhortation" was written by Alex Rogers, a singer and actor who was also the chief lyricist for some of Cook's shows. He also wrote the lyrics for "Rain-Song," a swinging, crowd-pleasing, comic song. "Swing Along," a favorite of the men's choruses of the day, was borrowed for this cycle from Cook's show In Dahomey and became the most widely performed and famous of the three pieces in the cycle. The three songs were brought together to form the cycle in 1912 and were published by G. Schirmer.

Burleigh's published works and his performances of art songs and spirituals made him both an exemplar of the tradition and an influence on composers and singers. His Album of Negro Spirituals (1917) put him in the vanguard of later race-preservation and promotion efforts and provided concert singers such as Roland Hayes, Marian Anderson, and Paul Robeson with a repertoire of arranged spirituals that would serve them well. In the 1910s, Burleigh wrote two impressive song cycles: Saracen Songs (1914) and Five Songs of Lawrence Hope (1919).

Cook and Burleigh were not the only highly significant figures of the period. The brothers James Weldon and J. Rosamond Johnson composed "Lift Every Voice and Sing" (1899), which was taken up as an anthem for the nationalist movement; Bob Cole collaborated with both of the Johnsons, together and singly, to write some of the most popular songs of the day, among which were "Under the Bamboo Tree" (1902), "The Old Flag Never Touched the Ground" (1901), and "The Maiden with the Dreamy Eyes" (1901).

Meanwhile, Ernest Hogan's orchestra, the Memphis Students (also referred to as the Nashville Students, both names serving as elliptical and exploitative references to the Fisk Jubilee Singers and their success), was introducing black secular music to America and Europe; Cook's American Syncopated Orchestra (also known as the New York Syncopated Orchestra and the Southern Syncopated Orchestra) was developing the beginnings of "symphonic jazz";[20] and the ragtime craze of 1898 to 1907 was in full swing, with its most famous composer, Scott Joplin, publishing his opera Treemonisha in 1911. And James Reese Europe was organizing his 369th Regiment "Hell Fighters" band, which would take France by storm during World War I.

In New York, Europe had already organized the Clef Club, which served as a social club, booking agency, and musicians' union and controlled the music and entertainment business.[21] Europe was supreme in New York. His recordings of "Castle House Rag," "Castle Walk," "Memphis Blues," and "Clarinet Marmalade," made in 1914 and 1918, are ambitious, exciting, and sensitive renditions of some of the popular songs of the century's second decade, reflecting social and musical changes, the beginnings of jazz dance, and the social optimism that prevailed in black society as a result of African American modernist thought and the participation of black men in World War I. Europe was the music director for the white dance team of Irene and Vernon Castle. He wrote "Castle House Rag" in tribute to the Castle House for the Teaching of Correct Dancing, where the more staid versions of black dance were introduced to white society and where the "rules of good taste were sufficiently strict to make the new dances acceptable."[22] "Castle House Rag" was introduced to the public by the Castles and Europe's Society Orchestra in 1914. It is a "trot and one-step," combining the one-step, the ubiquitous dance of the ragtime period, with elements of an African American animal dance called the turkey trot. The dotted shuffle rhythms of the one-step in the first part contrast sharply with the syncopated rhythms of the second, the latter clearly revealing its African American lineage. Europe's musical conception, based in the military march and in ragtime, made use of blues and jazz devices that he had probably heard in the various "syncopated orchestras" of Cook and Hogan and elsewhere.

The dancing of the Castles was called jazz dance. Although the music was not jazz as we know the genre today, jazz elements were made manifest in it. Europe's bands—at least the ones that were recorded—did not play jazz as we have come to know it. But whether or not Europe's band played jazz, it fairly *shouted*, with its brassy trumpets, smearing trombones, and additive and cross-rhythms, all of which can be heard on "Memphis Blues" and "Clarinet Marmalade." The prototype that Europe fostered in the second decade of the twentieth century should give him a place in the history of jazz.[23]

In the face of such accomplishments within the context of other Harlem-based nationalist activity then taking place, it was only a small step to musical culture-building by blacks across the United States.

Unlike the European Renaissance, which took place in western Europe from the fourteenth through the sixteenth centuries and was largely fueled by the rediscovery of the Greek cultural legacy, the Negro renaissance had no large body of written texts—no Plato or Aristotle—on which a new culture might be based. But African Americans were inspired by a growing awareness of the African civilizations that had once flourished along the Nile, Tigris, and Euphrates Rivers. They longed to restore African culture to a position of respect, and they used what they knew of African and African American folk art and literature of times past and current in an attempt to create new cultural forms. It is in this sense that the period was called a "renaissance." But the primary motive of the movement was political: If African Americans could demonstrate substantial abilities in arts and letters, then social, political, and economic freedoms would surely follow. As James Weldon Johnson wrote at the time:

> A people may be great through many means, but there is only one measure by which its greatness is recognized and acknowledged. The final measure of the greatness of all peoples is the amount and standard of the literature and art that they have produced. The world does not know that a people is great until that people produces great literature and art. No people that has produced great literature and art has ever been looked upon by the world as distinctly inferior.
>
> The status of the Negro in the United States is more a question of national mental attitude toward the race than of actual conditions. And nothing will do more to change that mental attitude and raise his status than a demonstration of intellectual parity by the Negro through the production of literature and art.[24]

The guiding assumption was that "excellence in art would alter the nation's perceptions of blacks, [leading] eventually to freedom and justice."[25] Patrons supporting or promoting this belief were wealthy black and white philanthropists, publishers, entrepreneurs, and socialites who wanted to promote the aesthetic advancement of the race; assist in blacks' social, artistic, and intellectual progress; or reap financial or social gain. Among the real patrons of the movement were A'Lelia Walker, the black beauty-culture heir, who provided a gathering place for musicians and writers alike on the third floor of her Harlem residence, known as the Dark Tower; Casper Holstein, the black "numbers" kingpin, whose Holstein Prizes for musical composition were offered through *Opportunity* magazine; J. E. Spingarn, who offered a gold medal for "musical achievement in any field";[26] David Bispham, sponsor of a prize medal of the American Opera Society, one of which was won by Clarence Cameron White for his opera *Ouanga* (1931); Julius Rosenwald, who offered prizes for creative work, apparently in any field; the Harmon Foundation, whose Harmon Awards—gold and bronze—were offered for high achievement in musical composition; the Wanamaker family, whose Wanamaker Music Contests were held under the partial auspices of the National Association of Negro Musicians (NANM); writer, photographer, and "Negrotarian" Carl Van Vechten; and the elderly and wealthy Charlotte Mason, who was the patron of writers Langston Hughes and Zora Neale Hurston.

The intellectual and artistic activity of writers, painters, sculptors, photographers, playwrights, and actors was feverish, and progressive organizations published magazines for the intellectual and political edification of black thinkers and strivers. Jean Toomer wrote the novel *Cane* (1923), Walter White wrote *Flight* (1926), Hughes wrote *Not without Laughter* (1930), and Hurston penned the short story "Sweat" (1926). Alain Locke edited the *New Negro* (1925). Aaron Douglas painted allegorical scenes, Archibald Motley painted *Syncopation* (1925), *Stomp* (1926), and *Spell of the Voodoo* (1928), and Palmer Hayden painted *Schooner* (1926) and *Quai at Concarneau* (1929). Eubie Blake and Noble Sissle wrote the musical *Shuffle Along* (1921), James P. Johnson wrote *Runnin' Wild* (1924), Johnson and Fats Waller wrote *Keep Shufflin'* (1928), and Donald Heywood wrote the operetta *Africana* (1933). Paul Robeson acted in *Simon the Cyrenian* (1920), *All God's Chillun Got Wings* (1923), *The Emperor Jones* (1925), and *Show Boat* (1928). The National Association of Colored People (NAACP) published *Crisis* magazine, and the National Urban League published *Opportunity*.

Musically, the idea was to produce extended forms such as symphonies and operas from the raw material of spirituals, ragtime, blues, and other folk genres. The movement's first successful effort in the transformation of folk music into "high art" was Dett's oratorio *The Chariot Jubilee* (1921). Still's *Afro-American Symphony* (1930) was the movement's crowning achievement. There were frequent concerts by the Harlem Symphony Orchestra and the Negro String Quartet (Felix Weir and Arthur Boyd, violins; Hall Johnson, viola; and Marion Cumbo, cello),

which played works by black and white composers. But the pride of the Renaissance leaders were the recital singers: Hayes, Robeson, and Anderson had magnificent voices, and they served as exemplars for the New Negro movement. Burleigh's *Album of Negro Spirituals*, which he had begun to write as early as 1916, probably served as the initial impetus for the black-music repertoires of these and other concert singers. In 1925, James Weldon and J. Rosamond Johnson's *Book of Negro Spirituals* appeared, followed in 1926 by their *Second Book of Negro Spirituals*. Also in 1925, Robeson became the first black solo artist to sing entire recitals of these songs, taking them to parts of the world that the Fisk Jubilee Singers had not reached in their tours from the 1870s to 1890s. Robeson was the son of a preacher and was steeped in black culture; he was nourished on the spiritual and on the sustenance of the ring.[27] His biggest contribution to African American musical nationalism was probably the influence he had on the recital artists of the period: After his 1925 concert of spirituals, nearly all black concert singers included them on their recital programs.[28]

And for entertainment, all danced the Susie Q, the lindy, the black bottom, and the Charleston at clubs such as Barron's, Rockland Palace, and the Bucket of Blood. Initially, entertainment music, including jazz, was ignored or dismissed by Renaissance leaders in favor of concert music; the blues and other folk forms (except for the Negro spiritual, which was held in high esteem) were rejected as decadent and reminiscent of the "old Negro." But many of the movement's entertainers were both amused and offended by the superior attitudes and posturings of some of the black intellectuals. So the entertainers subjected them to "Signifyin(g) revision" or "troping," commenting on them occasionally in speech, posture, gesture, and even song—for example, in Fletcher Henderson's "Dicty Blues" (1923) and in Duke Ellington's "Dicty Glide" (1929).

Ironically, however, it was jazz and the blues that provided the movement's aesthetic ambiance. Bands such as Henderson's and Ellington's were playing dance halls and floor shows; classic blues was ascendant, having first appeared in Harlem in the 1910s and now being recorded by female classic blues singers such as Mamie, Trixie, and Bessie Smith. When W. C. Handy arrived in New York from Memphis in 1918, the blues had been there for years among southern immigrants, and female professional entertainers from southern minstrel and vaudeville shows were already important in entertainment circles. These women had spent their apprenticeships and early professional careers in shows such as Silas Green from New Orleans and F. S. Wolcott's Rabbit Foot Minstrels. The Silas Green show had featured at different times future stars Ma Rainey and Ida Cox, and the Rabbit Foot Minstrels had headlined Rainey, Bessie Smith, and Bertha "Chippie" Hill. With her early start in southern tent shows, Rainey had defined the basic style for those who emerged as classic blues singers in the Harlem Renaissance, although that style was refined considerably for the sophisticated urban environment.[29] Singers such as Trixie, Mamie, and Bessie Smith, Chippie Hill, Lucile Hegaman, and Ethel Waters mastered the twelve-bar blues form and made it speak to the more sophisticated urban audiences. Bessie was dominant: her weighty voice, superb intonation, powerful emotional delivery, and subtle bending of blue notes were compelling and inimitable, setting her clearly apart from the other blues stylists of the period.[30] All these women sang the blues they had heard and learned in southern jooks and tent shows, songs they had composed themselves, and songs written by professionals such as Handy. Handy's songs were not strictly in the standard twelve-bar form. They were mostly Tin Pan Alley–type songs into which the structural and expressive characteristics of the blues were carefully set and integrated. "Memphis Blues"(1912), for example, is a simple A B construction, the A section being sixteen measures in length with a four-bar extension, the B section a twelve-bar blues. "St. Louis Blues" (1914) is ABC, with twelve, sixteen, and twelve measures, respectively. In spite of these structural aberrations, however, or even partly because of them, Handy's work was both different and familiar enough to make a strong and positive impact on the popular culture of the time; his blues songs became part of the classic blues repertory.

The blues tradition, with that of the spiritual, provided the basis for some of William Grant Still's work in the 1920s and 1930s. Throughout the 1920s, he heard many blues, spirituals, and African American secular folk songs. He absorbed the styles, made them part of his emotional and compositional arsenals, and experimented with them in works such as *From the Black Belt* (1926) while making his sketches for the *Afro-American Symphony*—the first symphony composed by an African American. That work, completed in 1930 and first performed in 1931, effectively

mirrors the ideals of the Harlem Renaissance. Still realized those ideals not by using existing folk songs but by creating stylized imitations of them, which he cast in conventional and not-so-conventional classical musical forms. Briefly, the four movements of the work can be described as bound together by an ever-prevailing "blues theme." The work's first movement begins with this trope; then a modified sonata form of this twelve-bar blues is presented in two "choruses" accompanied by a variety of riffs, walking rhythms, and call-and-response dialogues. The second theme is an ersatz spiritual. Then comes the requisite development section, where, in this case, the second theme and its accompanying figures are developed. In the recapitulation, the second theme returns first, with the first theme following on the heels of intervening riff signals; then follows a brief coda, which Signifies on the opening blues theme. The slow second movement, which begins with an introduction that tropes the blues theme of the first movement with fragments of itself, contains two themes, both tinged with blue notes and dance rhythms. Extensions, elaborations, and repetitions of the second theme appear, then the first theme returns in a statement that brings the movement to a close. The third movement is a "scherzo" in 2/4. A dance movement that appropriately employs the banjo, it features ring-based backbeats, a sprightly dance melody, an ersatz spiritual melody, approximations of the time line, and cross-rhythms. The fourth movement, slow and in triple meter, also has two themes, both of which are developed through Signifyin(g) revision; this final movement ends with a troping coda that Signifies on the work as a whole, with pendular thirds prominent and muted trumpets Signifyin(g) on classical trumpet timbres and African American timbral distortions. Fraught with dialogical, rhetorical troping, the entire work carries considerable semantic value, to use Henry Louis Gates's term. The *Afro-American Symphony* is of two lineages—African American and European—and these two lineages shine through the entirety of the work. The *Afro-American Symphony* effectively realized the goals of the Harlem Renaissance, with Still vindicating the faith of the movement's intellectuals and establishing himself as the first black composer of a successful symphony.

Stride piano was also flourishing in New York, and the amazing keyboard feats of James P. Johnson, Willie "the Lion" Smith, and Fats Waller were enthralling and stunning the cabaret-goers, house-rent-party revelers, and sophisticated white social set of the day. When Luckey Roberts (1890–1968) reigned as king of the Harlem ragtime pianists, the eastern school of ragtime was at its peak, and his "Nothin'" was "the last word in cutting contests from 1908."[31] Known especially for his composition and performances of pieces such as "Spanish Venus" and "Pork and Beans," the latter of which was published in 1913 and recorded by him around that time, Roberts was without equal in Harlem's gladiatorial cutting contests.

Around 1918, Roberts was succeeded as "king" by James P. Johnson, who broke with eastern ragtime and moved stride toward wide acceptance with his stunning performances, especially his recording of his own "Carolina Shout" (1921), a fast-moving, celebratory piece inspired by shout culture that was quite unlike any of the works of Scott Joplin, Eubie Blake, Jelly Roll Morton, or the other ragtime composers and pianists of the period. Willie "the Lion" Smith relates that Johnson "played a 'shout' and a shout was a stride. Shouts came about because of the Baptist Church and the way black folks sang or 'shouted' their hymns. They sang them a special way and you played them a special way, emphasizing the basic beat to keep everybody together."[32] Johnson had grown up in New York City's black community, where he saw southern black dances and heard southern black music as they were brought north by early black immigrants—the squares and jubas danced to mouth harps, bones, Jew's harps, and other makeshift musical instruments of the core culture—so he was wise to the musical ways of the culture.[33] Johnson confirmed that his music was "based on set, cotillion, and other southern dance steps and rhythms"; his songs were pianistic expressions of the actual sacred and secular "shouts" he had heard and seen danced in the northern black working-class culture.[34]

Yes, "Carolina" was a shout, yet it also foreshadowed the coming age of more advanced musical ideas. As an improvisational vehicle, it provided new latitude for the creative realizations and executions of the striders, the virtuoso party and cabaret professionals who would later revolutionize jazz piano with startling improvisations: newly invented melodies, rhythms, and harmonies, in seemingly endless variation, that were carried from key to more difficult key in two-handed voicings that cowed and drove away would-be carvers. "Carolina Shout" is a three-theme rag reflecting Johnson's impressions of the shout. It

begins innocently enough but quickly moves to tricky cross-rhythmic constructions that could confound a novice; and the melodic embellishments become more complex as the piece progresses. The piece is replete with call-response tropes: call-and-response figures, riffs, straight bass with tricky reverses that create cross-rhythms, and much imitative hand-to-hand action. "Carolina Shout" replaced Luckey Roberts's "Nothin'" as the cutting contest "separator." On May 13, 1941, Fats Waller recorded his version of "Carolina Shout" but did not play the cross-rhythms that are so clearly evident in the repeat of the first chorus of Johnson's performance (although he does approximate the device a little later in the piece). Waller's performance is much faster than Johnson's, however, and it displays an impressive technique.

After "Carolina Shout," Johnson, Smith, and Waller—the Big Three stride pianists—went on to revolutionize jazz piano, Smith with his wonderful two-hand melodic elaborations and Waller with his two-fisted, cadenza-like Signifyin(g). The lyric, expressive side of stride can be heard in other works by the Big Three—for example, Willie "the Lion" Smith's rendition of "Tea for Two," recorded much later, in an interview session. Although well past his prime at the time of this rendition, the Lion is in good form in this stride-based, inventive set of "melodic beautifications" (as he liked to describe his work and that of the other striders). He begins his performance with the verse out of tempo (rubato) and with much melodic filigree, then moves into the chorus, which is played four times. The first "chorus" is highly embellished, with more rhythmic activity and added-note chords than the verse. The second chorus (what he calls "first dressing") is dressed with much scale-like movement in the service of melodic elaboration. The two-measure phrases of the third chorus move to ever higher keys in a series of modulations ("changing apartments," according to the Lion) that continue throughout the sixteen measures of the theme. The fourth chorus, based solidly in shout-stride, is much more energetic, with Smith's left hand laying the foundation for his extensions and elaborations of the melody and bass line.[35]

With prodigious talent and technique, the Harlem striders remained ascendant until Art Tatum arrived in New York in 1931. According to a witness,

Tatum spread his hands out over the keyboard, feeling out the instrument. Finding the tension of the keys to his liking, he nodded ever so slightly and rippled off a series of runs. He played around with effortless grace for a short time, gaining speed and tempo. A breathtaking run that seemed to use up every note on the piano led to a familiar theme—*Tea for Two*. But something strange had happened to the tune. Just as suddenly as he gave them the melody he was out of it again, but never far enough away from it to render it unrecognizable. Then he was back on it again. The right hand was playing phrases which none of the listeners had imagined existed, while the left hand alternated between a rock solid beat and a series of fantastic arpeggios which sounded like two hands in one. His hand would start at opposite ends of the keyboard and proceed towards each other at a paralyzing rate; one hand picking up the other's progression and then carrying it on itself, only to break off with another series of incredible arpeggios. Just when it seemed that he had surely lost his way, Tatum came in again with a series of quick-changing harmonies that brought him back smack on the beat. His technique was astounding. Reuben Harris stole a look around the room. Everyone was exactly as they were when Tatum first sat down. Fats' drink halted on its way to his lips. Fats sat down as if turned to stone. A wrinkle had appeared between his eyes as he half frowned, half smiled at what he had heard. Nearby, James P. was likewise transfixed, small beads of perspiration showing on his forehead.[36]

The torch had passed. In this performance—reminiscent of the Signifyin(g) symbolism of Br'er Rabbit and Br'er Mockingbird, by the way—Tatum, with his new melodic and harmonic ideas and his superior technical ability, demonstrated his inimitable synthesis of ragtime, boogie-woogie, and stride piano, revealing his debt to Waller, Earl Hines, and the Chicago boogie-woogie men (some of whom we will encounter presently). He had brought together their disparate styles and molded them into a phenomenal composite that would launch a new school of jazz piano.

The range of Tatum's art can be heard on *The Best of Art Tatum* (1983), his extraordinary talent clearly evident on "Willow Weep for Me," a performance that is both elegant and eloquent in its semantic value. This rendition reveals Tatum's style as characterized by a level of melodic ornamentation and filigree that surpasses that of the striders; by frequent left-hand, right-hand, and two-hand runs, all superlative and incomparable; by considerable rhythmic, melodic, harmonic, and tonal variety; by quasi-rubato passages; by gestures approximating blue notes and other blues and jazz devices; and by more inventiveness—melodically, harmonically, and rhythmically—

than that in the striders' performances. The semantic value of Tatum's music is high, containing allusive gestures that analogously sigh, posture, gesture, and "breathe" at the end of "sentences." In much of this, he takes after Hines. In his prime, Tatum did not stop with pianists; he also sought out horn players, both to cut and to interact with cooperatively. On *The Best of Art Tatum*, he plays solo on four cuts and performs as a sideman and leader in groups with Roy Eldridge, Benny Carter, Lionel Hampton, Ben Webster, Jo Jones, and others. The harmonic and rhythmic support, filigree, flourishes, and countermelodic figurations and statements he contributes establish and significantly enhance the character and quality of the entire album. Tatum's unusual rhythmic devices, fantastic runs, phrasings, and bravura conceptions are evident on "Caravan," "A Foggy Day," "Elegy," and other cuts and suggest why he was able to best any musician he ran across. If the philosophers of the Harlem Renaissance were after artistic refinement and complexity, Tatum, like Ellington, clearly realized their desires (although belatedly and within a vernacular form—which, of course, in their view, may have disqualified the accomplishment).

As the 1920s progressed, jazz became, for renaissance leaders, the most acceptable of the secular vernacular genres. Before the renaissance, the earliest recognized general manifestation of jazz, New Orleans jazz, had been a collectively improvised, out-of-doors music, played primarily at "parades, picnics, concerts, riverboat excursions, and dances."[37] Drawing from the rich reservoir of the ring, it had spread quickly in the second decade of the century to most of the nation's major cities and to points in Europe (note, for example, Jelly Roll Morton's and Freddie Keppard's sojourns in California, King Oliver's permanent residence in Chicago, and the European tours of Sidney Bechet with Will Marion Cook's Southern Syncopated Orchestra).

In the renaissance period, the challenge of maintaining in jazz the continuity of this African American aesthetic expression within the framework of new and expanding technical resources as well as restraints was first faced, seriously and effectively, by Fletcher Henderson. New York's large dance halls required larger bands than the honky-tonks, nightclubs, and smaller halls that employed small jazz and society units. So Henderson devised a way to accommodate eleven pieces, initially, to handle the expanding requirements of the genre in its new setting. Henderson and his arranger, Don Redman, began making arrangements that would exploit the instrumental resources of a big band yet retain some of the flexibility and spontaneity of the small jazz ensemble. They accomplished this by placing the winds and brasses in contrast to each other, by employing composed riffs to create continuity and generate propulsive force, and by setting occasional solos against all of this. This process and structure started a new line of development that was to become and remain the standard in big-band jazz. The section-playing that Henderson employed was based on European principles (eschewing to some extent the heterogeneous sound ideal), but the riffs and improvisations and the character of the rhythmic propulsion were African American. The process of riffing had long been prominent in ring and ring-derived music, emanating from the recurrent and intermittent repetition of call-and-response figures and motivic interjections. In the Henderson band, the use of these devices was transformed into an organizing concept and, as a trope, underwent constant revision during a performance (and from performance to performance). In other words, the riff became both the object and a means of formal, Signifyin(g) revision. There was much of this troping in the Henderson band, and there was also much musical toasting, for improvisation was a prominent feature of the band. Dicky Wells, one of Henderson's sidemen, says, for example, that "when you hear some of Fletcher's old records, there may be just one jammed chorus, but on the job there'd be a lot more. They called it 'stretching it out.'"[38]

Henderson's innovations had far-reaching influence. His 1926 recording of his composition "Stampede" contains riffs and responsorial constructions: a clarinet trio, banjo accompaniment, carefully and effectively arranged section passages, and solos by tenor saxophonist Coleman Hawkins and trumpeters Rex Stewart and Joe Smith. "Wrapping It Up" contains fine and sophisticated, although tempered, ensemble playing of ring tropes: call-and-response constructions, riffs, and muted passages. By the late 1920s, Henderson had expanded his instrumentation to include five brasses, four reeds, and four rhythm instruments while continuing his riff-oriented, section-organized arranging structure. Nearly every active big band began to copy Henderson's successful formula, and by 1932 his work had launched the Swing Era. Henderson, the college-educated,

polished, urbane bandleader, became New Negro material, since some of the leadership, most notably Du Bois, had by the mid-1920s begun to recognize the legitimacy of jazz.

While Henderson eschewed the heterogeneous sound ideal as a primary organizing principle, Duke Ellington fully embraced it in an unsurpassed orchestral palette, with not only the instruments themselves providing timbral contrasts but also each of the musicians providing even more such contrast within the confines of his individual instrument. It is well known that Ellington selected his sidemen for stylistic and tonal *difference*. He surely recognized that *Signifyin(g) difference* powerfully enhances the heterogeneous effect. Timbre and rhythm, for Ellington, were inextricably bound, as Olly Wilson perceptively notes in presenting an example of the heterogeneous sound ideal:

> When Ellington followed the line "It don't mean a thing if it ain't got that swing" with the line "do-wah, do-wah, do-wah, do-wah, do-wah, do-wah," he illustrated the principle of swing by setting up the implied metrical contrast [that produces swing] and by tying this metrical contrast to a contrast in timbre. The line was not do-ooo, do-ooo, etc.; but do-wáh, do-wáh, which accents the affect of timbral contrast working in conjunction with a cross rhythm.[39]

It was during the Harlem Renaissance that Ellington recorded the works that established him as a composer of first rank—works such as "Creole Love Call," "Black and Tan Fantasy," and "East St. Louis Toodle-oo," of which the last concerns us here. Two of the several versions he recorded are examined—those from 1927 and 1937—both of which appear, side by side, in the Smithsonian Collection of Classic Jazz (1973). In the 1927 recording, "East St. Louis Toodle-oo" is structured just as Martin Williams points out in the liner notes (he calls the structure "a song-form section and a secondary theme"): A A B A C C A′ A″ C A. For my taste, it is a rondo-like structure with the opening succession of chords serving simultaneously as a returning theme over which improvisations take place. Viewed in this way, it is reminiscent of the French chaconne, which, we know, frequently appeared *en rondeau*. The intermittent intervening sections, B and C, provide melodic and harmonic relief from the repeating A section. The eight-bar chordal opening by the woodwinds and brass serves as the chaconne progression for the A section, over which the trumpet, baritone saxophone, and clarinet improvise in turn. The trumpet takes A, B, the repeat of the variation on C, and the final A; the baritone sax takes C; the clarinet, A′; the final C section is devoted to a trumpet trio in which the theme of that section is stated for the first time (having been improvised on in its first incarnation).

Several things are notable about this performance. First, it is influenced by New Orleans–style jazz, containing as it does the growls, elisions, and manner of soloing that are characteristic of, or derived from, that style. In the first A section, Bubber Miley's trumpet solo is accompanied, for six of the eight bars, by a countermelody remarkably like those of the New Orleans jazzmen; Fred Guy's banjo plays a steady off-beat accompaniment; Ellington strikes supporting chords in a percussive manner; and Sonny Greer's drums keep time—these last three instruments together functioning just as a New Orleans rhythm section would function. Second, and most notably for my purposes, the chaconne-like progression and the solos are fraught with semantic value: the ostinato seems to make a statement, or proposition, over and over; the soloing instruments are in a "talking" mode, with their improvisations seeming to comment on, "answer," "restate," make "by the ways," and confirm what has been "said" and "discussed." This "telling effect" is based, analogously, on black-culture ways of telling, answering, and discussing (except for the "siditty" chaconne-like chord progressions). Additionally, the trumpet trio Signifies on the society band and "symphonic jazz" of Paul Whiteman and other novelty musicians of the period, and the soloists Signify on aspects of New Orleans jazz-band technique. In these ways, this rendition of "East St. Louis Toodle-oo" comments on the state of jazz in 1927, a period during which Ellington and Henderson, most particularly, were making use of a variety of styles.

The 1937 version of "East St. Louis Toodle-oo" (treated here, although it takes us two years beyond the close of the Harlem flowering) features a few of the same players but also several others in an enlarged orchestra. It is a more sophisticated, more elegant rendition, giving proof of the continuing development of the Ellington band and of jazz in general. The structure of this version (A A B A A′ A″ A) is close to that of 1927, except that the C theme has been dropped. Other than that, the main differences between the two are that the band in the 1937 version is technically more advanced, and the arrangement is more elaborate, containing more sophisticated and varied articulations, more inner parts, more part-harmony, many harmonized doo-wahs, and more striking use of the capabilities of the full ensemble. This rendition is slower than the 1927 performance, and the New Orleans influences having disappeared, more appropriate to a New York nightclub than to a jook joint or core-culture dance hall. The intense and "pretty" vibrato of all the instruments in this rendition, contrasted with the almost straight tones and nearly subdued accompaniment of the 1927 version, evinces an increase in confidence and sophistication—even pretension—on the part of Ellington and his musicians and reflects the influence of the musical gains made by the band and the musicians in the intervening years. This performance also demonstrates Ellington's versatility, his ability to incorporate into his style whatever elements might contribute to its character, and his ever-creative artistry. This more elaborate and sophisticated version of "East St. Louis Toodle-oo" doubtless made the New Negroes proud, for the sharp line that divided the intellectuals from the jazz and popular musicians had dissolved by this time.[40]

The Duke Ellington Orchestra was followed in the Cotton Club by Cab Calloway's band. The Calloway band was considered to be one of the best of the big bands during the period 1939 to 1943, in spite of the prowess of those of Hines, Billy Eckstine, Ellington, and Count Basie. This sixteen-piece, exceptionally talented big band was in demand everywhere; through its radio broadcasts from the Cotton Club, it generated an appreciation for jazz among many segments of American society, ensuring the continuation of the tradition. In his performances, Calloway always made use of African-derived performance practices. The "hi-de-ho" phenomenon, for example, is a classic example of the African American call-and-response pattern. Aside from having a great instrumental aggregation, Calloway continued the scat-singing tradition introduced by Louis Armstrong in the 1920s. Discussing the African American basis for this technique and the technique's enhancement of instrumental music Willis Lawrence James wrote,

> Somehow, Armstrong and Calloway found the trick of using old folk cry principles to supplement the normal means of singing. . . . Being gifted in voice projection, Calloway invented or adopted a series of nonsense syllables and fitted them into

his songs of jazz rhythms. When this was done, people realized the thing as a part of themselves, but they did not know why. They did not realize that they were listening to the cries of their vegetable man, their train caller, their charcoal vendor, their primitive ancestors, heated in the hot crucible of jazz, by the folk genius of Calloway and Armstrong until they ran into a new American alloy. It is possible that neither Calloway nor Armstrong realized what took place. If so, the more remarkable. The response of the orchestra in imitating the cries of Armstrong and Calloway carried the cry into the orchestra itself. The rhythms and inflections have been picked up by the orchestras in general during the last two decades [1935–55]. This has caused a vital development in dance music.[41]

Armstrong and Calloway made calls and cries contemporary, to be picked up, enhanced, developed, and carried forth by the jazz singers of later years. The Calloway band was an experimental laboratory in which new musical techniques, devices, and procedures were explored; it had a profound impact on the future of jazz and, consequently, American music in general. It was in Calloway's band that Dizzy Gillespie began to develop his own style. The recordings he made with the band in 1940 include performances that reveal elements that would become unmistakable features of Gillespie's mature style—tunes such as "Pickin' the Cabbage," "Boo-Wah, Boo-Wah," and "Bye Bye Blues." Calloway's scat singing also must have had some influence on Gillespie.

All across the land, young black jazz musicians were listening to these bands over the radio, on records, and—the lucky ones—in live performances, inspired by their musicianship and Signifyin(g) prowess. These young aspirants used the performances of the musicians in these bands as measures of their own prowess, "woodshedding" constantly to gain control of their art; making efforts to be heard by top musicians and to become known in local, regional, and national jazz circles; hoping to be "sent for" by Basie, Calloway, Jimmy Lunceford, Chick Webb, or Ellington: "Being sent for was recognition and status. Usually it meant New York with a nationally known outfit."[42]

These bands and their leaders helped bridge the split that existed in Harlem between the strivers and the "show people" and contributed substantially to the eradication of the class distinctions that plagued the renaissance. Eventually, all the elements of black society found a place in Harlem's cultural cauldron, eventually closing ranks against the visiting white voyeurs and exploiters of the neighborhood.[43] This exploitation, together with other forces and developments, brought the Harlem flowering of the renaissance to an end.[44] The other forces included (1) the expatriation to Europe of some of the concert-hall musicians, such as Roland Hayes and Henry Crowder, and many of the entertainers, including Josephine Baker, Noble Sissle, and Ada "Bricktop" Smith;[45] (2) the arrival of radio and moving pictures, which reduced nightclub and concert attendance; (3) the establishment in many cities, by 1929, of "regulations prohibiting jazz from public dance halls," diluting much of the movement's force and ambiance;[46] and (4) the onset of the Great Depression, which dried up the patronage for the arts and letters. The Harlem flowering of the renaissance ended in the mid-1930s, as the Chicago flowering was beginning.

Robert Bone has posited the notion of a Chicago renaissance that spanned the years 1935 to 1950 and that featured ideals and practices that parallel those of the Harlem movement.[47] Bone's hypothesis is persuasive when one compares the main features of the Harlem flowering with the black cultural activity that took place in Chicago. As the Harlem Renaissance had been made possible by patronage, so the activity of black artists and intellectuals in Chicago was supported by public and private funding, primarily from the Works Progress Administration, as well as from some of the sources that had sponsored Harlem's literary activity of the 1920s (the Julius Rosenwald Fund, the Wanamaker family, the Harmon Foundation, and Casper Holstein). As A'Lelia Walker's Dark Tower had served as the primary gathering place for black intellectuals in Harlem, Horace Cayton's and Estelle Bonds's Chicago homes served a similar purpose in the Chicago flowering. As the Harlem Renaissance had the white Carl Van Vechten and the black intellectual Alain Locke as liaisons with white supporters of the movement, Chicago's nonblack supporters were encouraged and attracted primarily by Edwin Embree, the white administrator of the Julius Rosenwald Fund. As in Harlem, the Chicago renaissance was based on the premise that African Americans would "measure up" to the artistic, intellectual, cultural, and economic standards of the white world and eventually become part of a race-free society.[48] The Harlem Renaissance had been driven in part by the racial politics of Du Bois, and the activity in Chicago was stimulated to some extent by the revolutionary politics of Richard Wright, as reflected in his novels *Native Son* (1940) and *Black Boy* (1945).[49] The Harlem Renaissance had been fueled by the African American folk experience but sustained by an integrationist outlook; so was the activity in Chicago. The attitudes toward music that prevailed among middle-class blacks in Chicago in the 1930s were identical to those of the Harlem Renaissance intellectuals: Some accepted the spiritual as incomparable black folk music, to be used as the foundation for "high art," but rejected the blues and only tolerated jazz, considering the former as socially unredeeming and the latter as decadent; others viewed all vernacular black music as aesthetically valuable, if not socially acceptable. In Chicago, as in Harlem, the music of the rent-party, theater, and cabaret worlds was separate from, yet ironically supportive of, some of the New Negro ideals.

According to Grossman, Chicago in the early years was filled with "aromas of southern cooking . . . ; the sounds of New Orleans jazz and Mississippi blues; [southern] styles of worship; [southern] patterns of speech," all of which fit into "an interactive process" in which these cultural activities and values modified and were modified by new ideas, values, and habits within the context of northern discrimination, economic insecurity, and an urban lifestyle that was new to recent migrants.[50] This interactive process created among Chicago's African Americans an impulse toward an ardent self-affirmation that found its most public expression in the city's community of musicians, writers, and visual artists. In the music, it was probably manifest as early as the second decade of the twentieth century, when the blues and jazz began to make an impact on Chicago and when, in 1919, the National Association of Negro Musicians was founded there to effect "progress, to discover and foster talent, to mold taste, to promote fellowship, and to advocate racial expression."[51] But in spite of significant early activities by such figures as Kemper Harreld, Maude Roberts George, and Estelle Bonds, this great impulse for self-affirmation apparently did not flourish on a large and impressive scale until the 1930s.

On June 15, 1933, the Chicago Symphony Orchestra presented an evening of "Negro Music and Musicians," featuring Roland Hayes in a performance of Coleridge-Taylor's "Onaway, Awake, Beloved" from *Hiawatha's Wedding Feast*, pianist Margaret Bonds in a performance of white composer John Alden Carpenter's *Concertino*, and the premiere of Florence Price's *Symphony in E Minor*.[52] Because of the unprecedented

magnitude of this event, it should be taken as the landmark event for the musical aspect of the Chicago renaissance, preceding by more than eighteen months the year of commencement fixed by Bone. This concert had been preceded by two major accomplishments by black composers in Chicago: Florence Price's completion of her *Symphony in E Minor* (1932) and William Dawson's completion of his *Negro Folk Symphony* (1934).

Price's symphony has not been recorded or published, so I will not discuss it here. But another of her achievements can be discussed: the *Piano Sonata in E Minor*—the first major work of the Negro renaissance. Harmonically and melodically rich and well crafted, this unpublished but now commercially recorded twenty-five-minute work is filled with brief rhythmic motives and accompanying figures, typical African American rhythms, broad, heavy chords, flowing melodic lines, and ersatz spiritual and dance tunes. The first movement (Andante-allegro) consists of two themes reminiscent of African American dance tunes, treated here in a much more delicate, lyrical manner, developed and brought to conclusion in a dramatic close. The second movement (Andante), a rondo, begins with a tune reminiscent of the spiritual. It is based on the following rhythm, highly characteristic of the genre: ♫ ♩ . The third movement (Scherzo: allegro), also a rondo, begins with a theme made of rapid scale passages in triplets; this is followed by a broad, sweeping line that contrasts with all the other themes of the work. Dance rhythms abound in this section, which brings the movement, and the work as a whole, to a close with rapid scale passages and strong, insistent chords in a brilliant, bravura ending.

Dawson began his career in the mid-1920s with the publication of choral arrangements of spirituals, among which were "King Jesus Is A-Listening" (1925) and "I Couldn't Hear Nobody Pray" (1926). Among his other works are numerous arrangements of spirituals, the *Sonata in A* for violin and piano (1927), the *Trio in A* for piano, violin, and violoncello (1925), the *Scherzo for Orchestra* (winner of a Wanamaker Prize in 1930), and *A Negro Work Song for Orchestra* (1940), which was commissioned by the Columbia Broadcasting System. In the same year that Price's *Symphony in E Minor* was premiered, Margaret Bonds, who studied with Price and with Dawson and whose mother's home was one of the two principal gathering places for Chicago renaissance intellectuals,[53] won a Wanamaker Prize for her song "Sea Ghost." She later set texts by Hughes (for example, "The Negro Speaks of Rivers," 1946) and celebrated the Great Migration in her ballet *The Migration* (1964).

Chicago's vocal artists also actively contributed to the prevailing spirit of renaissance. On December 26, 1937, La Julia Rhea made her operatic debut with the Chicago Civic Opera Company, singing the title role in *Aïda*; in the same production, William Franklin debuted as Amonasro. The Chicago guild of the Pittsburgh-based Negro Opera Company presented *Aïda* in October 1942 and in February 1943. The second performance, before an audience "about equally divided between white and colored opera lovers," won "the highest praise" from critics.[54] Chicago baritone Theodore Charles Stone made his Town Hall debut in 1940 and began to tour regularly as a concert singer. In 1942, soprano Hortense Love, also of Chicago, debuted in New York City's Town Hall; Etta Moten, who had moved to Chicago in 1934, appeared as Bess in the 1942 production of George Gershwin's *Porgy and Bess*, after which she toured extensively in the United States as a concert singer.[55] These and many other events that took place between 1933 and 1950 give evidence of the abundant concert-music activity of the period.

In the vernacular arena, the Chicago renaissance years saw significant musical ferment in the development of black gospel music, the rise of urban blues, and important developments in jazz. After vocal blues became acceptable to record companies, so did a pianistic form called boogie-woogie, its first documents appearing in the 1920s and its first widespread urban manifestations taking place in Chicago. Pete Johnson, Roosevelt Sykes, Pine Top Smith, Cow Cow Davenport, Meade Lux Lewis, Jimmy Yancey, and Albert Ammons were masters of the style. In boogie-woogie, cross-rhythms are produced by the right hand playing triple figures against the duple divisions of the left hand's eight-to-the-bar, rumbling ostinato (which really swings when played by a boogie-woogie master). The rolling left hand is the key to the style, providing the propulsive, four-beat jumpy rhythm that gives the music its characteristic pump and flow. The I-IV-V chord progressions—delineated by the heavy, jerky, bass ostinato—support treble filigree, short runs, and sharp chords. By the 1920s, boogie-woogie had become enormously popular on Chicago's rent-party circuit, having originated in the late 1880s or 1890s in the jooks

and barrel houses of the south (although it was not called boogie-woogie until the 1920s) and brought to Chicago in the Great Migration.[56]

Developing and existing side by side with ragtime but used primarily as house-party music in small, intimate venues, boogie-woogie was more rhythm-oriented than ragtime, with its bass ostinato serving as the controlling element for all other, "resultant" musical activity[57] and a Signifyin(g) right hand producing figures that contrasted with and complemented the ostinato. Wendell Logan has pointed out the rhythmic and functional relationship between the ostinati of boogie-woogie and the African time-line concept, stressing that "much of the music of the black diaspora which is organized around the ostinato principle is dance music."[58] So although African time-line retentions can be found elsewhere in the music of African Americans, the technique as a *functional*, melodic bass-ostinato concept did not enter practice until the advent of boogie-woogie or its progenitors. As the time line functions in African music, so the ostinato functions for boogie-woogie—as a vehicle for other figures and lines. Wendell Logan, noticing that this principle has had broad and determinative effects on black music, concludes that it (1) influenced the change in jazz from a two-beat to a four-beat feel and (2) caused the eighth-note subdivisions of the beat to be interpreted as uneven durations, moving from ♫♫ to ♩♫ to ♩♪♪, the last coming to be known as swing eighths. Boogie-woogie was created by blacks in the American south but spread quickly to the northern urban areas when the Great Migration began. In the recorded performances of Meade Lux Lewis, Jimmy Yancey, and Albert Ammons, the genre can be observed in its formal guise. Lewis's "Honky Tonk Train" (1937), for example, contains all the elements typical of the style: a twelve-bar structure, eight beats to the bar; ostinato bass; improvised, vocally conceived right-hand figures; and a percussive approach. In this performance, as in others, the encounter of the right-hand figurations with the left-hand ostinato produces occasional polyrhythms that, together with the percussive attack and the blues mode, place the style squarely in the African American musical tradition. In its heyday, boogie-woogie was extremely popular in some segments of the black community; a nationwide craze prevailed in the late 1930s and early 1940s, after which the genre's popularity waned, ending in the early 1950s. The Chicago boogie-woogie pianists were the Windy City's counterparts of the Harlem striders, dominating the city's rent-party circuit. By the 1920s, a modified form of New Orleans jazz had developed in Chicago, created by the New Orleans musicians who had moved there—most notably King Oliver, Louis Armstrong, and Johnnie Dodds. Our knowledge of early jazz is extrapolated primarily from the body of recordings made by Oliver, Armstrong, and Jelly Roll Morton in Chicago from 1923 to 1929—specifically, the Paramount sides of Oliver's Creole Jazz Band, the Hot Five and Hot Seven recordings of Armstrong, and Jelly Roll Morton's Red Hot Peppers sides.

For my purposes, Morton's contribution can be heard best on his 1926 recording of "Black Bottom Stomp." This performance is governed to a large extent by the call-response principle, relying on Signifyin(g) elisions, responses to calls, improvisations (in fact or in style), continuous rhythmic drive, and timbral and pitch distortions that are retentions from the ring. At every point, "Black Bottom Stomp" Signifies on black dance rhythms and makes use of the time-line concept of African music. The latter is the rhythmic foundation for the entire piece but is kept in the background for the most part and sometimes only implied; it is a continuous rhythm that subdivides Morton's two beats per bar into an underlying rhythm of eight pulses. This continuous, implied, and sometimes sounded pulse serves the function of a time line over which the foreground two-beat metric pattern has been placed, and it serves as the reference pulse for the two-beat and four-beat metric structures and the cross-rhythms and additive rhythms that occur throughout the performance. The clarinet and banjo frequently emphasize this time line with added volume, thereby bringing it into the foreground as a Signifyin(g) trope. Over this time line, improvisation takes place—improvisation that Signifies on (1) the structure of the piece itself, (2) the current Signifyin(g)s of the other players in the group, and (3) the players' own and others' Signifyin(g)s on previous performances. These significations take place at the same time that the performers are including within their improvisations timbral and melodic derivations from the ring: the trombone's smears (elisions); the elided phrasings of the muted trumpet; tropes that revise, extend, and update call-and-response, calls, cries, hollers, and shouts—all accompanied by figures that Signify on foot-patting and hand-clapping after-beats, cross-rhythms,

breaks, stop-time tropes, and occasional four-beat stomp rhythms. The performance is fraught with the referentiality that Gates describes as "semantic value," exemplifying (1) how performers contribute to the success of a performance with musical statements, assertions, allegations, questings, requestings, implications, mockings, and concurrences that result in the "telling effect" that Murray has described and (2) what black performers mean when they say that they "tell a story" when they improvise.[59]

Morton's art clearly looked back to New Orleans, but that of Oliver and Armstrong looked forward. Oliver had as his model the legendary Buddy Bolden; Armstrong, notwithstanding other influences, took Oliver as his. Comparing Oliver's recorded work with the descriptions of Bolden's art, we can assume that Oliver appropriated Bolden's power and manner of improvising and added his own impeccable control and, perhaps, more scale-like passages. Armstrong built on Oliver's foundation and innovations, molding the art of jazz with his own conceptions and, in the process, revolutionizing it and setting standards that would guide all who were to come after him. Although there were few solos in the Oliver band's performances, the two-trumpet team of Oliver and Armstrong was superb, creating breaks, inventing ideas to fill them, and effectively voicing the intervals between their parts within the context of sensitive ensemble playing.

It was in Chicago that Armstrong became the world's most influential jazzman, developing his art and technique to a level that was then unapproachable by other trumpet players. We can get some idea of the artistic influence that Armstrong and other New Orleans players had on the elaboration of jazz and of the technical level Armstrong had attained by the mid-1920s, from four recorded performances: "Dippermouth Blues" (1923), "Hotter Than That" (1927), "West End Blues" (1928), and "Weather Bird" (1928).

"Dippermouth Blues," an instrumental in the style of the loose melodic heterophony of New Orleans jazz, showcases Oliver's improvisational style and ability. His wa-wa choruses and Johnnie Dodds's clarinet solo are good examples of the improvisation-by-paraphrase technique of early jazz. Apparently, Oliver was the first professional player to mute his instrument, employing bottles, cups, and utensils constructed specifically for distorting the sound of his cornet, a uniquely African-derived practice that surely must have been employed in African American folk music before Oliver made it common in professional circles.⁶⁰ On "Dippermouth," Armstrong was a sideman, but by 1928 he had emerged, with the Hot Fives, as "king." His "Hotter Than That," with Kid Ory on trombone and Dodds on clarinet, is an early example of extended instrumental and vocal improvisation. It is a sixteen-bar blues that makes use of a banjo shuffle-rhythm, elisions, riffs, polyrhythms, and call-and-response figures (the last on the seventh chorus). Ory and Dodds perform at a high level, and Armstrong is dazzlingly superb. His scat singing here is impressive, reminiscent of the way Africans teach rhythm through vocables. "West End Blues," with Fred Washington on trombone, Jimmy Strong on clarinet, and Earl Hines on piano, reveals movement away from the New Orleans ensemble tradition, with Armstrong having developed a virtuosity that showcases his out-of-tempo, cadenza-like introduction and enhances a linear complexity within the ensemble.

Armstrong had brought with him to Chicago, as had so many others during the Great Migration, the elisions, vocables, and other tropes of the blues. But from the Hot Five recordings onward, his unique and effective attacks and releases, his treatment of vibrato and rubato, and his way of phrasing and floating over, behind, and in front of the beat—that is, his *Signifyin(g)* on it—gave his performances a tremendous and unique swing. His movement away from the duple-beat divisions of New Orleans jazz to triple divisions created polyrhythms that added buoyancy and additional swing. His dominating lead cornet shifted away from the communal practices of the New Orleans ensemble to a leader/improviser–dominated practice that is also of call-response provenance. In addition, Armstrong began to move away from paraphrase toward the construction of new melodies—Signifyin(g) revisions—that opened the way for the more dramatic improvisations that would follow in succeeding decades. "Weather Bird" is a duet showcasing the impressive individual and collective improvisations of Armstrong and Hines. Armstrong's sureness and authority of tone, attack, and pitch are impressive here, and his effective use of terminal vibrato and subtle use of elision, turns, mordents, and hemiola figures demonstrate the level of his art in the 1920s. Hines's style is based somewhat on ragtime conventions, but it certainly transcends the strictness of that genre, making use of Signifyin(g) octaves in the melodic line and reverting

sometimes, however briefly, to a comping style that would be fully developed later. Employing advanced ideas of phrasing, accentuation, and rhythm, the level of imagination in the performance is high, elevated by the artistic stimulation of each player on the other. This solo-and-accompaniment performance of Armstrong and Hines began to move the music clearly away from both New Orleans– and Chicago-style jazz toward developments that would be more fully developed in the 1930s and 1940s.

To jump from the Armstrong-Hines "Weather Bird" collaboration of 1928 to the formation of the Earl Hines band in 1942 may seem a considerable leap, given the rapid change and elaboration of jazz and the difference in style and content between "Weather Bird" and the Hines band of the early 1940s. But since my focus here is on revolutionary high points, and not on the step-by-step evolution of the music, the developmental gap I leave between Hines's 1928 "Weather Bird" performance and his 1942 big-band activity is intentional and justified. For my purposes here, Hines is simply a convenient, logical connector of events because of his contribution of the comping piano style, which first appeared in "Weather Bird," and the musical freedom he allowed in his big band to the rise of that genre.

The Earl Hines band of 1942 to 1944, which included Dizzy Gillespie and Charlie Parker, was a hothouse of experimentation, an "incubator of bebop," according to Stanley Dance. Gunther Schuller confirms this by telling of the time, in 1943, when he "heard the great Earl Hines band. They were playing all the flatted fifth chords and all the modern harmonies and substitutions and Dizzy Gillespie runs in the trumpet section work." Cliff Smalls, a member of the band, reports, "Dizzy and Charlie [had solos], but they were not big stars then, although they were playing the way that made them famous," and Hines himself reports that Gillespie wrote the famous bebop tunes "Night in Tunisia" and "Salt Peanuts" while he was in the Hines band. Neither Gillespie nor Parker could have missed Hines's comping technique, which by that time he had probably developed beyond what he had demonstrated in "Weather Bird." In 1944, Gillespie and Parker left Hines to join Billy Eckstine, another "important pioneer of bebop," whose band included Miles Davis, Tadd Dameron, Dexter Gordon, Art Blakey, Fats Navarro, Gene Ammons, and other bebop notables. Gillespie remembers, "I'll never forget the record date Billy

Eckstine had at National after he left Early. He had me write one of the arrangements, for the *Good Jelly Blues*—Jelly, Jelly, you know. Talking about bebop, we were beeeee-boppin' behind him!"[61]

Throughout the history of African American music, the genres of the tradition have been created and developed through the synthesizing of their various elements by makers of black music. It was in Chicago that one of the most notable of these syntheses occurred: Thomas A. Dorsey's melding of blues elements with those of the religious hymn to make the gospel blues, spawning both what came to be known as the "Dorsey Song" and the choral gospel–blues style.[62] Dorsey had been assisted in his rise by the following individuals successively: the Reverend W. M. Nix, one of the singing preachers of the day, whose emotional, inspirational, improvisational singing of the song "I Do, Don't You" at the 1921 National Baptist Convention convinced Dorsey of the viability of blues tropes in the singing of religious music and spurred him to continue in that direction; the evangelistic singer Theodore Fry, who, between 1930 and 1932, teamed with Dorsey to present and promote Dorsey's songs on the church circuit; Sallie Martin, who, beginning in 1932, promoted Dorsey's songs and organized his publishing affairs; and Mahalia Jackson, who, between 1939 and 1944, sang and promoted Dorsey's songs on the church circuit and performed them at conventions. Jackson's voice was one of incomparable range and power, and her sound and delivery were equally distinguished.

Dorsey's relationship with Jackson in the religious realm may have been similar to his earlier relationship with Ma Rainey in the blues arena. For much of Rainey's career, Dorsey served as her pianist, bandleader, and songwriter. Sometime before 1920, he joined the church and began performing there as a pianist; he "backslid" in 1921, after his first gospel publication, "I Do, Don't You," to organize a band for Rainey, and again around 1928, when he wrote the blues hit "Tight like That."[63] Having been known variously as Texas Tommy, Smokehouse Charley, Barrelhouse Tom, and Georgia Tom, by 1924 Dorsey had not only become "one of the major blues composers in Chicago" but also was acquainted with the hymns of Charles Albert Tindley and the performance practices applied to them by performers such as Sister Rosetta Tharpe and Blind Joe Taggart, all of which fully prepared him to achieve what he desired.[64]

Tindley had smoothed the path for the develop-

ment of African American gospel music and the later crystallization of its style. He had created space in his songs to accommodate the call-and-response figures and improvisations that, together with flatted thirds and sevenths and other core-culture performance practices, would come to make the style. Tharpe's performance of Tindley's "Beams of Heaven," in which she accompanied her own conservative vocal delivery on the guitar, is a steady, rhythmic rendition of the sixteen-measure song, with accompanying figures that recall blues guitarists of the period. Taggart's 1927 recording of "The Storm Is Passing Over" is a more demonstrative interpretation of a Tindley song. A shouter, Taggart gives a fervent vocal rendition, and his guitar accompaniment is based squarely in ring values: polyrhythms abound, occasioned by Taggart's improvisatory, rhythmically free delivery of the vocal over a steady and repetitive guitar pattern.[65] The ground rhythm in this performance parallels—is almost identical to—those of juré and juba, particularly the former, and it closely approximates the ground rhythms in Mississippi John Hurt's "Big Leg Blues" and Rube Lacy's "Ham Hound Crave." Taggart's vocal delivery here also comes close to the blues singing of some of the Mississippi Moaners. Although I do not know that Dorsey was directly influenced by Tindley, it appears that by the late 1920s, Dorsey was prepared to exploit the possibilities suggested by Tindley's exemplary structures and to capitalize on certain of the compositional possibilities suggested by performers like Tharpe and Taggart (I would find it hard to believe that Dorsey was not familiar with their work).

Dorsey came to national attention after his song "If You See My Savior, Tell Him That You Saw Me" (1926) was performed by Willie Mae Fisher at the National Baptist Convention in Chicago in 1930.[66] But it was the publication, in 1932, of "Take My Hand, Precious Lord" that established him as a major figure. "Precious Lord" received a "resounding affirmation" in its premiere performance by Theodore Frye (with Dorsey at the piano) at Ebenezer Baptist Church in Chicago in 1932. Taken around to other churches by the duo, it apparently received equally rousing welcomes; those receptions led ultimately "to the rise of gospel blues as an established song form in old-line churches."[67] With this slow gospel song, Dorsey expanded on Tindley's practice of leaving gaps and spaces for "ring" play and added innovations of his own. Most of Dorsey's songs are composed of sixteen-measure sections and make use of blues inflections, favoring flatted thirds and sevenths and off-beat melodic accents, and "Precious Lord" is not an exception. The simple but unique melody line, accompanied by harmony that is advanced for the genre, is a gospel singer's delight; and the poetry and setting of the lyrics are superb. Marian Williams's 1973 recording of the piece is a powerful and moving rendition, with blue notes, bent notes, elisions, timbral variations, and moans delivered in a full, rich voice.[68] The supporting piano and organ frequently engage in call-and-response interplay and wordless yea-sayings of prodigious semantic value, bringing them into the foreground at appropriate points. The blues, jazz, and spiritual elements in this performance, including melodic and rhythmic paraphrase, are effectively and inextricably fused in a touching, fervent, and moving presentation. The instrumentalists on the recording—Lloyd Gary on piano, Paul Griffin on organ, Howard Carrol on guitar, and Earl Williams on drums—splendidly support the singer's powerful climaxes, the organist's swells combining with the pianist's repeated motives and single notes to enhance the singer's elevations; and there is splendid Signifyin(g) interplay between the piano and organ—real *interplay*—that complements Williams's effort. In her delivery, Williams intensifies aspects of Dorsey's text with repetitions of syllables and words, with bent notes, and with spoken interjections ("Lord, here's what I *want* you to do for *me*") and intensifies the music by displacing selected notes at the octave and by eliding certain grace notes.

Songs such as Dorsey's and precursors of performances like Williams's provided a new foundation for shout worship in black urban Protestant churches in the 1930s and beyond. Shout worship—which had continued since slavery in the Pentecostal and Holiness churches of the nation's cities—constituted, in Michael Harris's opinion, modern, urban "bush arbor" (or "brush harbor") worship, a throwback, or continuation, of the disguised and clandestine forest meeting places where slaves held worship and strategy meetings in which they had "a good time, shouting, singing, and praying just like we please." Eventually, Harris tells us,

This special communal gathering actually crept into the high worship hour itself in Baptist old-line churches, particularly with the deacon's prayer and song service that was held just prior to the high worship hour. But such a literal echo of the "bush arbor" prayer and shout threatened the new old-line aesthetic so much that a church like Pilgrim Baptist had to move it out of the main sanctuary into the basement—perhaps unaware that the cellar was a more authentic setting than the upstairs formal meeting hall by any stretch of the imagination.[69]

Harris suggests that Dorsey's Pilgrim Baptist Church chorus could be considered a resurrected version of the praying and singing bands of the nineteenth century, whose practice it had been "to carry on their shouting, clapping, and ring dancing after sermons or as an appendage to the formal worship." The gospel chorus originated in 1928 at Chicago's Metropolitan Community Church, when Magnolia Butler established a group to supplement the music of the senior choir; this led to similar choirs at Bethel AME and Quinn Chapel. But the gospel-*blues* chorus had its debut in that auspicious year 1932, when Dorsey and Frye established the chorus at Ebenezer, engaging the interest and participation of transplanted southerners who believed in the "bush arbor" aesthetic.[70] The gospel-blues choruses multiplied and became exceedingly popular. They would play increasingly important roles in black Protestant churches over the succeeding years and decades.

The importance of boogie-woogie, jazz, and gospel music in the Chicago renaissance is evident from references and allusions to it in some of the literature and other artistic output of the movement. For example, Gwendolyn Brooks's poems "Queen of the Blues" and "of De Witt Williams on his way to Lincoln Cemetery," both included in *A Street in Bronzeville* (1945), treat, in the first instance, the life of a blues singer and, in the second, the nature of black life itself, with a spiritual text at the end: "Swing low swing low sweet chariot. Nothing but a plain black boy." In Wright's *Native Son*, which makes no significant mention of music, Bessie, Bigger's girl, is a character whose "speech and life-style embodies in no simple way the spirit of the *blues*," according to Edward A. Watson. For Watson, "Bessie's blues are an extension of the earthly complaint in the tradition of Ma Rainey and Bessie Smith." In Bessie's speech—her "songs"—he finds "characteristic blues themes which fall naturally under the three divisions of the book."[71] In this way, Wright achieves a subtle wedding of literature and black music—a wedding that expresses the essentials of black life in early-twentieth-century America.

The magazines of the Chicago renaissance promoted such musical-literary interaction. The short-lived magazine *Negro Story* published Bucklin Moon's short story "Slack's Blues" (1944) and Vernon Loggins's "Neber Said a Mumblin' Word" (1944), a story based on the Negro spiritual of that name. Its final issue presented a column headed "Music," the first of what was to have been a regular feature, promising that "the current interest in the Negro's part in our jazz history started by *Lionel Hampton's Swing Book* will be exploited to the fullest."[72] The early issues of *Abbott's Monthly*, a literary magazine, carried features on and advertisements for musical solo acts and groups such as the Four Harmony Kings and Walter Barnes's Royal Creolians.

Lionel Hampton's Swing Book (1946), a quintessential product of the period, contained sections devoted to musicians, dancers, singers, arrangers, and blues music.[73] It also included sections such as "Literary Arts and Jazz," which featured poetry; "Fiction on Jazz," by James O. Wilson, Langston Hughes, Onah Spencer, and others; and "Notes on Jazz," "Swing and Listening," and "Swing and the Armed Forces." The book also featured biographies and photographs of the most prominent musical figures of the day, including Hampton himself, Ellington, Count Basie, Lucky Millinder, and Jimmy Lunceford; a column on jazz artists of the future; and a jazz bibliography. Revealing the contemporary values and perceptions of the music and other arts of the day, the book contains much ephemeral information, many obscure photographs, and brief biographical sketches and comments of a large number of black jazz musicians.

Certain figures of the Harlem Renaissance had strong influence on the Chicago activity. In 1940, for example, former Harlem Renaissance writer Arna Bontemps served as cultural director for a planned state-sponsored American Negro Exposition in Chicago. He brought with him Langston Hughes to write the book for *Jubilee: A Cavalcade of the Negro Theater.* Margaret Bonds and W. C. Handy assisted Hughes, and Ellington and gospel songwriter Dorsey set to music two sets of lyrics that Hughes wrote especially for the show.[74]

From all indications, the Chicago renaissance had less coherence, as a culture-building movement, than did the Harlem movement; it spawned no prevailing black string quartets or symphony orchestras and no black-composed operas, although it did have a branch of a black opera company. But during this period, the vernacular genres grew powerfully in influence and complexity. The blues was extended and elaborated in ways that would allow it to be transformed into rhythm and blues, rock 'n' roll, and, eventually, rock music; Chicago jazz served, in a specific case, as an incubator of bebop; and the Dorsey songs and their progeny extended and elaborated black gospel music, setting the stage for the emergence of modern gospel.

Like the Harlem movement, the Chicago renaissance was a flowering of African American arts and letters. Unlike the Harlem manifestation, however, in which recognition and theorizing took place simultaneously with its activity, recognition of and theorizing about the Chicago renaissance is only now beginning. But the Harlem and Chicago flowerings are all of a piece—aspects of a worldwide movement that had its beginnings in the 1890s and continued into the middle of the twentieth century. The Negro renaissance embraced Washington, D.C., Atlanta, Paris, London, and other large cities around the world—cities that served as bases for the dissemination of the art and ideas of Robeson, Du Bois, Dett, James P. Johnson, Hughes, Ellington, Roland Hayes, Wright, Edmund Jenkins, Still, Dorsey, Price, Hines, Locke, and all the other important figures of the movement.[75]

The way ragtime, blues, jazz, and gospel musics developed during the Negro renaissance was in some ways determined by the modernist mind-set and by New Negro philosophy. To what extent this is true I cannot prove—in part because of the absence of written confirmation of such influences, because of the participants' failure to have perceived or articulated such influences, and because the social posturing, dissembling, and denials that typically exist among competing class and caste groups make statements by some participants of the movement somewhat unreliable (many of the intellectuals and entertainers had a stake in denying such influences, since they tended to support their own particular and most pressing causes). As far as the concert music of the period is concerned, it is clear that in Harlem the initial artistic ideas of the Negro renaissance were best and most fully realized in Dett and Still and that in Chicago the same ideals were most fully realized in Dawson, Price, and Bonds. The Negro renaissances' greatest musical contribution to American culture was its exploration, extension, elaboration, and crystallization of the black aesthetic and the example that aesthetic set for the composers who would mature in the 1960s and beyond. There were certain casualties along the way, of course, most notably Will Marion Cook and William L. Dawson, both of whom had ambitions and talent that transcended what they accomplished. Both might have been prodigious composers of concert-hall music had real opportunities existed for them. But the fields of entertainment and education were the loci of whatever opportunities then existed, and in the face of continual resistance on the part of white culture, Cook and Dawson responded to the beckonings and seductions of Broadway and the teaching profession, respectively. Cook found it impossible to pursue a career as a concert violinist or composer of concert-hall music, and no one would or could take up and sustain the specific trail he blazed in writing show music. Dawson's ambitions were thwarted and redirected because of racial discrimination and because of the turn that the social, intellectual, and artistic climates took in the 1940s and 1950s.

In spite of the casualties, however, there were many successes. The accomplishments of Cook (in spite of being a casualty in the realm of concert-hall music), Joplin, Dett, Henderson, Ellington, and Still, for example, are culturally, socially, and humanistically significant, for in realizing some of the goals of the Negro renaissance, they vindicated the faith and the guiding and driving forces of the movement. Joplin, Dett, and Still, for example, *explored* the use of ragtime, spirituals, and blues, respectively, as foundations for extended composition; Tindley, James P. Johnson, Armstrong, Hines, Dett, Henderson, Ellington, Parker, Gillespie, and Still *extended* the reach of ring tropes, creating new possibilities and styles variously through the expansion of the heterogeneous sound ideal, more-extended troping, and the introduction of new tropes such as riffs, flatted fifths, and extended improvisations; Armstrong, Hines, Tatum, Ellington, Price, and Gillespie *elaborated* the tradition, bringing to it more-intricate revisions and articulations through the revision of timbre, rhythm, melody, and harmony; Dorsey *crystallized* the black gospel style by stabilizing the explorations of Tindley and others through his own stylizations of the extensions and elaborations of ring tropes. In the world of concert music, Dett, Still, and Price, in particular, aside from the developmental and crystallizing contributions they made, produced admirable works of concert music, Dett with the oratorios *The Chariot*

Jubilee and *The Ordering of Moses*, Still with the *Afro-American Symphony*, and Price with the *Symphony in E Minor*.

The leaders of the Harlem flowering of the Negro renaissance had felt certain that African American composers possessed the musical talents to achieve their goals—indeed, the fact had already been proved in the years before by Burleigh, Cook, and Joplin. But on the large scale, their goals were to some extent undermined by the imperatives of modernism. First, renaissance leaders apostatized the mythological foundations of black music: consciously or unconsciously, they expected ideology to replace myth, which they found incompatible with their modernist methodology (Joplin's *Treemonisha* was symbolic of this rejection). What they did not understand, however, was that their musical goals would not be adequately supported by or realized through the combined and rationalized principles of formalist composition and New Negro ideology. Of course, the formalist skills were necessary, but rather than ideology, the production of successful works of black music required the foundation of *myth*, which resides not in the mind, as does ideology, but in the intuitive images and metaphors of cultural memory and ritual. It is the supportive structure of myth, together with its ritual trappings, that drives cultural memory and its expression; and many of the composers' confusion of ideology with myth (as a result of their rejection of African American ritual) resulted in a dearth of artistic communication. This dearth was at the root of the composers' failure to produce in quantity the repertoire for which the movement's leaders had hoped, for when the genuine passions of myth are replaced by rationalized ideology, what results is vapid, or insincere, music. (Even *Treemonisha's* libretto was obliged to embrace myth in order to reject it.)

Second, as marginalized petitioners for entry into the larger social order, renaissance leaders were obliged—or they preferred—to accept the modernist distinction between high culture and low culture, for if privilege was to be given the high, they would eschew the low (and they had within their midst a capable articulator of the "high" in the person of Locke, who had the respect and ears of many of the renaissance's patrons and publishers). With most of the artists successfully negotiating the realm of the "low" and ignoring the "high," there was bound to be some consternation on the part of the intellectuals, and the entertainers were bound to be aware of this consternation. But some of the movement's younger artists would not accept this distinction as part of the prevailing ideology. As Hughes retorted in response to the admonitions of the leadership,

> Let the blare of Negro jazz bands and the bellowing voice of Bessie Smith singing Blues penetrate the closed ears of the colored near-intellectuals until they listen and perhaps understand. . . . We younger Negro artists who create now intend to express our dark-skinned selves without fear or shame. If white people are pleased we are glad. If they are not, it doesn't matter. We know we are beautiful. And ugly too. The tom-tom cries and the tom-tom laughs. If colored people are pleased we are glad. If they are not, their displeasure doesn't matter either. We build temples for tomorrow, strong as we know how, and we stand on top of the mountain, free within ourselves.[76]

Thus, Hughes and many of his peers also subverted the movement by undermining the leadership's attempt to focus on achievement in the realm of high art. The replacement of myth and ritual with ideology was part of the strategy (conscious or unconscious) to merge social, political, and artistic values in a frontal assault on access to the fruits of white society. But the individualistic values inherent in modernism (necessary, admittedly, for the rise of composers) were still foreign to the progeny of a culture in which communalism had been the norm and who were now experiencing various forms of alienation. All of this resulted in a social tension in which those accustomed to the organic unity of rural Afro-America could not or would not adjust entirely to the change and felt abandoned by the urban intellectuals and artists who were driven by the individualistic impulse. Thus, two cultural universes existed: one based on the values of the jook; the other, on those of the concert hall, the art gallery, the conductor's podium, and the composer's studio. Of course, there were those who successfully negotiated this breach, as evidenced by the collaborations of James P. Johnson, Waller, Still, and Handy on the performance of Johnson's *Yamakraw* (*A Negro Rhapsody*) and Cook's and Still's composition of works that included the values of both cultural universes.[77]

The musical goals of the Negro renaissance were realized but in ways that were not evident and certainly not planned. The "extended forms" that renaissance leaders wanted to see produced *were* produced by Ellington, although not as European-derived concert-hall music. But the New Negroes may not have perceived these accomplishments as relevant to their goals, since Ellington's works did not meet their social requirements: Renaissance leaders' use of the term *symphonic* (meaning "orchestra") was motivated by the politics of concert attendance, of "racial elevation," and of the high-minded aspirations of Locke and other intellectuals. One wonders whether in the face of such conflicts, the musical outcomes of the Harlem and Chicago flowerings would have been different and more substantive had there been gatherings and discussions between the musicians and the intellectuals similar to those that took place in the Dark Tower among literary artists, renaissance leaders, society leaders, and publishers. But these conflicts, differences, and paradoxes, significant as they may have been, should not obscure an essential unity that dominated the movement. That unity lay in black nationalism, for even with the movement's integrationist stance, black nationalism was its *real* ideology, and some of its imperatives gave direction to all who would embrace them. The problem was that this unity could not properly drive renaissance ideals because of the conflict between those values and the mythological values of the core culture. The primary contributions of black nationalism lay in its giving root to the movement, unifying all classes and castes of African Americans in their attempt, thwarted though it may have been, to build a culture.

The paradoxical nature of the movement—the ideologists' repudiation of black folk music in its pristine forms while embracing it in its more elevated ones, the desire to have the blues without Esu, art without myth—characterized it, exceptions notwithstanding. That the modernist rejection of the mythology of the past and the adoption and promotion, in exalted form, of its artistic progeny was a fundamental contradiction apparently never occurred to most of the players in the movement,[78] many of whom had an ambivalent desire to eat their cake and have it, too.

Notes

1. Tony Martin, *The Pan-African Connection: From Slavery to Garvey and Beyond* (Dover, Mass.: Majority, 1983), vii.

2. Peter Olisanwuche Esedebe, *Pan-Africanism: The Idea and Movement, 1776–1963* (Washington, D.C.: Howard University Press, 1982), 3.

3. Rainer E. Lotz, "The Black Troubadours: Black Entertainers in Europe, 1896–1915," *Black Music Research Journal* 10, no. 2 (1990): 264.

4. Esedebe, *Pan-Africanism*, 67, 70.

5. Ibid., 75.

6. The complete song text is in Esedebe, *Pan-Africanism*, 73–74.

Such Pan-African patriotic songs must have come into vogue around this time. In 1915, Harry T. Burleigh wrote the song "Ethiopia Saluting the Colors," and in 1920, F. A. Clark composed and published a song called "Ethiopia," which he referred to as a "race anthem."

7. Garvey's efforts, part of the New Negro movement's early years, ended in 1926, when he was deported for mail fraud.

8. Esedebe, *Pan-Africanism*, 81.

9. The term *Pan-Africanism* had become popular by 1897, and the first Pan-African conference was held in England in 1900.

10. Jeffrey Green, "'The Foremost Musician of His Race': Samuel Coleridge-Taylor of England, 1875–1912," *Black Music Research Journal* 10, no. 2 (1990): 61–62.

11. Jeffrey Green, "The Negro Renaissance and England," in *Black Music in the Harlem Renaissance: A Collection of Essays*, ed. Samuel A. Floyd Jr., Contributions in Afro-American and African Studies (New York: Greenwood, 1990), 156–57.

12. Coleridge-Taylor's *African Suite*, *Danse Nègre*, and "Onaway, Awake, Beloved," the last from *Hiawatha's Wedding Feast*, are available on a record in the Black Composers Series.

13. See, for example, William Grant Still, "A Composer's Viewpoint," in *William Grant Still and the Fusion of Cultures in American Music*, ed. Robert B. Haas (Los Angeles: Black Sparrow, 1975).

14. William Tortolano, *Samuel Coleridge-Taylor: Anglo-Black Composer, 1875–1912* (Metuchen, N.J.: Scarecrow, 1977), 73.

15. The term *black nationalism* refers here to movements in which blacks take pride in their African heritage and desire to control their own destiny and communities. It does not necessarily refer to separatist movement and thinking.

16. Sterling Stuckey, *Slave Culture: Nationalist Theory and the Foundations of Black America* (New York: Oxford University Press, 1987); Gayle T. Tate, "Black Nationalism: An Angle of Vision," *Western Journal of Black Studies* 12 (1988).

17. W. E. B. Du Bois, *The Souls of Black Folk: Essays and Sketches*, (Chicago: McClurg and Co., 1903), 190–91.

18. The appendix of Trotter's book contains sheet-music facsimiles of works by thirteen composers.

19. The overture to *In Dahomey* is recorded on *The Black Music Repertory Ensemble in Concert* (Chicago: Center for Black Music Research, 1993), sound recording, two cassette tapes.

20. Alain LeRoy Locke, *The Negro and His Music*, Negro Culture and History series (1936; Port Washington, N.Y.: Kennikat, 1968), 65; Eileen Southern, *The Music of Black Americans: A History* (New York: Norton, 1971), 345–47.

21. Jno W. Ellison, *Ellison's Clef Club Book for New York, Chicago and Boston Colored Musicians: A Standard Clef Club Diary and Daily Reminder for Members and Patrons* (New York: Ellison, 1916).

22. Peter Buckman, *Let's Dance: Social, Ballroom, and Folk Dancing* (New York: Paddington, 1978), 167.

23. For more on Europe, see R. Reid Badger, "James Reese Europe and the Prehistory of Jazz," *American Music* 7, no. 1 (1989).

24. James Weldon Johnson, ed. *The Book of American Negro Poetry, Chosen and Edited with an Essay on the Negro's Creative Genius* (New York: Harcourt, Brace, 1922), vii.

25. Arnold Rampersad, *The Life of Langston Hughes, Volume II, 1941–1967, I Dream a World* (New York: Oxford University Press, 1988), 6.

26. Maud Cuney-Hare, *Negro Musicians and Their Music*, Music Reprint Series (1936; New York: Da Capo,1974), 261.

27. Virginia Hamilton, *Paul Robeson: The Life and Times of a Free Black Man* (New York: Harper and Row, 1974), 12; Eslanda Goode Robeson, *Paul Robeson, Negro* (New York: Harper and Brothers, 1930).

28. For additional information about the intellectual and artistic ferment of the movement, see Samuel A. Floyd Jr., ed., *Black Music in the Harlem Renaissance: A Collection of Essays*, Contributions in Afro-American and African Studies (New York: Greenwood, 1990), 128; Nathan Irvin Huggins, *Harlem Renaissance* (New York: Oxford University Press, 1971; David Levering Lewis, *When Harlem Was in Vogue* (New York: Knopf, 1981), and Locke, *Negro and His Music*.

29. Rainey can be heard on *Ma Rainey*, Milestone M-47021 (1974). A discography and information about Rainey's accomplishments are found in Sandra Lieb, *Mother of the Blues* (Amherst: University of Massachusetts Press, 1981).

30. For examples of Bessie Smith singing, listen to her on *The World's Greatest Blues Singer*, Columbia GP33 (1970).

31. David A. Jasen and Trebor J. Tichenor, *Rags and Ragtime: A History* (New York: Seabury, 1978), 189. Luckey Roberts's "Nothin'" was recorded on *Harlem Piano Solos* (1958), Good Time Jazz M-12035.

32. Quoted in Maurice Waller and Anthony Calabrese, *Fats Waller* (New York: Schirmer, 1977), 26.

33. Ed Kirkeby, *Ain't Misbehavin'* (New York: Dodd, Mead, 1966), 36.

34. Scott E. Brown and Robert Hilbert, *James P. Johnson: A Case of Mistaken Identity*, Studies in Jazz, no. 4 (Metuchen, N.J.: Scarecrow, 1986), 22.

35. Willie (the Lion) Smith, "Tea for Two," *The Legend of Willie (the Lion) Smith*, Grand Award LP 33–368 (1958).

36. Kirkeby, *Ain't Misbehavin'*, 148.

37. Mark C. Gridley, "The Time-Life 'Giants of Jazz' Series: An Essay Review," *Black Music Research Journal* 3(1983): 53.

38. Dicky Wells, *The Night People: Reminiscences of a Jazzman* (Boston: Crescendo, 1971), 37.

39. Olly Wilson, "The Heterogeneous Sound Ideal in African-American Music," in *New Perspectives on Music: Essays in Honor of Eileen Southern*, ed. Josephine Wright and Samuel A. Floyd Jr (Warren, Mich.: Harmonie Park, 1992), 338. Elsewhere, in "Ring Shout! Literary Studies, Historical Studies, and Black Music Inquiry," *Black Music Research Journal* 11, no. 2 (1991): 273, I define swing as a quality that manifests itself when sound events Signify on the time line against the flow of its pulse, making the pulse freely lilt; this troping of the time line creates the slight resistances that result in the driving, *swinging*, rhythmic persistence that we find in all African American music, but this is most

vividly present in jazz. Swing is not a trope but an essential quality of the music that *results* from troping of a particular kind. My description is consistent with Wilson's.

40. Samuel A. Floyd Jr., "Music in the Harlem Renaissance: An Overview," in Floyd, *Black Music in the Harlem Renaissance*, 19.

41. Willis Laurence James, "The Romance of the Negro Folk Cry in America," *Phylon* 16, no. 1 (1955): 21.

42. W. O. Smith, *Sideman: The Long Gig of W. O. Smith* (Nashville: Rutledge Hill, 1991), 40.

43. Floyd, "Music in the Harlem Renaissance," 21–23, 25.

44. Ibid., 25.

45. Crowder was a pianist who was a "central figure" in Washington, D.C., Chicago, and New York music circles before World War I. He moved to Europe in the 1920s and lived with shipping heiress Nancy Cunard, who dedicated her *Negro Anthology* (1930) to him. He returned to the United States for good in the early 1930s. Henry Crowder and Hugo Speck, *As Wonderful as All That? Henry Crowder's Memoir of His Affair with Nancy Cunard, 1928–1935* (Navarro, Calif.: Wild Trees, 1987). Crowder's *Henry-Music* (1930), a set of six songs published by Cunard's Hours Press in Paris, included mediocre settings of two poems by Cunard and one each by Richard Aldington, Walter Lowenfels, Samuel Beckett, and Harold Action. A notation in *Henry-Music* claims that the songs were recorded on Sonabel, but all sources searched (OCLC, RILN, and the Rigler-Deutsch Index) reveal only one recording showing Crowder's involvement, as either composer or musician: "Honeysuckle Rose," with Crowder taking a piano solo, recorded by Jean Tany's Hot Club on the Belgium label in 1941.

46. Peter N. Carroll and David W. Noble, *The Free and the Unfree: A New History of the United States* (New York: Penguin Books, 1988), 321.

47. Robert Bone, "Richard Wright and the Chicago Renaissance," *Callaloo*, 28 (1986). This Chicago movement is not to be confused with the "Chicago Literary Renaissance" discussed by Dale Kramer, *Chicago Renaissance: The Literary Life in the Midwest, 1900–1930* (New York: Appleton-Century, 1966), which during the first four decades of the twentieth century embraced the works of white writers and poets such as Carl Sandburg, Floyd Dell, Theodore Dreiser, Sherwood Anderson, Edward Lee Masters, Vachel Lindsey, and Harriet Munro.

48. Bone, "Richard Wright and the Chicago Renaissance," 455–56.

49. Consider, for example, two passages in *Native Son*: "Goddammit, Look! We live here and they live there. We black and they white. They got things and we ain't. They do things and we can't. It's like living in jail." "Who knows when some slight shock, disturbing the delicate balance between social order and thirsty aspiration, should send the skyscrapers in our cities toppling." Richard Wright, *Native Son* (1940; New York: Quality Paperback, 1987), 23, 368.

50. James R. Grossman, *Land of Hope: Chicago, Black Southerners, and the Great Migration* (Chicago: University of Chicago Press, 1989), 262.

51. Cuney-Hare, *Negro Musicians and Their Music*, 242. The philosophy and efforts of the NANM carried forward the nationwide black concert activity dating from the mid-nineteenth century, which was exemplified by the Creoles of Color performing in New Orleans's Philharmonic Society Orchestra led by Constantin Duberque and Richard Lamber (1842); by Philadelphia's soprano Elizabeth Taylor Greenfield's concertizing between around 1850 and 1870; by Washington, D.C.'s Colored Opera Company (1872); and by the activity in 1876 of New York's Philharmonic Society.

52. Edward Moore, "Gershwin Plays with Orchestra; Some Sins of Jazz Forgiven," *Chicago Tribune*, June 11, 1933, 21 (ProQuest, *Chicago Daily Tribune*, June 15, 1933).

53. Helen Walker-Hill, *Piano Music by Black Women Composers* (Westport, Conn.: Greenwood Press, 1992), 11.

54. "Civic Opera Lauds 'Aida' Cast," *Chicago Tribune*, February 20, 1943; "Opera 'Aida' Ready for Curtain Call," *Chicago Defender*, February 20, 1943.

55. Eileen Southern, *Biographical Dictionary of Afro-American and African Musicians* (Westport, Conn.: Greenwood, 1982), 283.

56. For examples of the style, see *Original Boogie Woogie Piano Giants*, Columbia, KC 32708, (1974).

57. Compare A. M. Jones, *Studies in African Music* (Oxford: Oxford University Press, 1959), 1:53, 54.

58. Wendell Logan, "The Ostinato Idea in Black Improvised Music: A Preliminary Investigation," *Black Perspective in Music* 12, no. 2 (1984): 193.

59. Albert Murray, *The Hero and the Blues* (Columbia: University of Missouri Press, 1973).

60. It was well known that African villages traditionally have distorted and enhanced the natural sounds of musical instruments (perhaps in search of the heterogeneous sound ideal) by placing membranes over the amplifying tubes of marimbas, adding beads to the outsides of gourds that already contain seeds, adding rattles to the heads of drums, and the like.

61. Stanley Dance and Earl Hines, *The World of Earl Hines* (New York: Da Capo, 1983), 90, 290, 266, 90, 261. Unfortunately, the Hines band in which Gillespie and Parker played never recorded, but we do have Eckstine's recording of "Jelly, Jelly" (1940).

62. Michael W. Harris, *The Rise of Gospel Blues: The Music of Thomas Andrew Dorsey in the Urban Church* (New York: Oxford University Press, 1992).

63. Eileen Southern, *The Music of Black Americans: A History* (New York: Norton, 1971), 403; John W. Work, "Changing Patterns in Negro Folk Songs," *Journal of American Folklore* 62 (1949): 141–42. For examples of Dorsey's blues writing and performance, including "Tight Like That," see Thomas A. Dorsey, *Georgia Tom Dorsey: Come On Mama, Do That Dance, 1928–1932*, Yazoo, L 1041.

64. Harris, *Rise of Gospel Blues*, 75, 81.

65. This rhythmically free delivery is related to Armstrong's "floating" above the beat. It would be interesting to know the extent to which this practice was used in black folk music between the turn of the century and 1930. Although its "invention" is sometimes attributed to

Armstrong, I wonder if the practice had not already been present, to some extent, in core culture.

66. Harris, *Rise of Gospel Blues*, 175–79.

67. Ibid., 243–44.

68. Williams sings "Take My Hand, Precious Lord" on *Precious Lord: New Gospel Recordings of the Great Gospel Songs of Thomas A. Dorsey*, Columbia, KG 32151.

69. Former slave, quoted in Harris, *Rise of Gospel Blues*, 245, 187–200.

70. Ibid., 248, 207.

71. Edward A. Watson, David Ray, and Robert M. Farnsworth, "Bessie's Blues," in *Richard Wright: Impressions and Perspectives* (Ann Arbor: University of Michigan Press, 1971), 168, 168, 171.

72. "Music," *Negro Story*, 1946. *Negro Story* was published from May 1944 to May 1946. A full run of the magazine is at the Carter G. Woodson Regional Library, Chicago Public Library.

73. Alice C. Browning, *Lionel Hampton's Swing Book* (Chicago: Negro Story Press, 1946). I am grateful to Robert Bone for informing me of the existence of this book, whose cover is graced by the name of the great jazz and swing drummer and vibraphonist. Bone had brought it to my attention long before I ran across the reference in the April–May 1946 issue of *Negro History*. And I thank Dan Morgenstern of the Jazz Institute of Rutgers University for access to a copy of this rare document.

74. Unfortunately, it was never produced. See Arnold Rampersad, *The Life of Langston Hughes. Volume I, 1902–1941, I, Too, Sing America* (New York: Oxford University Press, 1986), 386.

75. Floyd, *Black Music in the Harlem Renaissance*; Green, "'Foremost Musician of His Race.'"

76. Langston Hughes, quoted in Lewis, *When Harlem Was in Vogue*, 191.

77. A version of James P. Johnson's *Yamakraw*, for piano alone, can be heard on *The Symphonic Jazz of James P. Johnson (1894–1955)*, William Albright, piano, Digital, MMD 60066A (1986).

78. Dett apparently realized and accepted the mythological underpinnings of the spiritual, although he did not flaunt or promote them; Still's success, I believe, to the extent that it was distanced from myth, was a rare triumph of ideology, probably facilitated by its tribute to ritual.

Chapter 3

The Problem of Race and Chicago's Great Tivoli Theater

CLOVIS E. SEMMES

The great palace theaters of the early twentieth century offered first-run feature films and stunning, live, variety performances to appreciative audiences but with racial and gender restrictions. One case in point involved the magnificent Tivoli Theater on the South Side of the great city of Chicago. On March 3, 1923, a young African American couple purchased tickets to attend the Tivoli, which was located at 6425 Cottage Grove (later given as 6329 Cottage Grove, as the building occupied significant space). Leon Headen of 4104 Vincennes Avenue, a dental student at Northwestern University, and Lillian S. Proctor, a resident of Brooklyn, New York, and daughter of the prominent clergyman Dr. Henry Hugh Proctor, entered the theater and proceeded to take seats located in the center aisle of the balcony. A white usher, Carl Linkenhoker of 6328 Greenwood, blocked access to this section and directed the couple to the extreme left aisle, indicating this is where black theatergoers were supposed to sit.[1] While the verbal sparring continued between

Headen and the usher, Proctor pushed past Linken-hoker and took a seat in the preferred section. When Headen attempted to follow, four to five ushers surrounded him. Linkenhoker struck Headen in the head with his flashlight, and three other ushers pummeled Headen in the face. Donald Bingham of 6442 Greenwood Avenue was one of the ushers who attacked Headen. Reportedly, the attack ceased when Proctor intervened or when the head usher arrived. The theater manager apologized to the couple but dismissed the matter as insignificant and made no effort to address the wrong that had been done. Headen subsequently filed suit.[2]

Two years later, a jury in the courtroom of Superior Court Judge Hugo Pam awarded dentist Dr. Leon Headen $2,000 in damages. Ultimately, Headen accepted a settlement through his attorney, William H. Haynes, of $1,200. Haynes had asked for $10,000 in damages for the assault and $500 in damages for discrimination. The jury acknowledged assault but not discrimination. Reportedly, this was the first recorded case of discrimination filed against the Tivoli Theater. However, black patrons previously victimized by Jim Crow policies at the theater had complained to Tivoli management, as ushers routinely directed black patrons to remote sections of the theater. This practice of segregated seating also was common at the Tivoli's sister movie palace, the Chicago Theater, located downtown in Chicago's central business district, known as the Loop. Both movie palaces and most of Chicago's elite movie houses were owned or managed by movie magnates Abraham Joseph Balaban, Barney Balaban, and Samuel Katz.[3]

The Tivoli Theater, like nearly all movie palaces in Chicago, was built primarily to service a white market from surrounding white neighborhoods. These neighborhoods and their movie theaters often discouraged black patronage and maintained racially discriminatory hiring practices. White-oriented theaters that had a policy of film and live performances utilized black talent selectively so as to not offend white audiences or challenge white racial hegemony.[4] The Tivoli, however, as would be the case for a number of Chicago's whites-only or whites-preferred movie palaces, would experience a marked shift in its surrounding demographics. Ultimately, numerous neighborhoods housing and servicing these white-oriented movie palaces would turn from white to black. For the Tivoli, the result would be, in the context of broader industry changes, a shift, beginning in 1959 and extending through 1963, to a policy of film and live performances that would showcase some of the best available entertainment talent to an enthusiastic black consumer market. Moreover, this policy of live entertainment and film would have a unique and organic relationship to the South Side's great Regal Theater, the most magnificent and only movie palace ever built exclusively for a black community.[5] Currently, the author has produced the only comprehensive study of this great movie palace and its social function in Chicago's black community.[6] But what are the roots of the movie palace and its film and live entertainment policy, particularly in Chicago and especially as they relate to black consumers?

The Roots of Vaudeville: Combining Variety Entertainment with Film

By 1890, live, variety entertainment called vaudeville was firmly established in this country, and big-time vaudeville became dominated by two large entertainment circuits. The Orpheum circuit controlled the West and extended from Cincinnati to the Pacific Coast, included significant portions of the South extending from Louisville to New Orleans, and encompassed western Canada. The Keith-Albee circuit dominated the East and extended eastward from Cincinnati to the Atlantic coast and south to Washington, D.C.[7] Vaudeville reached its pinnacle between 1890 and 1920 and, when most popular, attracted two million patrons a day. This entertainment form developed as an alternative to lewd, male entertainment in concert saloons and sought to create an amusement format that would be appropriate for women, children, and families. Many vaudeville theaters began to utilize the policy of continuous performances to attract crowds throughout the day. The public initially viewed vaudeville as a type of low culture that catered to the masses, while the legitimate stage was the province of high culture and the upper classes. Vaudeville moguls altered this perception by building large ornate theaters that could compete aesthetically with the higher-class legitimate theaters and opera houses. Managers often instructed vaudeville audiences in the proper behavior before the show and sought to provide an atmosphere characterized by comfort, cleanliness, and courtesy in their establishments.[8]

Organizationally, big-time vaudeville limited the presence of black entertainers on stage and banned them from its professional theatrical organizations.[9] However, alternative circuits and theaters (usually smaller in size) were available to black entertainers, audiences, and workers. White and some black businesspeople owned or controlled these theaters and circuits, and black owners developed their own professional theatrical organizations, most notably the Frogs and the Colored Vaudeville Benevolent Association.[10] Sherman Dudley created the first black-operated vaudeville circuit in 1912 that connected black entertainers with theater managers and owners. He later merged his efforts with white owners who controlled additional black-oriented theaters and circuits. These collaborations led to the creation in 1921 of the largest black-oriented vaudeville circuit, the Theater Owners Booking Association (TOBA). Dudley's efforts made this circuit possible, but he was pushed out of the organization.[11]

The evolution of vaudeville and movie presentation merged in important and unique ways. Movie exhibitors would embrace the vaudeville model for controlling markets; appealing to women, children, and families; and elevating their image and status. By 1890, when vaudeville was fully mature, the technology for film production was firmly in place. Film shorts became a feature at many vaudeville houses as early as 1896 and functioned as another act. However, as film technology evolved, which made feature films possible—longer presentations built around a major star—film exhibition became a primary and distinct form of entertainment. The film industry rapidly expanded during and after World War I; investment in the industry grew between 1922 and 1930, climbing from $78 million to $850 million. Weekly movie attendance between 1922 and 1928 advanced from 40 million to 80 million. Over time, film production, distribution, and exhibition became vertically integrated and dominated by a small group of corporations. There would also be a shift toward building larger, more elaborate, and ornate theaters to meet growing demand and to extinguish the image of film exhibition as a lower-class enterprise. Movie houses sought to sell the feel of being upper class while giving access to all classes and providing family entertainment. Some combined film and live presentations and implemented a policy of continuous performance.[12] In subsequent years, this combined format would decline generally but sustain itself selectively in black communities and experience a resurgence in the 1950s and 1960s. Black patrons would commonly refer to these live performances at movie houses as stage shows. Developments in the 1950s at Chicago's Tivoli Theater reflected this ferment, but we must first examine its connections to broader transformation in film exhibition.

From Nickelodeons to Palaces

Nickelodeons, cheaply equipped storefront establishments dedicated to film presentations, which only required a few chairs, a projector, and a screen (often a white sheet) and which usually charged a nickel, experienced rising popularity and rapid expansion between 1905 and 1910. One estimate placed weekly attendance at nickelodeons in 1910 at 26 million. These establishments replaced penny arcades and vaudeville houses as principal outlets for film exhibition. The mass appeal and low overhead brought significant profits, and the cash-rich enterprise began to attract the support of wealthy investors. Entrepreneurs and investors quickly began to refocus

their business objectives to exploit more upscale markets while preserving the mass appeal of movie exhibition. Notably, nickelodeons and related enterprises served as important entry points for Jewish immigrants and first-generation Jews into the movie industry. The revenue generated from nickelodeons supplied the capital to buy and construct more appealing theaters and to move into film production, exhibition, and distribution, providing the basis for an extraordinary Jewish presence, power, and influence in filmmaking and film presentation, including the creation of Hollywood. Examples are Carl Laemmle, who founded Universal Pictures; Adolph Zukor, who would build Paramount; William Fox, developer of Fox Film Corporation; Marcus Loew and Lewis Mayer of Loews-MGM (Metro-Goldwyn-Mayer); and Harry, Sam, Albert, and Jack Warner of Warner Brothers.[13] This Jewish presence, power, and influence would continue in the form of the Chicago-based Balaban and Katz (B & K) corporation, which would become the industry leader in building and managing theater palaces.

The construction of theater palaces, large ornate movie houses that typically had more than two thousand seats, predated Balaban and Katz, however.[14] The initial success of the theater palace was more associated with the techniques of Jewish American Samuel "Roxy" Rothapfel (later dropping the p to become Rothafel). Rothafel, a successful small-town movie operator, in 1910 helped Benjamin F. Keith turn around his struggling vaudeville theaters by adding film and enhancing the overall presentation of the moviegoing experience, including the interior décor and the appearance of the ushers. He turned around the struggling three-thousand-seat Alhambra Theatre in Milwaukee, previously only a legitimate theater, by bringing in a motion-pictures-only policy and adding an orchestra on stage.[15] It should be noted that music was an important accompaniment to the silent films of the era. Rothafel's innovations began to attract a more affluent clientele to movie houses while sustaining a mass market.[16]

New York became the next frontier for Rothafel. Here he could garner more national attention. Rothafel turned around in 1913 the fortunes of New York's newly constructed, two-thousand-seat, movie-only Regent Theater. He added a fifteen-piece orchestra to its stage. Rothafel connected upper-class music, which included a prologue to set the mood for the movie presentation, to high-quality motion pictures, and he provided a disciplined, attentive, uniformed, and entertaining usher corps. Rothafel would successfully manage other theater palaces in New York, including the four-thousand-seat Strand and his own cavernous, six-thousand-seat Roxy Theater. By 1914, opera houses, vaudeville theaters, and live theater venues began to convert to film, and many other entrepreneurs would begin to build theater palaces to profit from the popularity of this new film-entertainment venue.[17] Similarly, in Chicago, several first-generation Jewish immigrants would become seminal to advancing the growth of national theater chains and the character of theater palaces in Chicago and nationally. Ultimately, their efforts would result in the birth of the Tivoli Theater.

In 1916, brothers Abraham Joseph or A. J. (born 1889) and Barney (born 1887) Balaban partnered with Samuel Katz (born 1893) to create Balaban and Katz, which by 1924 became the most profitable theater chain in America and which ultimately set the standard for theater chains nationally. A. J. and Barney had already set up several nickelodeons in 1908, 1909, and 1914 and developed other related business ventures, before meeting Katz in 1914. Samuel Katz, with his father, Morris, had acquired three theaters by 1915. A. J.'s dream, which he shared with Katz, was to build great presentation houses (theater palaces with film and live entertainment) on each side of the city. The partners had observed that three other movie chains, the Ascher Brothers, the Marks Brothers, and Lubliner and Trinz had already begun to build large movie houses, and B & K needed to build comparable venues in order to compete.[18] Ironically, Balaban and Katz would eventually buy out or take over these chains.[19]

Nonetheless, the partnership between the Balaban brothers and Katz was a first step to realize their dream of building theater palaces in diverse neighborhoods and to compete effectively. The youthful collaborators began to plan a two-thousand-seat theater on Chicago's West Side in the North Lawndale community on Twelfth Street near Central Park. Architects Rapp and Rapp designed the theater, which would be called the Central Park. Katz obtained help from Julius Rosenwald, prominent philanthropist and president of Sears and Roebuck, the largest employer in the neighborhood. Rosenwald directed Katz to S. W. Straus, where he was able to secure a

mortgage to construct the new theater. The Balabans and Sam Katz put up their other theaters as collateral. The Central Park Theater opened October 27, 1917, and proved to be very successful. Reportedly, it was the first mechanically cooled theater in the world, and movie fans could comfortably attend the theater all year round.[20]

Birth of the Tivoli

The success of the Central Park venture led to larger projects. In October of 1918, Balaban and Katz opened the 2,000-seat Riviera at 4746 North Broadway on Chicago's Far North Side in the upscale Uptown district. A syndicate of investors backed this undertaking, which included Julius Rosenwald, William Wrigley Jr. of chewing gum fame, and John Hertz, who had established himself in the Yellow Cab business but later became successful in car rentals.[21] Next came the Tivoli Theater in February of 1921 at 6329 Cottage Grove and the Chicago Theater in October of 1921 at 175 North State Street. These two theaters had 3,520 and 3,861 seats respectively. After Balaban and Katz opened the 4,325-seat Uptown Theater at 4814 Broadway in August of 1925, the Tivoli, the Chicago, and the Uptown theaters became known as the big three.[22] More important, in 1925, Hollywood's largest film studio, Famous Players–Lasky, acquired controlling interest in Balaban and Katz. Additionally, Famous Players–Lasky had already taken over the company that distributed its films, Paramount, whose name would become the trade name of the merged company. This merger produced the first production-distribution-exhibition company with a truly national presence. The theater circuit portion of the company became Publix Theaters, and Samuel Katz became its president. A. J. Balaban would take national charge of all Publix stage presentations, and in subsequent years Barney would serve as president of Paramount Pictures.[23] The Tivoli Theater that Dr. Leon Headen sued in 1923 was connected to the largest and most powerful motion-picture-production-distribution-and-exhibition company in the country, and industry insiders called the Tivoli when it opened in 1921 "the finest theater in the world."[24]

Opening night at the Tivoli Theater in 1921 was another major advance toward fulfillment of the Balaban and Katz dream to build theater palaces in neighborhoods. The air-conditioned structure was on the cutting edge technically, and its architecture was awe inspiring. The *Exhibitor Herald* reported:

> The architectural plans for the Tivoli were inspired by the Chateau de Versailles. From the street a window with a clear height of 65 feet from the sidewalk radiates a welcome to the brilliantly lighted interior wherein is reproduced the chapel at Versailles where Louis XVI worshipped. Far overhead thousands of lights reflect their glow from magnificent chandeliers. At the end where the altar would stand is a beautiful staircase of marble. Giant columns rise on either side, broken on the various floors by alcoves, arches, windows and panels. There is not a single straight wall expanse in the building. The lobby will hold 1500 people and still will not interfere with outgoing patrons.
>
> Inside the theatre proper the ceiling is broken into units by a triple ceiling effect. Above the balcony there is a sunburst dome 65 feet in diameter, tinted in silver, while over the mezzanine floor is a dome edged by a hand decorated frieze. The forward part of the ceiling is domed and offset on each side by a rosette which tops the design leading into the pillared organ settings.
>
> Spacious aisles break up the immense floor expanse and ample room is given between rows of seats for everyone to pass in or out. Comfortable boxes and loges extend in horseshoe effect clear across the theatre. These are easily reached from the main entrance.
>
> The general architecture of the Tivoli is after the style of Louis XVI and the early Renaissance type, with late Italian treatment. Magnificent mural paintings and hundreds of oil paintings add to the beauty of the place.[25]

The Tivoli, besides its magnificent architecture, embodied all of the innovations that made Balaban and Katz industry leaders. Theaters were dedicated to people and their children and reflected classic artistic and architectural themes. The ladies' parlors and men's lounging rooms were exquisite. Live entertainment typically accompanied film and advanced a blend of jazz and opera, uniting aristocrat and worker. A neighborhood theater like the Tivoli had the same standard of beauty as downtown houses. The price was low enough for the masses. The Tivoli, like other B & K theaters, had the most modern equipment to ensure the convenience, comfort, and safety of its patrons, employees, and performers. The cooling system, for example, was the most advanced and washed and purified the air to a degree not found in other public structures. Moreover, management trained staff to deal with fires and other emergencies and equipped theaters with first-aid rooms, where a trained nurse or physician was on constant duty. Beautiful, expansive lobbies made waiting a stimulating rather than a tedious experience. Designers utilized the latest advances in lighting and paid great attention to line of sight, eliminating the use of support structures that could obstruct the view.[26]

Contradictions in Serving the Common Man and Woman

Despite these B & K innovations and progressive policies, deep contradictions based on race and sex remained, and ushers were a prime embodiment of these contradictions. B & K required its employees to serve their customers well and to treat the common man and woman like royalty. Ushers were central to this policy, and management paid great attention to their selection, appearance, and training. The principal requirements, however, were that ushers had to be white and male. Beyond these criteria, they must be similar in appearance and physical characteristics. Ushers had to be between 135 and 145 pounds, approximately five foot seven, and between the ages of seventeen and twenty-one. They wore military-style uniforms, which changed seasonally. If ushers failed to wear the appropriate uniform, they could be terminated on the spot. Ushers were to act with utmost courtesy in greeting and seating patrons. They also entertained the crowd with their military-style drilling. Ushers learned complex hand signals to communicate with one another and management so as to not disturb patrons during the entertainment experience. Ushers also aided in keeping the peace. They helped to quiet or remove unruly patrons and to dampen the activity of couples that might become too sexually enamored with one another. Ushers held positions of high visibility and status and were expected to come from "wholesome" and "refined" homes.[27] Commenting on the ushers at the Tivoli Theater on opening night, Carrie Balaban, wife of B & K cofounder Barney, observed:

> Another novelty was the military drilling of the ushers. White cotton gloves, swagger sticks, and some drilling of the ushers had been introduced at the Riviera, but in the Tivoli this was made all the more spectacular because of the larger corps of college boys, who were working their way through school. The "military" type of ushers control was now well developed. Boys were well drilled, smartly uniformed and coached continuously in their approach and service to patrons.[28]

Balaban and Katz management determined that only certain jobs were appropriate for black men and women at its theaters that served a predominantly white clientele. Black middle-aged men could be hired as footmen to assist patrons from their automobiles, and black boys could be hired as messengers and pageboys. Black boys had to be of slight build, and management preferred that they have light skin and physical features that were closer to white somatic norms. Management did not want to hire blacks it viewed as threatening to white patrons. Black women could be hired as maids to service the lounges and restrooms.[29] The jobs available to black persons also required uniforms, but these uniforms and positions could not communicate authority, only service, and helped to reify racial and gender stratification and stereotypes that existed in the broader society. Dr. Leon Headen and Lillian Proctor experienced firsthand how ushers and management at the Tivoli Theater routinely abided by these broader societal and racial norms.

Demographics and Racial Boundaries: The Tivoli and the Regal Theaters

Given the broader restrictions of race, opening day at the Tivoli brought a sea of white patrons and virtually no black presence among the throngs who clamored to enter the newly opened entertainment venue. Grand Boulevard, a community where the black presence was growing in 1921, was over a mile to the north. In 1920, black residents constituted 32 percent of this community. By 1930, Grand Boulevard's black population would reach nearly 95 percent.[30] Moreover, in 1920, the community between Grand Boulevard and the Woodlawn community, where the Tivoli Theater was located, was called Washington Park and had a black population of only 15 percent. Woodlawn itself was home to a black population of only 2 percent.[31] Many white residents and Balaban and Katz management were also secure in the knowledge that the Tivoli Theater was located on Cottage Grove Avenue, which constituted a racial dividing line. For years, blacks were not permitted to move east of this street. In addition, the community east of Cottage Grove and contiguous to north Woodlawn, called Hyde Park, which is also home to the University of Chicago, had waged a successful war to restrict its black residents, whose numbers barely exceeded 1

percent of the population by 1930.[32] Indeed, in prior years, white residents who opposed the black presence used vandalism to drive a black family from its home on Greenwood Avenue in Hyde Park.[33] Greenwood Avenue extended south into Woodlawn, the province of the Tivoli. Notably, two of the white ushers who confronted Headen at the Tivoli, including the one who admitted in court to striking Dr. Headen in the eye with his fist, lived on this street.[34]

Ultimately, however, Balaban and Katz would extend much of its entertainment concept to the black community and provide similar employment opportunities for black persons but without challenging existing racial norms. In 1928, after brothers Harry and Louis Engelstein opened a commercial and entertainment complex that included the famed Regal Theater, Chicago's Savoy Ballroom, and the South Central Department Store at Forty-Seventh Street and Grand Boulevard (later changed to South Parkway and then Martin Luther King Jr. Drive), Balaban and Katz managed the Regal Theater from 1928 to 1959. Initially, Lubliner and Trinz was the ostensible manager of the Regal at its opening in February of 1928. However, Balaban and Katz already maintained a controlling interest in this great chain and asserted its presence, as it relegated its prior competitor and then partner to obscurity. The Regal Theater had 2,798 seats and was the only theater palace ever constructed specifically to service a black community. It became famous for its combination of live entertainment and film and, throughout its forty-year existence, never had a year when it did not offer live performances. The Regal predated New York's Apollo Theater, was much larger, and significantly influenced the character of the Apollo's entertainment policy. But it was at the Regal Theater, located in the historic black community called Bronzeville or the Black Belt, that black persons could have access to the array of job opportunities and entertainment amenities, without restriction, available at other Balaban and Katz theaters that catered to white markets.[35]

Although white developers saw the Regal Theater and the commercial and entertainment venue of which it was a part as a lucrative business opportunity to meet the needs of an untapped and captive black consumer market, they also saw it as a way to slow black expansion into white enclaves. It was black persons who were better off financially who were generally at the forefront of an expanding black community and who proved most troublesome for white residents whose neighborhoods were near such blacks seeking to transcend racial restrictions. Veritably, it was black persons like Jesse Binga, real-estate entrepreneur and founder and president of a state bank, who had their businesses and homes bombed numerous times as they sought better resources and facilities in more-privileged and predominantly white communities.[36]

Lillian Proctor and Leon Headen were indicative of this search for a better life as they traveled into the Woodlawn community to enjoy the facilities of the Tivoli Theater in 1923. Indeed, the fact that dentist Headen lived on the 4100 block of Vincennes, north of the Woodlawn community, attested to an earlier quest for better housing. This neighborhood had been the center of racial violence a few years prior as white residents attempted to discourage black persons from living in this more attractive area. When opened, the Regal Theater served as a buffer between black persons to the north and white ones to the south, making it possible for black persons to seek quality family-oriented film and live entertainment without venturing south into Woodlawn and going to the Tivoli Theater. In addition, business mogul Julius Rosenwald, who had collaborated with Balaban and Katz previously, invested his personal funds to develop the Michigan Boulevard Garden Apartments, which became the most desirable housing complex in the black, South Side community and which opened in August of 1929, a little over a year after the opening of the Regal Theater. Also known as the Rosenwald building, Julius Rosenwald geared this apartment complex toward higher-earning black persons, and he constructed it several blocks north of the Regal, that is, deeper within the existing black community, where it served, like the Regal, to anchor more financially mobile black residents in the present black community, discouraging movement to white areas to the south.[37]

The Regal Becomes Independent, and the Tivoli Returns to Stage Shows

Thus, the Regal and the Tivoli (both managed by B & K) were intended for different audiences and had significant similarities and differences. Both venues were theater palaces in size and architecture. The Regal was not as ornate or as large as the Tivoli but was noted for its semi-atmospheric

interior, where the auditorium featured a lighted dome that created the illusion of being in a soaring, striped, multicolored tent. Through the tent's aperture one could observe the silhouette of Moorish castles under a North African sky with twinkling stars.[38] The Tivoli opened in 1921; the Regal opened in 1928. The Tivoli was at the beginning of a 1920s building boom in palace and deluxe theaters and in the growth of theater chains, and the Regal was at the end of this period of theater and film-industry expansion. The 1920s was also a period when major film companies, because of the blockbuster merger between Balaban and Katz and Famous Players–Lasky/Paramount, were forced to expand into film exhibition, and major theater chains (exhibitors) were forced to move into film production and distribution to remain competitive. The results were rapid expansion; risky speculation; mergers, including hostile takeovers; collusion; and monopolistic practices. Both theaters were part of a national and powerful, but shifting, film and live-entertainment circuit controlled by Paramount.[39] By 1950, Woodlawn, the community surrounding the Tivoli, was nearly 39 percent black; by 1960, it was 89 percent black.[40] Major changes were imminent.

Besides the demographic transformations taking place in the neighborhoods surrounding the Tivoli, major industry changes in film exhibition would profoundly impact the Regal and Tivoli, as well as the viability, ownership, and policies of movie theaters generally. The 1930s and Great Depression brought a reduction in many of the services and amenities associated with theater palaces. By 1940, many presentation houses went to film-only policies, including the Tivoli. Paramount experienced bankruptcy in 1933 but reorganized and regained its profitability in a few years. Paramount, however, would never lose its dominance in film production, distribution, and exhibition. Also, by 1930, five major film studios dominated the industry, including the control of theater chains. They were Paramount, Loews-MGM (Metro-Goldwyn-Mayer), RKO (Radio-Keith-Orpheum), Warner Brothers, and Twentieth Century Fox. Three minor film companies, Columbia, Universal, and United Artists, did not control a significant number of theaters but aligned themselves with the five majors. These companies colluded to control film distribution and release, which disadvantaged independent theater owners. Several anti-trust suits, culminating in the late 1940s, would break up monopolistic practices by the film companies mentioned above and require massive divestment in theater ownership.[41]

This broader context precipitated a management shift at the Regal and Tivoli that would result in the rebirth of live performances in 1959 at the Tivoli, which for two decades had operated on a film-only policy. This time the Tivoli's live performances would be directed toward the sensibilities of black audiences in a market that was predominantly black. Moreover, the Regal Theater had a series of white managers until 1936 when two black assistant managers, Ken Blewitt and Myron Wright, shared the job for several years on an interim basis. Balaban and Katz officials appointed Blewitt to the job permanently in 1939. Blewitt served as manager of the Regal until 1959 when B & K decided not to continue its managerial relationship with the Regal. Balaban and Katz transferred Blewitt to the Tivoli, where he led a resurgence in stage shows. Blewitt had been a legendary and respected figure at the Regal and was credited with maintaining its outstanding record of quality stage shows. The Regal became an independent theater in 1959, and for the first time since 1928, the Regal and the Tivoli became competitors, competing for a black audience, though no racial restrictions existed and white patrons freely attended both venues. The Tivoli, under the management of B & K's Blewitt, would sustain a policy of film and stage shows from 1959 through 1963, the year Balaban and Katz closed and demolished the theater. During this time period, the Regal provided a greater number of stage shows, but the Tivoli's productions were as noteworthy and spectacular.[42]

Stage Shows at the Tivoli: 1959–63

Excitement about the rebirth of live performances at the Tivoli had been building for several years. As early as 1956, the *Chicago Defender* speculated that the Tivoli would return to a policy of film and stage shows.[43] These rumors continued to rage in 1958, which included Blewitt leaving the Regal and moving to the Tivoli. Additionally, the *Chicago Defender* expressed excitement about the possibility of Chicago's major South Side presentation houses hosting big time shows like Larry Steele's *Smart Affairs* and Arthur Bragg's *Idlewild Revue*.[44] Long an advocate of the tradition of "flesh" (live) shows at movie houses, which were attractive to families and people from all

walks of life, the *Chicago Defender* paid attention to the status of the stage-show phenomenon nationally and reported the "encouraging note" that "several cities [would] open theatres to presentations by 1959" and that "Chicago [was] already set to go on the 'flesh' kick by changing the Tivoli from movie theatre to live shows." The newspaper did not hide its exuberance regarding what it felt Blewitt could bring to the Tivoli and the possibility of expanding the stage-show tradition that had been established at the Regal.[45]

1959

Blewitt resurrected the tradition of live performances at the Tivoli with the popular singer, dancer, actress, and comedian Pearl Bailey, who brought her own show. Opening March 27, Bailey's revue featured her husband, drummer Louis Bellson, and his seventeen-piece orchestra; the fourteen-voice Rhythm Choir; actress Helen Thigpen of *Porgy and Bess* fame; tap dancers Honi Coles and Cholly Atkins; singing groups, the Ambassadors, the Four Voices, the Flamingoettes; and others. The show claimed a contingent of fifty-five performers.[46]

Subsequent shows for the year were star studded and successful. The April stage show featured singers Fats Domino, Big Maybelle, Priscilla Bowman, and Joe Medlin; singing group, the Cadillacs; and guitarist Lefty Bates and his Rhythm Band.[47] Because of popular demand, Blewitt brought back Bailey and her revue for one week in May.[48] Also, for one day, May 9, the popular comedy team, the Three Stooges, was slated to appear at the Tivoli and several other B & K theaters (Uptown and Marbro) in concert with programs of film featuring the popular comedians.[49] A June production presented organist Dave "Baby" Cortez; guitarist and bassist Frank Virtue and the Virtues; singers Sam Hawkins, Valerie Carr, Arnold Dover, and Lula Reed; singing group, Harvey and the Moonglows; and pianist and vocalist Sonny Thompson.[50]

Entertaining productions at the Tivoli continued in July. The first show featured popular vocalists LaVern Baker and Roy Hamilton; two singing groups, Huey P. Smith and the Clowns and the Skyliners; and saxophonist Red Prysock and his band. A second show presented singers Brook Benton, Ruth Brown, Bobby Freeman, and Jesse Belvin; Jesse Powell and his orchestra; singing group the Heart Beats; and comedian Dave Friedman. A third production showcased saxophonist, vocalist Louis Jordan and his Tympani Five; vocalist Dottie Smith; the comedy dance team of Stump and Stumpy; the chorus line of the beautiful Dyerettes; singer Beverly Ann Gibson; sexy singing duo the Spence Twins; and the swinging Red Saunders orchestra.[51]

The Tivoli culminated the year with two weeklong stage shows in August, which appeared to end its live presentations for the year. The first production featured Eartha Kitt and her revue, which included saxophonist Reuben Phillips and orchestra.[52] Reportedly, autograph seekers mobbed Kitt at a jam-packed Tivoli Theater.[53] Later in the month, the Tivoli offered a spectacular program of gospel greats. Choral director Ralph Goodpasteur handled the staging and directing. Featured groups and soloists were the Caravans, the Swan Silvertones, Alex Bradford and His Men of Song, the Raymond Raspberry Singers, and R. L. Knowles. Albert Goodson was a featured organist, and Sally Martin served as mistress of ceremonies.[54] The *Chicago Defender* reported that the Tivoli was doing well. It saw the Tivoli as an important addition to an informal theater circuit that catered to an African American market and that included Chicago's Regal Theater, New York's Apollo Theater, and Washington, D. C.'s Howard Theater. The *Chicago Defender* also felt that there was a trend toward resurrecting stage shows at movie houses across the country.[55]

1960

In 1960, the stage-show season at the Tivoli began in January with the Dinizulu African Dancers appearing on stage with the Ahmad Jamal trio. The dance troupe of four men and two women was making its first Chicago appearance. Jazz pianist Ahmad Jamal and his trio were joined by jazz vocalist Carmen McRae, saxophonist Cannonball Adderly, and comedian Timmie Rogers. A second January production headlined Duke Ellington. Among the performers with Ellington were sensational one-leg dancer Peg Leg Bates and comedian Jackie "Moms" Mabley. Vocalists with Ellington were Lil Greenwood and Ozzie Bailey. Ray Nance, vocalist, violinist, and trumpet player with Ellington, was also a featured performer.[56]

In February, Tivoli management brought in Larry Steele's *Smart Affairs of 1960*. Steele's revue included singers Sallie Blair and Arthur Prysock; jazz organist Milt Buckner and trio; comedians Butterbeans and Susie; modern dancer Sir Lionel Beckels, who had a magnificent physique and who painted his entire body gold; tap dancers, the Leonard Brothers;

two stunningly beautiful groups of showgirls that performed superb routines, the Modern Harlem Girls and the Beige Beauts; and trumpeter Bobby Bryant and orchestra.[57]

After a break in March, the Tivoli management booked a new and different package show during the first week of April, the *Jewel Box Revue*, which proved to be very popular. It was the first racially integrated show of transgendered impersonators in the country and was well received in Chicago's Black Belt.[58] The *Chicago Defender* reported that the Broadway-style revue had only appeared in nightclubs, except for a recent engagement at the Apollo Theater in New York. The show featured twenty-five men who did female impersonations and one woman who impersonated a male and served as master of ceremonies. Elaborate costuming and humor characterized the production. Several notable performers were Jan Britton, a ballet artist, billed as the only male toe dancer in the country, and Billy Day, who did an impersonation of singer Billie Holiday. At the Tivoli, Lynn Carter, who impersonated noted entertainer Pearl Bailey, received star billing. The *Chicago Defender* called Carter's humorous exchange with the audience and impersonations as, by itself, worth the price of admission.[59]

In May of 1960, the Tivoli featured the sensational and soulful Sam Cooke and his revue. Included on the bill were doo-wop specialists, the Flamingos and the Crests, a racially integrated group, and solo vocalist Rose Hardaway. Singer Valerie Carr and the Red Saunders band rounded out the show.[60] The Tivoli briefly departed from its seven-day stage-show policy and brought in Ray Charles and the Raelets for one night on June 4. Also on the bill were the Drifters; versatile vocalist Ruth Brown; rhythm and blues singers Marv Johnson, Ron Holden, Billy Bland, and Preston Epps; bandleader Doc Bagby; comedian Redd Foxx; and pianist Ray Bryant and trio, whose record "Madison Time" was a top national seller.[61] After a summer hiatus, the Tivoli management brought back in September the racially integrated extravaganza of female and male impersonators, the *Jewel Box Revue*. The show proved to be so popular that it was held over for an additional week.[62]

The first of two stage shows in October featured vocalist Ruth Brown; singing groups the Drifters and Little Anthony and the Imperials; singers Joe Tex and Donnie Elbert; pianist, organist Doc Bagby and orchestra; and comedian Bob "Mumbles" Lewis. The Tivoli also invited fans for one day only to come to TV's Jim Lounsbury's "meet the stars party" in the lobby. Lounsbury, who was white, hosted a local dance program on television geared toward teenagers. Tivoli promoters encouraged young fans to bring their cameras and to seek autographs.[63] The second Tivoli stage show in October included noted entertainer Pearl Bailey and her revue. The show, which was direct from Las Vegas, was so popular that management held it over for an additional week.[64]

In November, the Tivoli hosted a local community event, the "Dance-O-Rama," a performance by seven Chicago dance schools. This was an annual benefit promoted by the Theta Omega chapter of the Alpha Kappa Alpha sorority. The proceeds were to go to the Chicago Urban League, the National Association for the Advancement of Colored People (NAACP), Provident Hospital, and the *Chicago Defender* charities.[65]

The final Tivoli stage show for 1960, which began in December and extended into January, was Larry Steele's annual touring production, *Smart Affairs of 1961*. Prominent performers in the 1961 edition of the show were vocal stylist Nancy Wilson; jazz instrumentalists the Three Sounds; comedian Slappy White; limbo dancer Roz Croney; dance groups the Cha Cha Taps, the Modern Harlem Girls, and the Beige Beauts; and others.[66]

1961

In 1961, there were at least seven weeks of live performances at the Tivoli. Stage shows began in January with song stylist Dinah Washington and her revue, which included singer Arthur Prysock; song and dance man Ray Sneed Jr.; singing group the Five Hi Fi's; female jazz organist Perri Lee and trio; chorines the Dancing Dinahettes; female saxophonist Lady Bird (Bert Etta Davis, who was compared to Charlie Parker) and combo; and more.[67]

After a break in February and March, strong stage shows continued in subsequent months in 1961. Theater management offered in April a show emceed by WHFC disk jockey Herb Kent the "Cool Gent." The show included singer Ernie K-Doe; comedian Willie Lewis; singing groups the Marcels and Little Anthony and the Imperials; blues guitarist and vocalist Freddy King; and pianist Sonny Thompson and orchestra, which featured vocalist Lula Reed. Singer Marv Johnson was an extra-added attraction.[68]

The second third of 1961 included two Tivoli stage shows. Appearing in late May were Count Basie and his orchestra, with vocalist Ocie Smith; the jazz vocal group of Lambert, Hendrix, and Ross; comedian Redd Foxx; and Norma Miller's Jazzette Steppers.[69] The second stage show in early June included jazz stylist Joe Williams and vocalist Gloria Lynne and trio; jazz trombonist Al Grey with tenor saxophonist Billy Mitchell and sextet; jazz trumpeter Harry "Sweets" Edison and quintet; bass player Johnny McAfee and orchestra; comedian and impressionist George Kirby; and singing group the Wanderers.[70]

In July and August, the Tivoli presented only film but booked the popular *Jewel Box Revue* for a week in mid-October and because of popular demand held the show over for an additional week.[71] After a hiatus in November, the Tivoli stage show in December was Arthur Bragg's *Idlewild Revue of 1962*. Featured were the Leon Escobar Dancers; dancer-singer Nichelle Nichols; blues guitarist and vocalist T-Bone Walker; rhythm and blues vocalists Buddy Lamp and Lonnie Sattin; singing groups the Simms Twins and the Falcons; dancing showgirls the Braggettes and the Fiesta Dolls; tenor saxophonist Choker Campbell and orchestra; and many more.[72]

1962

In 1962, the Tivoli had at least five stage shows and a one-night community event. The first of the Tivoli productions for 1962 was Larry Steele's *Smart Affairs of 1962*, which occurred in February. Among the many acts were comedian Dick Gregory; limbo dancer Roz Croney; vocalist Damita Jo; jazz trumpeter Lamar Wright; dancing showgirls the Beige Beauts and the Modern Harlem Girls; and more.[73]

The next Tivoli production occurred in early March and showcased singers Jackie Wilson and Joyce Davis and singing groups the Vibrations and the Four Tops. Comedian Timmie Rogers and several other acts rounded out the bill.[74]

In early May, Tivoli management featured singers Clyde McPhatter, Lavern Baker, and Nathaniel Mayer; dancer Bunny Briggs; singing group the Crests; and comedians Pigmeat Markham and Irwin C. Watson.[75] Later in the month, comedian Jackie "Moms" Mabley, singer Sarah Vaughn, dancer Peg Leg Bates, and singing group the Rockets were among the featured performers at another popular Tivoli stage show.[76]

The final stage show of 1962 at the Tivoli occurred in late August and early September. The talent included singers Della Reese, Adam Wade, and Billy Stewart; dancing girls the Twisting Parkettes; and comedian Redd Foxx.[77]

In October, the Tivoli hosted a one-night community affair. The Sixth Ward Democratic Organization held its annual "Night of Stars" show at the Tivoli on Friday, October 26.[78]

1963

In 1963, the Tivoli produced at least three weeklong shows. The first of the three Tivoli presentations in 1963 began in mid-February and featured jazz organist Jimmy Smith, Art Blakey and the Jazz Messengers, jazz pianist Billy Wallace, vocalist Gloria Lynne, and vocal group the Zeniths. The second Tivoli production was in March and featured comedian Dick Gregory, jazz vocalist Pat Thomas, the Ramsey Lewis Trio, comedian Godfrey Cambridge, and percussionist Olatunji and his company of traditional African dancers and drummers.[79] Pearl Bailey and her revue were the final Tivoli production in April, and the theater closed its doors for good in September.[80] Torn down shortly thereafter, the Tivoli Theater, born to service a white market while maintaining white racial hegemony, died in the service of a black community while catering to the sensibilities of black entertainment culture in the civil rights era.

The Tivoli Theater symbolized the fragility and futility of attempts at racial exclusion, both in terms of residential segregation and commercial segregation, directed at urban black communities. De facto segregation, which sought to preserve higher-quality facilities, economic advantage, and racial exclusivity for a white population, was challenged consistently by a black middle and upper class that sought access to a better way of life. Violence and other tactics, legal and illegal, would prove to be unsuccessful to restrict a black middle and upper class to so-called white neighborhoods. The demise of the Tivoli Theater, however, would portend a new phase of economic dislocation for black residents where major white-controlled commercial ventures, now desegregated, would emerge beyond the residential space of black citizens generally.

Notes

1. "Ushers at Tivoli Theater Attack Student and Girl," *Chicago Defender*, March 10, 1923, 4; "In Case against Theater," *Chicago Defender*, January 31, 1925, 4. Reverend Henry Hugh Proctor, the son of former slaves and a graduate of Yale Divinity School, was notable for developing unprecedented self-help initiatives through his church in Atlanta, Georgia, and for his efforts in supporting black American troops during World War I. See, for example, John Hope Franklin and Alfred A. Moss Jr., *From Slavery to Freedom: A History of Negro Americans*, 6th ed. (New York: McGraw-Hill, 1988), 259, 302; Edyth L. Ross, "Black Heritage in Social Welfare," *Phylon* 37, no. 4 (1976): 302; Roswell F. Jackson and Rosalyn M. Patterson, "A Brief History of Selected Black Churches in Atlanta, Georgia," *Journal of Negro History* 74, no. 1–4 (Winter–Autumn, 1989), 37.

2. "Ushers at Tivoli Theater," 4; "In Case against Theater," 4; "Tivoli Pays $1,200 to Dr. Headen," *Chicago Defender*, April 18, 1925, 1.

3. "In Case against Theater," 4; "Tivoli Pays $1,200 to Dr. Headen," 1. See also "B & K Record Sets Mark for Entire Industry," *Exhibitors Herald*, October 3, 1925, 25, 26.

4. See, for example, Douglas Gomery, *Shared Pleasures: A History of Movie Presentation in the United States* (Madison: University of Wisconsin Press, 1992), 155; Dempsey J. Travis, *An Autobiography of Black Jazz* (Chicago: Urban Research Institute, 1983), 86; Christine Basque, "The Paradoxes of Paradise: Elements of Conflict in Chicago's Balaban & Katz Movie Palaces," *Journal of the Theatre Historical Society of America* 27, no. 2 (1995): 7.

5. Clovis E. Semmes, *The Regal Theater and Black Culture* (New York: Palgrave, 2006), 163–69, 178–79.

6. Semmes, *Regal Theater and Black Culture*, 1–14.

7. Frank Arthur Wertheim, *Vaudeville Wars: How the Keith-Albee and Orpheum Circuits Controlled the Big-Time and Its Performers* (New York: Palgrave, 2006), 123.

8. Ibid.; Charles W. Stein, ed., *American Vaudeville as Seen by Its Contemporaries* (New York: Knopf, 1984), 3, 4, 15–17, 24.

9. Wertheim, *Vaudeville Wars*, 106–10; Anthony Slide, *The Encyclopedia of Vaudeville* (Westport, Conn.: Greenwood, 1994), 50.

10. Wertheim, *Vaudeville Wars*, 179. See also Henry T. Sampson, *Blacks in Blackface: A Source Book on Early Black Musical Shows* (Metuchen, N.J.: Scarecrow, 1980), 115–30.

11. Athelia Knight, "In Retrospect: Sherman H. Dudley, He Paved the Way for T.O.B.A.," *Black Perspective in Music* 15, no. 2 (Fall 1987): 153, 160, 163, 165, 171–72.

12. Kristin Thompson and David Bordwell, *Film History: An Introduction* (New York: McGraw, 1994), 5; Wertheim, *Vaudeville Wars*, 88–89; Gomery, *Shared Pleasures*, 3–17, 19, 22, 37–38.

13. Neal Gabler, *An Empire of Their Own: How the Jews Invented Hollywood* (New York: Crown, 1988), 3, 54–55, 126; Gomery, *Shared Pleasures*, 19, 22, 29–31; Ross Melnick and Andreas Fuchs, *Cinema Treasures: A New Look at Classic Movie Theaters* (St. Paul, Minn.: MBI, 2004), 12–13; Basque, "Paradoxes of Paradise," 4.

14. The parameter of a two-thousand-seat minimum is based on my own observations. In all cases that I have observed where scholars and experts have unequivocally labeled a movie theater as a palace, they have referred to the venue as a two-thousand-seat theater or more.

15. Gabler, *Empire of Their Own*, 95–100; Melnick and Fuchs, *Cinema Treasures*, 18–20.

16. Melnick and Fuchs, *Cinema Treasures*, 20.

17. Melnick and Fuchs, *Cinema Treasures*, 25–28; Gabler, *Empire of Their Own*, 100; Basque, "Paradoxes of Paradise," 4.

18. David Balaban, *The Chicago Movie Palaces of Balaban and Katz* (Charleston, S.C.: Arcadia, 2006), 31; Carrie Balaban, *Continuous Performance: The Story of A. J. Balaban* (New York: Putnam's, 1942), 15–45; Gomery, *Shared Pleasures*, 41.

19. See, for example, "B & K and L & T., Two Powerful Circuits in Chicago, Merge Forces," *Exhibitors Herald*, May 23, 1925, 39; "Chicago Personalities," *Exhibitors Herald*, March 26, 1927, 58; "Transfer of L & T to B & K Will Be Concluded This Week," *Exhibitors Herald*, August 20, 1927, 21; D. Balaban, *Chicago Movie Palaces*, 84.

20. C. Balaban, *Continuous Performance*, 47–52; Gomery, *Shared Pleasures*, 41, 43; D. Balaban, *Chicago Movie Palaces*, 38.

21. Gomery, *Shared Pleasures*, 41–44; C. Balaban, *Continuous Performance*, 57–69.

22. Carrie Balaban, "Opening Night at the Tivoli," *Marquee: The Journal of the Theatre Historical Society* 17, no. 14 (1985): 10; Michael Conant, *Antitrust in the Motion Picture Industry: Economic and Legal Analysis* (Berkeley: University of California Press, 1960), 157.

23. Irving Cutler, *The Jews of Chicago: From Shtetl to Suburb* (Chicago: University of Illinois Press, 1996), 151; C. Balaban, *Continuous Performance*, 81, 104; Conant, *Antitrust in the Motion Picture Industry*, 154–55; Martin J. Quigley, "The Famous Players Balaban-Katz Deal," *Exhibitors Herald*, October 3, 1925, 24.

24. "B & K Record Sets Mark for Entire Industry," *Exhibitors Herald*, October 3, 1925, 25.

25. "Chicago Boasts Two Finest Theatres in the World," *Journal of the Theatre Historical Society* 17, no. 14 (1985): 7.

26. C. Balaban, *Continuous Performance*, 159–61, 172–74; Basque, "Paradoxes of Paradise," 8.

27. D. Balaban, *Chicago Movie Palaces*, 45–48; Basque, "Paradoxes of Paradise," 6–7; C. Balaban, "Opening Night," 11.

28. C. Balaban, "Opening Night," 11.

29. D. Balaban, *Chicago Movie Palaces*, 47; Basque, "Paradoxes of Paradise," 7.

30. Chicago Fact Book Consortium, ed., *Local Community Fact Book Chicago Metropolitan Area: Based on the 1970 and 1980 Censuses* (Chicago: Chicago Review, 1984), 103–5.

31. Ibid., 109, 114.

32. Ibid., 112.

33. Allan Spear, *Black Chicago: The Making of a Negro Ghetto, 1890–1920* (Chicago: University of Chicago Press, 1967), 22–33.

34. "Tivoli Must Pay Damages to Dr. Headen," *Chicago Defender*, January 31, 1925, 4.

35. Semmes, *Regal Theater and Black Culture*, 3, 4, 16.

36. St. Clair Drake and Horace Cayton, *Black Metropolis: A Study of Negro Life in a Northern City*, rev. and enlarged ed. (Chicago: University of Chicago Press, 1993), 64, 79, 178–79; Spear, *Black Chicago*, 210, 211.

37. Semmes, *Regal Theater and Black Culture*, 20.

38. Ibid., 26.

39. See, for example, "Theater Building Takes Spurt in Latter Months of Year," *Exhibitors Herald*, January 3, 1925, vii; "B & K Take Over McVickers; Universal to Build in Chicago, Projects to Give Loop Five Big Film Theatres," *Exhibitors Herald*, January 24, 1925, 19; "Aschers Now in Complete Control of Chicago Chain," *Exhibitors Herald*, March 14, 1925, 21; "Balaban & Katz and A. H. Black Merge 100 Houses in Midwest," *Exhibitors Herald*, March 28, 1925, 23; "National Theatre Corp. to Build 3,000 Seat Chicago Theater, *Exhibitors Herald*, May 23, 1925, 42; "B. & K. and L. & T., Two Powerful Circuits in Chicago, Merge Forces," *Exhibitors Herald*, May 23, 1925, 39; "Marks Bros. Will Build New 5,000 Seat Chicago House," *Exhibitors Herald*, August 29, 1925, 122; "Cooney Brothers Promote Chicago Booking Combine," *Exhibitors Herald*, September 5, 1925, 29; "Paramount Theatre Interests Join with B & K in New Corporation, Record Deal Combines 500 Houses in One Ownership," *Exhibitors Herald*, October 3, 1925, 25; "$296,000,000 for New Theatres," *Exhibitors Herald*, January 21, 1928, 11; Semmes, *Regal Theater and Black Culture*, 43–45; Conant, *Antitrust in the Motion Picture Industry*, 21–29.

40. Chicago Fact Book Consortium, *Local Community Fact Book*, 115.

41. Conant, *Antitrust in the Motion Picture Industry*, 23–27, 84–177; Semmes, *Regal Theater and Black Culture*, 93–95; John Douglas Eames, *The Paramount Story* (New York: Crown, 1985), 114; Bernard F. Dick, *Engulfed: The Death of Paramount Pictures and the Birth of Corporate Hollywood* (Lexington: University Press of Kentucky, 2001), 37–38.

42. Semmes, *Regal Theater and Black Culture*, 26, 71, 73, 74, 86, 87, 163–69, 178–79.

43. Al Monroe, "So They Say," *Chicago Defender*, December 4, 1956, 15.

44. "Hear Tell: Tivoli to Make Change Over for 'Live Show' Stagings," *Chicago Defender*, January 3, 1958, 19: Al Monroe, "So They Say," *Chicago Defender*, November 11, 1958, 19.

45. "Predict Return of Flesh Shows in 1959," *Chicago Defender*, January 3, 1959, 18. Besides the Regal and the Tivoli, the *Chicago Defender* saw the Howard Theater in Washington, D.C., and the Apollo Theater in New York's Harlem community as major theaters that were central to a rebirth in the popularity of stage shows in black communities generally. "Hail Chicago Theatres Live Show Setup," *Chicago Defender*, July 11, 1959, 18. Moreover, the *Chicago Defender* asserted that black entertainers like Pearl Bailey, Eartha Kitt, and Sammy Davis Jr. —who had significant crossover appeal to white audiences—were cool to the idea of accepting engagements in theaters that serviced primarily black markets, because more money could be made in major (white-owned) nightclubs in New York, Chicago, and Las Vegas that serviced affluent white patrons. However, the success of the Tivoli and the policy of receiving a percentage of the gate encouraged Pearl Bailey, for example, "to make the rounds" at the Howard and Apollo. "Stars Find Gold in Theatre Dates," *Chicago Defender*, August 22, 1959, 19.

46. "Pearl Bailey to Tivoli Theatre with Great Bill," *Chicago Defender*, March 28, 1959, 18.

47. Movie section, *Chicago Tribune*, April 24, 1959.

48. Movie section, *Chicago Tribune*, May 1, 1959; "Pearl Bailey Revue Back," *Chicago Tribune*, May 3, 1959, F10.

49. "3 Stooges Will Appear on Stage at Six Theaters," *Chicago Tribune*, April 19, 1959, F12.

50. Movie section, *Chicago Tribune*, June 12, 1959; "Tivoli Sets 'Names' for Stage July, Aug.," *Chicago Defender*, June 9, 1959, 19.

51. Movie section, *Chicago Tribune*, July 12, 1959; "Brook Benton on Stage at the Tivoli Theater," *Chicago Tribune*, July 12, 1959, E12; "Rock 'n' Roll Rules Tivoli," *Chicago Defender*, July 18, 1959, 18; "Tivoli Rocks with Louis Jordan," *Chicago Defender*, July 25, 1959, 18.

52. Movie section, *Chicago Tribune*, August 7, 1959.

53. "Tower Ticker," *Chicago Tribune*, August 4, 1959, A3.

54. "Tivoli Theater to Present a Gospel Music Festival," *Chicago Tribune*, August 9, 1959, E10.

55. "New Outlets for Summer Season; Using Orks, Acts," *Chicago Defender*, July 11, 1959, 18; "Stars Find Gold in Theater Dates," *Chicago Defender*, August 22, 1959, 19.

56. "African Dancers at the Tivoli," *Chicago Tribune*, January 3, 1960, B9; movie section, *Chicago Tribune*, January 15, 1960, and January 22, 1960; "Tivoli's New Year's Show Star-Studded," *Chicago Defender*, January 2, 1960, 19; "Chicagoans 'Salute' Duke after Absence of 7 Years," *Chicago Defender*, January 30, 1960, 19.

57. "Larry Steele's 'Smart Affairs,'" *Chicago Defender*, February 27, 1960, 18.

58. Movie section, *Chicago Tribune*, April 1, 1960.

59. "'Jewel Box Revue' Tivoli Theatre April 1," *Chicago Defender*, April 2, 1960, 18.

60. Movie section, *Chicago Tribune*, May 20, 1960; "Stage Shows to Rock Regal and Tivoli," *Chicago Defender*, May11, 1960, 17.

61. "Ray Charles to Head One Night Show at Tivoli," *Chicago Tribune*, May 29, 1960, D10; "'Hit Makers' of 1960 Set for Tivoli, June 4," *Chicago Defender*, June 4, 1960, 18.

62. Movie section, *Chicago Tribune*, September 9, 1960, and September 16, 1960; "'Jewel Box Revue' Awes Theatre Goers," *Chicago Defender*, September 10, 1960, 19; "Impersonation Show Held Over in Chicago," September 24, 1960, 18.

63. Movie section, *Chicago Tribune*, October 7, 1960; "Ruth Brown Heads All-Star Bill to Tivoli," *Chicago Defender*, October 8, 1960, 19.

64. Movie section, *Chicago Tribune*, November 4, 1960.

65. "Dance Students to Aid Charities with Benefit," *Chicago Tribune*, November 6, 1960, S4.

66. Movie section, *Chicago Tribune*, December 30, 1960.

67. "Big Dinah Washington Show to Rock Tivoli," *Chicago Defender*, January 28–February 3, 1961, 18; movie section, *Chicago Tribune*, January 27, 1961; Antoinette D. Handy, *Black Women in American Bands and Orchestras*, 2nd ed. (Lanham, Md.: Scarecrow, 1998), 178, 179.

68. Movie section, *Chicago Tribune*, April 28, 1961; "'Stars of the Swinging Sixties' at the Tivoli," *Chicago Defender*, April 22–28, 1961, 18.

69. Movie section, *Chicago Tribune*, May 26, 1961.

70. Movie section, *Chicago Tribune*, June 9, 1961.

71. Movie section, *Chicago Tribune*, October 13, 1961, and October 20, 1961.

72. "Arthur Bragg's 'Idlewild Revue of 1962,'" *Chicago Defender*, December 30–January 5, 1962, 10; movie section, *Chicago Tribune*, December 29, 1961.

73. Movie section, *Chicago Tribune*, February 2, 1962.

74. Movie section, *Chicago Tribune*, March 2, 1962.

75. Movie section, *Chicago Tribune*, May 11, 1962.

76. Movie section, *Chicago Tribune*, May 25, 1962.

77. Movie section, *Chicago Tribune*, August 31, 1962.

78. "Singer Jo Ann Henderson to Head 6th Ward's Show," *Chicago Defender*, October 6–12, 1962, 10.

79. Movie section, *Chicago Tribune*, March 1, 1963.

80. Movie section, *Chicago Tribune*, April 26, 1963.

Every citizen of my race who can should travel.
Travel is broadening.
—ROBERT S. ABBOTT to PATRICK B. PRESCOTT JR.

Chapter 4

The *Defender* Brings You the World

The Grand European Tour of Patrick B. Prescott Jr.

HILARY MAC AUSTIN

Much has been written about the *Chicago Defender* and its importance in American history. The newspaper's influence on the Great Migration is well documented. In addition, *Defender* reports and editorials were a vital source of information and helped spark race activism locally and nationally. It could even be argued that the *Defender* helped create a wider, national African America by publishing society news about every black community in the country from Pocatello to Harlem. It is not surprising, therefore, that the *Defender* played a powerful role in the Black Chicago Renaissance. The paper promoted and published major figures of the renaissance; Langston Hughes wrote for the *Defender* as did Willard Motley and St. Clair Drake, among many others. Gwendolyn Brooks's early poetry was published in the paper. In addition, the paper was an important source of information about the activities and successes of Chicago artists and musicians.

These elements of the renaissance and the *De-fender*'s history have been well documented. However,

one area has been more neglected: The paper's role in creating a sense of the black Chicagoan, indeed the black American, as a member of the world community. Foreign reporting by African Americans in the black press helped place American racism in a larger context and likely gave African Americans a sense of being part of a larger community. It is certain that this international reportage was an essential element in the cosmopolitan identity of black Chicago.

Throughout its history, the *Defender* regularly reported international news. Like most other black papers, the *Defender* used wire services, such as Associated Press (AP) and United Press International (UPI), for most of its foreign news. It augmented these sources by printing articles by African American students, tourists, and artists overseas. In Chicago in the 1920s, readers could learn something about the Middle East with "Letters from Cairo, Egypt," written by "Two Performers Who Went Abroad in 1878 and 'Never Came Back.'" Among many columns reporting on Europe, from 1926 until late 1939, "Across the

Pond" relayed the social and theatrical news of African Americans. During the mid-thirties, one of the many authors of "Across the Pond," Edgar A. Wiggins, also wrote about Montmartre under the name "The Street-Wolf of Paris." Probably to compete with Claude Barnett's Associated Negro Press, the *Defender* from 1929 until 1940 had a formal foreign news service. News on Africa was steady, and there were regular reports from Russia, South America, and Asia as well. Not surprisingly, many of these articles included information on the existence, extent, or lack of the color line.

In addition to these more traditional kinds of news reports and columns, *Defender* readers could experience the world outside the United States through series written by African American travelers. Though not strictly "foreign reporting," the articles written by overseas travelers served to introduce readers to new cultures and important events. These travel series gave black Chicagoans a sense of their place in a broader, more diverse world and showed them that the racism of the United States was not universal. In addition, some of these travelogues allowed black Americans to participate in a traditionally white, upper-class adventure—the European Grand Tour.

Obviously, the perspective of a black American traveler to Europe would, on many occasions, be starkly different from that of a white traveler, but the ability to take a Grand Tour, to know the ins and outs of international travel, to have first- (or even second-) hand knowledge of the founding places of "culture" and "civilization" were important to black Chicago's, and particularly the black elite's, cosmopolitan identity.

Travel writing as a genre is not unique to the *Defender*. The travelogue is an important element of African American letters, and the form has received a fascinating review and analysis in *Stranger in the Village: Two Centuries of African American Travel Writing* by Farah Griffin and Cheryl Fish (1998), among others. In addition, African American internationalism and diasporic identity in general are burgeoning fields of study with important contributions by many scholars including Brent Edwards on African Americans and interwar Paris in *The Practice of Diaspora: Literature, Translation, and the Rise of Black Internationalism* (2003), Tina Campt on black German identity in *Other Germans: Black Germans and the Politics of Race, Gender, and Memory in the Third Reich* (2004), and Penny Von

Eschen on anticolonialism in *Race against Empire: Black Americans and Anticolonialism, 1937–1957* (1997).

Over the past two centuries, many African Americans who ventured overseas wrote of their experiences in memoirs, diaries, pamphlets, and essays. Among the most famous travelers who wrote about their time in Europe and beyond during the interwar years were W. E. B. Du Bois and Langston Hughes. In addition, a variety of biographies of prominent African Americans detail their subjects' overseas travel.

However, it is the travel reporting in the popular press that deserves a closer review. Articles published in the black press reached wide audiences, comprising all classes and educational levels. In the 1920s and 1930s, in addition to the *Defender*, travel writing appeared in the *Crisis* and *Opportunity* magazines. Travel writing also appeared in *Ebony* and *Negro Digest* in the 1950s and 1960s. More research needs to be done on the other major black newspapers, particularly the *Pittsburgh Courier*. In the case of the *Defender*, the question is: Did these travel articles affect or change typical readers, whether in a kitchenette or a mansion, whether in Chicago or Clarksdale?

The first example of a travel series in the *Defender* appears to be three articles written in 1912 by Dr. U. G. Dailey on his time in Europe as a postgraduate student. In 1923, Abbott himself wrote a series of ten articles on his trip to South America, and in 1929, he wrote a thirteen-part series on his trip to Europe. In 1932–33, Roberta Thomas and Flaurience Sengstacke (both nieces of Robert Abbott) wrote a nineteen-article series on their year abroad.[1]

In late 1934 Patrick B. Prescott Jr. also wrote a series of articles on his and his wife's seven-week European tour. Prescott and his wife, Annabel Carey Prescott, were community leaders. He was an attorney. She was an administrator in the Chicago public school system and the daughter of Bishop Archibald J. Carey of the Woodlawn AME Church.

Patrick B. Prescott Jr.

Patrick B. Prescott Jr. was born on November 24, 1889. in New Orleans, Louisiana. It appears that he was the illegitimate son of Emma Mills and Patrick Prescott Sr. In 1900, eleven-year-old Patrick was living in New Orleans with his mother, Emma (now Redmond), his stepfather, John Redmond, and his half-sister, Cora, as well as various uncles and aunts. His mother worked as a laundress, his stepfather as a laborer at a lumber mill, and the young Prescott attended school. He was a Southern University normal graduate in 1907, and by 1910, he had moved to Chicago.

In the early days in Chicago, Prescott worked as a clerk in the post office and was rooming at 3134 Forest Avenue with other "mulattoes." It seems that he was an aspiring writer at this time. He published at least one story, "The Dormitory Tragedy," in Top-Notch magazine in 1912.[2] He was also a columnist for the Chicago Whip and wrote under the name "The Grist Mill."

There is no information on whether Prescott as a child had a relationship with his father, Patrick Sr. However, it is clear that after Patrick Sr. moved to Chicago around 1917, the two had a fairly close relationship. According to family lore, Patrick Sr. and his wife Josephine Baumann Prescott took in Patrick Jr., and he lived with the family for some time. The 1920 census has Patrick Jr. still working at the post office and living with his father, stepmother, and his four half-siblings. At the same time, he was studying law privately. In 1924 Prescott was admitted to the bar and married Annabel Carey.

After his marriage, Prescott's career flourished. He served as assistant corporation council from 1927 until at least 1931. He later served as special assistant traction attorney and special commissioner of the circuit and superior courts. In 1928, he was awarded a doctor of laws degree from Wilberforce University for his "distinguished service in the promotion of Mississippi flood control legislation" and for his legal service in Chicago. In 1940, a Chicago Daily Tribune article listed him as a "specialist in constitutional law." By all accounts, Prescott was an honest and able attorney. In 1943, the Chicago Bar Association wrote that he was "a man of integrity and good legal ability . . . patient, courageous, diligent and conscientious."[3]

Like other members of the black elite, Prescott was involved in a variety of community organizations. He joined the Criterion Club in 1914, and by 1940, he was a director of the Chicago Urban League and chairman of the board of directors of the South Side Community Arts Center. He was deeply involved in local Republican politics. In 1932, he was a delegate-at-large to Republican convention, and in 1934, he ran for Third Ward committeeman but lost to Oscar De Priest.[4] In 1940, he ran for the First District congressional seat

but did not get the GOP nomination. According to the Chicago Daily Tribune, Prescott's chances were hurt in part by his connection to the Democratic Kelly-Nash machine (possibly because Prescott was on the city payroll at the time as assistant traction attorney).[5]

In 1941, Prescott's career reached its apex. Republican Governor Dwight H. Green named Prescott associate justice in the municipal court. Prescott was chosen to fill a vacancy created when Edward Scheffler was elected to the position of chief justice. In being so named, Prescott became the second black judge in Chicago's history. He was also the only Republican judge on the municipal court at the time.

Sadly, Prescott's greatest achievement was also his greatest heartbreak. Scheffler refused to recognize the appointment, arguing that the governor did not have the right to appoint judges to posts that lasted longer than one year. Green countered by saying that although Scheffler had submitted his resignation on November 5, Green had refused to accept the resignation until December 10. The commission only ran until the following December 7, therefore the post was open for less than a year, and the appointment was legal.[6] Prescott spent the next year fighting to gain his place on the bench. In June 1942, the Illinois Supreme Court ruled in Scheffler's favor, but Prescott moved for a rehearing. Finally in November, the court ruled in Prescott's favor. Less than a month was left of the term. He was then replaced by Wendell E. Green, also a black man and a Republican but nominated by Democrats.[7] Prescott ran for the position of municipal judge in the following two elections but never won a seat. He died shortly thereafter, on December 20, 1945. In 1950, Edgar A. Jonas, Republican congressman and a former judge, told the Chicago Tribune that the Democrats "drove Patrick Prescott to his grave" by denying him his seat on the bench.[8]

The Grand Tour

However, in 1934, when they took their Grand Tour through Europe, Patrick and Annabel Prescott were at the height of their respective careers. Prescott was a partner in the law firm of Prescott, Burroughs, and Taylor, which had offices at 188 West Randolph Street. Annabel was the dean of Wendell Phillips High School.

In true Defender style, the paper reported that it had "prevailed upon" Prescott to undertake the series "so that the thousands of citizens who may never go will nevertheless feel the joy of European travel." Prescott wrote fifteen articles, each starting with a byline and the words "for the benefit of those readers of the *Chicago Defender* who desire a glimpse of Europe as it is today. It is in keeping with this paper's policy to give its readers the best."

An initial survey of the paper indicates that Prescott's series is the last of its type. He wrote it when American unemployment was at 21.7 percent, (down from 24.9 percent the previous year).[9] Franklin Delano Roosevelt was in the second year of his presidency. Many of Roosevelt's New Deal agencies had been created including the National Recovery Administration (which the Supreme Court declared unconstitutional the following year). The *Defender* had already published at least one article on inequities in the new government policies, "What the NRA Is Doing to the Race! 'New Deal' Rapidly Becoming 'Raw Deal' for Dark Americans," by Lewis Caldwell Jr.[10] Prohibition had recently ended with the passage of the Twenty-First Amendment. The folk criminals John Dillinger, Baby Face Nelson, and Bonnie and Clyde were front-page news—at least in the white papers. *Imitation of Life*, with Louise Beavers and Fredi Washington, hit the movie theaters, as did the first Fred Astaire–Ginger Rogers musical *The Gay Divorcee*. The Apollo Theater opened its doors that year, and Charles Hamilton Houston recommended that the NAACP focus its legal efforts on ending discrimination in education, which led, in twenty years, to the Brown decision.

In Chicago, the World's Fair: A Century of Progress, which had run from May 27 through November 12, 1933, reopened for another summer. The attendance for the two years was close to 40 million.[11] At the same time, unemployment in Chicago stood at almost 385,000.[12] As a community, African Americans suffered the most. By 1932, 40 to 50 percent of black workers in Chicago were unemployed.[13] However, Bronzeville, black Chicago's main business and residential district, was still the center of black America. By the end of the 1920s, according to the *Encyclopedia of Chicago*, "black Chicagoans gained unprecedented access to city jobs, expanded their professional class, and won elective office in local and state government."[14] This then was the diversity of black Chicago—and the *Defender*'s readership—old settlers and migrants, the unemployed as well as laborers, entrepreneurs, civil servants, and professionals.

New York

Prescott begins his travelogue in New York prior to the couple's departure for England. He reports on two things: the sight of a black ticket-seller in the subway and Ethel Waters's performance in *As Thousands Cheered*. For him, the ticket-seller is a beacon of hope and call to action for more African Americans to enter the public work force.

> In New York City the first rounds of the fight for racial recognition in this particular field had been won. Colored people were at work in decent jobs for the corporations which they helped support. It was an opening wedge. From this splendid example others must follow. Back in the third century before Christ, Archimedes, the great mathematician of ancient Syracuse, in Sicily, declared, "If I had a fulcrum, a lever and a place to stand I could move the world!"

The fulcrum in this case, Prescott argues, is the employment of African Americans; the lever is the "tremendous political, industrial and purchasing power" of African Americans. Then "all that we need is a place to stand to move the world of proscription and prejudice."

Next, Prescott raves about Waters's performance and discusses her improvement as an actress over the years. He spends particular time on Waters's rendition of "Suppertime" in the scene "Unknown Negro Lynched": "[I]t is our guess that there will not be any lynchers—thanks to her—among the thousands who saw *As Thousands Cheer*."

Having established his perspective and politics, Prescott admonishes himself, "My task is a tale of travel. . . . May I say at the outset that I am NOT setting myself up as an authority on ocean-wide travel or on things European." He goes on to make clear that his intent in the series is to give a "green-horn's" perspective on the sights he and his wife will see. And he does so immediately.

Of the activity at the pier, he writes, "All is haste. Baggage is flying. Flower vendors everywhere. Ah!" Then they board the ship:

> Confetti is flying. A group of young folk are singing Russian folk songs at the tops of their lusty voices. . . . Now good German ballads rend the crowded air. Someone has begun singing "The Sidewalks of New York." . . . A whistle blows—not loud, not long—a rather small whistle for this giant of the deep. . . . [W]e are going, going . . . It's a strange feeling, like the first

second of the skyride at the World's Fair. . . . The magic lights of the harbor blink everywhere within eyesight. The Statue of Liberty, with her magnificent torch, stands at the mouth of the harbor. Ellis Island with her dark buildings just opposite across the channel. . . . Whatever may be my feelings about this ocean it is too late now. We are definitely on our way across three thousand miles of trackless water.

So ends Prescott's first installment, leaving the reader breathless for more.

At Sea

The next two installments of the series are both about the journey on the ocean liner. The first of these, headlined, "The Prescotts Learn a Few Things about Steamship Travel," begins:

I had been aroused by a "toot." Now a toot may not mean a thing to you when you are on a railroad train, all of the tracks of which are firmly annexed to dry land. . . . But a "toot" on an ocean liner is a serious thing, because away out there in no man's swimming pool there is nothing to toot at, or toot about—unless it be trouble. . . . Certainly no self-respecting ship will go tooting all over this ocean, without good rhyme and better reason. So at once I concluded that the captain needed me to help watch this thing through.

He discovers that the ship is surrounded by a deep fog.

We were tooting to see if we were the only ones in and about these parts of the sea. We were tooting to let the world know that we were coming straight on with more than 50,000 tons displacement; not looking for trouble of course, but coming. We were the tooters so far. But if any tootee gave us answering toot, and thus became the tooter and we became the tootee; and if there wasn't time to stop the engines of both ships and get the question of rights of way straightened out—Boy, what a headline! What a HEADLINE! As I stood by the porthole of my stateroom the ship kept up its warning blasts every minute or less. It sounded like the crack of doom. After about an hour of this watchful waiting I realized that my heart was ticking between toots, and the ship was tooting between ticks.

Nothing came of my fears. Mrs. Prescott, of course, got a good laugh out of it. She thought it very funny that a full grown man should be afraid of only three thousand little miles of water 25,000 or so feet deep. Mere trifle.

Prescott's description, though much lighter in tone, mirrors a snippet from the Thomas-Sengstacke series, where a dangerous Channel crossing in a deep fog is described.

The fog must have eventually dissipated because Prescott then moves on to his surroundings. He describes the couple's stateroom in great detail. The room is large and carpeted. The beds are box springs, not bunks, and have fresh, clean linens. There are two wash stands not just one and, "delight to the ladies," a full dressing table with an enormous variety of adjustable mirrors. In addition he gives a wonderful description of a bath aboard ship:

These are the longest and deepest tubs I have ever seen. You can't touch the bottom except by definitely trying, nor reach the foot except by extending yourself. . . . And it is filled to the brim—almost—with hot salt sea water, which leaves the victim very fresh and fine, but a bit sticky. To remedy this a shower of fresh water is overhead subject to the turn of a handle. Ah! how thoughtful these shipbuilders are.

Later, he paints just as vivid a picture of the ship as a whole, including its enormous size and many amenities. He pauses to comment on the elevators (called lifts by the English, he informs the reader) and writes of "that most important task at sea—to eat heartily and well." He includes, verbatim, a full menu and explains the ritual of English tea.

One cannot get off the ship without having had his four o'clock tea. It just isn't done, don't you know. Breakfast at 9, bouillon at 11, luncheon at 1 and dinner at 7. But ah! my friends, tea—English tea!—at 4. It is a ceremony and a rite. The English would stop the war to have tea at four. And it's ra-w-ther funny. Funny to see big, strong men with their cup of tea, fingers crooked and taking it quite adroitly as the ladies while an orchestra plays soft strains of classical offerings.

Among the other amusements described are the games on board: shuffleboard, deck tennis, ping-pong, and deck golf.

But the outstanding pastime of all is "deck chairing." That is played by all—old and young, male and female, well, sick and sea sick. It is done by renting a long reclining chair labelled with your name, and a heavy woolen blanket for about $2.50 for the voyage. Drop down into it and permit the uniformed "deck steward" to wrap up you and your legs—that's deck chairing.

Early on in the articles, Prescott explains the variety of stewards (and stewardesses) aboard the ship, their various duties, and the fact that those terms are used instead of "servant." He even takes the time to detail the finer points of English versus American pronunciation. At one point, he writes of the stewards, "They talk like college professors for the most part."

In fact, reporting on the quality of service is one of the through lines of the series. There is not one country or city the Prescotts visit where the service is not discussed. Of the stewards on the ship, he writes:

> They make it appear that it is a pleasure to them to be called on to serve you. It is peculiarly a European accomplishment, as we were to learn. They take such an interest in serving that you almost feel embarrassed if you have no task at hand. That is elevating personal service to an art.

Prescott also serves as something of a traveler's guide during the series, giving future Grand Tourers the benefit of his experience. When traveling on an ocean liner, he suggests, "If you are early in making your selection [of a stateroom]—and you should be—you will get an outside room (at a small added cost), with its additional space and air." On dining, he advises, "If you have been wise you have made a written reservation for the type and location of the table that you want in advance. Naturally, the best tables are the small one[s] seating two, three, or four persons, and near a porthole."

He also answers a few hypothetical questions. He takes the fifth on his opinion of ocean travel. Yes, there is a swimming pool on board. Gambling? "Well, if you look for trouble, no doubt you could find it." Dinner clothes? Absolutely, if you are in first class. You might squeeze by without them in tourist class, and "[i]n third class anything within the bounds of decency goes." (This is the only time he mentions the existence of the "classes" on the ship.)

Despite his obvious fear of ocean travel, Prescott paints a picture of supreme ease and leisure. However, early in the description of the ocean crossing, Prescott pulls back for a moment. The joy of travel is not "unalloyed": "Then, too, a great desire to 'share' comes over you. You want to organize a general migration—to have all of your friends along to help enjoy the many wonders that you are sure will be yours." This leads to ruminations on the shortness of life and losses the couple recently experienced. He tells of friends who have recently died: a woman "snuffed out before we could realize she was ill," an older woman "driven to an untimely close by the cruelty of a criminal," and a child "called as a little lamb to higher greener pastures."

However unlikely, it is tempting to think that this passage was written to reconnect with the *Defender* readers, many of whom have also been part of a migration and left loved ones behind, who possibly share the desire to have their friends and family with them, and who suffer painful loss as part of life.

No matter their economic status, Prescott can and does connect with his readers with regard to race. At the end of the first article aboard ship, Prescott deals with the color line. His report: There is none. The reason: There is strict discipline aboard a ship. Further, he says, the ship is British, and the British "are perhaps the most disciplined nation on Earth."

> Since the ship's owners have issued a passage to a colored person there is no one on board who would dare take responsibility for offending a guest that the company saw fit to accept. That's discipline. Americans would not understand that. But the British do.

In addition, the couple felt no antagonism from other passengers because:

> nobody wants any trouble at sea. Everybody tries to be nice to everybody else. After all this little spot in this big ocean is all that is between everybody and the great tumbling waves. Who's going to offend who, I ask you? Create hostility in some poor meek passenger? NEV-V-VER . . . the danger of this unbelievable mass of dark, deep water makes it "One for all and all for one."
> I am for bigger and better oceans.

Later, Prescott describes the various nationalities on board—mostly English and American but with representatives from Japan, China, Siam, New Zealand, South America, and Europe. He gives special note to an American woman who travels the transatlantic journey like a commuter. This woman, he reports, prefers traveling on English ships. On American ships, "the petty officers attempted to regulate her meals and the like because she was unaccompanied. She paid her own passage, but they were the bosses instead of the servants. She could not understand it. But I could. It's just an old American custom."

He then moves seamlessly to "Three Kinds of 'Colored' People." The text under this subhead begins, "Then, of course, there are colored people on board—three kinds." The first he notes "are the just plain colored people. They are easy to define and understand." Next, he says, are "the colored people who are colored but do not know they are." He defines these people as those whose grandparents or great-grandparents crossed over the color line.

> The child never knew it was colored and usually (very sincerely) ascribes its "curly locks and dark complexion" to the effects of the Chicago fire, or to shock, fright, aenemia, bad powder,

sun tan, or any of the hundred fool notions that its helplessness in a color-mad America may conjure up. Usually they are perplexed and irritated over their sugar-brown situation, but, because they are definitely established as "white," it does not become a tragedy.

The final category is the people who are passing and know they are. He describes these people as walking the deck "like a hunted animal, hoping that no one aboard will recognize the hidden strain." In particular, he describes one woman that he felt was passing. As proof, he points to the fact that she took great care over her "crispy hair and tawny complexion." He also notes that she avoided certain kinds of lighting and certain situations. Her children (members of class number 2—see above) won all the fancy-dress contests onboard. This was the final proof: "Only colored people have such outstanding native histrionic ability."

Just prior to landing, Prescott reminds his readers of an African American success story. He is describing a concert onboard given by passengers for passengers. This reminds him of a story he heard about Florence Cole-Talbert. During a different transatlantic journey, Talbert participated in this shipboard ritual as well. In fact, he reports, she was so successful that the rest of the concert was scrapped, and "with her nightingale sweetness, for the rest of the evening she sang and sang." The following night, at the captain's request, she gave a special concert for the disabled sailors: "So much for one brilliant brown girl among a thousand music hungry souls!"

Thus far in the series, Prescott has made a few things crystal clear: his class, his race consciousness, and his sense of humor. He is not writing an exposé, he is writing an amusing and generally light-hearted travel guide. He makes no bows to the poorer people among his potential readers. There is no blush at the mention of $2.50 paid for the deck chair, no desire to unearth the servant's perspective or to report on the lives and experiences of the third-class passengers. While the color line will be faithfully reported at every juncture, and politics plays a major role in some installments, Prescott stays true to this quality throughout the series.

England and Scotland

The fourth article in the series finally has Mr. and Mrs. Prescott on land but not before he gives a detailed account of the landing and disembarking, including the rules on tipping all the many various stewards who have served the couple during the ocean journey. Prescott then relates the activities of the customs officials. This is the first of many such descriptions. Prescott gives detailed information on the customs officials at each border crossing. Nor is this element unique to Prescott. Thomas and Sengstacke also describe their experiences with customs several times in their series. However, Prescott sums it all up quite well this first time out, "'Customs is customs' the world over. It consists of letting some very narrow-minded men in uniform know your most intimate personal secrets."

At the time of the Prescotts' arrival in England, the country was in recovery from the world depression, though many British citizens were still suffering. Admittedly travel-weary, "disappointed, almost depressed," Prescott's first impression of London is that it is "grey, drab, dingy, smoky, and old." The next day he is in a better mood.

> London is almost too difficult to attempt to even describe. It is old but not too old; grey but not too grey; dingy but not too dingy. It is a city of contradictions. It has the earmarks of antiquity everywhere, and yet it has the throb, hustle and bustle of vigorous young manhood. It has landmarks galore which show that it is the capitol of a warring nation, and yet in the manners of the people there is something of quiet refinement which suggests an avoidance of conflict.

Throughout the British installments, Prescott educates the reader on the differences between Britain and the United States. He writes about how the trains are different in England, that all the traffic is "on the wrong side of the road," that the steering wheel is on the wrong side of the car, and that the taxicabs are strange, black, and boxy. He notes that there are no tall buildings in London, and that the English public transportation system is more sensible than the American: You pay for how far you go, not one flat rate.

Prescott admonishes readers not to make the same mistake he does: People don't look different in England nor do the surroundings: "I somehow half-way expected to see a strange weird place about as far different from our style of architecture as are the pagodas of Japan. This is not the case." He writes that the biggest difference is that the streets are so curved that there is no sense of the entire city as one might get looking down Broadway or Fifth Avenue in New York, "State Street, Chicago; Michigan Avenue, Detroit, or Canal Street, New Orleans." He tells the reader that there is (thankfully) no noise in London, unlike in America, no blaring radio advertisements and no honking horns. The English "seem to drive with their heads and steering wheels rather than with their horns. It is a lesson we might learn." He explains that the policemen are called bobbies and are very picturesque. They are polite. Again the servant issue pops up: "They appear to know that they are the servants of the taxpayers rather than their bosses."

America is having an influence, though. Prescott mentions a Woolworth's on the Strand, the availability of cream for coffee, and American breakfasts. However, do not try "the attempted soda water" or "the counterfeit ice cream sodas." "Save your money and your digestion," he advises. The movies—called cinemas, he notes—are the most obvious source of American influence. This influence extends to the way African Americans are portrayed in film. He argues that the British are subconsciously absorbing American attitudes about race from the portrayals they see in American movies. "Unquestionably, the greatest influence toward race prejudice in England is the visiting of Americans there and the showing of American movies." He pauses at this point and notes:

> We did not see any prejudice anywhere in England or Europe. . . . And yet I must be honest with my readers. When Miss Valaida Snow said a few weeks since that she had seen no prejudice in London, Mr. A. Ward, president of the Negro Welfare association of that city, retorted that she had "merely been lucky."

Prescott goes on to point out that the real test is not whether he is able to eat in the best restaurants but whether people of color have access to occupations, can succeed in any kind of business, and can live wherever they choose. Ward says this is not so, and Prescott will not argue with him. He reiterates, though, "Whatever prejudice there is in England against Americans of color has undoubtedly been inspired by white Americans."

Prescott gives no nod to British colonization, which was reported on and editorialized about in the *Defender* as well as other national newspapers. This is interesting but not surprising. Other *Defender* travel writers do not examine European colonial policies very closely either. Most of the time the reason is stated quite clearly: The depth and violence of American racism have no comparison. However, at least one *Defender* travel article of the period did report on a slightly different English experience.

In 1933, William Gillett wrote one article for the *Defender* on a trip he took through England and Europe with a large group of women, most of them teachers. Gillett's experience puts a slightly different cast on the Prescotts' positive experience, at least in England if not throughout Europe. Gillett wrote that his group was denied a hotel in London because the group was too big: "The English hotels will generally accept one or two Colored persons provided that they are not too dark."[15]

The remainder of the Prescotts' British sojourn is decidedly literary and historic. First, they visit the home of "the immaculate genius of the written word," William Shakespeare. Prescott is obviously a fan. He uses the Bard's own words to describe him, first quoting Cassius from *Julius Caesar*, "he doth bestride the narrow world like a collosus; and we petty men walk under his huge legs." Then, at Shakespeare's grave:

> you stand suffused and overwhelmed and finally turn and walk out into the deep shade of the three hundred year old oak trees that seem to feel as you do, you think of how fitting to Shakespeare are his own immortal worlds in Hamlet: "What a piece of work is a man! How noble in reason! How infinite in faculty! In form and moving how express and admirable! In action how like an angel! In apprehension how like a god!"

Prescott next bonds with Sir Walter Scott by traveling to the "exquisitely rich and well-kept" Warwick Castle and the "mass of ruins" that is Kenilworth Castle. He describes and relates the histories of each. Of Kenilworth he writes:

> Here, then, is history in the raw, walls 14 feet thick in places, which make you go back to Sir Walter Scott's "Kenilworth," to repopulate it properly with all of the great who once defended its gates and roamed its fair pastures.

Next, Edinburgh, Scotland, "bleak, harsh, and cold," brings another castle and more historic and literary figures. Prescott informs the reader that no real sense of the castle can be given in less than ten thousand words. It has everything anyone could want in a castle, including moats and crown jewels. "On every hand memories of Sir Walter Scott, of Bobby Burns, of John Knox, of Mary. . . . You realize that you cannot take it all in. You simply love it—and leave it." Of the city itself, its streets always look windswept:

"Its hills and crags mark it as a place which saw the siege of many a Scottish chief during the centuries of its existence." He also describes a Scottish Bible, enlightens his readers on the source of the phrase "burning a candle at both ends," and reviews the history of John Knox, the Protestant reformer. This includes explaining that the doors in Knox's house are four feet high and two feet wide in order to slow any invaders or assassins who attempted access.

While history and literature dominate the reportage of the couple's time in Britain, Prescott does not leave out humor or landscape. At Kenilworth Castle, he writes:

> A little woman with a cart stand asked us if we would have refreshment. I ordered the one which seemed most satisfying—milk and soda water. She poured out a glass of milk and squirted into it about a tablespoon or so of seltzer water. Need I describe it? I paid my sixpence in silence, took a mouthful and quietly poured the rest on the ground. Strange, strange England, I thought . . .

On the train up to Edinburgh, he gives the reader a view out the window:

> You start in the warm, green pastures of southern England and watch nature grow sterner and sterner until your train skirts the bleak rock-ribbed coast of northeastern England where the cliffs are steep and harsh, and where the bare promontories overlook the cold North Sea. . . . Perhaps the most noticeable thing that strikes you as you reach the northwest part of England on this road is the long stone fences about four feet high that have been there two, three, four, and five hundred years. The remarkable thing about these fences is that they are not held together by mortar. They are made of stones one laid upon the other. They run up hills too steep for any kind of vehicle, and curve and wind, but with all this they have stood the storms of centuries, and still serve to separate the sheep and cattle of one farmer from that of another.

In Scotland, Prescott spares a moment to describe the largest cantilevered bridge in the world, which crosses the Firth of Forth. (Soon, though, to be outdone by the "one across San Francisco Bay.") He gives a nod to the modern city of Glasgow and takes a breath to paint a picture of the acres and acres of "orchid-hue[d]" heather on the mountainsides between Loch Lomand and Loch Katrine.

He spends a bit more time on the couple's quick stop in the Lake Country. He notes that he wanted to stay longer, it being "the most beautiful spot in Europe," and continues, "the grandeur of nature and the civilized development of man [are in] perfect symmetry and harmony" there. The end of the British portion of the tour brings the reader back to literature when Prescott quotes Southey, the poet laureate of England, on the beauties of an apple orchard.

Already, Prescott has referenced Archimedes, Shakespeare, Sir Walter Scott, Robert Burns, and Robert Southey, among others. Soon, more names will be added to the list including de Maupassant, Clemenceau, Dumas, and Henry O. Tanner. While references to the classic writers and artists of Europe are not unexpected in a travelogue such as this, it is interesting that during this period, literary references were not unusual for the *Defender* in general. In 1934 alone, twenty-four articles referenced Shakespeare and twelve Walter Scott.

France

The next stop on the couple's itinerary is France. France felt the effects of the depression later than many countries and in the summer of 1934 was still facing steep unemployment and low production levels. It was also still reeling from the effects of the Stavisky scandal and the ensuing riots. The Radical government had lost power, and a conservative government succeeded it. The number of ultranationalist and fascist groups in France was increasing.

These events were to some ominous signs of coming disaster. Yet, for most African Americans, including Patrick Prescott, France continued to represent sanctuary and freedom. Even before the couple gets to the country, when their boat stops on the French coast before continuing to Britain for the first part of the trip, Prescott devotes some space to a rhapsody on France:

> the vast great hinterland so dear to the hearts of all true lovers of liberty for mankind regardless of race, or creed, or color— France, France, the land of Biset, and Saint Saens, of Hugo and de Maupassant, of Napolean and Clemenceau. France whose fertile bosom could nurture such giants of our own race as Alexander Dumas and Henry O. Tanner.

When the couple finally actually gets to France, the headline says it all: "American Travelers Finally Land on Soil of France; and Prescott Finds Himself Boyishly Excited Over Country." Prescott writes:

> The English are cool, quiet, serene. But as the boat landed at Calais, you realized at once that the French people had a lot of

excitement, personality and color. This was no ordinary country. This was FRANCE.

Not surprisingly, it is not France in general that really grabs Prescott but Paris. He quickly remarks on the disappointing countryside of northern France, and then:

> three or four hours out of Calais you are rewarded. You do not have to be told it is Paris. Gay, glamorous, interesting gateway of the world! You recall at once (at least I did) the admonition to all civilized people, "Go to Paris; see Venice—Then die!"
>
> For the first time on the trip I began to feel boyishly excited. I suppose I expected to see Eiffel Tower, Tombeau de Napoleon (Napoleon's Tomb), Place de la Concorde, the Tuilleries and River Seine—all seated on the railroad station steps. I guess I sort of looked for apaches to be doing muscle dances in the middle of the streets. You know how it is. This was Paris. And in Paris anything can—and should—happen.
>
> [Paris is] strange, weird, in spots, beautiful, gracious, grave, gay, glamorous and altogether indescribable. It reminds you of a fresh fig. If one has never eaten a fully-ripe fresh fig there is no way to describe it to him because there is no other standard of comparison. There is nothing else in the world like it. So with Paris. Paris is—Paris. . . . Shade trees growing on the busiest business boulevards . . . sidewalk cafes as thick as buses in London, with colored awnings and brightly decorated small tables, where the weary, the thirsty and the just plain cussed sit in midday (or midnight) and watch the world go by; comfort stations perched gaudily in the middle of respectable thoroughfares and making themselves (and their patrons) known to at least three of the senses; theatres, art galleries, hotels, of the purest forms of artistic creation; boulevards that are made for a people used to centuries of ceremony and promenading; forests, ages old, located right in the heart of the city; stores in which the elevators have transparent glass backs so you might see through them into each floor as you pass; shops, shops, shops—"parfum" shops, pastry shops, "parfum" shops, pastry shops, "parfum" shops, pastry shops—that's Paris.

Sadly for the modern reader, Prescott and his wife do not seem to be jazz fans. No mention is made of Bricktop's, Josephine Baker, or any of the many jazz musicians—including Louis Armstrong, Cab Calloway, Duke Ellington, and Alberta Hunter—who are performing all over Europe at this time.[16] In their travelogue, Thomas and Sengstacke also don't give much space to black music and art in Paris or anywhere in Europe. They have the opportunity to see Baker per-

form in Copenhagen: "Was she good!"[17] In their Paris installments, they mention that there are many cafés where a person can "eat, drink and dance to the fine French music which is sometimes played by our own people." They also give a short and somewhat elliptical description of "the famous night life of Paris":

> Some people like it, some people don't, but no person can claim to know Paris unless he has seen it. It is a gay, easy going sort of life, with none of the unpleasantness which is often associated with it.[18]

Thankfully, *Defender* readers could get more information on the goings-on of black artists from checking out the column "Across the Pond."

Despite this gap in the record, Prescott's Paris is a fascinating glimpse of a legendary city. He does momentarily pull back on his excitement to explain that Paris is usually so extravagantly described there is no way it can match anyone's expectations. He reminds his readers that Paris has its share of poor and middle-class people just like everywhere else. The main example he gives is that not all the women are dressed in the highest style. He continues by relating some of his more mundane experiences in Paris. An example: he is charged 20 centimes for choosing to sit in a chair on the Champs Elysées as opposed to a bench, which is free. As in London, he spends a few words describing the public transportation system: The inner city buses have three sections (classes) of seats—"How's that for class distinction." He also soberly explains that there are a variety of meals to be had in Paris at a variety of prices depending on a person's desire for luxury and quality.

Having done his duty depicting some of the everyday elements of Paris, Prescott happily returns to the extravagant City of Lights. His verve returns when writing of the luxury of a meal at Delmonico's, "Hors d'oeuvres? . . . hors d'oeuvres at Delmonico's are an event, a ceremony and a rite." He goes on to write of the couple's confusion when their waiter produces twelve plates of hors d'oeuvres piled on top of each other in a pyramid. "Only the French would have imagination and daring enough to make a spectacle out of a preliminary course. And all this was even before soup was served!"

He goes on to explain other key details of Parisian life. Sidewalk cafés are described down to how they are created and the size of the tables. He gives helpful tips on café etiquette:

When you arrive, always order something . . . After the first order you may sit all day, chat and watch the passersby. No one will pester you to order again. If you wish something you yourself beckon the waiter. It all seems so civilized.

He describes the French attachment to wine and champagne:

You are not quite prepared for . . . the avid thirst of the small intelligent children who quaff two water glasses of wine before dinner as a means of slaking same. It is a novel experience. Here is plain and fancy drinking in its most colorful aspect. You may have heard of wine flowing like water, but it is only in France that it is drunk like water.

And he quickly explains the French idea of theater: Shows "seem to be planned on the theory of the battle royale" and last from 8 p.m. until midnight. He also notes that you are expected to tip the ushers who have shown you to your seats.

By far, the largest amount of space in the French articles is spent on describing the lack of prejudice in Paris and Prescott's theories on why this is the case. His thoughts on the matter are particularly poignant when one thinks of the current racial/ethnic problems in France:

There is no color line in France. They do not know—or care— what a man is. France is cosmopolitan. There is every race and creed there, and in many instances there are people who do not subscribe to the doctrines of liberal France. The Frenchman is so truly without prejudice that colored people are not even a curiosity to him. He never discloses by any word or act his recognition that the thousands of colored people in France are not of his own blood.

Frankly a careful observer must come to the conclusion that there could not be a color line in France. The French and Italians are the strangest assortment of people you have ever seen. Thousands upon thousands of French men and women look like thousands upon thousands of colored people you have seen in the United States. My hat was always half-off, ready to be tipped to someone I was sure I knew at home, only to find that the crinkly hair and tawny skin belonged to a native of France. Ah that Mediterranean Sea—and across it—in centuries long since gone, our people must have known these Latin people, and from their friendship forever made a color line impossible in France. If French people ever draw a color line, a good percentage of French people themselves would be caught in it by the sheer fact of its being impossible to tell them from the people who were supposed to be set aside. Unquestionably the French know this. Undoubtedly their enemies have

reminded them of it. Indisputably the "100 per cent Nordics" have already classed them as "non nordic." Thus, fate in her mysterious way, has by strange devices created a haven of peace and protection for the colored people who come within the borders of this land of sunshine and liberty.

Thus, Prescott not only takes his reader to an almost magical land where life is free and African Americans feel totally at home but at the same time he introduces an ominous note preparing the reader for his next installment.

Germany

Upon entering Germany, the tone of the series changes dramatically.

Suddenly your train comes to a sharp halt. Grey uniforms and stern faces appear in the aisles of the train. It is customs inspection in Germany. You must remember that we were entering Germany very shortly after Hitler's "blood purge" of all the enemies of Nazism.[19] And it was midnight. This combination was not very reassuring. . . .

The German officers were civil and courteous. But they were firm and business like. They did not display any great sense of humor. This then, was a close-up glimpse of another great nation. As before related, there was a great change when we came the short distance across the English channel from England to France. There was just as great a difference in entering Germany. The English are easy, quiet, reserved and very sure of themselves. The French are sparkling, spirited, aggressive with suggestion about them that they intend to take care of themselves. The Germans are erect, serious and militaristic. I am speaking only of the officials of England, France and Germany, understand. The officials of France, for example, always look as if they are tired of looking official and would unbend and lower their shoulders and subside at shortest provocation. But German officialdom is trained to the hilt—a holdover of the incomparable training given them in their line by Wilhelm II before the debacle of Armistice, 1918. They are put up erect, square shoulders, heel-in toe out, with chin stiff, to stay. The military precision born of the dream of Empire under the Kaiser is the same military precision now maintained as a defense against the ring of steel encircling her by her enemies throughout Europe.

It is difficult to tell when exactly the couple entered Germany. They left the United States on July 31, and Prescott notes that they "entered Germany but a few days after the German people had approved the Hitler regime by an overwhelming vote." This probably means that the couple entered Germany after the August 19 plebiscite that made Hitler legally the chancellor and president, that is, the führer. At this time in the rise of Nazism, the army had sworn a personal loyalty oath to Hitler, and the Law for the Prevention of Hereditarily Diseased Offspring had been passed. (The "hereditarily diseased" included the approximately four hundred so-called Rhineland bastards, children of German women and African soldiers.) Government-sanctioned persecution of Jews and other minorities had begun. Among other things, Jewish people were no longer allowed to serve in the German civil service, their ability to attend universities was limited, and there had been several national boycotts of Jewish businesses.

In this light, Prescott's reporting on Germany in general and Munich in particular is interesting. He begins by remarking that he prefers the German scenery to the French: "It appears more modern in its buildings and roadways."

He also notes a detail regarding the role of women under Nazism: "A little surprising however was the number of women working in the fields, behind plows, swinging heavy scythes and handling hoes." Prescott concludes this observation with a statement that comes across as quite odd: "It is something that the women of American could not possibly understand—this wholesale use of their sex in the tilling the soil." That Prescott, an African American (born and raised in the south, no less) would choose to write these words for an African American audience seems either amazingly naive or supremely disingenuous. Yet, another traveler the year before, Mrs. Henry McCrory, also noted how hard the peasant women in Europe worked. According to a *Defender* article in September 1933, Mrs. McCrory felt that women in rural Europe worked "even much harder than the Colored women in the South."[20]

Beyond Prescott's interpretation of rural women, his description of Nazi Germany is revealing.

All along the way you realize there is something going on in Germany. The swastika, or Nazi emblem, is visible everywhere on flagpoles along the route of the train. . . .

You do not have any doubt when you get [to Munich] that there is a Hitler in Germany. His lithographs are everywhere, big as sin, with that puckered leer on his face. . . . Thousands of Nazi flags and emblems: hundreds of Nazi soldiers with their

brown shirts with red bands around the left arm: hundreds of signs, slogans and what-nots reminding you of the "great qualities" of "der fuehrer" —these are the strange new things that stamp Germany as a changed place. . . .

Heaven alone knows or understands the Germany of today. Suspicion is rife everywhere, men doubt, fear and mistrust one another. A neighbor may be a traitor, and a stranger, a spy. When Mrs. Prescott and I sat on a bench in the public park the man next to us took very good pains to see that we did not speak German before he began to talk to his neighbor. Talk is dear and heads are cheap in these trying times in central Europe and one can take no chances. Everywhere the city of Munich appeared as an armed camp. Brown shirts strutted up and down the streets or flashed by on bicycles. These Nazi guards were young enough, but certainly drunk with the notoriety that world comment has thrust upon them. It must be remembered that these are only the personal soldiers of Hitler—his own political followers who have joined his guard for the purpose of enforcing the dictates of his regime. The army of Germany is another thing entirely. It is the grey-uniformed instrument of the German people trained and organized to defend German honor and liberty against the world. The brown shirts are created to defend Hitlerism in Germany against all other Germans who might oppose it. The one is the national army of the great German people. The other (the brown shirts) is a political army personally attached to the Nazi politicians who organized it. If ever there is a clash between them, just bet on the German army. All it needs is a great leader. . . .

The German people are not happy. They seem tense, strained, worried, bowed and bent. It is only a question of time when some sort of change will come. This is not the permanent form of government in [Germany] you may be assured of that.

In hindsight, Prescott's differentiation between Nazis and Germans just a few days after the plebiscite where 89 percent of Germans voted in support of Hitler seems strained. Interesting also is Prescott's lack of attention to the Nazi restrictions placed on Jews and people of color, which had been reported in the *Defender* as well as in other papers.[21]

However, Prescott was not the only traveler to report that Germany in the 1930s did not exhibit prejudice. In 1931, Thomas and Sengstacke visited relatives in Bremen, Germany, and stayed with them for months. They reported, "[A]fter living with the Germans and enjoying their society for a year, we could not believe the mean things said about them." The women found "no traces of cruelty or prejudice."[22] They went to numerous dances and parties, "where everyone wanted to dance with us."[23]

However, they were stared at more in Germany than anywhere else, particularly in areas where "the darker people seldom visit."[24] In 1933, William Gillett wrote, "The German people, as I know them, are as free of color prejudice as any of the other Europeans."[25] Also in 1933, Mrs. McCrory was quoted as saying, "Even in Germany with its Nordic propaganda, we met none of it [color prejudice]."[26]

Happily for the Prescotts, they do not spend much time in Munich, and they are quickly on their way to see the Passion Play performed in Oberammergau in the Bavarian Alps, a far more pleasant experience. Prescott describes this part of the Alps as "one of the most poetic spots in the world" and the play as "the greatest drama known to man—the drama of Christianity." True to his duties as travel guide, he explains how to arrange attending the play and its cost ($8). He also explains that every ten years, the townspeople of Oberammergau mount the extravaganza. People from all over the world attend, and all of the attendees stay in local people's homes.

The actual article about the Passion Play is written by Annabel Prescott. She begins it by juxtaposing the experience of Munich with the Bavarian Alps. This juxtaposition brings to life the atmosphere of early Nazi Germany and provides a perspective that could only be from a woman who works with children every day.

> Oberammergau—and you are in another world, another age. You cease to worry about the unchaperoned band of adolescents, straggling, unwashed and underfed in and out of the Munich railway station at every train call. You cease speculating at even this sample of the "Youth Movement" and its effects on the future of Germany. As from under a cloud, you slip from the menace of the huge lithographs of a glowering Hitler that have hung from every shop window and in almost every home.

She writes that Oberammergau is "a peaceful New Testament village nestling joyously and tranquilly in the heart of seething Germany." Now that she is in this small town, the Europe she has seen so far seems "sophisticated and effete." The Prescotts stay with Anton Lang, who for many years played Christ but is now too old and has the role of reading the prologues. He is described as the "beloved and reverenced patriarch of the country-side." The house layout and color scheme are described ending with, "It is comfort to the nth degree, without one note of luxury."

The couple heads out early the morning after their arrival to attend the play. They are among thousands of others who are walking through the small town toward the amphitheater:

> You get a kaleidoscopic effect of Astrokan turbans of Russian priests mingled with Bedouin veils, Tyrolean feather-cocked hats, Parisian models, fascist uniforms and American tweeds. And everywhere your eye is caught by the black vestee and flat-topped hat of the Catholic clergy. . . .
>
> [The play is a] series of tableaux, all reproductions of masterpieces, all illustrative of some story in the Old Testament which was prophetic of a parallel event in the New and the parallelism is explained and interpreted by the prologue preceding each scene and the chorus.

She did not expect to enjoy the Passion Play. They were in Europe in a Passion Play year, she explains, so she really had no choice but to attend: "It should not be missed just as a matter of course and common sense." She writes that she had expected to see a play much like other Passion plays that she, "as a good minister's daughter," had already seen. However, her reaction surprises her: "I was not prepared to live, yes, and to suffer, this thing as I did for the eight hours duration of the performance." She says that she was "totally unprepared for the intensity with which I was made to live [the play.]" She calls it "the most stupendous dramatic spectacle ever staged."

Austria

Prescott retakes the narrative as the couple leaves Bavaria and heads to Austria. He begins this installment by describing his attempt to communicate via mime with two young boys ("urchins") of the town. The boys will carry the couple's luggage but need to know whether they are to go to the train or bus station. Prescott communicates the correct answer—successfully and much to the boys' delight—with the international language for train: "choo choo." This leads Prescott to comment:

> I had been noticing how, under their skin, human beings are pretty much the same the world over. Tongues may differ but human nature reacts basically alike everywhere. A smile means the same in every language. So do a frown, a scowl, and a harsh voice. . . . The world after all is small.

However, the international brotherhood of the Passion Play quickly ends. The couple is on their way to

Austria, which in the summer of 1934 is facing its own political crisis. Just a month previous to the Prescotts' arrival, Austrian Nazis had assassinated chancellor Engelbert Dollfuss during a failed coup attempt. Prescott relates this information to the reader and points out that "all the way coming from America, people had asked if we intended visiting Germany and Austria in their unsettled condition." He then goes on to relate the only "unsettling" event of the trip:

> About a half hour [after the train crossed into Austria] a group of men got into a brawl the like of which I have rarely heard. They seemed intelligent which made it worse. It made it "appear" political to me, since I could not understand a word of their vociferous German. Nothing came of it, happily, and I do not yet know what it was all about. But as I look back over the stretch of months it still seems dangerous to me. That was, I believe, the only time I felt one should use a little discretion traveling about these unsettled countries at midnight.

However, based on the remainder of his installment, this experience is an aberration:

> Vienna is different from any city in Europe. It is the epitome of grace and good breeding. Its civic spirit is of the highest. . . . And Vienna is to my mind the politest and most civilized city in the world.

As a traveler from Depression-era Chicago, a polluted manufacturing city that had "a virtually insolvent municipal government,"[27] it is not surprising that Prescott is taken with the visual charm of Vienna. He notes the efforts made by the Viennese municipal authorities to beautify the city. The flower baskets hanging from the lampposts get particular mention, as do the municipal apartment buildings on the outskirts. This housing is for poor residents, and Prescott compares it favorably to the new housing being built by the government in the United States. He is also astounded by the city's cleanliness (as was Annabel by Oberammergau).

As always, Prescott remarks on the excellent service he and his wife receive, and he rhapsodizes about the food. Never willing to let historic significance slip by, he reminds the reader that Vienna is the home of Strauss and informs them that the Danube is not blue but brown. The couple visits Schonbrunn, Emperor Franz Joseph's castle, and Prescott goes into great detail describing its unbelievable luxuries. However, after all the positives, Prescott ends on an ominous note:

> Somehow the little country seemed pitiful. It seemed not to know which way it was drifting or to which port it was bound. Yet it was brave, cheerful, hopeful, civil and courteous. . . . We could not help but think that Austria, with such a stout heart and smiling face, must certainly pull herself out of the morass of messy political intrigue.

Italy

The next stop on the Prescotts' itinerary is Italy and the fabled city of Venice. To a modern reader, the headline of this article is somewhat startling: "Travelers Leave Vienna for Land of Mussolini: Greatly Impressed by Picturesque Fascist Italy." The headline does not mislead. Prescott writes very positively of Benito Mussolini. In the *Defender* in general, Mussolini and the Fascisti get a mixed reception until Mussolini threatens Abyssinia (Ethiopia) in late 1934, when the dictator loses all support. Prior to that point, some *Defender* articles point positively to Il Duce's relations with Africa and the fact that his armed forces are not segregated. For example, a 1926 article about Mussolini's alliance with Africa says in part, "No color line has marred Italy's dealings with the darker races."[28] In addition, in the early 1920s, just after he came to power, Mussolini publicly disassociated himself from certain members of the Ku Klux Klan who were calling themselves American Fascisti. This was another point in his favor as was his praise of the Fisk Jubilee Singers in 1928.

Even when Mussolini published an appeal to "his countrymen and to the white race in general" that expressed concern about declining birth rates among whites and "black and yellow . . . fecundity," the *Defender* expressed no outrage. At the time (1928), Mussolini's statements were blamed on "Nordic propagandists" and "American informers."[29] In March 1934, the issue came up again when Mussolini wrote an editorial in his own newspaper, part of which was published in the *Chicago Daily Tribune* and later reported in the *Defender*:

> From Rome comes the information that the premier of Italy, Mussolini, has been somewhat worried as to who will be president of the United States 100 years from now. His alarm is predicated upon the diminution of births in this country among the white race.
>
> Says the premier: "The yellow peril is nothing. We will encounter an Africanized America in which the white race, by the

inexorable laws of number, will end up being suffocated by the fertile grandsons of Uncle Tom. Are we to see within a century a Negro in the White House?"[30]

This time the *Defender* did not defend Il Duce but responded with an attack on Italian immigrants and the Mafia in the United States.

> It is fortunate to be forewarned that we may be prepared to meet our new responsibilities. But at the present time we are not so much concerned about the president 100 years hence as we are in guarding against those foreigners that invade our country bringing with them insidious desire to live by pelf and plunder through what appears to be a traditional instinct of throwing bombs, and committing massacre and murder.[31]

It is possible that Mussolini's comments may be the reason that—for all the compliments—there seems at times to be a wry, backhanded quality to Prescott's reporting on the Italian leader. However, the majority of the time his tone is glowing:

> As soon as you reached Italian soil you realized that the new Italy of Mussolini is something that the world might as well make up its mind to recognize as one of the greatest nations on the earth. There is construction going on everywhere. . . . On your train are two Fascisti guards—the Black Shirt troopers of Mussolini. They are on every train in Italy for the purpose of keeping order. In former years, B.M.—Before Mussolini—all types of thieves and beggars infested the trains of Italy. . . . [The Guards] not only keep order, but they also keep a weather eye for political busy-bodies, who might be inimical to Il Duce's regime.

Of passing a barracks, Prescott says:

> Black Shirt boys from 10 to 17 years of age, wave merrily as we pass. Mussolini takes 'em young, treats 'em kind and teaches 'em plenty. They come out believing that Italy is the greatest nation on earth.

In Venice, he writes:

> Out in the harbor an Italian warship and cruiser lay at anchor, an object lesson by the far-sighted Mussolini to the thousands of visitors who are bound to see. Little black-shirts almost take [over] Venice. They are given this tour free. When they grow up these chaps, most of them very poor, will most certainly remember the Fascist regime which made this fairyland vacation for them a reality.

Apart from Mussolini, Venice is the magical city that most tourists experience, and Prescott carefully describes its strangeness for the benefit of his readers:

There is no question that Venice is a topsy turvy land. It is everything the books tell you that it is. It's crazy. It's different from anything that you have ever seen. It is almost unbelievable even after you have seen it. Water washes right up the steps of the hotels and houses—no joking. And you cannot wade in that water either. For it is an average of 15 feet deep. So Venice is no toy water city. Every boat and gondola that it has is really needed.

He explains that one can tour the city on dry land as well:

> You can walk over much of the town by following these back streets which are connected by some 450 bridges, which span the smaller canals. And it is quite a little jaunt through these narrow streets, which are only 8 or 10 feet wide. . . . [Y]ou can readily see that horses and carriages are unknown.

He lists the various luxury goods produced for tourists: leather, lace, porcelain, mirrors, handmade glass, silk, velvet, and Italian linen. The couple attends a concert in St. Marco Square, eat two vanilla ices for $1.20, and ride in a gondola to celebrate their tenth anniversary, where Prescott serenades his wife with the "Barcarole"—the Boat Song. Finally, he summarizes the city:

> Such was ancient Venice, started back in the 5th century as a place of refuge from the Huns of Attila. Old are its walls, broken are some of its peaks of beauty, decayed are many of its treasures, but it fires the imagination and touches the heart strings for the fading grandeur that was, and sets you to thinking of the plaintive words of Lord Byron in "Childe Harold's Pilgrimage."

He then quotes—in its entirety—the third stanza of the fourth canto of the famed epic poem.

Prescott begins the next installment saying, "Leaving Venice is like leaving a party. Everything seems to be an anti-climax after the breath-taking experiences in the city of water." The next stop is Milan:

> It served to confirm our opinion that Italy has been remade under Mussolini. A big vigorous, clean city of wide streets and a million souls. A few years ago it was ridden with beggar[s] and petty larceners. Mussolini has made it the symbol of New Italy—a city of promise and possibilities.

The couple then heads from Milan to Switzerland, and Prescott comments upon the Swiss customs officials waiting on Italian soil, "The mutual peace and happiness of those two nations was something to be enjoyed in this age of jealousy and strife."

Switzerland

Prescott spends less than one installment describing the couple's stay in Lucerne, Switzerland. In summary:

> Switzerland is a toy country. It is spotlessly clean. It is so tiny that you can ride across it in a few hours. Its inhabitants are kindly, honest, industrious, intelligent, sober, with costumes that look like they were made for the stage.

To help the readers imagine the country, he reminds them of the Black Forest Village at the World's Fair. He then compares the city of Lucerne with Glacier Lake in the Rocky Mountains. In so doing, he betrays his sensibilities:

> Lucerne and its Alps breathe the acme of civilization, refinement and culture. Not only is nature grand, rugged and magnificent, but man has subdued the rough edges, and everywhere you turn are landscaped gardens, comfortable hotels, and cultivated amusements.

This is all there is of Switzerland. Far more interesting is the return to Paris, and Prescott wastes no time getting there.

France (Again)

Beginning the second section of the series that has the travelers in Paris, Prescott writes that African Americans and the French have a great deal in common.

> The French are not only cosmopolitan, they are "universal." They are much like Colored people. For instance, I believe Colored people are the best "mixers" on earth. Any person of any nationality can and will feel close to a person of color under advantageous circumstances. I think the same is true in large measure with the French. . . .
>
> Americans of color will notice this French trait especially, because it is the call of temperamental kinship. The French people are warm, effusive, easily excited, kindly, voluble, very expressive, original, dramatic and easy to make acquaintance. What other nationality, or race can answer this description save our own? Add to that those dark eyes, swarthy cheeks, full features and a hundred different complexions of the French people, and you can see why colored Americans pick France as their favorite spot on earth.

And a final Paris rhapsody:

> Ah! Paris by night. Lights, lights, lights across the gay spots that make 42nd and Broadway gasp for the comparison. It was Saturday night. Everyone seemed to be afoot. The hotels bustled with gay merrymakers, the streets teemed, the cafes did their full part to take the load off the sidewalks.

Again Paris in 1934 does not mean Bricktop's or jazz to Prescott. It means shopping. Virtually the entire installment is about shopping: "Small shops abound. The French tend very strongly to selling one thing at a time. Another characteristic very common in colored people." He argues that the French have developed their five senses more highly than any people on earth. As proof he points to French perfumes and wines, which satisfy a highly developed sense of smell. The art at the Louvre and Versailles satisfies the French sense of sight. Fine laces and tapestries delight the sense of touch. The French ear can be seen to be "highly developed and educated" by visiting the opera and the academies of music. The sense of taste is obvious: French is synonymous with fine. He reminds his readers not to "expect too much of Paris." It is not "bright and new all over." However, "Paris has its way about it of warming itself into your heart. You will leave it but you can never forget it."

Across the Pond

In his last installment, Prescott summarizes the places the couple visited. London was the "greatest"; Oberammergau, the most "sacred"; Venice, the "most startling and surprising"; Vienna, the "most cultured and civilized"; Lucerne, the "most beautiful"; and Paris, the "most gay and interesting." The British, he adds, are "the most stable people in the world."

Prescott also uses his summary to address the effects of the Depression. He notes that England seems economically healthier than any other country, including America:

> Poverty as we see it in the United States was at a minimum. There were no extraordinary flashes of prosperity: and, on the other hand, there were not the throes and depths of economic ruin. The English are an even-keel people.

He writes that France, Italy, and Switzerland do not seem to be suffering economically as badly as the United States. He clarifies this point by saying that the people there lead a simpler life, and while they have fewer luxuries, their financial position is more secure. His summarization continues.

> But please remember that France is on the gold standard and has the richest national treasury today; that England

had her depression five years ago and is now well on the road to recovery; that Switzerland, through industry, thrift and a marvelous ability to mind her own business always manages to keep abreast of civilization; and that Italy, under the lash of Mussolini, is enjoying an unprecedented era of building and manufacturing prosperity.

Germany and Austria alone, of the countries of Western and Central Europe, are having economic and financial troubles that have reduced their populations to misery. This sad situation is largely due to the political unrest of these nations rather than to a fundamental breakdown in their economic fabrics. Hitler rides Germany like the Old Man of the Sea, and Austria flounders helplessly in a morass of political intrigue and governmental indecision.

He then makes the point vital in much of the travel writing published in the *Defender*.

In these two countries you notice and miss the personal liberty that is such a much vaunted privilege in America. In Germany and Austria you have a distinct reaction that the average American has a better lot at home. But in the other more or less normal countries of Europe we did not find the wild advantages of living in the United States of which Americans are wont to boast.

And he summarizes the color issue.

Unquestionably the American of color is far, far better treated in Europe than in the United States. Certainly an individual, as an individual, would be better off there, provided he could provide himself a means of livelihood. . . . [W]e did not see prejudice in England, but we are forced to admit that it must exist in acute quantities because of the complaints of Colored people more familiar with the country than we are. But even in England the prejudice is not—could not—be of the same violent, unreasoning nature as to be found in many parts of the United States.

The late Bishop A. J. Carey, in talking to an English statesman over there, asked, "How does your little country hold in such subjugation two giants like India and Africa?" "Oh," said the Englishman, "that's easy, we keep them fighting among themselves." In a word, English prejudice is as likely to be a matter of "policy" as not—the deliberate subjugation of color to the purposes of empire.

In France, Germany, Austria, Switzerland and Italy, prejudice, as we know it, does not exist. If you had seen, as I did, those unbelievably dark Latin Europeans running over every country, you could know that Europe could not have a color line unless it wanted war every day. But the European does not feel as the American does. He does not think of a Colored person as a former slave, but rather as a person of a different skin.

. . . It is speculative, but I venture to say that even large numbers of Colored people in Europe would not engender the same type of prejudice that they now do in America. I do not think they could be as thoroughly absorbed in an economic sense as they now are in the United States and for that reason a large migration (which nobody is thinking of, anyway) would be futile and silly. But on the question merely of prejudice as you and I know it, I do not think the American variety is to be found anywhere except in the States. And I base my belief on just one thing—that the association of the races on a plane of equality does not create resentment, furore, comment or notice in Europe. Which is a pretty fair indication that while they might [not] love the Colored man (any more than they do themselves) yet they do not regard him as a pariah to be shunned and scorned.

Reading these articles seventy-five years after they were written, one is often reminded of the musicals of the era. In many ways, despite the political turmoil, Prescott describes a world where nothing goes wrong and nothing is hard. The living is supremely easy, very dignified, and frequently amusing. How was this received? Did these articles, like the movies, serve as an escape for many readers? Or was the mention of $2.50 for a deck chair or $1.20 for vanilla ice a painful reminder to many *Defender* readers that this was more than they made for a day's work? (Even the relatively well-off Pullman porters averaged only $16.92 per week at that time, and domestic workers in the south averaged only $3.50 per week.)[32]

In terms of the tone of the series, money was no problem. More important, neither was race. The author of these articles was unashamedly a black man, a Race man, though a member of the "light-skinned elite." In addition to experiencing the world as a rich man, he experienced it as a black man. And he related to a wider African American public that there was a part of the world with no color line. This is the central importance of the *Defender's* travel narratives. They exposed the singularity of white America's race obsession.

Mrs. McCrory expressed it very succinctly a year earlier, "I wish it were possible for large numbers of our people to come to Europe just to get this larger vision—just to see the lack of color prejudice in the white race in its native home. . . . More than ever we are convinced that color prejudice in America is artificial—it has been deliberately cultivated."[33] Through international reporting and travel narratives, the *Defender* built a citizenry informed about essential international news of the day, but more important, it provided its readers with an alternate reality—one that proved through lived experience "that color prejudice in America is artificial." There could be no more powerful news to impart.

Notes

1. These articles appear to have been misnumbered, so while the paper reports nineteen installments with a final "extra" article containing tips for planning a trip abroad, there are in fact only eighteen articles in the series itself. For even more news on the women's time in Europe, Roberta G. Thomas also wrote a separate column called "A Little about Everything," and many of these are also about her experiences in Europe.

2. *Chicago Defender*, July 20, 1912, 8.

3. "Bar Approves 2 for Municipal Bench Position," *Chicago Daily News*, April 3, 1943, 2.

4. Harold Smith, "Anti-Dies Vote Rises to Plague 2 Congressmen," *Chicago Daily Tribune*, February 18, 1940, S1.

5. Wayne Thomis, "Congress Foes to Enter Final Drive This Week," *Chicago Daily Tribune*, March 31, 1940, S1.

6. "Refuses to Seat Negro Named to Bench by Green," *Chicago Daily Tribune*, Dec. 27, 1941 9.

7. "Induct Prescott as Judge; G.O.P. Stages a Rally," *Chicago Daily Tribune*, November 25, 1942, 16.

8. George Tagge, "Negro Is Slated by G.O.P. for Circuit Court," *Chicago Daily Tribune*, January 28, 1950, 9.

9. Gene Smiley, "Recent Unemployment Rate Estimates for the 1920s and 1930s," *Journal of Economic History* 43, no. 2. (June 1983): 488.

10. *Chicago Defender*, May 26, 1934, 10.

11. Robert W. Rydell, "Century of Progress Exposition," in *Electronic Encyclopedia of Chicago*, Chicago Historical Society, 2005, http://www.encyclopedia.chicagohistory.org/pages/225.html.

12. "Chicago during the Great Depression," module 3, chapter 2, *History of Chicago from Trading Post to Metropolis*, External Studies Program, University College, Roosevelt University, http://web.archive.org/web/20090316062717/http://www.roosevelt.edu/chicagohistory/mod3-chap2.htm.

13. Tracey Deutsch, "Great Depression," *Electronic Encyclopedia of Chicago*, Chicago Historical Society, 2005, http://www.encyclopedia.chicagohistory.org/pages/542.html.

14. Christopher Manning, "African Americans," *Electronic Encyclopedia of Chicago*, Chicago Historical Society, 2005, http://www.encyclopedia.chicagohistory.org/pages/27.html.

15. William Gillett, "Some Observations Made on Sailing to Europe," *Chicago Defender*, August 5, 1933, 10.

16. Except, it seems, Germany. A musician named Joe Cork had been contracted to play in Berlin for a season, but, according to Ivan Browning in "Across the Pond," Cork was back in Montmartre in mid-

June "having received a short notice from the police to 'clear out' after working three weeks." *Chicago Defender*, June 16, 1934, 9.

17. Roberta G. Thomas and Flaurience Sengstacke, "Find Architecture of Denmark Very Interesting," *Chicago Defender*, February 4, 1933, 11.

18. Roberta G. Thomas and Flaurience Sengstacke, "Find Paris Is True to Reputation for Beauty," *Chicago Defender*, March 4, 1933, 10.

19. Presumably, the "Night of Long Knives," June 30–July 1, 1934, when Hitler's SS purged the SA (Sturmabteilung), the original paramilitary arm of the Nazi Party.

20. The Rambler, "Streets of Paris," *Chicago Defender*, September 30, 1933, 11.

21. *Defender* articles on the subject include "Hitler Expels Africans from Germany in Race Hate Tilt; Orders Black Race to Follow Jews Out in Nazi Drive," April 15, 1933, 1, and Pembroke Stephens, "How Jews Fare under Hitler Regime; Noted English Correspondent Reveals Inside Facts of Horrors Perpetrated by Germans on Defenseless Minority Groups," June 16, 1934, 10.

22. Roberta G. Thomas and Flaurience Sengstacke, "American Express Is Aid to Tourists," *Chicago Defender*, December 24, 1932, 11.

23. Roberta G. Thomas and Flaurience Sengstacke, "Bremen Holidays Prove Delightful," *Chicago Defender*, January 7, 1933, 10.

24. Thomas and Sengstacke, "American Express," 11.

25. Gillett, "Some Observations Made," 10.

26. Rambler, "Streets of Paris," 11.

27. Deutsch, "Great Depression."

28. Cable to the Defender, "Mussolini in Secret Pact with Africa," *Chicago Defender*, April 24, 1926, 1.

29. "Italian Dictator Warns White Race; Gives Alarm after Being Misinformed Mussolini Listens to Propagandists," *Chicago Defender*, October 6, 1928, A1.

30. "Mussolini Seems to Be Worried," *Chicago Defender*, April 7, 1934, 14.

31. Ibid.

32. Edward Berman, "The Pullman Porters Win," *Nation*, August 21, 1935, 217, *New Deal Network*, http://newdeal.feri.org/nation/na35217.htm (accessed November 11, 2011); Phyllis Palmer, "Black Domestics during the Depression: Workers, Organizers, Social Commentators," *Prologue Magazine*, Summer 1997, *National Archives and Records Administration*, http://www.archives.gov/publications/prologue/1997/summer/domestics-in-the-depression.html (accessed November 11, 2011).

33. Rambler, "Streets of Paris," 11.

Bibliography

PATRICK PRESCOTT'S TRAVEL ARTICLES FOR THE *CHICAGO DEFENDER*, IN CHRONOLOGICAL ORDER:

"Patrick B. Prescott Begins Series on Trip Abroad," October 13, 1934, 1.

"The Prescotts Learn a Few Things about Steamship Travel," October 20, 1934, 5.

"The Prescotts Learn about Travel Aboard Ship," October 27, 1934, 5.

"Traveler Reveals Facts Gained by Trip Abroad," November 3, 1934, 5.

"Travelers Find England Being Influenced by American-made Moving Pictures," November 10, 1934, 5.

"Real Thrills Come to US Citizens Touring England for the First Time," November 17, 1934, 11.

"American Travelers Finally Land on Soil of France; and Prescott Finds Himself Boyishly Excited over Country," November 24, 1934, 5.

"Prescotts Reveal European Thrills; Tourists Agree That France Is without Color Prejudice, Americans Find Complete Equality in French Republic," December 1, 1934, 5.

"Prescotts Compare Fatherland with Romantic France," December 8, 1934, 5.

"American Travelers Tell of Trip to Europe; 'Passion Play' in Germany Thrills Mrs. Prescott," December 15, 1934, 5.

"Tourists Continue Trip through Old Country; Prescotts Leave Scene of 'Passion Play' for Calmer Spots," December 22, 1934, 5.

"Travelers Leave Vienna for Land of Mussolini; Greatly Impressed by Picturesque Fascist Italy," January 5, 1935, 5.

"Tourists Get First Hand Facts on Swiss Culture," January 12, 1935, 5.

"Paris Stores Hold Interest of U.S. Travelers," January 19, 1935, 10.

"Prescotts End Series about Travels to Europe; Sum Up Experiences in Final Article," January 26, 1935, 12.

SECONDARY SOURCES

Buni, Andrew. *Robert L. Vann of the Pittsburgh Courier: Politics and Black Journalism*. Pittsburgh: University of Pittsburgh Press, 1974.

Farrar, Hayward. *The Baltimore Afro-American, 1892–1950*. Westport, Conn.: Greenwood, 1998.

Griffin, Farah J., and Cheryl J. Fish. *A Stranger in the Village: Two Centuries of African American Travel Writing*. Boston: Beacon, 1998.

Hogan, Lawrence D. *A Black National News Service: The Associated Negro Press and Claude Barnett*. Haworth, N.J.: St. Johann Press, 2002.

Wright, Julie Adesina. *The Role of International News in the Black Press*. Boston: Boston University, 1983.

Part II

Black Chicago's Renaissance

Culture, Consciousness,
Politics, and Place

Chapter 5

The Dialectics of Placelessness and Boundedness in Richard Wright's and Gwendolyn Brooks's Fictions

Crafting the Chicago Black Renaissance's Literary Landscape

ELIZABETH SCHLABACH

As black Chicagoans and the most prominent figures of Black Chicago's Renaissance movement in the 1940s and 1950s, Richard Wright and Gwendolyn Brooks led a vibrant period in Windy City life—a period, Adam Green stresses, engendering a unique cultural consciousness, fostering ideas of racial identity that remain influential today.[1] African Americans found themselves involved in complex and compelling debates on the future of their identities—identities paused at the precarious intersection of domestic and transnational politics, modernity, urbanism, segregation, and cosmopolitanism. These intersections result, in part, in the massive migration of African Americans from the south to northern cities, revealing the creation of "a city within a city" in Chicago following the Depression, as Bronzeville became the capital of black America.[2] The migrants' heritage encompassed slavery, virtual serfdom after emancipation within the agricultural system of the south, and wage slavery in unskilled industrial and service jobs for those who migrated north over successive generations.

From these urban spaces spring interesting and poignant conversations on the tensions of black modern life, consciousness, and racial geographies. Amid these floods of chaos always surging erosively at the roots of black life, Black Chicago Renaissance poets and writers engage in a mission of coherence acted upon these tensions through an investigation of black Chicago's metalevels of space, place, and time. Brooks and Wright figure forth a "new expressive world,"[3] illuminating African American artists' struggle against traditional dynamics of African American place. This figures as one of the many projects of the Black Chicago Renaissance. The Black Chicago Renaissance stands as an artistic and cultural exercise in mining coherence from these uncertainties; this coherence converges at the dynamism of African American society's step toward radical and modern consciousness on the pavement of the South Side's streets.

Typically, Wright sits at the center of the Black Chicago Renaissance, the towering figure whose achievement first forced the world to pay attention to what was taking place in black Chicago. Wright used Chicago as a starting point in his epochal novel *Native Son* and in his *12 Million Black Voices*, the great essay and photographic work on the black migration. Both drew from his experience on Chicago's South Side. It was out of this experience that he wrote the introduction to Horace Cayton and St. Clair Drake's *Black Metropolis*, the 1945 sociological classic. His career is one of the prime examples of the remarkable interplay among creativity, scholarship, and radical politics that formed the core of the Black Chicago Renaissance.[4]

Talented poets, however, emerged during the Black Chicago Renaissance as well. Brooks's first book of verse, *A Street in Bronzeville*, appeared in 1945. In 1949, Brooks appeared at the "Book Review and Lecture Forum" at the George Cleveland Hall Branch Library to read from *Annie Allen*, her second book of poetry. The next year she was to win the Pulitzer Prize for poetry. Brooks became the first black writer to win the most prestigious creative award in the United States, an achievement that marked the culmination of the extraordinary literary output of black Chicago during the Black Chicago Renaissance.[5]

Brooks and Wright, themselves migrants, mine struggle, beauty, and a pantheon of emotions from this urban landscape. They commence an investigation of place, coherency, and consciousness in Chicago's flats, alleyways, blocks, and one-room kitchenette apartments. These are the prescriptive elements of their fictions: how to impose coherence, how to impose and set boundaries, how to give place and craft image upon the fortunate but adventitious, upon the terrifying struggles of forebears, upon the comrades provided by black institutions, upon the adventitious resources suddenly coming from white society, upon both the health of black society and the ways in which black society stepped forward into its experiential radical uncertainties.[6]

Houston A. Baker, in *Workings of the Spirit: The Poetics of Afro-American Women's Writing*, draws from a scene from Wright's *Native Son* to explain the geopolitical elements of these uncertainties:

Bigger and his friend Gus meet on a South Side Chicago street. Leaning against a building, comforting themselves in sunshine warmer than their kitchenette apartments, their attention is suddenly drawn upward. An acrobatic skywriter is spelling out

the bold, commercial message: USE SPEED GASOLINE. Bigger gazes in childlike wonder and says, "Looks like a little bird." Gus responds, "Them white boys sure can fly." Bigger continues, "I *could* fly a plane if I had the chance." Gus promptly responds, "If you wasn't Black and if you had some money and if they'd let you go to that aviation school, you *could* fly a plane."

The skywriter in Wright's novel suggests the enormous confinement of black life; it is not a disruption of place but a signifier implying black placelessness. It has the effect of making African American geographies into placeless places. Why placeless? Because Bigger's South Side lacks the quality of place as it is traditionally defined. For a place to be recognized by one as actually PLACE, as a personally valued locale, one must set and maintain the boundaries. If one, like Bigger, is constituted and maintained by and within boundaries set by a dominating authority, then one is not a setter of place but a prisoner of another's desire. Baker stresses that under the displacing impress of authority, even what one calls and, perhaps, feels is one's own place is, from the perspective of human agency, placeless. Bigger Thomas and the other myriad characters in the literature of the Black Chicago Renaissance occupy authorized boundaries and are therefore insecure in their worlds but maximally secured or incarcerated by interlocking, institutional arrangements of power.[7]

Such spatial realities set black life and its coherency apart from all others. Black life's rites of coherence, enacted after the displacements of slavery, migration, and urban segregation, perform in the area where the radical uncertainties of existence festered most densely and most acutely—the physical surfaces of Chicago's South Side. Thus, this life and its relationship to all those rituals and institutions by which society orders its center remained estranged, orphaned, or in Brooks's own words, "unpredictable, ambivalent, and adventitious."[8] Brooks and Wright carry these threads throughout their fictions problematizing notions of locality, nationhood, and belonging.

What resulted from the Black Chicago Renaissance artists' labors were complex and distinct articulations of the future of African American identity. I wish to engage in a recovery of this radicalism, putting into dialogue articulations of racism with a strict geographic notion of space that is the city of Chicago. Taking a cue from Darlene Clark Hine, in her book *Hine Sight: Black Women and the Re-Construction of American History*, I move to craft a theoretical understanding of African American cultural output and consciousness that reflects the shaping of ideologies of the "New Negro" "not only in Harlem but also in Midwestern cities."[9] Toward this end, I compare Wright's 1941 photographic essay 12 Million Black Voices and his final literary publication—The Outsider, set in Chicago and Harlem, to Brooks's 1945 collection of poetry, A Street in Bronzeville, and her only novel, published in 1953, Maud Martha. Brooks's and Wright's narratives rest on an axis of place and on assertions of racial identity and consciousness.

Wright and Brooks offer a virtual tour of African American urban life at street level, and oftentimes one can imagine their characters brushing past one another on the streets. W. E. B. Du Bois introduced this technique in his famed study The Philadelphia Negro, and Cayton and Drake used it in Black Metropolis. Consider, for instance, this famous passage from Black Metropolis:

> Stand in the center of the Black Belt—at Chicago's 47th Street and South Parkway. Around you swirls a continuous eddy of faces—Black, brown, olive, yellow and white. Soon you will realize that this is not "just another neighborhood" of Midwest Metropolis. . . . In the nearby drugstore colored clerks are bustling about (they are seldom seen in other neighborhoods). In most of the other stores, too, there are colored salespeople, although a white proprietor or manager looms in the offing. In the offices around you, colored doctors, dentists, and lawyers go about their duties. And a brown-skinned policeman saunters along swinging his club and glaring sternly at the urchins who dodge in and out among the shoppers.[10]

Here the sense of vibrant human community and space, the array of sturdy public institutions—a variegated professional and merchant class, an alert office of the law—evoke a captivating sense of functionality in the central black district of Bronzeville.[11] An extended walk in any direction from this crossroads would have brought other key institutions of local black life into view—the Wabash YMCA west on Thirty-Ninth Street and the Provident Hospital east along Fifty-First Street, Supreme Liberty Life Insurance up on South Park at Thirty-Fifth, and the offices of the Defender and the Associated Negro Press just west along Thirty-Fifth, and a progression of churches and spiritual homes, from Olivet Baptist Church at Thirty-First and South Park, to Metropolitan Community Church ten blocks south, to the small but growing Second Temple of the Nation of Islam further south and west of Sixty-Third and Cottage Grove.[12]

The barometers of urban wellness that indicated a high quality of life within Bronzeville—institutions, interaction, exchange—serve as a counterpoint to a dystopian portrayal of black life in the city. But what about that dystopia and what about the urchins mentioned by Cayton and Drake, Brooks, and Wright? The fiction of Wright and Brooks profoundly challenges the functionality and autonomy of this "city within a city" functioning "well, on its own terms, and of its own accord."[13] In Wright's view, the forces of slavery and segregation left the personalities of modern black folk numbed, partially deformed, and half-articulate:

> Three hundred years are a long time for millions of folk like us to be held in such subjection, so long a time that perhaps scores of years will have to pass before we shall be able to express what this slavery has done to us, for our personalities are still numb from its long shocks; and, as the numbness leaves our souls, we shall yet have to feel and give utterance to the full pain we shall inherit.[14]

As a result, the African American immigrants explored in Wright's as well as poet and cultural activist Brooks's fiction, exist between two "vastly different plains of reality"—one determined by material conditions and bound by immediate circumstances, its truths dependent upon surface appearances and direct perceptions—the other by the internal, intangible, expansive possibilities of consciousness.[15] As a consequence, migration to the city and its unkept promise of freedom left African Americans on Chicago's South Side suspended between two planes of existence.

Wright engages in an investigation of this suspension with the photographic image. Responding to the massive migration of African Americans from the south to northern cities, 12 Million Black Voices, authored by Wright with Edwin Rosskam as director of photography, gives visibility to the socioeconomic injustices that perpetuated the existence of the black underclass of northern cities in the early twentieth century. Wright's poetic text coupled with the Rosskam photographs present the South Side's misery and struggle, a neighborhood whose "humble folk" swam in the depths of poverty and despair.[16] Wright and Rosskam capture this marooning in their photographs and prose of the South Side's kitchenette buildings, its sidewalks, alleys, and subways.

In his introduction to Black Metropolis: A Study of Negro Life in a Northern City (1945), the sociological investigation authored by Drake and Cayton, Wright identifies Chicago as the American place that most powerfully encompasses this suspension. As sociologists of the Chicago School, Drake and Cayton saw the city of Chicago as a laboratory for the scientific investigation of the social, economic, and historical forces that create and perpetuate economically desolated and isolated urban communities. Originally, theirs was a project designed to study the problem of "juvenile delinquency on Chicago's South Side"; soon this problem ultimately became subordinated to the "larger problem of description and analysis of the structure and organization of the Negro community, both internally, and in relation to the metropolis of which it is a part." On the one hand, Chicago is the quintessential "self-conscious" and "known" city; on the other, it is the place where the contemporary facts of African American experience take "their starkest form [and] crudest manifestation." Wright stresses, "[T]here is an open and raw beauty about that city that seems either to kill or endow one with the spirit of life. I felt those extremes of possibility, death and hope, while I lived half hungry and afraid in a city to which I had fled . . . to tell my story."[17] For Wright, the segregated urban landscape forces an economics of self-preservation, in a material sense, as a prerequisite to the acquisition of self-consciousness or knowing one's "story." The results of migration and urban segregation show African Americans marooned between these planes of disembodied existence, between their material and metaphysical selves. Wright's brilliant blend of text and image evidences that there is a discrepancy or a discontinuity between what African American migrants thought and what they were living. Wright and Rosskam come to the conclusion that this incongruence causes a suspending effect to occur: where black bodies are frozen in the spaces of the photograph and caught between lines of poetry—as both aesthetic mediums oscillate around the image of the kitchenette. The kitchenette building becomes a locus of urban segregation; the kitchenette is the material embodiment of the suspending conditions of segregation in the mid-twentieth-century American city—specifically Chicago, Illinois.

Viking Press published 12 Million Black Voices in 1941, one year after Wright's novel Native Son provoked national attention toward race matters. The book's "photo-direction" is credited to Rosskam, a German immigrant who studied painting at the Philadelphia Academy of Fine Arts and who took the position of picture editor with the Farm Security Administration in 1938. As Rosskam later explained it, the collaboration with Richard Wright followed the working principle that "whatever would normally be description is a picture. And whatever is abstraction or concept is written." Exposition in 12 Million Black Voices was written entirely by Wright; the choice and format of photographs, by masters such as Russell Lee, Dorthea Lange, and Jack Delanao, was principally Rosskam's. The book's limited number of captions consists of phrases that Rosskam extracted from Wright's accompanying prose. Aside from four news-agency photographs and two personal photographs (one taken by Wright and one by Rosskam's wife, Louise), the book's other eighty-two images all came from FSA files.[18]

The book provides a powerful commentary on three centuries of oppression. It begins with an account of the slave trade and follows the course of slavery to the point of the Civil War, when the inevitability of industrialization made slaves and the "inheritors of slavery" seem "children of a devilish aberration, descendants of an interval of nightmare in history, fledglings of a period of amnesia."[19] Wright details the sharecrop system, African American life in the south, and the Great Migration. Throughout, Wright expresses his view of black migration out of the south, a journey he himself experienced. This bittersweet migration often traded the harsh, rural repression of the south for the overcrowded, anonymous ghettoes of the north. He begins his third chapter, "Death on the City Pavements," with one of the book's few statistics: "From 1890 to 1920, more than two million of us left the land."[20] The steady influx to the city brought about serious complications. Maren Stange, author of Bronzeville: Black Chicago in Pictures, provides startling demographic data piecing together Chicago's migration story: As African Americans had continued the northward migration begun in the teens, becoming more urban than rural by the 1960s, Chicago absorbed wave after wave of newcomers. The Depression years saw a 20 percent increase in the city's black population, who lived for the most part mercilessly overcrowded. Population density was seventy thousand per square mile on the South Side; the death rate exceeded the birthrate by 2 percent. The war years, a moment of renewed migration, saw some 60,000 more new arrivals between 1942 and 1944, swelling the black population to 337,000, one-tenth of the city's total and double what it had been before World War II. Buildings abandoned and condemned in the 1930s were reinhabited during the war years as the Black Belt remained, in Richard Wright's words, "an undigested lump in Chicago's melting pot."[21]

The volume 12 Million Black Voices sets the migrants' first contact with "the brutal logic of jobs," the northern "world of things," and "the beginning of living on a new and terrifying plane of consciousness" in the cramped and deteriorating "kitchenette" apartments sequestered "beyond the business belt, a transition area where a sooty conglomeration of factories and mills belches smoke that stains our clothes and lungs."[22] Drake and Cayton stress that Bronzeville was a community of stark contrasts, the facets of its life as varied as the colors of its people's skins.[23] The rickety frame dwellings, sprawled along the railroad tracks, "bespeak a way of life at an opposite pole from that of the quiet and well-groomed orderliness of middle-class neighborhoods."[24] Unscrupulous landlords subdivided buildings into the tiniest possible apartments, and as impoverished newcomers who could afford no better, black migrants were forced to cope with overpriced, substandard housing as best they could. Kitchenette apartments, as these units were called, were essentially old houses or larger apartments, long since abandoned by Chicago's wealthy whites, converted into multiple apartments, each installed with a communal restroom, small gas stove, and one small sink. Subject to the desire of northern landlords, or what Wright terms "Bosses of the Buildings," African American migrants soon found themselves entangled in the games of price gouging: "The Bosses of the Building rent these kitchenettes to us at the rate of, say, $6 a week. Hence, the same apartment for which white people—who can get jobs anywhere and who receive higher wages than we—pay $50 a month is rented to us for $42 a week! . . . The kitchenette is the author of the glad tidings that new suckers are in town, ready to be cheated, plundered, and put in their places."[25]

Wright and Rosskam accompany this prose with a stark photograph of several kitchenette buildings perilously sitting in the foreground of over twenty smoke stacks that emit white billows of smoke clouding the city's faint horizon line (see figure 5.1). A few visible bodies, along with several automobiles, traverse a thin, steel bridge serving as the sole barrier separating the industrial from residential spaces. A single visible face occupies the photograph—a

small, black child, with hands gently rested on his or her windowsill, gazes out the third- or fourth-floor window of the kitchenette apartment closest to the camera's lens. The child squints as the sun glares off the kitchenette's dry, dilapidated siding. Its windows hang wide open, combing the stale humid air for a faint breeze, as the heat scorches the worn wooden roofs of the apartment building—what Wright termed "[o]ur death sentence without a trial."[26]

The juxtaposition of the overcrowded city landscape with the solidarity of the lone visible face exacerbates Wright's sense of African Americans being "put in their places." As if to acquire some respite from the interior goings-on of the kitchenette, the child flees to the window but instead of catching a brief moment of freedom from the overcrowded space of kitchenette life, the child finds a densely packed city landscape from which he or she cannot escape. Home, for our weary window-gazer, is thinly separated from work; the apartment building rests "just beyond the factory areas, behind the railroad tracks, near the river banks, under the viaducts, by the steel and iron mills, on the edge of the coal and lumber yards." This child sought refuge from the overcrowded interiors of "crowded barn-like rooms, in rotting buildings where once dwelt native whites of a century ago," only to find his or her respite, a gaze from a window, assaulted by clouded and hazy skies, dilapidated buildings, and dozens of smoke stacks.[27] There is no space in this photograph, but the image clearly articulates a definite place and function for the African American migrant in this dismal cityscape. Every inch of the photograph is overcrowded: factory buildings, smoke stacks, or apartment buildings dominate the frame. Every inch of the kitchenette bears the trace of these urban elements and, moreover, a colorline that runs deep into both the kitchenette and its inhabitants' compositions. Such is the case for our small window-gazer. Segregation on Chicago's South Side affords no respite for this small child burdened with crying babies, chores, or simply the hot stifling heat of the kitchenette apartment.

"Sometimes five or six of us live in a one-room kitchenette, a place where simple folk such as we should never be held captive." Home, for black Chicagoans, is a place where emotions wage war:

[O]ne part of our feelings tells us that it is good to be in the city, that we have a chance at life here, that we need but turn

5.1. "Slums, Pittsburgh, Pennsylvania," July 1938. Photograph by Arthur Rothstein. Credit: Farm Security Administration—Office of War Information Photograph Collection (Library of Congress), Library of Congress Prints and Photographs Division Washington, D.C.; Reproduction Number: LC-DIG-fsa-8a09907 (digital file from original neg.) LC-USF33-002819-M3 (b&w film nitrate neg.).

a corner to become a stranger, that we no longer need bow and dodge at the sight of the Lords of the Land [plantation owners]. Another part of our feelings tells us that, in terms of worry and strain, the cost of living in the kitchenettes is too high, that the city heaps too much responsibility on us and gives too little security in turn.

Wright captures the pace of the kitchenette's congestion, its desolation, and psychological ruin in fifteen sentences or "verses" poised carefully between seven

stunning images of women, children, and, although infrequently, men crammed inside these dark and dismal living spaces. For example, the third verse, "The kitchenette, with its filth and foul air, with its one toilet for thirty or more tenants, kills our black babies so fast that in many cities twice as many of them die as white babies," rests beneath a photograph of a seatless toilet crammed in the corner of a room, shards of porcelain and splinters of wood surround its base, plaster peels off a wall anchored by

5.2. "Toilet in the Basement of an Apartment House Rented to Negroes. Chicago, Illinois," April 1941. Photograph by Russell Lee. Credit: Farm Security Administration—Office of War Information Photograph Collection (Library of Congress), Library of Congress Prints and Photographs Division, Washington, D.C.; Reproduction Number: LC-USF34-038617-D (b&w film neg.).

a stack of wood resting near the toilet's amputated seat (see figure 5.2). It seems only natural that verse 3 is followed by verse 4's delineation of the medical perils of the space: "The kitchenette is the seed bed for scarlet fever, dysentery, typhoid, tuberculosis, gonorrhea, syphilis, pneumonia, and malnutrition." Most disturbing, however, is the fact that these verses straddle a photograph of three small children nestled peacefully under a quilt on top of a dirty mattress (see figure 5.3). The mattress, sheet-less and

without pillows, lies crudely on a concrete floor, a hamper full of laundry resides in the corner near an exhausted child's shoes—strewn absentmindedly on his way to bed. Verse 5 follows this mélange of image and verse: "The kitchenette scatters death so widely among us that our death rate exceeds our birth rate, and if it were not for the trains and autos bringing us daily into the city from the plantations, we black folks who dwell in northern cities would die out entirely over the course of a few years." Here, Wright

5.3. "Negro Children Asleep. Southside of Chicago, Illinois," April 1941. Photograph by Russell Lee. Credit: Farm Security Administration—Office of War Information Photograph Collection (Library of Congress), Library of Congress Prints and Photographs Division, Washington, D.C.; LC-USF34-038820-D (b&w film neg.).

gives no indication that this cycle will end. In each "verse," the kitchenette acts: it "poisons," "scatters," "blights," "jams," "fills," "piles," "reaches out," and "funnels." The photograph unmasks the actor while the text reveals its crimes: Wright identifies the kitchenette as criminal and its inhabitants its victims. The crimes of the kitchenette, "our prison, our death sentence without a trial, the new form of mob violence that assaults not only the individual, but all of us, in its ceaseless attacks," do not issue a call for justice by Chicago's forgotten—no one is willing to listen: the kitchenette is the "funnel through which our pulverized lives flow to ruin and death on the city pavements, at a profit."[28]

According to Stange, the chosen pictures, she stresses, in the photo essay were meant to represent features of northern urban life in general and cropped to exclude sky, horizon, or recognizable landmarks.[29] The images are printed quite dark, so that backgrounds of the cityscapes, or images of walled-in spaces, read as gray or gray-black tones—as a result they are overwhelmingly grim. Stange also stresses that Rosskam extended all images to the edges of the page, rather than setting the pictures off with a white border. She points to two photographs specifically employing this technique. The first photograph, captioned "Chicago, Illinois. Scene in Negro Section," taken by Russell Lee, April 1941, shows

5.4. "Chicago, Illinois. Scene in Negro Section," April 1941. Photograph by Russell Lee. Credit: Farm Security Administration—Office of War Information Photograph Collection (Library of Congress), Library of Congress Prints and Photographs Division, Washington, D.C.; LC-USF34-038720-D (b&w film neg.).

a three-story kitchenette building flanked to the left by a neighboring kitchenette apartment building and to the right by a brick church with worship times boldly printed on its front door (see figure 5.4).[30] In the foreground, a makeshift fence separates camera from subject: three tall, steel or wood posts adjoined by strands of crudely affixed steel rods comprise the boundary. The fence continues off the page along with the buildings. Viewers cannot see the edge of the church building or the far-left wall of the kitchenette apartments. This never-ending fence lines a narrow dirt path traversing the picture from side to side continuing, one is to guess, along down the street; a stroll down the path, viewers could guess, would provide a never-ending cycle of similar scenes.

The fourth photograph attributed to Lee pictures four African American children bundled up in their winter clothes (see figure 5.5).[31] They play under the subway, what, evidenced by the photograph's caption, "Street Scene under the Elevated," Chicagoans term "the elevated."[32] A four- or even five-, viewers are left to question, story kitchenette building flanks the children to their right as its stairs wind to the top of the photograph. The "el" juts, violently, across the photograph's middle, shooting from the scene's hazy horizon in the lower-left corner out over the four children, dwarfing them in the process, only to quickly recede off the top-right corner of the page. Viewers see neither the elevated's beginning nor its end. Stange posits that this suggestion of indefinite extension, rather than specific containment in the images, implies the dialectics of placelessness and boundedness—both of which call to mind Wright's dislocating planes of diasporic reality or conscious-

5.5. "Children Playing under the Elevated on the South Side of Chicago, Illinois," April 1941. Photograph by Russell Lee. Credit: Farm Security Administration—Office of War Information Photograph Collection (Library of Congress), Library of Congress Prints and Photographs Division, Washington, D.C.; LC-USF34-038601-D (b&w film neg.)

ness.[33] Wright's text, emphasizing the kitchenette as the migrant's death sentence, with, Rosskam's and collaborators' use of full-page bleed techniques, emphasizing the unprotected and overly cramped nature of the kitchenette's urban landscape, both reiterate the inadequacies of the kitchenette and its inability to serve as a protective domestic space against the harsh physical and subconscious realities of Chicago's migration story.

In 1945, four years after the publication of *12 Million Black Voices*, Brooks's examination of an unknown street in Bronzeville appeared.[34] In a series of poems, she explored both the hope and hopelessness of a people caught in the maelstrom of urban migration and segregation. The power of this collection of poems, such as "The Mother," "Kitchenette Building," "A Song in the Front Yard," "The Ballad of Chocolate

Mabbie," "Sadie and Maud," and "Ballad of Pearl May Lee," resides in their concern with social issues, such as abortion, poverty, the limitations of class restrictions, restrictive gender roles, and lynching. Similar to Wright's photo essay, *A Street in Bronzeville* presents material concerned not with a talented tenth but poetic renderings of the people she observed from her kitchenette apartment navigating the city's South Side ghetto. Brooks's Chicago is not one of the elite, not the city of spectacular boulevards and buildings.[35] This is a city of black streets and back alleys, of kitchenettes and vacant lots. Brooks wrote, "If you wanted a poem, you had only to look out a window. There was material always, walking or running, fighting or screaming or singing."[36]

Brooks's Bronzeville is symbolic of the impersonality of the overcrowded ghetto ignored by those caught in the activities of their own lives—as a result she offers a different lens through which to explore the material world's relation to or inspiration for consciousness.[37] Her first poem in *A Street in Bronzeville*, the "kitchenette building," finds her looking through a window from Bronzeville's streets to the dark, dim interiors of its kitchenettes. This poem is set literally and figuratively next door in Brooks's overcrowded and subdivided cityscape:

> We are things of dry hours and the involuntary plan,
> Grayed in, and gray. "Dream" makes a giddy sound, not strong
> Like "rent," "feeding a wife," "satisfying a man."
>
> But could a dream send up through onion fumes
> Its white and violet, fight with fried potatoes
> And yesterday's garbage ripening in the hall,
> Flutter, or sing an aria down these rooms
>
> Even if we were willing to let it in,
> Had time to warm it, keep it very clean,
> Anticipate a message, let it begin?
>
> We wonder. But not well! not for a minute!
> Since Number Five is out of the bathroom now,
> We think of lukewarm water, hope to get in it.[38]

She sought, through poems such as this, to explore the lived-in spaces of urban segregation. Few realized that existing behind the facades of the multitude of kitchenette buildings were ordinary people leading ordinary lives, not daring to dream their dreams. The kitchenette, as a product of segregation, isolated Chicago's forgotten psychologically and physically from the rest of the city.

Brooks possesses a clear vision that permits her to observe her people in a particular setting that articulates recognition of the relationship between place and life.[39] Her characters, many of them unnamed, are urban figures who exist in an environment that does not care about them. That many of them live in a kitchenette building where dreams "fight with fried potatoes / And yesterday's garbage ripening in the hall" adds to a general sense that her people are bound by their immediate circumstances at the expense of their dreams. This poem follows a character's stream of consciousness, verse by verse. Readers move with a tired narrator, perhaps while she scrubs her concrete floors, from fact—dry hours—to fantasy—fluttering dreams singing arias—back to fact—lukewarm bathwater and dripping children.

Brooks captures in this short sketch the "misery of place."[40] The suffering inside the kitchenette is irrefutable evidence that the rituals that give meaning and substance to human lives problematize the daily struggle to survive.[41] In the kitchenette, a dream, "even if we were willing to let it in, had time to warm it, keep it very clean," is fleeting—"we wonder / But not well! not for a minute!" Survival, down to mundane bathwater, remains the key to existence. As a consequence, that is where Brooks ends her poem and where her character rests her thoughts: "we think of lukewarm water, hope to get in it." Brooks's people are challenged when they seek to project their identities beyond the harsh realities of their environment—an environment that does not care about them yet strictly defines them. They are bound yet placeless.

Brooks's work delineates lines of caste, race, gender, and class difference on the South Side in a manner providing a critical feminist dimension to the photographs and poetics of Wright's photo essay. Brooks's passionate portraiture of women inhabiting this domestic space carves room for their solace and security amid the urban crisis of segregation. The diverse nature of Brooks's females enables her to reveal the many facets, complexities, and paradoxes of the urban black experience. Although their worlds are drab and ordinary, they go about their daily lives, accepting their plight and somehow managing to survive.[42] There is an acceptance of the realities of life, no matter how unpleasant—therein lies her characters' power. It is Brooks's aim, then, to show that the struggle to survive is the meaningful ritual, or that thing that imbues rituals with meaning. Brooks does not romanticize life inside the kitchenette. Clearly aware of its ugliness and oppression, she chooses to defy it with grace, allowing her characters to live as best they can.[43] The miracle she does present is the very fact that her people—in spite of everything—can exist from day to day.

Brooks captures this grace most poignantly in her poem "The Mother." The poem portrays the difficult and intimate conversations between a mother and her aborted children. Brooks explores, through a series of magnificently thoughtful and provoking verses, a mother's feelings of anxiety, guilt, impotence, and anguish. Literary critic Beverly Guy-Sheftall points out that Brooks, in the appendix of her autobiography, later referred to this mother as "hardly your crowned and praised and 'customary' Mother; but a Mother not unfamiliar, who decides that *she* rather than her World, will kill her children."[44] Although she realizes that she has shielded her unborn babies from the harsh realities of the life they would have lived as residents of the kitchenette, the mother admits she has stolen from them whatever joys they might have been able to experience:

> . . . if I sinned, if I seized
> Your luck
> And your lives from your unfinished reach,
> If I stole your births and your names,
> Your straight baby tears and your games,
> Your stilted or lovely loves, your tumults, your marriages, aches,
> and your deaths,
> If I poisoned the beginnings of your breaths,
> Believe that even in my deliberateness I was not deliberate.[45]

Throughout the poem, one has the feeling that if circumstances were different, if she had been able to provide for these children, they would have been allowed to live. Ironically, Guy-Sheftall stresses, "It was her deep concern for them as well as her own situation, which caused her to have the abortions."[46]

> Believe me, I loved you all.
> Believe me, I knew you, though faintly, and I loved, I loved you.
> All.[47]

She knew what life would have brought them and her own fate.

> You will never neglect or beat
> Them, silence or buy with a sweet.
> You will never wind up the sucking-thumb
> Or scuttle off ghosts that come.
> You will never leave them, controlling your luscious sigh,
> Return for a snack of them, with gobbling mother-eye.[48]

In this powerfully succinct and sincere poem, Brooks affords her female character a moment of agency. This agency, however, comes at a deep emotional price; the mother suffers psychologically: she struggles with the responsibility for the death of her children in a world where her existence is bound by her sex and race. She takes full responsibility for her actions: "Though why should I whine? Whine that the crime was other than mine?" all the while conscious of her own powerlessness: "Believe that even in my

deliberateness I was not deliberate." Born into the world that would have killed them, born into homes unable to provide them with the protection they need, the world of kitchenette apartments, where "twice as many" black babies "die as white babies," where "Black mothers sit, deserted, with their children about their knees," where "crimes against women and children" happen commonplace, both Wright and Brooks agree, this is no place for a child.[49] The mother, in this case, does the best she can; in a moment of feminist agency, Brooks's "mother" takes away the boundedness and the placelessness of the ghetto by refusing to birth any more victims into the tangled world of urban segregation. This is evidence that Bronzeville's populace can, at a cost, project their identities beyond the harshness of place—testaments to their resilience.

An obvious difference between Brooks and Wright is the greater amount of attention she devotes to the experiences of females. For example, in her poem "A Song in the Front Yard," the female voice finds itself in combat against the confines of space. The narrator, a girl, stayed in the front yard her whole life and now wants "a peek at the back" or "to go in the back yard now / And maybe down the alley" or "strut down the streets." Brooks crafts a poetics of enclosure juxtaposed against the openness of the dangerous places of urban life. Her narrator pivots between the front yard and the inside of her house, where her mother calls her in at a "quarter to nine," where she has stayed her all her life, with rough and untended back yards, winding alley ways, and public streets. She wants to play in the backyard "where the charity children play," "do wonderful things," "have wonderful fun," where children do not have to go in at a quarter to nine. This salacious backyard is "rough and untended," rife with opportunity and adventures; with hungry weeds and seemingly unending in that it has no back gate—George, one of the charity children, sold it. But along with these freedoms come her mother's moralist and heeding warnings that charity children such as Johnnie Mae will "grow up to be a bad woman" or that "George'll be taken to jail soon or late." The narrator concludes that this would be fine; that she would like to be a bad woman, dress like one, "wear the brave stockings of night-Black lace / And strut down the streets with paint on [her] face." In this juxtaposition between the safety and boredom of the enclosed spaces—the front yard and house— and the enticing expanse of the backyard that leads to alleyways and streets, Brooks remaps safety to the black matriarchal home—spaces in which women can control their children—placing danger and moral disdain beginning with untended open backyards, that lead to alleyways, that take young girls and boys to lives of crime and sexual promiscuity on Chicago's city streets. But Brooks leaves us with an interesting twist at the end of this poem, in that these unsafe city streets is exactly where a little girl wants to be—she wants to strut the street with paint on her face. In one verse, Brooks tosses readers back out on to the street, adding further complexity. The young girl wants the life her mother does not warn her against—she thinks it would be just "fine."[50]

The heroes and heroines of Wright and Brooks are uprooted and orphaned from any sort of sanctuary or protective patronage. Affiliation with protective philanthropic institutions, communities, families, or chivalric male companions usually turns sour, leaving them stranded and isolated, with little hope of redemption or prospective acceptance into any collective shelter. The fates of these modern, uprooted protagonists would seem to spell out an "essential sadness [that] can never be surmounted" that Edward Said ultimately attributes to the condition of exile.[51] I believe, however, that Wright and Brooks cope with racial exile and confinement in their crafting of an "aesthetics of impermanence."[52] They develop characters who have fallen out of synchrony with normative white American culture and its "myths" of belonging. Their literature articulates African Americans' sense of homelessness or impermanence—their living at once within and out-of-sync with white normative frameworks of aesthetics, modernity, urbanism, cosmopolitanism—echoing questions W. E. B. Du Bois asks in the closing chapter of The Souls of Black Folk, "Your country? How came it yours?" and "Why did God make me an outcast and a stranger in mine own house?"[53] This aesthetics of nonsynchronicity or impermanence challenge the ideologies of belonging or nationality. Brooks and Wright, as projects of the Black Chicago Renaissance, craft an aesthetic that works to restructure notions of ethnic and national identities to include paradigms of nationhood and definitions of African American identity determined but not overdetermined by the mutilations of American racism.

Wright crafts his epically tragic figures as the only African American author wealthy enough at the time to traverse the globe. Despite this literary success,

Wright was not totally satisfied even after becoming the great black American writer, since the color of his skin still imposed limits on him. His climb up the social ladder had only caused him to confront the racial problem on a larger scale. He realized he would never enjoy all his rights as an American citizen and that not all the readers of his country were ready to consider him a full-fledged author—thus, in 1946 he left the United States for Paris, where he would eventually die of a heart attack in 1952. In his essay "I Choose Exile," written six years after his arrival in Paris, Wright found himself imbued "with a new sense of social confidence," concluding, "The sharp contrast between French and American attitudes demonstrated that it was barbarousness that incited so militant a racism in white Americans."[54]

Wright published The Outsider thirteen years after his famous novel Native Son, with a marked shift in his fiction. Contemporary reviews saw Wright moving away from a literary reputation based on works sparked by anger, anger at indignities and racial discrimination toward an existentialist vein. For example, Arna Bontemps, in his review of the book, terms Wright as having "had a roll in the hay with existentialism of Sartre" and apparently liking it.[55] Written from Paris, France, but set in Chicago and Harlem, The Outsider opts for an individual struggle against white racism—highlighting Wright's personal, existential struggle as an alienated black intellectual. The Outsider has African American "Cross Damon" for its hero; his is the story of a mail sorter on the night shift in a south Chicago post office. Cross is consumed with despair, guilt, shame, and self-loathing, trying to anesthetize his overpowering sense of the drudgery of city life imprisoning him with whiskey and women. When Cross had the chance to let another man's body mistaken for his in a subway wreck, he never hesitates. He flees all personal responsibility, feeling no obligations toward wife, children, mistress, or mother. And to make good his escape, he murders his best friend.[56]

Wright juxtaposes this violence against Cross's presentation as a meditative, introspective man, addicted to self-analysis and philosophical speculation. Cross arrives at these intersections of self-reflection because he is, regardless of his new identity via the subway wreck, an outsider in American society. The realities of this racism, as he lives them daily, lead him to the conviction that existence was senseless, that society had no moral claims on him, that there were no divine or traditional laws that applied to him. Cross believes that life is an incomprehensible disaster, and human beings are "nothing in particular." So, if no ideas were necessary to justify his acts, he could kill impulsively to satisfy a passing whim or for his own convenience. Cross's dilemma in his story is that "each act of his consciousness sought to drag him back to what he wanted to flee" [57]—his body, more important, his skin. Cross's real concern lies in his awareness of "his body as an alien and despised object over which he had no power, a burden that was always cheating him of the fruits of his thoughts." [58] Each episode following the subway wreck allows Cross, to a certain degree, the opportunity to start from scratch—at first he enjoys the newness of anonymity, but eventually he finds he cannot overcome what becomes *the* insurmountable obstacle, more so than any other urban element—the color of his skin. Racism, grafted onto the physical surfaces of Chicago's imprisonment, follows him, relentlessly, as the plot twists and turns finding its conclusion with Cross's dying words from prison, "I wanted to be free. . . . To feel what I was worth . . . What living meant to me. . . . I loved life too . . . much." [59] But that life, defined by American racism, functions, as Said states, as a kind of orphaning sadness where dwelling is impossible. His family and the monotony of the South Side of Chicago are problematic; they do not function as sources of resilience or beauty because they are irreparably mutilated by racism.

Brooks's only novel, *Maud Martha* (1953), finds its characters navigating the same streets Chicago's Black Belt: Washington Park, Cottage Grove, Forty-Seventh Street, and State Street—what would become the Black Chicago Renaissance's landscape. But, as Barbara Christian asserts, Brooks's work does not sacrifice setting to the inner realities of her characters, who may be hampered by the environment but are not completely made of or by it. Her protagonists exist in process, flowing in and out of themselves and their worlds around them—locally, globally, and epically manifested. Brooks elucidates this process through her fiction's unwavering devotion to the present, its ability to sense, perceive, and translate her characters' perceptions into precise words. These words are not dramatic. There are few grand topics in her works; instead, her themes are commonplace and therefore great. And always the tone is understated, dramatic because it is muted. [60]

One of Brooks's feminine perceivers is Maud Martha—a young, married African American woman experiencing the impact of racism as Brooks subtly weaves it throughout the stories and streets of Chicago's South Side. As Maud Martha navigates this racism, she attempts to know herself, exhausted by the seeming trivia of the commonplace yet finding truths through continuously experiencing everyday life. Maud Martha is an ordinary woman; she is neither an aspiring lady nor necessarily a doomed heroic beauty. The novel is a revelation of her thoughts and her reflections on her limited world. Brooks shows her small South Side world, her relation to other people and her physical environment. For example, in a chapter entitled "The Kitchenette," Maud and Paul move into their first home:

> Paul, after two or three weeks, told her sheepishly that kitchenettes were not so bad. Theirs seemed "cute and cozy" enough, he declared, and for his part, he went on, he was ready to "camp right down" until the time came to "build.". . . . [T]he Owner would not allow the furniture to be disturbed. Tenants moved too often. It was not worth the Owner's financial while to make changes, or to allow tenants to make them. . . . [H]aving to be satisfied with the place as it was—[was] not the only annoyance that had to be reckoned with. She was becoming aware of an oddness in color and sound and smell about her, the color and sound and smell of the kitchenette building. The color was gray, and the smell and sound had taken on a suggestion of the proprietors of color, and impressed one as gray, too. The sobbings, the frustrations, the small hates, the large and ugly hates, the little pushing-through love, the boredom, that came to her from behind those walls (some of them beaver-board) via speech and scream and sigh—all these were gray. And the smells of various types of sweat, and of bathing and bodily functions (the bathroom was always in use, someone was always in the bathroom) and of fresh or stale love-making, which rushed in thick fumes to your nostrils as you walked down the hall, or down the stairs—these were *gray*.
> There was a whole lot of grayness here. [61]

The kitchenette serves as the basis for the world she knows and imagines. The grayness begins to consume her, nearly all of her until one day she encounters a mouse she had been hunting for three weeks:

> There. She had it at last. . . . It shook its little self, as best it could, in the trap. Its bright Black eyes contained no appeal— the little creature seemed to understand that there was no

hope of mercy from the eternal enemy, no hope of reprieve or postponement—but a fine small dignity.[62]

Maud Martha wonders what the little mouse might be thinking—she imagines that it has similar worries as herself if she were near death: "that there was not enough food in its larder," housework "would be left undone," or that "Bobby's education was now at an end." Maud Martha could not bear its little black eyes; she urges, "go home to your children," "to your wife or husband." Suddenly, with this act of mercy, this "small fine dignity," Maud Martha extends herself beyond the harshness of her kitchenette apartment:

> [S]he was conscious of a new cleanness in her. A wide air walked in her. A life had blundered its way into her power and it had been hers to preserve or destroy. She had not destroyed. In the center of that simple restraint was—creation. She had created a piece of life. It was wonderful. "Why," she thought, as her height doubled, "why I'm good! I am *good*." She ironed her aprons. Her back was straight. Her eyes were mild, and soft with godlike loving-kindness.[63]

Maud Martha spares the mouse even as the author of its fate, for she sets and maintains the boundaries over the mouse. It echoes Baker's commentary that for a place to be recognized by one as actually PLACE, as a personally valued locale, one must set and maintain the boundaries. Instead of imprisoning the mouse, as Maud Martha herself finds it inside her gray kitchenette apartment, she sets it free. In this short episode, Brooks records the impact of city life but reduces its power in Maud Martha's ability to extend beyond the harshness of the kitchenette apartment to act mercifully. Brooks does not hold the city completely responsible for what happens to people; its effects are still tragic, but the city is simply an existing force with which people must cope.

Maud Martha's musings on this life evidence the efficacy of her coping strategy:

> On the whole, she felt life was more comedy than tragedy. . . . The truth was, if you got a good Tragedy out of a lifetime, one good ripping tragedy, thorough, unridiculous, bottom-scraping, *not* the issue of human stupidity, you were doing, she thought, very well, you were doing well.[64]

Maud Martha, then, is a woman caught in the existential dilemma familiar to Cross Damon. But Brooks replaced the intense drama of Damon's story with a careful rendering of the ordinary, careful

rending to the rituals, the patterns of the particular, where racism, Barbara Christain interprets, is experienced in sharp nibbles rather than the screams of a subway wreck.[65]

Brooks juxtaposes making do to small significant dreams.[66] Maud Martha helps to transform her own world through her thoughts and imaginings. Maud Martha's sensitivities to her situation become her. For example, Maud Martha has come to work as a maid at the home of a rich white couple, the Burns-Coopers:

> [S]o these people looked at her. As though she were a child, a ridiculous one, and one that ought to be given a little shaking, except that shaking was not quite the thing, would not quite do. One held up one's finger (if one did anything), cocked one's head, was arch. As in the old song one hinted, "Tut, tut! now now! Come come!" Metal rose, all built, in one's eye.
>
> I'll never come back, Maud Martha assured herself when she hung up her apron at eight in the evening. She knew Mrs. Burns-Cooper would be puzzled. The wages were very good. Indeed, what could be said in explanation?
>
> Why, one was a human being. One wore clean nightgowns. One loved one's baby. One drank cocoa by the fire—or the gas range—come the evening, in the wintertime.[67]

This passage evidences the human, physical, local, correlative of Cross's dilemma in *The Outsider*. Maud Martha's response to the Burns-Coopers's "now nows" are tangibles: clean night gowns, cocoas, and fireplaces prove her household is just as good as theirs. Brooks does not romanticize her life as a maid or as a wife fighting with mice in her small, dingy, kitchenette apartment. Clearly aware of racism's ugliness and oppression, Brooks empowers Maud Martha with defiance through grace—she allows her to live the best life she can with tangible clean nightgowns, loved babies, and cocoa. Maud Martha's resilience illustrates the many facets, complexities, and paradoxes of the female urban black experience. Although her world may be drab and ordinary, Maud Martha goes about her daily life, accepting her plight and somehow managing to survive. There is an celebration of the realities of life, no matter how unpleasant—therein lies Maud Martha's power.

Maud Martha does not attempt to overcome these realities through a didactic plot. Rather than faking her death in a subway wreck, Maud Martha takes hold of the resources she does have and uses them for self-affirmation. It appears that Brooks's character sees this process through, more clearly, in the simple—that which already exists and has sustaining value. Maud Martha finds her advantage in the everyday, the already, the present, where Cross Damon lunges, unsuccessfully, toward affirmation through fabrication and evasion, through an identity he crafts for himself. The trouble with Cross Damon is that his journey must end. He could not change his self—that which he could not escape—his existence as a black man is not a negotiable point of resistance.

Gwendolyn Brooks's subtle and nuanced observations of racial struggle in *Maud Martha* measure African Americans' resistance to racial exile through the triumph of simplicity. Her feminine and localized challenge labors to defy the representation of African Americans as a socially problematic group without resources to shape American culture and history actively. She instead shows how displacement, poverty, racial subordination, and racial exile in modern mass culture are not necessarily mutilating forces—as they figure in Cross's fate—instead she celebrates this life—a life out of sync with white culture—evoking a sweet sense of contentment, a soothing victory of the simple.

Wright and Brooks essentially view a particular place, such as the kitchenette apartment building on Chicago's South Side, as symbolic not only of black ghettos across the country but also of the isolation wrought by urban segregation and the unkept promises of migration. Their photographs, text, and poetry record, commemorate, and interrogate the struggles, styles, and structures of black urban life in segregated America.[68] In rising above the specificity of locale and through their thoughtful examination of the inner recesses—physically and psychologically—of tortured human souls, Brooks and Wright demonstrate the inadequacies of the kitchenette as a place to gain immunity from the racial insults of everyday life.[69] Inside the kitchenette, the new home between the margins of slavery and segregation, black consciousness surrendered to material actuality; as a result, Wright felt, African Americans were "not allowed to react to life with an honest and frontal vision."[70] Both Wright and Brooks explore these dialectics of placelessness and boundedness through their visual and poetic imaginations. Brooks's feminist vision, however, at once artistry and advocacy, apportions the women of Bronzeville more agency than Wright's blend of image and text. The overwhelming dominance of female bodies throughout Wright's kitchenette imagery concomitant with its absence of

men fixes poverty to the body of the back matriarch. Brooks alleviates the strain of this blame by affording the mothers and daughters of Bronzeville grace and beauty within their daily struggle to survive. Within the beauty of the commonplace, Brooks allows readers to see and feel the effects of racism and capture the struggle to survive against grayness and hate.

Notes

1. Adam Green, *Selling the Race: Culture, Community, and Black Chicago: 1940–1955* (Chicago: University of Chicago Press, 2006), 1.

2. St. Claire Drake and Horace R. Cayton, *Black Metropolis: A Study of Negro Life in a Northern City*, 3rd ed. (Chicago: University of Chicago Press, 1970), 379.

3. Houston Baker, *Workings of the Spirit: The Poetics of Afro-American Women's Writing* (Chicago: University of Chicago Press, 1991), 50.

4. Michael Flug, "Chicago Black Renaissance: An Introduction," Vivian Harsh Digital Collections, January 2000, http://www.chicagohistoryfair.org/for-teachers/curriculum/chicago-black-renaissance.html, accessed November 11, 2005.

5. Ibid.

6. Baker, *Workings of the Spirit*, 104.

7. Ibid., 103–4, 103, quoting Richard Wright, *Native Son* (New York: Harper and Row, 1966), 19.

8. Gwendolyn Brooks, *Report from Part I*, 1st ed. (Detroit: Broadside Press, 1972), 32.

9. Ibid., quoting Darlene Clark Hine, *Hine Sight*.

10. Drake and Cayton, *Black Metropolis*, 379.

11. Green, *Selling the Race*, 8.

12. Ibid., 8–9.

13. Ibid., 9.

14. Richard Wright, *12 Million Black Voices*, 3rd ed. (New York: Thunder's Mouth Press, 1992), 31.

15. Ibid., 40; James Goodwin, "The Depression Era in Black and White: Four American Photo-Texts," *Criticism* 40, no. 2 (Spring 1998): 283.

16. Richard Wright, introduction, *Black Metropolis*, by Drake and Cayton, xix.

17. Ibid., xiii, xviii.

18. Goodwin, "Depression Era in Black and White," 281, 281, 282.

19. Wright, *12 Million Black Voices*, 30.

20. Ibid., 93.

21. Maren Stange, *Bronzeville: Black Chicago in Pictures 1941–1943* (New York: New Press, 2003), xxi, quoting Richard Wright, "Shame of Chicago," *Ebony*, 7, 1951, 24.

22. Wright, *12 Million Black Voices*, 101.

23. Drake and Cayton, *Black Metropolis*, 382.

24. Ibid., 383.

25. Wright, *12 Million Black Voices*, 104, 105.

26. Ibid., 101,107.

27. Ibid., 105, 103.

28. Ibid., 105, 106, 107, 111.

29. Stange, *Bronzeville*, xxiv–xxv.

30. Wright, *12 Million Black Voices*, 115.

31. Ibid., 139.

32. Ibid., 152.

33. Wright, introduction, *Black Metropolis*, xxv.

34. Kenny J. Williams, "The World of Satin-Legs, Mrs. Sallie, and the Blackstone Rangers: The Restricted Chicago of Gwendolyn Brooks," in *A Life Distilled: Gwendolyn Brooks, Her Poetry and Fiction*, ed. Maria K. Mootry and Gary Smith (Urbana: University of Illinois Press, 1987), 53.

35. Ibid., 55.

36. "Gwendolyn Brooks," *The Norton Anthology of African American Literature*, ed. Henry Louis Gates Jr. and Nellie Y. McKay (New York: Norton, 1997), 1577.

37. Williams, "World of Satin-Legs," 55.

38. Gwendolyn Brooks, "the kitchenette," *Selected Poems: Gwendolyn Brooks*, 6th ed. (New York: Harper and Row, 1963), 3.

39. Williams, "World of Satin-Legs," 57.

40. Ibid., 62.

41. Gary Smith, "Paradise Regained: The Children of Gwendolyn Brooks' Bronzeville," in *A Life Distilled: Gwendolyn Brooks, Her Poetry and Fiction*, ed. Maria K. Mootry and Gary Smith (Urbana: University of Illinois Press, 1987), 130.

42. Beverly Guy-Sheftall, "The Women of Bronzeville," in Mootry and Smith, *Life Distilled*, 154.

43. Patricia H. Lattin and Vernon E. Lattin, "Dual Vision in Gwendolyn Brooks' *Maud Martha*," *Critique* 25 (Summer 1984): 183.

44. Guy-Sheftall, "Women of Bronzeville," 154, quoting Brooks, *Report from Part I*, 186.

45. Brooks, "the mother," in *Selected Poems*, 4.

46. Guy-Sheftall, "Women of Bronzeville," 157.

47. Brooks, "the mother," in *Selected Poems*, 5.

48. Ibid., 4.

49. Wright, *12 Million Black Voices*, 106, 108.

50. Gwendolyn Brooks, "song in the front yard," in *Selected Poems*, 12.

51. Edward Said, quoted in Delia Caparoso Konzett, Caparoso. *Ethnic Modernisms: Anzia Yezierska, Zora Neale Hurston, Jean Rhys, and the Aesthetics of Dislocation* (New York: Palgrave/Macmillan, 2002), 2.

52. Ibid.

53. W. E. B Du Bois, *The Souls of Black Folk* (New York: Norton, 2001), 162, 10.

54. Wright, "I Choose Exile," quoted in Michel Fabre, *The Unfinished Quest of Richard Wright*, 2nd ed. (Urbana: University of Illinois Press, 1996), 296.

55. Arna Bontemps, "Review of *The Outsider*," *Saturday Review*, March 28, 1953, 15.

56. Orville Prescott, "Review of *The Outsider*," *New York Times*, March 18, 1953, 29.

57. Richard Wright, *The Outsider* (New York: Harper Collins, 1993), 109.

58. Ibid., 16.

59. Ibid., 585.

60. Barbara Christain, *Black Feminist Criticism* (New York: Teachers College Press, 1997), 13–14.

61. Gwendolyn Brooks, *Maud Martha* (Chicago: Third World, 1993), 62–64.

62. Ibid., 69.

63. Ibid., 70–71.

64. Ibid., 165.

65. Christain, *Black Feminist Criticism*, 129.

66. Ibid.

67. Brooks, *Maud Martha*, 70–71.

68. Stange, *Bronzeville*, xv.

69. Williams, "World of Satin-Legs," 69.

70. Wright, *12 Million Black Voices*, 130.

One aspect of any renaissance is experimentation
against a background of tradition.
—CHINWEIZU, *Africa and the Rest of Us*

Either it [Negro writing] crept in through the kitchen in the form
of jokes; or it was the fruit of the foul soil which was the result
of a liaison between inferiority-complexed Negro "geniuses" and
burnt-out white Bohemians with money.
—RICHARD WRIGHT, "Blueprint for Negro Writing"

Chapter 6

Richard Wright and the Season of Manifestoes

JOHN McCLUSKEY JR.

Richard Wright's ten years in Chicago (1927–37), before the publication of *Native Son* and the completion
of his full autobiography, *American Hunger*, were years
of dazzling challenges and growth. He found work
in the post office after a bout of gorging; he joined
the Federal Writers' Project and shrank smartly and
swiftly from the open blade of a confused actor.
He started composing blues and haiku poetry. He
befriended eminent sociologists at the University
of Chicago. He joined the John Reed Club, later the
Communist Party, and helped launch the South Side
Writers' Group. He crafted his first short stories.
These experiences culminated in the development of
his novels, *Native Son* and *Lawd Today*, as well as the
story collection *Uncle Tom's Children*. The lessons from
these encounters resonate also through his nonfiction, such as *12 Million Black Voices* and early essays.
This essay explores the early journalistic writings,
primarily through the *Daily Worker*, and the culmination of the diverse Chicago influences to his 1937
manifesto, "Blueprint for Negro Writing." The essay

will also place Wright's essay into an ever-widening
circle of contemporaneous black diaspora mani-
festos struggling with issues of color, caste, and
nationalism.

Often, the lead article or essay in an early, if not
the first, issue of a small journal, the manifestoes
were typically direct assaults on preceding traditions.
The earlier traditions were the result of disruptions—colonialism in the cases of Caribbean and
African nations—and literary expressions regarded
as inauthentic. A new direction promised a bold
return to a purer expression, a core from which new
literary expressions reflect a more assertive group
ethos. Such statements were often sweeping literary
and cultural declarations of independence. They have
served as urgent and crafted assertions of shifts in
aesthetics and ethics. The new would be built upon a
recovery and extension of the old. For some, it took
the shape of experimentations against the traditional
rhythms of music, as in the work of Nicolas Guillen
utilizing the rhythms of the Cuban *son* or Sterling

Brown's use of classic blues. For others, it might have meant the locating within a folk tradition the heroic gestures and rhetoric of primary characters, as in the case of Jacque Roumain in *Masters of the Dew*. Further, it was a set of assertions of a nationalist spirit and an imagined past, as with the Negritude poets. In most statements, whether for ideological or strategic reasons, the call was to end provinciality and to align themselves with other writers/thinkers, regardless of color, who wished to join in common cause against the forces of injustice. Thus, the stance of the manifesto was very similar to the tradition of the published open letter—a declaration of the limitations of the old and an invitation to the glories of the new. Wright's manifesto collected and foreshadowed much of this urgency. If Wright's major fiction achieved none of the above, his early poems and essays certainly acknowledged the vitality of a past folk tradition and its possibilities for literature.

According to his autobiographies, Wright arrived in Chicago with an adventurous syllabus of nonfiction and fiction examined in an embattled solitude in Memphis, Tennessee, and Jackson, Mississippi. Eager to grow intellectually, he was soon attracted to the debates among the young communist sympathizers in Chicago and would join the John Reed Club and later the Communist Party. At nearly the same time, he helped to shape the small but influential group of African American writers, the South Side Writers' Club. His account of his first meeting with the John Reed Club borders on the apocryphal.

In *American Hunger*, Wright relates that he accepts the invitation to the meeting out of boredom and has planned to look on upon the meeting as an amused outside observer. He is quickly given back issues of Marxist-oriented journals and newspapers to read and has given his promise to read them. His host gives him a quick tour: "He took me to an office and introduced me to a Jewish boy who was to become one of the nation's leading painters, to a chap who was to become one of the eminent composers of his day, to a writer who was to create some of the best novels of his generation, to a young Jewish boy who was destined to film the Nazi invasion of Czechoslovakia. I was meeting men and women whom I would know for decades to come, who were to form the first sustained relationships in my life."[1]

The accounts by his biographers are equally dramatic.[2] In every instance, the moment is liberating for Wright in that he was supplied with a new and global vocabulary, one that stretched his trust in the impact of material conditions for shaping the character of individuals and communities. Yet, it is the ensuing conversation with his mother and the urgency in one of his first poems, "I Have Seen Black Hands," that would demonstrate the goals for him as a writer, at least in his 1934–45 period.

After he fails to clarify the goals of communist activity to his mother, he broods upon his possible role as a writer: "The Communists, I felt, had oversimplified the experience of those whom they sought to lead. In their efforts to recruit masses, they had missed the meaning of the lives of the masses, had conceived of people in too abstract a manner. I would make voyages, discoveries, explorations with words and try to put some of that meaning back. I would address my words to two groups: I would tell Communists how common people felt, and I would tell common people of the self-sacrifice of Communists who strove for unity among them."[3]

Wright makes this same point with equal zeal in his long poem in the very last stanza. The poem's sweep of images of black labor and suffering in the south and urban north culminates in this declaration as stanza 4.

> I am black and I have seen Black hands
> Raised in fists of revolt, side by side with the white fists of
>   White workers,
> And some day—and it is only this which sustains me—
> Some day there shall be millions and millions of them,
> On some red day in a burst of fists on a new horizon![4]

This ideal of a color-blind brotherhood and this zeal to demonstrate the corrosive assault of class conflict through the drama of his fiction would be profound even when the contradictions, more experiential than theoretical, would arise. If the South Side Writers' Group provided a small community of fellow black writers, as shown later, the John Reed Club provided a venue for his early poetry and ultimately his first efforts as a journalist. Wright's earliest publications were poems in small radical journals, *Left Front*, *The Anvil*, *New Masses*, and *Midland Left*, among others.

Wright and fellow members would weather a demise of the Chicago chapter of the John Reed Club due to a turn in Communist Party politics during 1934–35. At the same time, as a bystander of the few blacks in the Chicago chapter of the party, Wright was eventually made an editor of the *Daily Worker*. Before and during his new assignment as editor,

Wright became a close observer of black proletarian life across regions. Again, this is evident from his memories shaped and shared in his autobiography, as well as in the text of the photo documentary *12 Million Black Voices*. His early journalism was a window on cultural and economic disruptions and adjustment to new settings, rural and urban, to the struggle for educational and economic equity, to the quest for political participation.

The *Daily Worker*

During late 1937, Richard Wright wrote forty signed articles for the *Daily Worker* at the same time he was crafting the final revisions for the 1938 edition of *Uncle Tom's Children*. Certainly, there is the possibility of many unsigned articles, as well. His readings of Marxist materials and social realist fiction, his experience as a black male in America during the Depression, his forays into poetry and short fiction—all together would summon a cultural and critical position not articulated in any substantial way among his fellow African American writers. As suggested above, this would culminate in the then little-known "Blueprint for Negro Writing," a clear break with the credos of the Harlem Renaissance and a call for a new and tougher direction in black life and writing. This would not vary much throughout the remainder of Wright's life and has clear application from works as varied as his major novel, *Native Son*, and his first book-length travel memoir, *Black Power*, the record of his trip to Ghana, the former Gold Coast. His years of organizing in Chicago were profoundly important as the starting basis for his maturing work as a reporter in New York. After commenting on Wright's early interest in folk forms, I cite and briefly discuss several of the columns that are representative in demonstrating Wright's development.

Wright's earliest attempts at writing blues poems reflect his incipient and intense interest at expanding the political, if not revolutionary, possibilities of African American folklore. Wright was not the first writer to embrace the social implications of oral expression. One of the markers of the Harlem Renaissance writers was the acceptance of black folklore on the part of its major writers, such as Langston Hughes, Sterling Brown, and James Weldon Johnson in poetry and Zora Neale Hurston in prose. W. E. B. Du Bois's celebration of the spirituals in *The Souls of Black Folk* (1903) and Johnson's prose celebration of folklore and spirituals in *The Autobiography of an Ex-Coloured Man* (1912) and his expansive preface to the second edition of *The Book of American Negro Poetry* served as early signals for the elaboration on themes and forms. Closer to Wright, Hughes's "Negro Artist and the Racial Mountain" and Zora Neale Hurston's "Characteristics of Negro Expression" were contemporaneous attempts to rescue folklore from the too frequent corruptions of black speech and song in fiction, musical theater, and early film. Yet, for Wright, except for Hughes's 1930s poems and plays, too often the application and demonstration of folk expression did not go far enough. Perhaps for Wright, it is logical to explore those moments during which the folk expressed revolutionary ideals of a restless working class.

In an August 12, 1937, article Wright profiles the eventful career of the singer Huddie Ledbetter, aka Leadbelly. In the first paragraphs of the article, Wright summarizes Leadbelly's encounter with the legal system—his first incarceration and the parole after the second. He applauds the range of the performer's song lyrics. Ever the native son to his region and claimed by those who still live near his old "address," Wright excoriates folklorist Alan Lomax for exploiting to gain entry and trust in the southern prisons in order to record work songs, blues, and other seculars. In sharp terms, Wright accuses Lomax, an official at the Library of Congress by then, for attacking the character of Leadbelly. Yet, Wright pleads no simple sympathy here; instead, he insists upon a tragedy that deepens understanding. This impulse would inform his response to a letter from Eleanor Roosevelt years later regarding her reaction to the first edition of *Uncle Tom's Children*. Instead, Wright is awed by the possibility of lyricism in the face of personal catastrophe. In addition, he finds Leadbelly's repertoire as inexhaustible.

> Blues, spirituals, animal songs, ballads and work songs pour forth in such profusion that it seems he knows every song his race has ever sung. . . .
>
> He makes his songs out of the day-to-day life of his people. He sings of death, of work, of balked love, of Southern jails no better than hell-holes, of chain gangs, of segregation, and of his hope for a better life.[5]

Ledbetter gained an apparent reprieve later in New York when he applied for relief and joined the Workers' Alliance. Still, relief officials seemed incredulous that the singer had little savings and threatened to withdraw his food ticket. Under threat of publicity through the singer's lyrics, the officials relented. As in subsequent profiles, it is the generosity and support by members of the Workers' Alliance that wins Wright's approval and that of those saved: "The folks in the Workers' Alliance are the finest I've ever known. . . . I feel happy when I am with the boys here in the Workers' Alliance. They are different from those Southern white men."

Wright ends the article by quoting the lyrics of two Ledbetter compositions, "Scottsboro Boys Got Here" and "Bourgeois Blues." The first is a celebration of the release of the young men accused of rape in southern Alabama. This was a cause célèbre for the Communist Party. Ledbetter composed the song after listening to a radio broadcast of a meeting welcoming the four Scottsboro boys to a rally in New York.

The latter, better-known song, focuses on racism in the nation's capital.

> Me and my wife went all over town
> And everywhere we went people turned us down
> Lord, in a bourgeois town
> It's a bourgeois town
> I got the bourgeois blues
> Gonna spread the news all around
>
> Home of the brave, land of the free
> I don't wanna be mistreated by no bourgeoisie
> Lord, in a bourgeois town
> Uhm, the bourgeois town
> I got the bourgeois blues
> Gonna spread the news all around

Though Wright generally ignored the more sensual aspect of the form, he was consistent in his celebration of the blues impulse—tenacity and resilience coupled with the comic, despair in the glare of the hopeful. The musical form could not liberate or change on its own power. Yet, it could carry the residue that, when shaped by discipline and a clear social vision, supports communal and individual relief. The folk artist here emerges as a hero with an intimacy with the communal experience none of Wright's fictional characters dared to carry.[6]

Another article, dated August 30, 1937, focuses on the exploits of a southern migrant who becomes a Communist Party advocate after coming north. The article is entitled "Born a Slave, She Recruits 5 Members for the Communist Party." Wright focuses on Eleanor Ross, seventy-one, called "Mother" Ross in the Harlem community. Wright profiles her harsh life as a laborer in the deep south before her move north and work as a domestic: "She spent 23 of the best years of her life slaving in a tobacco factory, from the time she was 16 until she was 39. During those years she had eight children, six of whom died in infancy because she did not have time enough to give them the attention they needed. But there is in her no bitterness when she speaks of this; she talks of it calmly, matter-of-factly—she spoke of it like a worker who knows that certain conditions of life are inescapable under capitalism."[7] According to Wright, she was failed by "Negro organizations" in her search for a better life. She eventually joined the Unemployed Councils in 1930 and soon the Communist Party. Wright is clear in his attention to the detail of blacks and whites united: "When the Young Communist League of Harlem, composed of Negro and white youth, meets this Wednesday it will extend to Mother Ross the honor of becoming an honorary member and the adopted mother of the group. 'I am glad to accept the honor. I like to see Negro and white youth fight together.'" She is proud to have recruited five black laborers into the party during a recent membership drive and, as Wright hopes, will recruit many more. The example of this woman belies the notion that uneducated laborers/migrants could not absorb the tenets of the party. This contrasts with Wright's depiction of his mother's original response, as reported in *American Hunger*, to literature brought home from the first meeting at the John Reed Club. Frustrated by his seemingly failed explanations to her of Marxist concepts, Wright's mission is shaped in terms that complement those in "I Have Seen Black Hands."

A testament to the possibility of change and sustained resistance, the article also has literary implications. Mother Ross is what An' (Aunt) Sue of Wright's "Bright and Morning Star" might have become. In that story, first published in *New Masses* in 1938 and added in 1940 to the first four stories in *Uncle Tom's Children*, an elderly woman transitions from a quiet Christian matriarch to an uneasy sympathizer to Communist Party organizing. Yet, her sympathy and her later killing of a traitor are based on her love for her grandson. Ideology did not triumph over simple love. Despite the fact that both grandson and grandmother are ultimately martyred for the party's cause, reviews in the party venues were critical of the story.

An article dated August 16, 1937, expands in interesting ways upon the story of "Mother Ross." Entitled "What Happens at a Communist Party Branch Meeting in the Harlem Section?" Wright gives a behind-the-scenes look at a meeting. Perhaps his intention is to contrast the procedures and their seriousness with those of other organizations black or white. The introduction is instructive.

> Before you have time to sit down your eyes are drawn to a huge black placard.
>> "IN MEMORY OF OUR BELOVED BROTHER, ALONZO WATSON, WHO DIED FIGHTING FOR DEMOCRACY IN SPAIN."
>
> So you know, even before the meeting starts and you hear them talk, that there are people here who will give their lives for what they believe.
>
> The Nat Turner Branch has a membership of about 20; of that 20, 16 were present. The composition according to class and sex were as follows: 9 women and 7 men. Of the 7 men, 2 were white. The Negro men and women were of the working class in manner, accent, and deportment. There is absolutely no difference between the Negro and white in the Communist Party. They participate on an equal footing in the carrying out of their tasks.

Wright focuses on the closeness of the party members, demonstrating a zeal just short of that in a southern Baptist church. The business agenda is moved through crisply, inspired in anticipation of a report on the international scene with emphasis on the political situation in China. The report is met with energetic questioning and excited discussion. Wright editorializes for the fictional onlooker.

> These black people who meet here in Harlem are hungry more than in one sense. They love this Communist Party which is the only organization caring enough for them to give them this world-view of things. It is through such meetings as these that Bolsheviks are forged, men and women with guts and courage enough to take the world into their hands and mold it and in molding it remake themselves.
>
> And it is through such meetings as these that for the first time in American history the Negro is receiving his *highest pitch of social consciousness* [my emphasis]. When you listen to them talk, you know that the future is fraught with conflict, but you feel that here are people capable of dealing with that conflict.[8]

Wright describes the weakest moment in the meeting as one in which a "comrade" refused to take responsibility for getting copies of the *Daily Worker* to members of his branch and failed. He finally realizes that such a failure was his fault and his fault alone.

His conclusion to the article is rousing.

> Denied university educations, they are receiving an education from the vanguard of the working class, the Communist Party. Farmers, intellectuals, and middle-class people who drifting about in a shoreless sea, wondering what straw they can grasp, should look here, for this is a new pole of strength about which the life of the whole world can regroup itself.[9]

Wright's description of the meeting and its import is in sharp contrast to a meeting in Chicago first published in *I Tried to Be a Communist* in 1956 but already embedded in the unpublished American hunger. At this meeting, Wright has arisen to make a report to a group of black communists. He describes his activities as a writer, a member of the party and John Reed Club.

> I finished and waited for comment. There was silence. I looked about. Most of the comrades sat with bowed heads. Then I was surprised to catch a twitching smile on the lips of a Negro woman. Minutes passed. The Negro woman lifted her head and looked at the organizer. The organizer smothered a smile. Then the woman broke into unrestrained laughter, bending forward and burying her face in her hands. I stared. Had I said something funny?[10]

In contrast to the earlier meeting, however, is hope not humiliation. Though Wright in the article is not the center of attention, he finds purpose and meaning far more significant than the artifice of half-hearted believers.

Among the more sensational headlines for a Wright story appeared in early August 1937: "Negro, with 3-Week-Old Baby, Begs Food on Street." The story recounts how a mother with three starving children and an infant walked the streets of Harlem, begging for food. The husband and father lost his assignment with the WPA two weeks earlier, and, in Wright's words, "rather than face the harrowing task of feeding five children with no job he ran away and has not been seen or heard from." Relief through established channels is delayed until the husband is located. Just three weeks after a childbirth, the mother spends her days alternately waiting in the relief office or walking the streets with her starving children. Wright cites the case of a young couple waiting in that same office with their infant child deprived of nutrients. Wright insists in his first lines that these scenes are real, not scenes from, say, a Dickensian portrait of nineteenth-century London: "Trekking into the headquarters of the Workers' Alliance at 326 Lenox Ave., is an endless stream of black people looking for help. They come here because someone has told them that the Alliance will help them. Usually their pride keeps them back until the last moment then they make this their desperate 'court of final appeal.'"[11]

In both episodes, Wright demonstrates what he has judged the deliberate callousness of the government bureaucracy. In these pieces, he is consistent in reporting, then arguing that it is the urgent, tough-minded yet sympathetic efforts of the Communist Party in the shape of the workers' alliance that sustain hope during the late years of the Depression.

A later piece signed by Wright (December 6, 1937) reports the ultimate sacrifice: A white truck driver saves two babies from a burning building in Harlem. He died when he rushed back into the building to save others. Wright excoriates the investigators for their suspicion of the rescuer—what was he doing in Harlem?—and the living conditions of the family. His overriding intent is clearly to show the potential of unity among working-class blacks and whites, even to the point of the ultimate self-sacrifice.[12]

As a whole, the pieces dramatize Wright's zeal regarding working-class unity, the callousness of the state and its minions, an indomitable spirit, and the heroism of the members of the Communist Party. His own growing doubts regarding the efficacy of the organization's leadership is well masked in the party organ. He continued to produce his fiction despite the tiring newspaper work, however. He would need another venue, not a daily newspaper, to present his plan outlining the relationship of the committed black writer to a national literary tradition, with other contemporary writers, with an emerging audience.

Challenge/New Challenge

While Wright was beginning his intellectual sojourn in Chicago, another project that he would later join and provide a venue for his work was developing in New York. Dorothy West launched *Challenge* in March 1934. Its announced aim was to recapture the spirit and eloquence of the Harlem Renaissance. She prevailed upon James Weldon Johnson to write the introductory editorial and challenged him to both chide the older writers for not fulfilling their promise and to inspire the younger writers. Johnson delivered promptly. In its foreword, Johnson was blunt.

> The term "younger Negro writers" connotes a degree of disil-
> lusionment and disappointment for those who a decade ago

hailed with loud huzzas the dawn of the Negro literary millennium. We expected much; perhaps, too much. I now judge that we ought to be thankful for the half-dozen younger writers who did emerge and make a place for themselves. But we ought not to be satisfied; many newer voices should be constantly striving to make their voices heard. But these younger writers must not be mere dilettantes; they have serious work to do.[13]

It is intriguing that so soon after the end of the renaissance, generally signaled with the onset of the Depression, that the voices of disillusionment would spring up. Yet even earlier, a major champion of the renaissance, Alain Locke, began to voice his doubts in commentaries lasting well into the 1930s. Rudolph Fisher in a 1932 review of Wallace Thurman's *Infants of the Spring* comments that the New Negro had not delivered: "Perhaps the New Negro is dead. Or perhaps in the warm sunlight of publicity, he stretched himself out and dozed off to sleep."[14] Others remarked wistfully at the end of an era. These seemed to be of the same spirit as F. Scott Fitzgerald's comment in his "Echoes of a Jazz Age." The long sentence that ends the elegy to the "Lost Generation" concludes—"it all seems rosy and romantic to us who were young then, because we will never feel quite so intensely about our surroundings any more."[15] By 1940, the same year as Wright's *Native Son*, Hughes would claim in *The Big Sea*: "The ordinary Negroes hadn't heard of the Negro Renaissance. And if they had, it hadn't raised their wages any."[16]

Thus in a time of regrouping and fitful nostalgia, West sought to recapture a moment of high promise. West was justly proud of individual pieces throughout the brief life of the journal, especially the entire third issue. However, by the sixth and final issue of the journal, she despaired the quality, originality, and liveliness of the younger cadre of writers. She had begun to chide the writers in increasingly sharper terms and invited more radical poems and stories of social indictment. Also, her frustration at the lack of financial support through subscriptions and donations is palpable in the last issue's "Dear Reader" column. Black colleges and universities have failed to distribute and publicize the journal to faculty and students. Yet all is not lost. She has discovered Chicago: "Yet we are not entirely discouraged, for we have become greatly interested in a young Chicago group, one of whose members appears in this issue. These young Chicagoans hold meetings regularly, where their work is read for open discussions. The meetings, we are told, are lively and well attended." She concludes by informing her readers that the Chicago group has been especially critical of *Challenge*.[17] In turn, she offers the Chicago writers a special section in a future issue as her editorial challenge. Richard Wright had been a key member of the Chicago group, the South Side Writers' Group. Biographers Michel Fabre and Hazel Rowley note that as Wright departed from Chicago, one of his interests was to revive *Challenge*. The problem perhaps might have been an overzealousness that took West aback. Yet, it was clear to her that a sharper, more radical edge was necessary to revive the magazine and keep it attractive to younger writers.

The organization of the National Negro Congress in 1936 emboldened Wright to found the South Side Writers' Group. The first meeting of the group was during May 1936. At the time, he was still a member of the John Reed Club. However, his effort on the South Side might be seen not as a sudden nationalist turn for Wright but as an effort to address the isolation of black writers at the same time craft issues were explored. The group met regularly for two years under Wright's leadership before that of Margaret Walker. In her biography of Wright, Walker relates that the most consistent attendees included Frank Marshall Davis, Edward Bland, and Ted Ward.[18] The group was never large, six to eight, according to Walker. Yet, the group became both a writing workshop and a seminar on culture and class. Wright read drafts of "Big Boy Leaves Home" and "Down by the Riverside." Walker suggests it was Wright's social-political orientation that was his lasting legacy to the group: "Dick Wright's social-political orientation began in Chicago, and it was this that he passed on to us in the South Side Writers' Group."[19]

Thus, it was one of Wright's ambitions to transplant some of his Chicago experience in a little magazine based in New York. In the June 8, 1937, issue of the *Daily Worker* under the headline "Negro Writers Launch Literary Quarterly," Wright announced the birth of *New Challenge* and its purpose. Citing the early example of the South Side group, Wright stated that a similar group in New York had recently met to draft a statement that called for "an active struggle on the part of Negro writers against war, fascism, and reaction in general." Wright relates that the organizational plan, "similar in purpose and structure to that of the old John Reed Clubs which influenced so many young white writers during the past seven

years," would be launched with the new magazine as its venue. As an editor, he welcomed white writers who deal "definitively" with black themes and issues. Wright would reemphasize these points in the two-page editorial for the first edition published a few months later.[20]

Blueprint for Negro Writing

The "Blueprint" was Wright's most complete statement of the confluence of literature and politics, of the union of aesthetics and propaganda, of craft and theme, and for Wright a happy confluence of New York and Chicago. Presented in ten brief sections, the original essay was the centerpiece for the first issue of *New Challenge*. The first issue could be seen as Dorothy West's concession to the "Chicago group." As it turned out, it would be her last foray into little magazines.

In the first two paragraphs of his manifesto, Wright early dismisses the optimism and any residual sense of achievement of the Harlem Renaissance.

> Generally speaking, Negro writing in the past has been confined to humble novels, poems, and plays, prim and decorous ambassadors who went a-begging to white America. They entered the Court of American Public Opinion dressed in the knee-pants of servility, curtsying to show that the Negro was not inferior, that he was human, and that he had a life comparable to that of other people. For the most part these ambassadors were received as though they were French poodles who do clever tricks.
>
> White America never offered these Negro writers any serious criticism. The mere fact that a Negro could write was astonishing. Nor was there any deep concern on the part of white America with the role Negro writing should play in American culture; and the role it did play grew out of accident rather than intent or design. Either it crept in through the kitchen in the form of jokes; or it was the fruit of the foul soil which was the result of a liaison between inferiority-complexed Negro "geniuses" and burnt-out white Bohemians with money.[21]

There was a gulf between the artists of the period and the masses for whom they purportedly spoke. Healing the breach would be the realization that there are genuine sources for black art—the church and black folklore. Wright's assumption here was that a closer demonstration of the profundity of the church and folklore would close the gap. The writers would thereby achieve the class unity and integrity too often missing from works that sought the praise of an audience unappreciative of the significance of black expression.

Just as important is both the social and intellectual isolation of black writers during the two decades after World War I. Wright implies a debilitating insularity and provinciality of theme. This effect is closely tied to dependence upon a fawning and uncritical white audience. Wright argues for an autonomy from such audiences, yet does not claim a black audience as the staple for young radical black writers. The note on supporters in the introductory editorial is instructive: "We are dependent upon subscriptions, support of benefit affairs, and outright donations. We are, in this respect, responsible only to ourselves, a fact which is contrary to the belief of the skeptics and agonizing to our enemies." In the "Blueprint," Wright extends the note of independence to include freedom from any -ism, though he generously mentions Marxism as a complete ideological system worthy of close study by black writers.

The isolation Wright decries very neatly parallels the isolation he has carefully nurtured in the creation of a persona that comes alive most forcefully in *Black Boy*. Wright's personal profile is that of a lone intellectual at odds with his environment: a viciously racist white south and an apathetic and helpless black community. He is a young man whose early writings and expressed thoughts are censored or nearly so by various authorities in and outside of the home. He seeks solace in literature. (This is not completely true, as his letters to Joe C. Brown easily attest.)[22] Once in Chicago, he achieves community through the radical teachings of Marxism and the company of members of the John Reed Club. He helps to establish a black intellectual community through the South Side Writers' Group and alliances with Horace Cayton and John Gibbs St. Clair Drake. In this way, his perspective of the world is broadened beyond strict binaries of black and white to include sensitivity to class struggles in the United States and around the world. He insists upon a collective growth and evolution along similar paths. In this way, writers will move beyond the emotional and political confines that hampered true maturation and growth during the Harlem Renaissance.

Intellectual and emotional discipline is key for Wright. The apparent exoticism of some of renaissance writings—hedonist joy, spontaneous exuberance, and the like—was not true for the majority of black people. This note is as true for his pieces in the *Daily Worker* as it was true for his earliest pub-

lished stories. Except for the early playful moments in "Big Boy Leaves Home," the life of the southern black male was grim business. Yet, that life, any life, demanded close, conscious rational thought and self-control. Without these, the lives would be "soft" responses to social forces. This point would be a hallmark in all of Wright's future work, whether the family of Bigger Thomas as Bigger views them through Wright's perceptions or the inhabitants of the Gold Coast (later Ghana) as developed in his 1953 travel memoir *Black Power*. As with the citizens, so with the writers—the discipline of hard work wedded to a tough social ideology was important to the individual writer and a collective literary movement.

Again, the foundation is the location within the black experience of a source for literature. Wright identifies the black church and black oral expression as sources for the writer and nation-building. From these sources must come the terms for progress and heroism, though in their present forms they may be seen as the source for ridicule and a mindless leisure Wright often seems to place this folklore in the rural south; thus, he cobbles it into a grand category of Tradition. Like so many writers the late twentieth century, Wright is asking the old American question—what is to be done with the past, or how can one make the past usable, even after a clear sense of the past has been shaped? Though Wright was not successful in responding even partially to this question in his own fiction, this does not vanquish a question that Baldwin, Ellison, Hurston, Gaines, Morrison, and others have confronted. How does one shape a contemporary story set in the rural south or urban north with the looming social forces and drawing from folklore, demonstrate a heroism with lessons for resolution to class conflict on a national and international scale?

Which brings Wright to the "vexing question" of nationalism. Harold Cruse is most pointed in his criticism of Wright's inability to resolve the question based on his loyalty to CP ideology. His words carry the weight of the dilemma at the same time he repeats a key phrase from an earlier journal piece: "They (negro writers) must accept the concept of nationalism because in order to transcend it, they must *possess* and *understand* [Wright's emphasis]. And a nationalist spirit in Negro writing means a nationalism carrying the *highest possible pitch of social consciousness*" (my emphasis). Yet, even after Wright's formal break with the party, it is clear that the transcendence of nationalism was no easy task for him. Racial experience made such a transcendence irreconcilable as a stated goal for fiction, at least. An article that follows the "Blueprint" in the first issue of *New Challenge* is entitled "A Note on Negro Nationalism" by Allyn Keith, a pseudonym for a member of the South Side group. The article suggests the importance of the issue of nationalism at the time. Keith agrees with Wright that nationalism must be approached and articulated as a phase for resolving broader class issues. The case remains as to how his position on nationalism gets demonstrated in fiction without compromising the complexity of characterization.

Wright's essay joins Pauline Hopkins's regular editorials in *Colored American Magazine*, Hughes's "Negro Artist and the Racial Mountain," Du Bois's "Criteria for Negro Art," and Locke's "Art and Propaganda" as among the most significant African North American manifestoes of the early twentieth century. Wright's piece is especially important here as it helps to shed light on other manifestoes of the period in other parts of the diaspora. Examples that follow are from the francophone world Wright would connect with in 1947. Perhaps it is worth noting here that when his blueprint was published, Wright was barely twenty-nine years old.

Wright and his family left the United States in 1947 to live in Paris, where he would live for the rest of his life. He soon joined with a cadre of intellectuals and artists to establish *Presence Africaine*. Overlapping his move to Chicago, his stay in New York, and his arrival in Paris, there were a number of small journals published throughout the diaspora, especially in the French-speaking colonies and Paris. Many of the editorials and public pronouncements in these journals reflect a wrestling with nationalism, traditional forms, and radical politics similar, though not always identical, to Wright's. For Wright, his ever-widening language and culture circle included the founders and editors of journals dedicated to linguistic and cultural independence. Their manifestoes are often identical in their urgencies.

Haiti

In his seminal book, *So Spoke the Uncle (Ainsi Parla l'Oncle)*, ethnographer Dr. Jean Price-Mars provided the cornerstone for the Haitian Indigenist (sometimes Indigenous) movement when the book was published in 1928. This was a movement of young

Haitian writers who wanted to break from French models of poetry and to include a newfound respect for their own folk traditions. An earlier journal, *La Revue Indigene*, sounded the alarm clearly from its first issue. However, the point was most sharply drawn in the early pages of its second number in the fall 1927. Norman Sylvain's "La Jeune Litterature Haitienne" begins as follows:

> There has never been, truly literary schools in Haiti. The great French movements, the methods of the inner circle, have not brought together enough adepts to create genuine currents. Haitian writers remain isolated, and if the influence of a master can sometimes be perceived, it emanates from a particular preference. . . . Haitian poetry should purport more at being human than at limiting itself to a temporary picturesque, which is subjective besides. It was more French than anything else and whether we like it or not, it was more or less an imitation.[23]

With the occupation of Haiti by U.S. forces, with a seeming exhaustion with a poetics that honored the French romantics of the nineteenth century, a call to the contemporary through the gaze to the traditional was loudly made. Price-Mars's work leavened the movement and put it on a solid foundation. From its beginning chapter, "What Is Folklore?" Price-Mars's work analyzes while celebrating the complexity of Haitian thought and life. At the core of the nationalizing of Haitian literature was the vernacular-vodun, folklore, dance, and an appreciation of things African. Moving beyond a cool detachment of an anthropologist, as Zora Neale Hurston would in years ahead during her studies in Florida, Louisiana, Haiti, and Jamaica, Price-Mars is insistent on folk and expressive culture being appreciated as an important way to knowledge far beyond a simple exoticism. He places it at the center of a new national literature. Freed from the Marxist constraints that confined Wright, he pushes on to suggest patterns for a literature in chapter 7 as James Weldon Johnson would in his introduction to *The Book of American Negro Poetry*: "[S]omething else is necessary that is greater, more faithful to Haitian and human verities; it is necessary to draw the substance of our works sometimes from this immense reservoir of folk-lore in which the motives for our decisions are compressed after centuries, in which the elements of our sensibility are elaborated, in which the fabric of our popular character, our national mind, is structured."[24]

Thus girded intellectually, Haitian writers were liberated to discover their voices. However, none quite met Price-Mars's challenge in poetry. The figure who would come closest, Jacques Roumain, would do it in the form of the novel *The Masters of the Dew*, published in 1944. Carolyn's Fowler's *Knot in the Thread* is a careful study of the career and works of Roumain. Fowler documents Roumain's shift from a cosmopolitanism to a far more nationalist agenda in his poetry before the publication of the novel. The shift was dramatic. Building on a 1939 speech, Roumain comments on the poet's role in a December 1940 speech: "The poet is at the same time a witness and an actor in the historical drama. He is engaged in it with full responsibility; specifically, at present, his art must be a first-line weapon at the service of the struggle of the masses. . . . Poetry today must be a weapon as effective as a leaflet, a pamphlet a poster. If we succeed in fusing with the class content of the poem the beauty of form . . . we will be able to create a great human revolutionary poetry worthy of the cultural values we have the will to defend."[25]

Yet, the point drawn throughout his master work is instructive. Returning from years in Cuba, the protagonist enlists the *coumbite*, collective efforts at land cultivation and house construction, as a means resurrect a failing economy in his native land. Thus, an import from another site in the black diaspora proves to be critical. The very fact of the book in English is also key. The most popular translation of the book is Hughes's in 1947. By this time, Roumain had left his work as a journalist and was studying ethnography. He had also begun to translate the works of Countee Cullen and Hughes into French. From journalist through poet, social scientist, and novelist/translator, Roumain displayed a versatility demonstrated by Hurston, Wright, and his mentor and intellectual liberator Jean Price-Mars. The issue for Haitian writers, however, was the issue of form informed by folklore as well as the sense of the heroic beyond Dessalines, Christophe, Boukman, and L'Ouverture, its earlier liberators.

In *La Releve* in 1932, Price-Mars in a three-part article showcased the North American "Negro Renaissance." Throughout its pages during 1932 to 1938, the journal offered a number of translations of works by U.S. writers. Still, as shown, in an early editorial, the project was urgent.

> We are stretching out a loyal hand to our seniors in the career, to those whose ideas agree with ours, but also to those whose ideas will be in disagreement with ours. We will have nothing

> but only the courage to be weak when confronted with our colleagues' reasonable arguments whenever they emanate from a thorough analysis of different questions that life's circumstances will expose to common sense and to everyone's conscience. . . . With the sole concern of helping the deprived Haitian population to gain consciousness of itself, to turn and walk resolutely toward order, and to laugh at the perfidious spites with which it has been associated, here we are ready to struggle. And we will face things.[26]

The students who were still in Paris during the early 1930s launched journals important to the birth of Negritude. The names of Leon Damas, Leopold Senghor, and Aime Cesaire have long been familiar to researchers of this topic. Less-well-known are the names of Paulette Nardal and Etienne Lero introduced relatively recently and given important discussion in several places. Though issues of extensions of folk forms might appear to be less urgent, essential to the essays in these journals prior to 1940 was the break from colonial poetics and the reach for a more creative synthesis of the traditional and the modern in a tone that could critique a restrictive political and linguistic order and still demonstrate the vitality and complexity of a new "sound."

The three journals below have received close attention in recent studies. I wish to merely excerpt from their editorials common chords. In his superb study of black internationalism, *The Practice of Diaspora*, Brent Edwards identifies the origins of each and their relationship to one another. For example, *Légitime Defense*, which lasted for one issue in June 1932, was founded one month after the demise of *La Revue du monde noir*. Edwards argues and cites supporting evidence that, despite its heightened rhetoric, the younger might have indeed been a step back in narrowing its focus and moving from a sharp political analysis to the platitudes of surrealism.[27] *L'Etudiant Noir* published a single issue in 1935. Despite its seeming force in all discussions of Negritude, Edwards points out the lack of a unified voice. Yet, the assertions of humanism and nationalism, objectivity, and intuition are pointed.

L'Etudiant Noir (Black Student)

In *The Black Student*, Cesaire describes the situation:

> The colonizer soon gets disgusted with his or her creation. Since the copies are nothing but copies, the models have nothing for them but a hatred feeling similar to the one we have for

a monkey or a parrot because the truth is that if a man fears the other, he also despises the similar. The same applies to the colonized. Once he starts acting like his or her trainer he fails to understand the contempt that the maker has for him or her, and he starts to hate the maker. That is how I come to learn that some disciples hate the master once the former ceases to be a disciple.

It is true, then, that assimilation resulting from fear and timidity is conducive to contempt and hatred. Moreover, it carries with it seeds of conflict; it brings about the conflicts of the same with the same which is the worst of the conflicts. It is for this reason that the young black generation turns its back on the clan of the old Black generation. The old generation experienced assimilation but we want resurrection. What does the Black youth want? Nothing but life.[28]

Légitime Defense

The urgency is clear in the pages of *Légitime Defense*.

This is nothing but a warning. We intend to thoroughly commit ourselves. We are convinced that there are young people other than us capable of signing what we write but refuse—in as much as it is still compatible with the continuation of life—to compose with the surrounding ignominy . . .

This small journal is a temporary intellectual tool, and if it stops working, we will find other instruments. We are accepting with indifference the temporal and spatial circumstances that, defining us as French speakers from the West Indies, have marked off, without limiting, our prime scope of operation. . . . If its content targets young black men it is due to the fact that we consider that they have particularly suffered from capitalism (beyond the African borders, we can consider Scottsboro), and that they likely offer—as long as they have ethnic personality that can be materially determined—a potential for revolt and joy generally more elevated.[29]

La Revue du monde noir

As with the journals above, the aims of *La Revue du monde noir* are

Our Aim:
To give to the intelligentsia of the black race and their partisans an official organ in which to publish their artistic, literary and scientific works.

To study and to popularize, by means of the press, books, lectures, courses, all of which concerns Negro Civilization and the natural riches of Africa, thrice sacred to the black race.

The triple aim which *La Revue du monde noir* will pursue, will be: to create among the Negroes of the entire world, regardless

of nationality, an intellectual and moral tie, which will permit them to know each other, to love one another, to defend more effectively their collective interests and to glorify their race.[30]

Thus when Wright joins the group that would launch *Presence Africaine* in 1947, there was a foundation of efforts at a cultural break from colonial forms of education and cultural production. As the most celebrated black writer in the world, Wright joined the board of editors organized by Alioune Diop, a Senegalese instructor. The board would include Aime Cesaire and Leopold Senghor, among other French-speaking black representatives. It would also include Jean-Paul Sartre and Andre Breton and an equal number of non-black writers. The thinking is alleged to have been that prominent white scholars would form a phalanx around the black thinkers to avoid censorship or trials for subversion. The very idea of a cosmopolitan journal to unite black thinkers during a colonialist regime was a daring one, no doubt. In its first issue, Diop spells out the mission Wright helped to translate that statement from the French into English and apparently supported it.

Diop's editorial for the first issue of *Presence Africaine* is instructive in the many echoes it has collected from the diaspora and Chicago. Wright assisted in the translation and presumably agreed with the principles and the mission set forth. He was no longer a lone apostle bringing to a fledgling journal his zeal as a black Marxist writer describing the travails of being black in the North American rural site of Mississippi and the urban locales of Chicago and New York City. He was a world-famous writer now on a broader stage. Yet, the points of nationalism, autonomy, isolation, and a folkloric basis for writing were still issues of much urgency.

As much as Wright's "Blueprint" and Dorothy West's journalistic agenda, *Presence Africaine* in its earliest days moved along a generational axis. Unlike *Challenge* and *New Challenge*, it has enjoyed a much-longer life. The journal was launched to demonstrate and articulate the position of young African intellectuals and artists who were unwilling to assimilate themselves completely to Europe, unable to fully embrace either traditionalism or any version of black exotica, and were not yet clear how to confront European technological advances.

Diop is inclusive.

Being neither white, nor yellow, nor black, incapable of returning completely to our ancestral traditions or of assimilating ourselves to Europe—we had the feeling of constituting a new race, mentally crossed, but which had not acquired an awareness of its own originality and had not made that originality known. Were we then uprooted beings? To the degree that we had not defined our position in the world, we had abandonned (*sic*) ourselves between two societies, without a recognized meaning in either, being strangers to both. Such a situation could be tolerated only when ethical considerations are stifled. It is because of our refusal to renounce thought that we believe in the usefulness of this review.[31]

Diop's conclusion is rousing and harks back to Du Bois's conclusion in "Of Our Spiritual Strivings."

> We Africans need to develop a relish for the elaboration of ideas, the evolution of techniques,—and thus to understand western civilization which, without crushing natural civilizations, will preserve just those portions of them that its vital impulse and our effective presence can allow it to spare.
>
> . . . We should occupy ourselves with present questions of world importance, and, in common with others, ponder upon them, in order that we might one day find ourselves among the creators of a new order.
>
> The intellectual collaboration that we appeal for can be useful to all. Europe creates the leaven of all future civilizations. But we men of overseas, from ancient China, from pensive India to silent Africa, possess immense moral resources which constitute the substance to be fecundated by Europe. We are indispensable to each other.[32]

Thus, in a decade, Wright has shifted his axis from the United States. In experience, it has been from south to north—Mississippi to Chicago and New York—and from Paris from south to north again— Africa to Europe. Though his discovery and inclusion of the *Presence Africaine* cadre is not freighted with the drama of the John Reed Club in Chicago, it does signal another major move in the web of race, culture, and literature. The problem of nationalism or now internationalism and an incipient pan-Africanism remains vexing. How does one close ranks around color and not dilute one's cause in a universalism that dissipates the focus of all causes and dilutes the urgencies of movements whether political or artistic (or, better, both conjoined)?

Not bound by one individual -ism—Marxism, surrealism, Negritude or even pan-Africanism—the journal would cast its intellectual and aesthetic net broadly. This must have been gratifying to Wright, for could he have imagined the twists and turns in his own

"adventure with western culture" (to modify George Kent's gorgeous phrase)?

As the ever loyal Chicagoan, he included Gwendolyn Brooks's poem in the first issue. In addition to pieces by Frank Marshall Davis, he would also lobby for pieces by Samuel Allen and C. L. R. James while still an active member of the board until 1950. The argument here is not for an unbroken circle but for the evolution of a theory and practice of literature and the pronouncement of its intentions. If Wright did not regard himself as African, he was very quiet on that point in the founding moment of the journal. He was very clear that, like the young students from the French colonies, he was a man between two worlds. He was western and black. What he would do with that in fiction was his greatest challenge and biggest loss. The fact that he could say it so forcefully and vividly during the 1937–47 period is one of his several achievements in letters.

Coda: "Blackness Ahead"

Beyond Wright, there would be other manifestoes throughout the diaspora during the last decades of the last century. They will continue as past literary/artistic achievements are weighed by a younger generation. It can be argued that manifestoes seek to *will* literary movements into existence. Robert Hayden's powerfully simple phrase from "Runagate, Runagate," describing the fearful night, is instructive here. For there would be and will be variations on "blackness ahead." Based in Chicago under the indefatigable leadership of Hoyt Fuller and Carole Parks, *Black World* was central to the existence of the black arts movement; *In Praise of Creoleness* mapped out still another strategy from the Caribbean.

Black World (Chicago, 1970)

In its premiere issue, *Black World* magazine focuses, appropriately, on the two principal centers of black population in the world, the African continent and the United States of America:

> It is the hope of the editors of *Black World* magazine that black people everywhere—in Brazil, Venezuela, Colombia, and the islands of the Caribbean, as well as in Africa, Europe, and North America—have reached a level of political maturity where they understand that the empowerment of black people of Harlem is not possible until black men in the Congo are in

full control of the vast mineral wealth of that country, that the millions of black people who grovel under the boot of the white minority of Zimbabwe (Rhodesia) will remain debased until Nigeria evolves into the economic and military giant that is her potential, and that the *favelas* of Rio will continue to house a disproportionate number of blacks until black men control the governments of Angola and Mozambique.[33]

In Praise of Creoleness

The journal *In Praise of Creoleness* introduces the complexity of creoleness with no less urgency than the previous statements.

Neither Europeans, nor Africans, nor Asians, we proclaim ourselves Creoles. This will be for us an interior attitude—better, a vigilance, or even better a sort of mental envelope in the middle of which our world will be built in full consciousness of the outer world. These words we are communicating to you here do not stem from theory, nor do they stem from any learned principles. They are, rather, akin to testimony. . . .

Caribbean literature does not yet exist. We are still in a state of preliterature: that of a written production without a home audience, ignorant of the authors/readers interaction which is the primary condition of the development of a literature. This situation is not imputable to the mere political domination, it can also be explained by the fact that our truth found itself behind bars, in the deep bottom of ourselves, unknown to our consciousness and to the artistically free reading of the world in which we live. We are fundamentally stricken with exteriority. This from a long time ago to the present day.[34]

Richard Wright packed what he needed from Chicago and in turn honored his once "sweet home" while a citizen of the world. He did not do this in the isolation deplored in his blueprint and the intellectual exile painstakingly demonstrated in his autobiographies. He made his pronouncements on the politics of culture within a growing community of writers and thinkers seeking the sources and defining the goals of a national literature. On both generational and ideological grounds, that search has continued.

Notes

1. Richard Wright, *American Hunger* (New York: Harper & Row, 1977), 61–63.

2. See Michel Fabre, *The Unfinished Quest of Richard Wright* (New York: Morrow, 1973), 96–97; Hazel Rowley, *Richard Wright: The Life and Times* (New York: Holt, 2001), 75–77; Bill Mullen, *Popular Fronts: Chicago and African American Cultural Politics, 1935–46* (Urbana: University of Illinois Press, 1999), 25–30.

3. Wright, *American Hunger*, 66.

4. Wright, "I Have Seen Black Hands," *New Masses* 11 (June 26, 1934): 16.

5. Wright, "Huddie Ledbetter, Famous Negro Folk Artist," *Daily Worker*, August 12, 1937, 7.

6. In my article "Two Steppin'": Richard Wright's Encounter with Blue-Jazz," *American Literature* 55, no. 3 (October 1983), I attempt to show Wright's reach for the blues form and themes with his anxiety over one of the prevailing themes—sexual love.

7. Richard Wright, "Born a Slave, She Recruits 5 Members for Communist Party," *Daily Worker*, August 30, 1937, 2.

8. Richard Wright, "What Happens at a CP Branch Party Meeting in the Harlem Section?", *Daily Worker*, August 16, 1937, 6.

9. Ibid.

10. Richard Wright, "I Tried to Be a Communist," *Atlantic Monthly*, August 1944.

11. Richard Wright, "Negro, with 3-Week Old Boy, Begs Food on Street," *Daily Worker*, August 4, 1937, 3.

12. Richard Wright, "'He Died by Them,' Hero's Widow Tells of Rescue of Negro Children," *Daily Worker*, December 6, 1937, 1

13. James Weldon Johnson, *Challenge* 1, no. 1 (1934): 2.

14. Rudolph Fisher, "Harlem Manor," review of *Infants of the Spring* by Wallace Thurman, *New York Herald-Tribune*, February 21, 1932, 16.

15. F. Scott Fitzgerald, "Echoes of a Jazz Age," in *The Crack-Up*, ed. Edmund Wilson (New York: New Directions, 1945), 22.

16. Langston Hughes, *The Big Sea: An Autobiography* (New York: Hill and Wang, 1940), 228.

17. Dorothy West, "Dear Reader," *Challenge* 2, no. 1 (1937): 41.

18. Margaret Walker, *Richard Wright: Daemonic Genius* (New York: Warner, 1988), 61.

19. Ibid., 77.

20. Richard Wright, editorial, *New Challenge* 2, no. 1 (1937): 4.

21. Richard Wright, "Blueprint for Negro Writing," *New Challenge*, 2, no. 1 (Fall 1937): 4.

22. Richard Wright, *Letters to Joe C. Brown*, ed. Thomas Knipp (Kent, Ohio: Kent State University Libraries, 1968), esp. 8–11. In most of the ten letters in this collection, not authorized by Wright's widow, Ellen, Wright is asking for or relaying news on the "old crowd" he grew up with in Jackson, Mississippi.

23. Norman Sylvain, "La Jeune Litterature Haitienne," *La Revue Indigene* 1, no. 2 (Autumn 1927): 42.

24. Jean Price-Mars, *So Spoke the Uncle* (repr., Washington, D.C.: Three Continents Press, 1983), 178.

25. Carolyn Fowler, *A Knot in the Thread* (Washington, D.C.: Howard University Press, 1980), 209.

26. "A Nos Aimes dans la Carriere," editorial, *La Releve* 1, no.1 (1931): 1.

27. Brent Edwards, *The Practice of Diaspora* (Cambridge: Harvard University Press, 2003), 178–79, 195.

28. Aime Cesaire, "Jeunesse noire et Assimilation," *L'Etudiant Noir* 1, no. 1 (1931): 1. Adrien Pouille translated the excerpts from this journal, *La Releve*, and *Légitime Defense* from the French.

29. Etienne Lero, Thelus Lero, Rene Menil, et al., [untitled], *Légitime Defense* 1, no. 1 (1932): 1–2.

30. Editorial, *La Revue du monde noir* 1, no. 1 (1931): 2.

31. Alioune Diop, *Presence Africaine* 1 (November–December 1947): 186. Wright was a translator of Diop's essay.

32. Ibid., 192.

33. Hoyt Fuller, "Editorial Note," *Black World*, May 1970, 5.

34. Jean Bernabe, Patrick Chamoiseau, and Raphael Confiant, eds., *In Praise of Creoleness*, trans. M. B. Taleb-Khyar (Paris: Gallimard, 1993), 75–76.

Chapter 7

Horace Cayton

No Road Home

DAVID T. BAILEY

Black Metropolis has maintained its position in the pantheon of African American scholarship even though it is sixty years since its publication. Yet, Horace Cayton, one of its authors and the director of the WPA research project on which it was based, has faded from memory. He is one of the lost figures of the Black Chicago Renaissance. At least part of the reason for his disappearance from our collective memory was self-inflicted. More than many of his contemporaries, Cayton struggled constantly and profoundly with what it meant to be a black man in midcentury America. His *personal* turmoil often took him away from the main stages of intellectual life. It is particularly important to place him in the context of the Black Chicago Renaissance, however, because it was in Chicago, for almost two decades, that he seemed to find a place for himself, a home.

When Cayton arrived there, Chicago seemed to him a world of endless wonders. Born in Seattle, Washington, in 1903, he came east in 1931 to begin graduate work in the University of Chicago sociology de-

partment. Much later, he recalled his reaction: "Never had I seen so many Negroes; it came as a shock to see so many dark faces." In the Seattle of his youth, the largest minority group was Native American. According to the 1930 U.S. census, 328,972 African Americans were in Illinois, most living in a small area south of the Chicago Loop. In Seattle in 1930, the census reported 6,840 "Negroes," with about two-thirds living in King County. Cayton's father, Horace Sr., the leading black journalist in Seattle, and his mother, Susie, a social reformer and clubwoman, knew or knew of most black families in Seattle. Cayton felt "unprepared for this sea of black, olive, and brown faces" overwhelming his senses on the South Side of Chicago.[1] W. E. B. Du Bois, who had grown up in the small black community of Great Barrington, Massachusetts, first came to understand what it meant to live in black America when he went to college in Nashville, Tennessee. Almost as a cultural echo forty years later, Cayton felt similarly disoriented and confused by his confrontation with black Chicago.

Just as Du Bois would plunge into an intensive investigation of black Philadelphia in part as a way to begin to understand himself, Cayton knew that if he learned from Chicago, he would know a lot about what it meant to be black in America: "Understand Chicago's black belt and I would understand the black belts of a dozen other large American cities." He soon understood that pluralism was no less present on the South Side of Chicago than it was anywhere else in America. There was no singular black community; rather, "the lives of the people were as varied as their faces." Black men and women provided many of the services, from nurses to undertakers. Churches seemed everywhere, some with unfamiliar names: What did the Hebrew Baptists believe? Although the depression was reaching high tide, there was a puzzling vibrancy to life in South Side Chicago: "[T]he vigor with which these people lived belied the obvious fact that it was a poverty-stricken ghetto."[2] He later told Studs Terkel, "I had a romantic notion about the black belt, the cabarets, the jazz, the life . . . but the grimness of hunger, of cold and no place to sleep, people actually freezing, it shocked me to my death."[3]

One of his first experiences in Chicago was to witness a rent strike. It led to his first publication, an essay in The Nation, that he called "The Black Bugs." He looked out the window of a restaurant, he said, and "saw a number of Negroes walking by, three abreast, forming a long uninterrupted line." He went outside to find they were Communists, and, out of curiosity, he joined in line. The marchers were trying to force landlords to let evicted tenants back into their apartments, and the march ended in a rally, which the police violently broke up. Cayton's tone is one of sadness, resignation, and quiet anger. "Then I realized," he writes, "that all these people had suddenly found themselves face to face with hard, cold reality."[4]

Early Life

Cayton had already learned a bit about hard, cold reality. His route to Chicago was a complicated one. He spent his youth in 1920s Seattle, searching for his place in society. He dropped out of school to work on steamships heading north to Alaska and south to Mexico. After a couple of scrapes with the law, he was briefly sent to reform school, and when he finally returned to high school, he was much older than his fellow students and had the reputation as

a tough kid; he soon dropped out again. In an early autobiographical essay, he called this "a period of unadjustment and despondency, which finally turned into dissipation."[5] After more wandering from job to job, Cayton finally decided to finish high school through courses offered by the Seattle YMCA. When he finally received his high-school diploma, Cayton was twenty-two, and he now felt that time was slipping by. He immediately enrolled at the University of Washington, where he initially took the practical route of a business administration degree. In part to support himself, he took a job as a deputy sheriff for Kings County, where he worked on the vice squad, a particularly busy part of law enforcement during prohibition. Both his past experience with delinquency and his new job led him to a class with a young and exciting professor who had just arrived on campus, Norman S. Hayner.

Born in Beijing of missionary parents, Hayner had been an undergraduate at the University of Washington after serving in France during World War I. He decided to take a PhD in sociology, and in the wake of the publication of The Polish Peasant in Europe and America, William Thomas and Florian Znaniecki's monumental study, the University of Chicago seemed to be the place to be. Hayner's diary entries of his first years in graduate school are filled with anxiety, excitement, and a search for both spiritual and secular meaning, along with more mundane concerns about getting ahead in his newly chosen profession. Among these was the quest for an adviser, and eventually, a little reluctantly, he joined the growing cadre of young men and women following Robert Park on his travels around Chicago.[6]

Park was the center of the emerging Chicago school of sociology, and students like Hayner came in a flood to engage in the interview-based research that Park championed. The place seemed all the more exciting when, with Park's encouragement and support, Charles S. Johnson wrote the monumental study of the causes and results of the postwar race riots in Chicago, The Negro in Chicago. At first, Hayner found Park a bit fuzzy to understand, but when he spent a day walking through Chicago and seeing how essential shoe leather was to the techniques Park was pioneering, Hayner became more and more a true believer. His 1921 master's thesis, "The Effects of Prohibition on Packingtown," whetted his appetite for the rich and dense research in his 1923 dissertation, "The Hotel: the Sociology of Hotel Life." The students working with Park and his colleague Ernest Burgess left little unexplored in Chicago life. Hoboes, gang members, and taxi-hall dancers received the same careful study that Hayner deployed in looking at hotel denizens.

When Cayton encountered him in the classroom, Hayner was bursting with the evangelical message of Chicago-style sociology, and Cayton was beginning to study Seattle-area criminals with the same rigor he had brought to hotel tenants. Hayner's enthusiasm was contagious, and Cayton entered the graduate program in sociology. His early autobiographical sketches for Hayner suggest that he thought sociology might begin to answer questions that had been swirling around in his mind for much of his youth.

Through academics, Cayton began to look backward into his family history to attempt to understand the nature of his rebellious adolescence. He spent much of his life haunted by the collapse of his family's fortunes. Perhaps even more important, his maternal grandfather was Hiram Revels, who had been elected in 1870 as the first African American member of the U.S. Senate. The Caytons lived in a comfortable house on Capitol Hill in Seattle, and Horace Sr. was, for a time, reasonably well-accepted in both black and white society. When Booker T. Washington came to Seattle in 1909, he stayed with the Caytons, and over the dining room table, Horace Sr. and Washington debated the issues of the proper role of blacks in American society. Horace Sr. took the Du Bois side of the debate.[7]

Cayton recalled that, at least when he was a child, the racial divide was muted in Seattle: "At that time there were not many Negroes here and for the most part my brother and sisters and I lived and participated in the general culture of the area to an extent which is not possible now, for with the increase in the Negro population the race line sharpened and toughened to set them apart from the rest of the people." Nevertheless, in ways big and small, he was made to understand that he was different; "one's difference was rather like an accident, like having some slight physical deformity, like being slightly deaf, tongue-tied, or having a misshapen foot."[8] When he proudly told his fifth-grade class that his grandfather had been a U.S. Senator, his teacher refused to believe him. When he insisted, she answered that perhaps he was telling the truth, because "a lot of 'ignorant darkies' were elected to the Senate during the reconstruction days."[9]

In the middle of the 1910s, however, this somewhat genteel existence collapsed for the Cayton family, while young Horace began to see that his vague "otherness" had deeper and more profoundly painful meaning. When, in 1894, Horace Sr. founded his newspaper, the *Seattle Republican*, he viewed it as only partly a paper devoted to the tiny African American community in the Puget Sound area. Just as important, it served as a party organ, expressing the views of the reform wing of the Republican Party in Seattle. He would soon become a great advocate of Theodore Roosevelt. The *Republican*, at its peak, was the second most widely circulated newspaper in Washington State.

As race relations in both Seattle and the nation as a whole began to deteriorate dramatically after the turn of the century, Horace Sr. devoted more and more space to the coverage of lynchings, riots, and other racial atrocities. His readership gradually began to shift, and by the 1910s, he was experiencing regular resistance to his views. When he was refused service at the Epler Cafeteria in Seattle (whose motto was "serves you right"), he sued to force into the open the increasing bigotry of the merchants in the city. The suit, with attendant unpleasant revelations about his arrest long before in Kansas, fanned the increasing antagonism toward Horace Sr. in the white community. By 1917, he was forced to shut the presses down, and although he continued to be active in publishing, he was in many ways a crushed man.

As the family fortunes collapsed, young Horace found that the racial divide was much more powerful than he had understood as a child. Horace was told by his high school principal that he could not dance with a white girl. He went to a cheap restaurant in Portland and was told, "We don't serve niggers here." He was dragged out of the whites-only section of a theater and jailed for violating the color line. Seattle, for all of its vaunted radicalism, proved to be fully part of the American racial system, and Cayton felt, for the rest of his life, a persistent sense of anxiety and despair over the loss of his innocence and his emerging sense of his identity as one of the many oppressed members of American society.

The more he studied sociology at the University of Washington, the more he began to have tools with which to understand and analyze his anxieties. Cayton began to see that the issues that so troubled him were not the results of psychological maladjustment but were indeed subjects worthy of scholarly study:

"Then I discovered that my problem was no different from any other Negro's except that it was perhaps intensified by the fact that the relative freedom of the Northwest in those early years had allowed me to gain more acceptance and hence to develop more completely the aspirations which all Americans have."[10] He came to temper his naive view of endless possibility with an understanding of the realities of the complex social system and his place in it. When he took Roderick McKenzie's course on the complex nature of American racism, he learned of the Chinese exclusion act and other ways in which the political and social system conspired to place whites above all other groups in society.

When Robert Park came to Seattle, one of Cayton's professors arranged an interview for Cayton. He knew by now that Park was the central figure in the transformation of sociology that had been taking place in Chicago. Later, Cayton recalled the meeting as tense and confrontational:

> I first met Park on the Pacific coast when I was an undergraduate at the University of Washington. One of the professors had arranged an interview for me with Park during which I told him that I was interested in Negro history. He replied that Negroes didn't have any history, which angered me a great deal and I replied that everyone had a history, even the chair that he was sitting in. I made a great fuss and finally left under not too polite circumstances. I had decided that I would never look him up, but when I ventured into his office a few years later he welcomed me with open arms. He'd been trying to feel me out, to get a rise out of me.[11]

> Cayton was a risk lover. Clearly, Chicago was the right school for anyone wanting to pursue a sociological study of racial oppression in America. Even though his meeting with Park had gone poorly, Cayton had the backing of two important advocates in McKenzie and Hayner, and by the early thirties Chicago sociology was much more than Burgess and Park: "When I finished college I had the determination to leave the place of my birth, to find a larger group with which to work, to assume a more responsible and satisfying position that it was possible for me to have in the small black ghetto of Seattle or in the twilight zone between the races."[12]

Early Career at the University of Chicago

The Chicago Sociology department of the interwar period was unique in its group commitment not only to scholarship about race but also to scholarship by members of racial minorities. Johnson had come to graduate school at Chicago in 1917, and he found that Park altogether lacked "the usual condescension and oily paternalism of which I had already seen too much."[13] Park not only embraced Johnson as a student, he provided crucial support in Johnson's first major research project, the report on the Chicago riots of 1919 that would eventually become the massive volume *The Negro in Chicago.* Park's role as mentor and friend was equally important in the career of E. Franklin Frazier. Park had written Frazier an enthusiastic letter attempting to recruit him into the graduate program at Chicago, where Park anticipated that Frazier could undertake a "thoroughgoing study of the Negro family."[14] When he took his master's degree at Clark University, Frazier had to tolerate the "scientific" racist theories of Frank Hankins, the author of *The Racial Basis of Civilization.* In sharp contrast, Park and his colleagues had created an atmosphere dominated by a spirit of serious and generous inquiry about race.

Ellsworth Faris chaired the department starting in 1925, and he brought in a rich array of scholars who could enhance and support the central concerns of Park and Burgess. When Cayton began his coursework, he was encouraged to range broadly, taking appropriate classes in economics and political science as well. In particular, Harold Gosnell took an interest in Cayton and hired him to help with research on Chicago politics. Like so many early social scientists, Gosnell came from a religious background; his father was a Methodist minister in Lockport, New York, where Gosnell was born in 1896.[15] In the 1920s, first as a graduate student and then a faculty member in Chicago's political science department, Gosnell puzzled over the origins and value of political machines. While Matthew Josephson and other writers decried machines as fonts of corruption, Gosnell saw, as early as 1923, that political machine bosses provided a crucial service in the mix of political interests; the boss was "busily engaged behind the scenes doing his part to bring about some kind of continuity out of a disintegrated administrative system, to pick out the least objectionable of the office-seekers, and to secure the cooperation of the governor and a two-chambered legislature made up of two hundred localists."[16] By the 1930s, Gosnell fully understood that machine politics served as a means of distributing power to those who might not get noticed in less "corrupt" systems, and Chicago became, for him, an important test bed for

his ideas. Goswell, along with his colleagues in political science, Harold Lasswell and Charles Merriam,
began to work closely with Park's Society of Social
Research. Cayton, along with other like-minded sociology students, moved back and forth among the offices of members of the society, less concerned than
most graduate students at the time with establishing
a fixed location within a discipline.

When he asked Cayton to work with him, Gosnell
had already begun to see the advantages that machine government in Chicago had for residents of the
South Side. Not only were black migrants from the
south mostly of voting age and, unlike immigrants,
the black migrants, already citizens, also quickly
made up an enormous percentage of voters. "When
it is considered that one in every twelve of the adult
citizens in Chicago [in 1930] is a Negro," Gosnell
said, "it is clear that here is a factor of great political significance."[17] Cayton proved an energetic and
enthusiastic assistant, as he was sent off to interview
policemen and learn about the nexus between politics
and crime: "This took me to police precinct stations
and into the homes of black policemen from the rank
of patrolman to lieutenant. It also made me aware
for the first time of the ramifications of the numbers
rackets, which reached out beyond the black belt to
the offices of the mayor, the governor, and perhaps
even beyond."[18] Cayton's work in the sheriff's office
in Seattle had given him a level of comfort with police
often lacking in a community where police were
sometimes seen as a hostile occupying force, and in
particular he was fascinated by using this subset of
South Side Chicago life to begin to understand the
ways in which urban and rural sensibilities continued
to interact. He was particularly intrigued by those
older policemen who had never fully accommodated
themselves to life in the big city, "for in their lives one
saw clearly the stresses and strains which accompany
a change from peasant life in the South to urban
existence in this jungle of concrete and steel."[19]

The excerpts from his interviews that appear in
Negro Politicians demonstrate how well Cayton managed to gain the trust of the police. One, for example,
told Cayton, "They wanted to get me for two reasons,
first, I was a Negro and they didn't like Negroes, and
second, I didn't stand for any foolishness. I believe
that the law was made to enforce, not to make money
out of."[20] Cayton had the unusual ability to make
people from all layers of Chicago black society open

up to him, perhaps because he was simultaneously
an insider, a black man, and an outsider, a migrant
from the exotic northwest.

A small number of the manuscript interviews
Cayton undertook for Gosnell have survived, and they
demonstrate yet one more of his talents. Cayton had
always resisted his status as a member of Seattle's
black elite, yet he could talk to the "talented tenth" in
Chicago almost as an intimate. Throughout his life,
he retained an ambivalent relationship with the black
elite, and in Chicago he tried to navigate between his
status as a researcher and graduate student at the
University of Chicago on the one hand and an activist for the needs of oppressed blacks on the other.
This ambivalence is reflected in the small number of
interviews he undertook in 1932 concerning Archibald J. Carey. AME Bishop Carey had wielded enormous social and political power on the South Side
for almost two decades, but by the 1930s his coziness
with corruption had started to grate on some younger
black leaders. One of Cayton's interview subjects told
him, "Of course as I said before, some of the Negro
leaders are pretty lax. Take for example Bishop Carey,
he was supposed to be a man of God and a force for
uplift in the community. But he was a bad egg. He
was a bad influence both for the Negro community
and for the city as a whole."[21]

Cayton quickly became known as an excellent
researcher, and because he was slightly older and
more experienced than many of his colleagues, he
found himself flooded with opportunities. The most
attractive came from Johnson, who continued to keep
an eye out for excellent talent at his alma mater. After
his work in Chicago, Johnson had edited *Opportunity*
for the National Urban League in New York, and in
1927, he moved to Fisk University, Nashville, Tennessee, where he created a nationally noted center in
research on the sociology of black America. In 1933,
Johnson had been asked by Harold Ickes, Franklin
Roosevelt's Secretary of the Interior, to create a Committee on Negroes in the Economic Reconstruction
to study how much blacks benefited from New Deal
policies. Johnson was already busy on a number of
assignments, especially the research for *Shadow of
the Plantation*. Because he viewed this as an important opportunity, he was willing to collaborate with
Will Alexander and Edwin Embree on a study of the
agricultural sector, which would serve as the basis
for *The Collapse of Cotton Tenancy* (1935). Johnson also

encouraged Arthur Raper to look closely at the plantation system in Georgia, which resulted in *Preface to Peasantry* (1936).

Johnson asked George S. Mitchell to write the sections of the industrial volume concerning the south. Mitchell, an economist, a Rhode Scholar, and son of the former president of the University of South Carolina, had all of the credentials necessary to undertake the project. He had already published *The Industrial Revolution in the South* (1930) with his brother Broadus. In 1931, he published *Textile Unionism and the South*. Cayton could offer no similar resume, but he was, by now, a full member in the Robert Park network. That was apparently enough recommendation for Johnson, and Cayton began a yearlong research project, during which Cayton interviewed hundreds of workers, with a primary emphasis on the steel and meatpacking industries. Mitchell and Cayton worked in parallel rather than in collaboration, and when *Black Workers and the New Unions* was published in 1939, Cayton had written about two-thirds of the text.

Cayton's first section in *Black Workers and the New Unions*, a study of blacks in the iron and steel industries, runs well over two hundred pages. It is a small masterpiece. In the first pages, he coolly presents statistical data that highlight job stratification. The detached tone soon gives way, but with a particular flair, as Cayton uses the voices of the hundreds of men and women he interviewed to lay out an indictment of the racial line on the shop floor. One worker in Duquesne, Pennsylvania, for example, told Cayton

> In the labor department the colored has a hard way to go. They leave the white get more time than the colored. There was nothing you could do about it. They were given hot and dirty work and they rushed you. They would bawl you out and make you work fast. You have to crawl into the checkers with a hoe; the checkers are about 2 ½ to 3 feet high. You are hot already and that dust and soot—First you get a headache and then the stomach bothers you and then you have to come out or someone will have to carry you out. You always have to put boards down and bags around your knees and you still feel the heat on your knees. Colored and white are given this work but colored are given this type of work mostly. They put colored in the hot checkers especially on hot days.

Cayton's analysis gains greater focus as he details the long history of organized labor in the steel industry. As he describes each attempt to bring unions to factories, he explains, again with telling use of

testimony of black workers, how solidarity collapsed over the issue of race. In a particularly fascinating account, he describes how company unions used the threat of communist organizing drives to prevent any meaningful representation. The threat the communists posed was not their Marxist ideology but rather their insistence that blacks must be full members of the union. Black workers, Cayton notes, felt caught between the racial prejudices of their fellow workers and the bigotry of management. Early Depression attempts by unions amalgamated with the American Federation of Labor (AFL) promised little to black workers: "After the passage of the National Industrial Recovery Act (NIRA) (1933), the union officialdom went through its customary superficial gestures of accepting the Negro steel worker, but it was not anxious either to accept him as a full and equal member or to face the problems incident to his organization."[22]

Cayton ends his section on the iron and steel industry on a note of cautious optimism, as he describes the ways in which the Congress of Industrial Organizations (CIO) attempted to break from past racial practices of organized labor. To be sure, he notes, the rhetoric of the leadership decried racist practices of job segregation. To be sure, the CIO had hired a number of black labor organizers. But distrust still flowed under the surface: "The Negro has been isolated from the main body of white workers for years and has considered whites his implicit enemy." How could workers give up well-earned distrust for their new union brothers? At the same time, whites "had not overcome their antipathy to Negroes in many instances, and although the union had adopted the policy of including Negroes in all social events, this was usually tolerated only because it was generally felt that for the present it was necessary."[23]

In the last section of the book, Cayton tries to lay out an argument for a future in which race will play an ever-decreasing role in the story of labor. He allows himself a moment in which he imagines that education and regulation can go a great distance toward curing the evils that the book so carefully articulates. Good will and intellectual leadership, he argues, are available and important. Ultimately, however, he asserts that change will come only when black workers conclude that they will no longer accept their status at the bottom of the wage scale. For him, the idea of a separate black economy is a myth, "just another escapist mechanism" like Garveyism.[24]

Perhaps Cayton's greatest problem as a young black intellectual in the 1930s is that he had little use for the sometimes clear but simple solutions to social problems posed by radicals of the era. His younger brother Revels had joined the Communist Party, and he had even convinced their mother to join at the end of her life. However, Cayton argues in *Black Workers and the New Unions* that communists used black workers for their own ends no less than did management when it rounded up blacks to be strikebreakers. Becoming a pawn in a white chess game had no appeal for Cayton. His increased sophistication as a social scientist left him seeking concrete answers, not answers that led to further troubles and questions. Underlying his training was the philosophical tradition of pragmatism coming out of William James and John Dewey.

The Chicago School, at least at its height when Cayton first arrived at the university, derived a certain degree of its intellectual power from pragmatism. Park had worked with Dewey and had been a student of James; he remembered when James read "A Certain Blindness in Human Beings" to his Harvard class.[25] James insisted on generosity, on taking seriously the desires and dreams of others, no matter how confusing we might find them. James's analysis "absolutely forbids us to be forward in pronouncing on the meaninglessness of forms of existence other than our own; and it commands us to tolerate, respect, and indulge those whom we see harmlessly interested and happy in their own ways, however unintelligible these may be to us."[26] Park taught his students that experience, in all its richness and myriad manifestations, must be taken seriously. Within this intellectual community, policy proposals should be based upon a dense understanding of human needs and desires, weighed against what might actually work in the real world.

Cayton did not find this knowledge easy to take. Indeed, the more he learned about working life in Chicago and the more he understood about the still somewhat foreign life of South Side Chicago, the more it weighed on him. Perhaps he had used up his font of anger in his youthful rebellion against his parents. He had struggled with depression, and it returned with a vengeance, and he sought comfort or escape in alcohol and drugs. He had married Bonnie Branch, a white woman from Olympia, before he had come east, and they had found that mixed-race marriages did not sit well with either black or white

sensibilities in Chicago. They fought, and this added to Cayton's depression. He began a series of affairs, and Bonnie finally walked out on him. By the fall of 1934, Cayton came close to a total collapse. Park arranged for time off, and Mitchell arranged for a stay in an Ontario lodge east of Sault Ste. Marie. He then returned to Chicago, where his sister nursed him back to a modicum of mental health, and he developed a new romantic relationship with a fellow graduate student, a white woman named Elizabeth Johns. (She would later marry St. Clair Drake, Cayton's collaborator on *Black Metropolis*.) Cayton, Johns, and a Swedish exchange student hit on the idea of a trip to Europe. They sailed on a ship flying the Nazi flag, but Cayton showed little interest in the coming disaster in Europe. Instead, he used the time to learn about Paris and to be treated as something of a celebrity because of his race. Nancy Cunard, the heiress to the shipping fortune, showed him around Paris. In his fascinating and unreliable memoir *Long Old Road*, Cayton describes the encounter as all but a mortal combat for his identity. Cunard, he recalled, wanted him to express outrage at the treatment of blacks in the United States. Cayton had just come off a year of personal crisis, and he did not need a rich English woman explaining his blackness to him. He also resented the fact that she seemed to be willing to sleep with him if he would only agree with her. "There was such superiority about her manner, as if she were dealing with a child," he said. "Underneath this preoccupation with Negroes, she was still the haughty upper-class Englishwoman telling an inferior what he should do."[27]

When he returned to the United States, Cayton was immediately offered a job at Fisk by Charles Johnson. He had taught one summer at Tuskegee Institute, so southern race relations did not come as a complete surprise, but once again Cayton found himself in a place where he wasn't sure he belonged: "There was less fear of physical violence from white people there than at Tuskegee, but the possibility was always in the air. Nashville was rigidly segregated, and accommodations for Negroes were crude and inadequate."[28] On a personal and professional level, however, Fisk was fine. He met and married his second wife, an engaging black woman, Irma Jackson, who was working on a master's degree in social work. Johnson and the other sociologists were stimulating. Most important, Park had retired from Chicago and was now teaching at Fisk. Park's optimistic assumption that assimilation would be the inevitable result of the "race relations cycle" still had some appeal for Cayton, but more important, he simply enjoyed the fellowship with an elder whom he deeply admired.

While at Fisk, Cayton met Du Bois; it was a somewhat more complicated experience than Cayton might have expected. His father had considered Du Bois to be the true leader of black America, and Cayton had much in common with the great old man, intellectually and personally. Du Bois had somewhat different interests. He was meeting Shirley Graham, an instructor at Tennessee Agricultural and Industrial College for a brief extramarital fling, and Graham had asked the Caytons if she might use their spare bedroom. To be sure, there were no appropriate hotels available in Nashville, and Du Bois did not want to be seen at Fisk. Cayton did get an evening's conversation with Du Bois out of the experience.[29]

The Cayton-Warner Research

After a year at Fisk, Cayton was ready to return to Chicago and finish his work in graduate school. Though Park was gone, a next generation of Chicago sociologists carried on the tradition, most notably Louis Wirth, who had already developed a close relationship with Cayton. A German-Jewish immigrant, Wirth was deeply concerned with the experiences of minorities in America, and he had written his dissertation under Park. *The Ghetto* was a study of the Jewish community in Chicago. He was currently working on his major theoretical work, "Urbanism as a Way of Life." Influenced by Durkheim, Wirth argued that urbanism had fostered alienation and artificiality in relationships, but he also emphasized the ways in which voluntary organizations served to ameliorate some of the psychosocial effects of city life.[30]

Cayton also met a new faculty member, W. Lloyd Warner, who would prove equally important in his career. In the tradition of interdisciplinary work Park had fostered, Warner, with a PhD in anthropology from Harvard, was in fact jointly appointed in sociology and anthropology. Warner had begun a long and complex study of Newburyport, Massachusetts, as something of a response to the work of the Robert Staughton Lynds in Muncie, Indiana. Ultimately, this project, known as the Yankee City, yielded five volumes, and Warner also had the unusual distinction of being satirized by John Marquand in his novel *Point of No Return*. Allison Davis, one of the few black

students at Harvard, began working with Warner, and Warner helped arrange funding for Davis to begin the field work in Mississippi and Louisiana that would ultimately produce *Deep South and Children of Bondage*.[31]

Warner had good connections for the just-created Writers' Project of the Work Projects Administration (WPA), and he envisioned a thorough-going study of black life in Chicago. When Warner asked Cayton if he would like to participate, he jumped at the possibility. The massive scale of the project they first envisioned seemed to both Warner and Cayton somewhat hard to pitch to the WPA: "What Warner and I actually had in mind was too complex and sophisticated to submit as a project, so we decided to say that we planned to study the problem of juvenile delinquency in the Negro community and under that specific authorization proceed to study the entire social structure of the Negro community and its relationship to the rest of Chicago."[32]

Warner quickly ceded day-to-day control of the project to Cayton, who began to hire a staff of interviewers, researchers, and typists. Many were graduate students, but Cayton also included undergraduates and people from the community in his attempt to bring local knowledge to the project. He estimated that over the life of the project, the government employed over 150 workers to help gather data, process it, and begin to analyze it. This WPA project was in fact only one of two underway in Chicago. The major project, associated with the creation of several "American Guides," ran out of an office in the Loop. Although a few black writers worked there (most notably Richard Wright, Margaret Walker, Katherine Dunham, and Arna Bontemps), it was dominated by such young white intellectuals as Jack Conroy, Nelson Algren, and Saul Bellow.

The Negro in Illinois project remained more than a mile south and, in many ways, a world away from the intellectual excitement in the downtown office. Thousands of interviews were conducted, including a large number of life histories. Cayton found it hard to manage by himself, and a young anthropology graduate student had just arrived on campus who proved more than able to take on some of the burden. John Gibbs St. Clair Drake was born in Virginia in 1911, the son of a schoolteacher and a Baptist minister. His father was from Barbados, and he briefly had worked as an organizer for Marcus Garvey's Universal Negro Improvement Association, taking the family north to Pittsburgh, Pennsylvania, and then back to Virginia.

Drake went to Hampton Institute, where he joined student rebellion against the paternalistic attempts to control their every action. Although he majored in biology, he came under the powerful influence of Allison Davis, who had taken time away from Harvard to reconsider his place in academics.

Davis became Drake's first mentor. He was only nine years older, but Davis had been to Harvard and had a network of important contacts. Davis had concluded that anthropology provided a richer set of possibilities than literary criticism for understanding black experiences. Drake was at first puzzled. Why would a brilliant teacher of literature shift to anthropology? Much later, at the end of his own career, he decided it had to do with the Depression and the ways in which Davis and his peers "became very self-conscious about what obligations black intellectuals had to the masses."[33]

After Drake graduated, Davis arranged in 1935 for him to teach at Pendle Hill, a remarkable Quaker school where Richard Gregg was teaching students the ideas of Mohandas Gandhi. This led to a year teaching at Christiansburg Normal Industrial Institute, a Quaker school in western Virginia. The problem, Drake found, was that this segregated education, however well-meaning on the part of the Quakers, simply supported the regime in Virginia. When Davis asked him to join his research team in Natchez, Mississippi, therefore, Drake jumped at the opportunity.

The Deep South project was supported and nominally run by W. Lloyd Warner, Davis's mentor at Harvard. Warner had rather rigid theories of how caste worked in the south, and Davis and his wife lived in the black community while their partners in the project, Burleigh and Jackie Gardner, lived in the white community. Davis was so identified with upper-class black members that the project was getting skewed toward the elite. Warner wanted to study caste in the south, and this system was not as apparent from discussions mostly with highly educated black professionals. He wanted Drake to interview the rest of Natchez black society: "It was my job to move to the black lower-class community and do that part of the ethnography on the bars, juke-houses, shouting churches and general lower-class areas."[34]

As the fieldwork in Mississippi slowly wound down in 1937, Davis encouraged Drake to apply for a Rosenwald Foundation fellowship and begin graduate work in sociology and anthropology. Davis and

Warner also vouched for Drake with Johnson: "No one got grants unless Charles Johnson agreed, which he did in my case."[35] Warner was now at the University of Chicago, so Drake found himself joining in the excitement and seriousness of Hyde Park. Cayton needed someone who could help bring sense out of the Negro in Illinois project, and the partnership was forged from necessity and a common desire to cover Chicago as carefully as Muncie, Newburyport, and Natchez.

Both men found the project a wonderful opportunity and yet a great burden. Drake recalled that his "first five years of graduate work involved a shuttling between classrooms of Chicago and the streets, churches, and kitchenettes of *Black Metropolis*. What I gained from intensive participant-observation, I lost in diminished contact with peers in the anthropology department and a reduced volume of reading."[36] Although Drake ultimately did receive his PhD, Cayton never quite could find the time to complete the requirements for the program. He did apply for a Rosenwald grant to allow him to focus on graduate work, but activism of a different kind caught his attention. He had been seeking more of a place in the South Side communities, and he found what he had been seeking in the creation of the Parkway Community House.

Parkway Community House

Good Shepherd Baptist Church was one of the older and better-established South Side congregations. Reverend Harold H. Kingsley had built it into a middle-class enclave in a fairly poor neighborhood, and the very active women's organizations within the church decided that a community center would help deal with some of the problems for children in the neighborhood. There was some local sentiment that the Good Shepherd members thought that they were just a bit superior; one of the interviewees in the Negro in Illinois project said, "There are some people who have gone to Good Shepherd church and have never returned because they think the congregation is too stiff, stating that the congregation didn't seem to accept them along with the other church people."[37] Another felt certain that the community center would help: "I think it will be one of the best things that has happened to the community in general, and with Reverend Kingsley heading the campaign I can see no reason why it will not be realized."[38]

After a successful fund-raising drive, the center opened in 1938, with several of the leading black clubwomen, educators, and professional women serving on its board. The Negro in Illinois project had received its WPA funding through the sponsorship of the American Youth Commission, and although the research had taken Cayton and his staff far beyond their initial mandate, he saw the Good Shepherd Community Center as a wonderful ally, and gradually he moved the staff and the ever-increasing volume of paperwork off campus and into this community location.[39]

Almost immediately, the center had outgrown its space, and Cayton seized the opportunity to expand its program to include a training center and dormitories. He helped raise money to buy the somewhat deteriorated Chicago Orphan Asylum at South Parkway and Fifty-First Street and create the Parkway Community Center. After some complex negotiations with the board, Cayton was named director in December 1939.[40]

Cayton's ambition was to make Parkway into much more than just another variant on the settlement-house theme. He viewed Parkway as a centerpiece for the thriving black intellectual and social scene in Chicago at the end of the Depression. He wanted it to be a place where visiting scholars, artists, writers, and performers could feel at home. Perhaps he was remembering that when he first arrived in Chicago, there was no good place for a visiting black man to hang his hat. "Our intimate friends," Cayton recalled, "were the younger intellectuals. They were a mixed lot of Negroes and whites, many with left-wing leanings. Prominent among them was Langston Hughes, who on his annual speaking tour would often stay with us for a month at a time."[41]

Cayton expanded his net to include any bright, young black persons in Chicago as members and participants in the life of the Parkway Center. A member of the WPA staff in the Chicago Loop, Arna Bontemps, had not yet met Cayton, but he received a letter asking him to come to Parkway. "We do not assume," Cayton wrote, "that this HOUSE is the only answer to working out a program of racial amenity. We do feel, however, that we play a vital role in interpreting to the larger white community and to the smaller Negro community, the hopes, fears, and aspirations of each other."[42]

Cayton also helped develop a wide range of performances that brought music and theater to the community, whose members were less than likely to head north to the opera house or the concert halls and theaters in the Loop. Helen Spaulding based her Skyloft Players at Parkway, who then performed in a variety of venues throughout the South Side.[43] Cayton soon discovered, however, that a part-time impresario had more headaches than he had expected. He wrote Bontemps about one well-known visitor, the "father of the blues": "I am not particularly interested in having a press conference for Mr. [W. C.] Handy, as I found him very cheap. Last time he was here we went to considerable expense and trouble and put him up for some time without charge, and he has never made even a contribution of a dollar to the Center."[44]

Cayton enjoyed the excitement he had fostered at the center, and he even seems to have enjoyed sparring with Reverend Kingsley over the political views of some of the speakers.[45] More and more, however, he seemed again torn by two opposing tendencies. On the one hand, he enjoyed the group project of building a community center, the complex webs of association and activism that developed, almost for the first time, on the South Side. Yet, at the same time, Cayton wanted to stand apart, as critic, observer, analyst. In a column in the *Pittsburgh Guardian*, Cayton wrote admiringly about A. Phillip Randolph, "(O)ne of the darker clan cannot help but look at Randolph's career and think of him sitting in the White House and talking to two Presidents in the same calm, crisp, cultured English, and telling them what 'God loves' without feeling a surge of admiration."[46] Cayton hoped he would be able to use his many accomplishments as an organizer and writer so that he, too, could be received by the leading powers in America, and they would listen to what he had to say. He knew the value of cooperative action, but he also desired individual success. The Parkway Center ultimately did not provide him with enough of the latter.

Black Metropolis

The enormous quantities of raw data that the Cayton-Warner project produced soon became the source material for a remarkable number of books and dissertations. Two mimeographed volumes came out at the end of 1939 as reports of the WPA, one by Mary Elaine Ogden providing a statistical analysis of the black community, the other by Estelle Hill Scott, describing occupational status among black residents of Chicago. A third WPA mimeographed volume was Drake's first major publication, a careful study of black churches in Chicago, peppered with extensive quotes from the interviews. Drake also produced an even more extensive report based on the Negro in Illinois materials for Gunnar Myrdal's research, which would eventually serve as the underpinnings for part of *An American Dilemma*. Warner, with two collaborators, mined the interviews for material that was virtually the entire underlying data for *Color and Human Nature: Negro Personality Development in a Northern City*, published in 1941.

Cayton felt a bit put out when Warner went to Washington, D.C., to report on the project, leaving the day-to-day director behind.[47] To be sure, finishing *Black Workers and the New Unions* took whatever writing time he could spare. Soon, he had also begun to write one of the regular weekly columns for the *Pittsburgh Courier*, which he would continue for almost twenty years. But the eight thousand interviews provided enough material for many more volumes. Warner, Drake, and Cayton agreed to begin to draft as complete a study of Chicago as the materials would allow, but only Drake found the time to work on the manuscript. By 1944, he had completed over six hundred pages, and Cayton wrote to Warner that the book should have only two authors. Like the *Deep South* project, Warner had been crucial in providing the initial support, but the project had moved beyond him. Cayton wrote, "I have talked to Drake about this and he and I both feel that as the writing of the book will be done by us that this is a fair procedure which will acknowledge us as writers and you in your capacity as director." Warner understood collaborative projects, and he chose simply to provide a methodological note.[48]

Black Metropolis was published in 1945 to all but universal acclaim. Carter G. Woodson, always hard to please, noted that the book was "written in the language of the new social scientists," and he hoped that a more accessible version might follow.[49] More typical was Bucklin Moon's review in *The Nation*: "[I]t contains the clearest picture of what it means to be a Negro in America that I have ever encountered."[50]

Cayton wrote part 2 of the book, 241 dense pages covering the racial line in Chicago, job segregation, black access to the political system, and the development of what he may have first termed "the black ghetto," borrowing the term from the first book by his mentor Louis Wirth. The originality and depth

of the thinking in *Black Metropolis* have been well understood by scholars since its publication. What is perhaps most important is that neither Cayton nor Drake had much interest in maintaining the Park model anymore. Nor were they particularly careful to acknowledge Warner's ideas about caste. For them, the most important lesson of their more than eight hundred pages is that the color line exists in Chicago as much as in the south. Black residents responded to their exclusion from white institutions by creating their own separate, parallel structures. Yet, black persons also needed to compete for social and economic resources. It was the combination of competition and separation that creates the ghetto and sets the terms, they argue, for the future.[51]

Richard Wright

Everything seemed to be working well for Cayton in the early 1940s. His professional writing had begun to bring him enormous acclaim. The Parkway Center gave him a significant role in South Side culture. He began to meet and become friends with some of the major figures of black intellectual life. The most important of these, and the man who became a central part of Cayton's self-image, was Richard Wright. Wright remembered meeting Horace Cayton long before the publication of *Native Son*. Cayton was working in Wirth's office, and Wirth's wife was the social worker for the Wright family. "According to Dick, she made an appointment for him to talk with Wirth, and when he knocked I opened the office door because Dr. Wirth was out," Cayton recalled. "He claims I invited him in and showed him our files on Chicago and that he never forgot the enormous collection of facts and figures we had assembled or the methodological manner in which we had organized, classified and catalogued them."[52] Mary Wirth had already arranged for Wright to work cleaning everything from operating rooms to bed pans at Michael Reese Hospital,[53] and the connections with the Wirths led to his appointment as a member of the Chicago branch of the Federal Writer's Project when it began in 1935.[54]

It was only after *Native Son* became a cultural sensation that Cayton and Wright developed an intense, ultimately painful friendship. As part of his promotional tour for the book, Wright had arranged with *Life* magazine to do a photographic background article of Wright's Chicago, for which Wright contributed the words. Cayton served as host, and these two quite different men soon began to plan a variety of collaborations. Wright remembered the vast store of materials he had seen in Wirth's office, which had by now vastly expanded. Cayton happily offered to share them for Wright's 12 Million Black Voices, a collaboration with the photographer Edwin Rosskam. Wright was particularly gracious in the acknowledgments: "I take this opportunity to extend my thanks and appreciation to Mr. Horace R. Cayton, director of the Good Shepherd Community Center of Chicago, for his making available his immense file of materials on urban life among Negroes and, above all, for the advice and guidance which made sections of this book possible."[55] Cayton's influence seems strongest in the section on black labor, where Wright describes the ways in which management manipulated racial tensions to prevent unionization.[56] Wright had, by this point, broken with the Communist Party, and he had clearly begun to seek out alternative interpretations of capitalism. While Wright was working on 12 Million Black Voices, Cayton arranged a dinner party where Wright renewed his relationship with Louis and Mary Wirth. He asked Wirth for a bibliography so he could become more conversant with the ideas that had been pouring out of the University of Chicago.[57]

Upon its publication, Cayton reviewed 12 Million Black Voices in his column for the Pittsburgh Courier. He notes that he had been engaged in a huge research project on black persons in urban America but that his project would remain mostly the concern of specialists. Wright, on the other hand, brings all the skills of a "great writer" to the same material. The book, Cayton asserts, is "magnificent in its simplicity, directness and force." It serves, moreover, as a complement to Native Son, through articulating "the habitat, the social matrix from which warped social personalities such as Bigger Thomas arise and will continue to arise until there is some fundamental change in the position and social status of the American Negro." Cayton's column ends with a moving glimpse into the self-doubt that never left him for very long: "The society about which Wright wrote and which Rosskam illustrated just couldn't exist in America. . . . [B]ut it does, and for years my associates and I have tried to describe it by figures, maps and graphs. Now, Wright and Rosskam have told the story as it has never been told before."[58]

Although Wright was five years younger, Cayton began to look on him for emotional support and counsel. Increasingly, the intensity of Cayton's feelings for Wright reflected his deteriorating emotional state. From Seattle, Cayton wrote, "Dick, I've lived so many lives that I fear even psychoanalysts won't be able to orient me to the reality which is me." In another letter, he proclaims, "I have never met anyone with whom I could talk as freely and who seemed to understand what I was trying to do as yourself."[59] In many of his essays from the period, Cayton seems bound to the work and thought of his friend. "Frightened Children of Frightened Parents" begins with the assertion that "Richard Wright has had but one story to tell. That story is how it feels to be a Negro in the United States."[60] In another essay, Cayton begins by insisting "Richard Wright . . . has written more profoundly upon [racial] subjection than any other American student of the question."[61]

While there is more than a hint of obsession in Cayton's desire for an increasingly intimate relationship with Wright, there is little inkling from Wright's side that he viewed Cayton as much more than a good friend. To be sure, they talked about collaborating on a journal, American Pages, and Cayton had lined up part of the financial support from Claire Florsheim, daughter-in-law of Milton S. Florsheim, founder of Florsheim Shoe Company. Unfortunately, Marshall Field III, grandson of the famous retailer Marshall Field, ultimately decided not to provide the rest of the backing, and the project fell by the wayside. They had taken a trip to Fisk together, sharing an intense reaction to segregation. Most important, Wright agreed to write the introduction to Black Metropolis, providing it an intellectual and cultural cache that few scholarly works could claim. The introduction exceeded the best hopes of the authors. Wright proclaimed, "It is with a sense of keen pride that I undertake to introduce Black Metropolis, a landmark of research and scientific achievement, to the reading public."[62]

Margaret Walker, in her fascinating memoir/biography/critique of Wright, takes a characteristically tough-minded view of the Cayton-Wright friendship: "If Wright had become a lion, Cayton was a lionizer. In the den of the young lions, Wright had learned his way to be a lion. With Cayton there was a fraternizing like unto that of a blood brother."[63]

Walker also touches briefly on one other shared interest that drew Wright and Cayton together: "Both men shared a passion for high living, good food, wine, women and song, and had great sexual curiosity." Cayton was married four times, twice to the same woman. Wright was married twice, both to white women. According to Cayton (not, in such matters, a particularly reliable source, unfortunately), his relationship with Wright broke in part because of their rivalry for the attentions of a young woman. Wright had been visiting over Thanksgiving and stayed with Cayton. Two young women from Antioch College came to stay at Parkway. "One was an attractive Negro girl of possibly nineteen, the other a pretty, blond white girl," Cayton wrote. "When they heard that the author of *Native Son* was staying with me, they asked to meet him." The next day, Wright ducked out of a dinner date with Cayton to sleep with the young white woman, and then the next day he left town. The woman came to Cayton to ask where Wright had gone, and she was devastated to discover he had skipped town.

> She acted as if she had been struck by a blow and, walking over to my desk, she sat down and began to cry. On some strange impulse I led her through to my apartment and into my bedroom. She didn't utter a word or put up any resistance as I undressed her and took her to bed. I was as flabbergasted as she at my strange behavior.[64]

When they next met in New York, Cayton told Wright what he had done, and the relationship was never the same. When Wright died in France in 1960, the two men had barely had any contact in over a decade.

The Final Years

Cayton's behavior in breaking with Wright was only one example of dozens in which he seemed to lose his emotional balance. Indeed, almost immediately after the publication of *Black Metropolis*, Cayton fell into a tailspin of drugs, drink, and mental illness. Many of us pursue linear lives. Horace Cayton did not. He left Chicago in 1948 and moved to New York. Almost as if he were a character in his own picaresque novel, Cayton bounced from career to career, from failure to success to failure again, with sometimes alarming, almost-instantaneous transitions from one stage to the next. His name should be immediately recognized by anyone interested in African American history. His obscurity, however much it was self-inflicted, stands as one of the saddest facts of his often-sad life. I recently asked an African American student preparing for her orals in sociology what she thought of Horace Cayton. "Never heard of him," she replied.

Cayton rebounded somewhat when he moved to California in the 1960s. He taught occasionally at the University of California Berkeley, and he found the strength to write his memoir. J. Herman Blake, a black graduate student at Berkeley, found Cayton fascinating, and for several years they developed an intense friendship. Blake took a job at the University of California Santa Cruz, and Cayton moved nearby. Early in his time at Santa Cruz, Blake hosted a poetry reading by Leroi Jones, "and Horace came by to renew their acquaintance. Roi always showed great respect for the older warriors, and it was beautiful watching the two with each other." Another session was with Eldridge Cleaver, who said he read *Black Metropolis* while in prison "and came to really admire and respect Horace for the high quality of that work."[65]

Cayton had become fascinated with the idea of writing his own account of Richard Wright, and he threw himself into the project. He collected his own material; he undertook a set of interviews. He went to Paris filled with enthusiasm that he could continue the research, but in January 1970, he died alone in his hotel room. In his eulogy, Blake tried to make sense of a man who had so much to offer, who had accomplished so much, and who had spent so much of his life in such unhappiness: "This was a land most strange for Horace, he was truly a sojourner looking for a home. Yet what he sought was a peace of mind, an inner harmony which does not exist for any black man in this society. He sought it most diligently and in many ways believed that it was there to be found, if not by him then perhaps by others."[66]

Cayton's lost quest for "inner harmony," for a place in society that allowed him to be Horace Cayton but also to be a self-confident and self-expressive black man, may satisfy some who want to understand his role in the Black Chicago Renaissance. He was, by this interpretation, a tragic figure who lost himself in drugs, alcohol, and despair. Yet, key to the end of his life and the ways in which he seemed adrift and alone was the crucial choice he failed to make. Cayton understood, when he went to the University of Chicago, that academics fit him, and he fit well into academics. He loved the give-and-take of the classroom, the discussions with his colleagues, the myriad ways in which the life of the mind receives constant reinforcement in the university. His letters abound with a desire for just the connections that academics provide. Indeed, he regularly reengaged in academics throughout the over twenty years after he left Chicago, lecturing at City College in New York (1957–58), Berkeley (1962–64), and the University of Illinois (1967–68).[67] By the end of his life, Cayton seemed to have understood how much the discourse of intellectuals mattered to him.[68] Moreover, he sorely wanted to have a role in national policy, especially with the excitement of the Great Society programs. He wrote Ben Zimmerman, who was in charge of the Community Services Division of the Office of Economic Opportunity, providing his advice on race relations in San Francisco, Oakland, and Richmond. Zimmerman politely rebuffed any further offer of assistance Cayton might have made.[69]

The choice to enter more fully into the world of academics was not, of course, wholly Cayton's to make. Why his mentors at Chicago never convinced him to finish his PhD is impossible to say. Perhaps Cayton rebuffed them. Yet, his work on his two major books surpassed research that often passes for a dissertation. *Black Metropolis* is, arguably, the crowning achievement of the Chicago school of sociology. It is possible, had Cayton taken a position as a professor of sociology, that he could have taught a generation of black scholars how to continue in the tradition he had learned from Park and Wirth. By the mid-1960s, he had begun to envision a new project about Los Angeles, "Black Metropolis—West," but it went nowhere without the institutional support a university could provide. In the post–World War II era, a status as independent intellectual became less and less common, and Cayton simply needed an intellectual home.

The question is what home? At the University of Washington, he had learned what it means to be the only black student in a room. When Cayton first started college, he wrote a callow, self-important but wonderfully revealing autobiographical sketch for a sociology class. "I came to college," he wrote, "with ideals: ideals of college life—the work, the study, the play; ideas of my individual ability and social position. Need I say that I am now thoroughly disillusioned." He then described his background: "My family has always held among our group, as well as other groups in the city, a very high social position. My grandfather was the first colored senator to the United States Senate and took the seat left open by Jefferson Davis immediately following the Civil War. This fact alone gave us quite a place of distinction in the community." He tells that before college he never had to study, that school work came easily to him.

Then he came to college, where suddenly he knew no one, where no one seemed to care what he did. Most important, he discovered, he said, that he was different: "Along with this feeling of nothingness there came the realization that I was a colored boy. . . . There are certain things that I as a colored boy must do; others that I should not. There is a certain way that I am expected to dress. Any achievement or even ordinary intelligence is looked upon in amazement."[70] Although he struggled to find a place for himself in the white-dominated academy as a very young man, and he continued to struggle for the next four decades, Horace Cayton never succeeded in finding a home in white-dominated universities.

His dilemma was that he found little appealing in historically black colleges either. In his first trip to Tuskegee, to teach summer school, he found low pay, a heavy teaching load, and ill-prepared students. He also saw his first lynching.[71] After his year at Fisk, he never returned to black academia.

Cayton was, like so many black intellectuals, a man caught between two worlds. He had seen Richard Wright's solution—escape to Europe. Even that had been hard for Cayton, though. He disliked having to be a representative of his race to people like Nancy Cunard. Everywhere he turned, he felt isolation, even when he was celebrated for his many great successes. Horace Cayton's life and career served as a testament to the tragedy of the black intellectual in interwar America. For him, there was no road home.

Notes

1. Horace Cayton, *Long Old Road* (New York: Trident, 1965), 175.

2. Ibid., 176–77.

3. "Interview with Horace Cayton, an African American, on Poverty," interview by Studs Terkel, 1971, *Chicago History Museum*, http://www.studsterkel.org/.

4. Horace Cayton, "The Black Bugs," *Nation* 133, September 9, 1931, 255–56.

5. Horace Cayton, autobiographical essay, box 1, Horace Cayton Papers, Vivian G. Harsh Research Collection, Carter G. Woodson Regional Library, Chicago (hereafter Cayton Papers).

6. Norman S. Hayner, diary, Norman S. Hayner Papers, Special Collections Research Center, University of Chicago.

7. Richard S. Hobbs, *The Cayton Legacy. An African American Family* (Pullman: Washington State University Press, 2002), provides the best account of the family and its relation to Seattle society.

8. Horace Cayton, "The Bitter Crop," in *Northwest Harvest: A Regional Stock-Taking*, ed. V. L. O Chittick (New York: Macmillan, 1948), 175.

9. Horace Cayton, autobiographical essay, Cayton Papers.

10. Cayton, "Bitter Crop," 178.

11. *Pittsburgh (PA) Courier*, February 26, 1944, 7.

12. Cayton, "Bitter Crop," 181.

13. Martin Bulmer, *The Chicago School of Sociology. Institutionalization, Diversity, and the Rise of Sociological Research* (Chicago: University of Chicago Press, 1984), 76.

14. Anthony M. Platt, *E. Franklin Frazier Reconsidered* (New Brunswick: Rutgers University Press, 1991), 79.

15. Horace Cayton obituary, *New York Times*, January 25, 1970, D25.

16. Harold S. Gosnell, "Thomas C. Platt, Political Manager," *Political Science Quarterly* 38 (September 1923): 469.

17. Harold F. Gosnell, "The Chicago 'Black Belt' as a Political Battleground," *American Journal of Sociology* 39 (November 1933): 330.

18. Cayton, *Long Old Road*, 184.

19. Ibid., 185.

20. Harold F. Gosnell, *Negro Politicians: The Rise of Negro Politics in Chicago* (Chicago: University of Chicago Press, 1935), 255.

21. Horace Cayton interview with Reverend Philip Yarrow, Illinois Vigilance Committee, February 15, 1932, 35 North Dearborn Street, Chicago, folder "Chicago," box 59, St. Clair Drake Papers, Schomburg Center for Research in Black Culture, New York (hereafter Drake Papers). For more information on Carey, see Milton C. Sernett, *Bound for the Promised Land: African American Religion and the Great Migration* (Durham: Duke University Press, 1997), 169–76.

22. Horace R. Cayton and George S. Mitchell, *Black Workers and New Unions* (Chapel Hill: University of North Carolina Press, 1939), 33, 159.

23. Ibid., 210, 221.

24. Ibid., 433.

25. Fred H. Matthews, *Quest for an American Sociology: Robert E. Park and the Chicago School* (Montreal: University of Toronto Press, 1977), 32.

26. William James, "On a Certain Blindness in Human Beings," 263–64.

27. Cayton, *Long Old Road*, 217.

28. Ibid., 235.

29. David Levering Lewis, *W. E. B Du Bois: The Fight for Equality and the American Century, 1919–1963* (New York: Holt, 2000), 385–86. For more information on Horace Cayton Sr.'s relationship with Du Bois, see Hobbs, *Cayton Legacy*, 95–96.

30. Louis Wirth, *The Ghetto* (Chicago: Transaction, 1928); Louis Wirth, "Urbanism as a Way of Life," *American Journal of Sociology* 44, no. 1 (July 1938): 1–24.

31. Daniel W. Ingersoll Jr., "A Tale of Two Cities: Warner and Marquand in Newburyport," *Anthropology and Humanism* 22, no. 2 (1997): 137–49; Michael R. Hillis, "Allison Davis and the Study of Race, Social Class, and Schooling," *Journal of Negro Education* 64, no. 1 (Winter 1995): 33–41; W. Lloyd Warner obituary, *New York Times*, May 24, 1970, 81. A somewhat critical evaluation of Warner is Stephan Thernstrom,

"'Yankee City' Revisited: The Perils of Historical Naivete," *American Sociological Review* 30, no. 2 (April 1965), 234–42.

32. Cayton, *Long Old Road*, 236–37.

33. St. Clair Drake, "Reflections on Anthropology and the Black Experience," *Anthropology and Education Quarterly* 9, no. 2 (Summer 1978): 92.

34. St. Clair Drake, "Studies of the African Diaspora. The Work and Reflections of St. Clair Drake," in *Against the Odds. Scholars Who Challenged Racism in the Twentieth Century*, ed. Benjamin P. Bowser and Louis Kushnick (Amherst: University of Massachusetts Press, 2002), 92.

35. George Clement Bond and John Gibbs St. Clair Drake, "A Social Portrait of John Gibbs St. Clair Drake: An American Anthropologist," *American Ethnologist* 15, no. 4 (November 1988): 769.

36. Ibid., 277. For a brief account of the complexity of the project, see Henri Peretz, "The Making of Black Metropolis," *Annals of the American Academy of Political and Social Science* 595 (September 2004): 168–75.

37. Interview with Benjamin A. Gore, box 58, Drake Papers.

38. Interview with Pearl Managree, box 57, Drake Papers.

39. A careful account of the development of the center can be found in Anne Meis Knupfer, *The Chicago Black Renaissance and Women's Activism* (Urbana: University of Illinois Press, 2006), 34–49.

40. Ibid., 35–38.

41. Cayton, *Long Old Road*, 247.

42. Horace Cayton to Arna Bontemps, July 2, 1943, box 4, Arna Bontemps Papers, University of Syracuse (hereafter Bontemps Papers).

43. Knuper, *Chicago Black Renaissance and Women's Activism*, 46–47.

44. Horace Cayton to Arna Bontemps, July 5, 1944, box 4, Bontemps Papers.

45. Knupfer, *Chicago Black Renaissance and Women's Activism*, 40–41.

46. *Pittsburgh Guardian*, April 17, 1948.

47. Hobbs, *Cayton Legacy*, 114.

48. Horace Cayton to Lloyd Warner, January 10, 1944, folder 24, box 5, Drake Papers.

49. C. G. Woodson, review of *Black Metropolis: A Study of Negro Life in a Northern City*, St. Clair Drake and Horace R. Cayton, *Journal of Negro History* 31, no. 1 (January 1946): 115.

50. Bucklin Moon, review of *Black Metropolis*, *Nation*, November 17, 1945, 526.

51. St. Clair Drake and Horace R. Cayton, *Black Metropolis. A Study of Negro Life in a Northern City* (New York: Harcourt, 1945).

52. Cayton, *Long Old Road*, 248.

53. Michael Fabre, *The Unfinished Quest of Richard Wright* (Urbana: University of Illinois Press, 1993), 93.

54. Margaret Walker, *Richard Wright Daemonic Genius. A Portrait of the Man. A Critical Look at His Work* (New York: Warner, 1988), 69.

55. Richard Wright, *12 Million Black Voices. A Folk History of the Negro in the United States* (New York: Viking, 1941), 6.

56. Ibid., 118–23.

57. Richard Bone, "Richard Wright and the Chicago Renaissance," *Callaloo* 28, Summer 1986, 454.

58. Horace Cayton, "Black Voices," *Pittsburgh (PA) Courier*, November 15, 1941, 13.

59. Quoted in Hobbes, *Cayton Legacy*, 136–37.

60. Horace Cayton, "Frightened Children of Frightened Parents," *Twice a Year* 12–13 (Spring–Summer, 1945, Fall–Winter, 1945): 262.

61. Horace Cayton, "The Psychology of the Negro Under Discrimination," in *Race Prejudice and Discrimination: Readings in Intergroup Relations in the United States*, ed. Arnold M. Rose (New York: Knopf, 1951), 276.

62. Drake and Cayton, *Black Metropolis*, xvii.

63. Margaret Walker, *Richard Wright Daemonic Genius, a Portrait of the Man: A Critical Look at His Work* (New York: Warner, 1988), 168.

64. Cayton, *Long Old Road*, 262–63.

65. J. Herman Blake memorial address in *Carry On! The Carli and Stanley Stevens' Collection of Correspondence and Memorabilia from and about Horace Roscoe Cayton Jr.*, trans. Stanley D. Stevens (Santa Cruz, Calif.: Stevens, 2003), 60.

66. Ibid., 61.

67. Horace Cayton, resume, box 1, Cayton Papers.

68. For an important essay on the ways in which intellectuals depend upon contact with one another, see David Hollinger, *In the American Province: Studies in the History and Historiography of Ideas* (Bloomington: Indiana University Press, 1985).

69. Horace Cayton to Ben Zimmerman, box 14, General Correspondence, Cayton Papers.

70. Autobiographical sketch, box 1, Cayton Papers.

71. Cayton, *Long Old Road*, 185–207.

Chapter 8

"Who Are You America but Me?"

The American Negro Exposition, 1940

JEFFREY HELGESON

"American Negro history," Harold Cruse wrote in *The Crisis of the Negro Intellectual* (1967), "is basically a history of the conflict between integrationist and nationalist forces in politics, economics, and culture." Cruse admonishes his readers to recognize the fundamental tensions between integrationist goals— "civil rights, racial equality, [and] freedom"—and the commitment to nationalist ideals, "separatism, accommodationist self-segregation, economic nationalism, group solidarity and self-help."[1] Cruse goes on to describe how the tensions between integrationist aims and the commitment to the African American community as a national group played out in Harlem in the middle of the twentieth century—between, for example, black artists in Harlem and the bohemian West Village, or between African American and West Indian leftist activists. While Harlem retained much of its economic, political, and cultural prominence for African Americans nationwide, there was another center of black life growing in importance. Beginning in the 1930s, African

American Chicago experienced what cultural historians describe as a renaissance of black arts, intellectual production, and politics that arguably vaulted the city's black population to the head of a national African American community.[2] One event, the 1940 American Negro Exposition, announced Chicago's ascendance and displayed in dramatic fashion the tensions running through black Chicago's politics. Struggles for control of the planning and content of this celebration of the seventy-fifth anniversary of the Thirteenth Amendment revealed political divisions within Chicago's black community and created a stage for diverse Black Chicago Renaissance figures and their views on African American history and the best paths for racial progress.[3]

Black Chicago was a very different place from Harlem—its population was from the Deep South rather than the East Coast and the West Indies; its black neighborhoods were even more starkly segregated than those in New York; black workers in Chicago more often found jobs in large steel, packing, and manufacturing plants; and Harlem was farther from Manhattan's centers of white financial and cultural power. In 1940, both Harlem and black Chicago were, as Cruse puts it, "just beginning to emerge from the depths of the Great Depression," and they both "seethed with the currents of many conflicting beliefs and ideologies."[4] However, Chicago's population, economic and cultural opportunities, and mix of ideas were unique.

By 1940, most black middle-class "race leaders" and black working-class activists in Chicago were not sharply divided between those seeking integration and those pursuing separate economic, political, and cultural paths. Ultimately, both groups sought integration and racial equality. At times they even reached across class and ideological lines to try to combine the influence of middle-class racial leaders with the mass militancy of the 1930s. It was not a neat fit; the established black leaders and those active in the leftist political and cultural movements of the 1930s differed greatly in their political styles and immediate goals. It is significant, though, that both groups combined integrationist and nationalist rhetoric and tactics in movements for economic power and civil rights. African American labor activists, for example, used appeals to Marcus Garvey–like nationalism to build support within black communities but celebrated the larger industrial union movement's commitment to interracialism.[5] Similarly, African American business and media leaders dreamed of recreating the separate economy of the black metropolis of the 1920s but used their connections to white philanthropies, politicians, and businesses to improve the "Black Belt."[6] Black artists also took advantage of white-run philanthropies such as the Julius Rosenwald Foundation and the Harmon Foundation, as well as positions in the Federal Writers and Arts Projects to continue writing, painting, and sculpting through the Depression. Yet, they used their opportunities to articulate a class- and race-conscious critical perspective on racial inequality and oppression in the United States. Remarkably, all of these groups made their mark on the exposition.

The exhibits in the Chicago Coliseum—a large venue about ten blocks north of the city's segregated South Side, African American neighborhoods—showcased both moderate and radical versions of African American history, and visions for racial progress.[7] An interracial group of politicians, intellectuals, entrepreneurs, and religious leaders sold the show as "the history of the Negro in the United States; the present position of the Negro in American civilization; and trends which would indicate the further integration into the fabrics of American life and achievements which show a rise in his social, economic, and political status."[8] The organizers were determined to make the exposition a display of the achievements and potential of African Americans that would be suitable for an interracial audience. Many of the exhibits, therefore, consisted of dry descriptions of African American history and institutions working for racial uplift. The exposition's organizers also needed to draw crowds, but instead of including the equivalent of a carnival-like midway, they turned to young black writers and artists both to show off African Americans' cultural sophistication and to create a display that would appeal to a wider public. By including black writers and artists, most of whom were active in the leftist political and cultural movements of the 1930s, the exposition's planners created a stage for the more militant, working-class-inspired versions of black history and racial politics. By bringing together racial moderates and radicals, the exposition opened a window onto the cultural politics and ideological tensions that shaped a broad revision of race relations and the development of civil rights unionism in the late 1930s and early 1940s.[9]

The exposition is most interesting because the event's organizers attempted to reconcile competing liberal and radical perspectives on African American history and the best path for racial progress in the United States. There were, of course, important differences within the two groups, but the liberal organizers' core messages emphasized an older model of racial uplift and gradual integration, while the exposition's more radical contributors—black artists and writers—articulated a militant civil rights consciousness that combined a class-based critical perspective on racial oppression in the United States with demands for immediate integration and equality. The fair's interracial group of liberal organizers shaped the exposition's respectable tone and focused its messages on gradual racial progress. The exposition's organizers also included some of the most radical contemporary voices on racial politics, but they pushed the more radical groups out of the event's management and packaged the artists' and writers' radicalism in terms of African Americans' ability to create sophisticated art works and historical narratives that captured the fundamental truths of American race relations.

Previous historical accounts of the exposition tend to underemphasize the significance of the reciprocal relationship between liberals and radicals in the exposition's planning stages and in the content of the exhibits.[10] On the contrary, historians Robert Rydell and Adam Green dismiss the more radical elements of the exposition. In *World of Fairs: The Century-of-Progress Expositions* (1993), Rydell argues that the federal government's support differentiated the event from previous fairs, which excluded or segregated African Americans, while often including harsh racist portrayals of Africans and African Americans.[11] Nonetheless, he writes, the exposition "failed to mount a radical critique of the dominant culture."[12] Green concurs, arguing in his PhD dissertation, "Selling the Race" (1998), that the exposition foreshadowed the postwar rise of Chicago's African American community to the "leadership of [a] national racial community. [Yet,] viewed from a present vantage point as an attempt at resonant and expressive public culture, the event seems a profound failure."[13] On the other hand, literary scholar Bill V. Mullen emphasizes the radicalism of the exposition's art exhibit and the role of the exhibit in the making of a local black art scene. In *Popular Fronts: Chicago and African American Cultural Politics, 1935–46* (1999), Mullen highlights the "Popular Front-style cultural politics," which in a "swirl of giddy entrepreneurialism and vanguard cultural production had made the exhibit . . . Chicago's *own* Negro People's Front avatar: a progressive cultural and political party drawing enormous mixed-class crowds from black Chicago eager to realize the city's potential to supplant New York as the capital of Negro progressive culture."[14] The exposition certainly showed that the federal government's relationship to racial politics was changing or merely foreshadowed black Chicago's wartime and postwar *political* and cultural rise. Yet, it also revealed the tensions between and within integrationist and nationalist forces in Chicago in 1940, especially in struggles over whether the fair would be held in a venue inside the Black Metropolis. At the same time, the exposition's exhibits highlighted the differences between liberal and radical integrationist perspectives on black history and racial progress.

The crucial questions for liberal and radical African American politicians, intellectuals, activists, and artists during the late 1930s, and at the exposition, revolved around what they saw as the challenges of African American modernization, especially the causes and effects of rural to urban migration. Were African Americans better off in rural or urban communities, and what were the best means to improve life in the country or the city? Five exhibits most directly addressed these questions. The U.S. Department of Agriculture's exhibit, shaped by Secretary of Agriculture Henry A. Wallace and U.S. Representative from Chicago Arthur W. Mitchell, pushed an optimistic vision of black Americans' rural future as a solution to persistent black unemployment and poverty in the nation's cities. In contrast, the exhibits of African American–run urban businesses, media outlets, and religious institutions promoted what they saw as the opportunities for social mobility in urban political, economic, and social networks. Similarly, prominent black sociologists Horace Cayton, St. Clair Drake, and E. Franklin Frazier highlighted African Americans' chances for economic and social progress in cities. Unlike their contemporary business, media, and religious leaders, however, the social science exhibit argued that black industrial workers needed to adjust to urban life for the race to progress. Finally, the exposition's widely distributed pamphlet *Cavalcade of the American Negro* (1940), produced by the Illinois Writers' Project (IWP), and the Henry Ossawa Tanner Art Exhibit articulated class-based, Marxist-inspired views on racial oppression in the south and inequality in the north, countered dominant gender stereotypes, and looked to movements led by African American farmers and industrial workers as the best hope for racial progress.

The ninety-five-page *Cavalcade of the American Negro* summarized the exposition's major themes—the editor, Arna Bontemps, worked closely with members of the IWP to create a history of blacks' achievements in education, religion, music, literature and art, theater, industrial labor, agriculture, business, sports, the media, and formal politics. Curtis D. MacDougall, state supervisor of the IWP, called it "the story of a brave people forced to become a part of the American scene."[15] This narrative, however, included references to the most militant aspects of African American history, from the work of radical black abolitionists like Martin Delaney to recent black labor movements for equal treatment for sharecroppers and industrial workers. Little has been written on the New Deal's state writers' projects, but as Adam Green points out, the IWP's Negro Division was "the most prolific marriage of Black intellect and state patronage to come out of the New Deal."[16] Members found both an opportunity to support themselves with their writing during the Depression and found links to local political and artistic circles that included people such as Richard Wright, Katherine Dunham, Horace Cayton, St. Clair Drake, and Langston Hughes, among many others. The cultural radicalism IWP writers took from these experiences is evident in the Cavalcade of the American Negro, as is the tension between their perspectives and the exposition's liberal emphasis on uncontroversial, evolutionary racial progress. This is perhaps most significant because the pamphlet was so widely distributed, with two original printings of more than fifty thousand each.[17]

More than any other display, the Tanner Art Exhibit blurred the lines between the exposition's respectable tone and the more militant attitudes toward racial inequality and progress. Much like the exposition as a whole, organizers couched the art exhibit as a display of African American achievement. In the art exhibit, however, the organizers could not hide the more radical perspectives on black history and the paths for racial progress. Nonetheless, in large part, the organizers intended the art exhibit to be a stage for black artists whose works otherwise went unseen. Few major American museums displayed black artists' work in their general collections in 1940, and during the American Negro Exposition there was an extended debate about whether to include black artists' work in the 1940 World's Fair in New York.[18] Individual artists struggled against the art world's color line. Charles White, for instance, twice won scholarships during the mid-1930s only to be denied the opportunities when the scholarship committees discovered he was black.[19] Similarly, the Carnegie Institute of Technology in Pittsburgh, Pennsylvania, denied Elizabeth Catlett's application for admission, despite the fact that school officials praised her work during the entrance examinations.[20] Overall, African Americans in the mid-twentieth century were "confined to exhibiting their works in 'all Negro' art exhibitions and left out of the national forums on American art," writes art historian Richard J. Powell.[21]

The Tanner Art Exhibit was more than merely a display of marginalized art; it was also a chronicle of black artists' developing politics. Art exhibit adviser Alain Locke, an eminent African American art critic and intellectual and editor of one of the cornerstones

of the Harlem Renaissance, The New Negro (1925), introduced the exhibit as "the most comprehensive and representative collection of the Negro's art that has ever been presented to public view." To this extent, the assemblage of art itself was the main point. The exhibit also showed that black artists "were painting in colonial America, when American art itself was in its swaddling clothes" and that this emphatically American art continued to engage life with sophistication through the 1920s and 1930s. For Locke, the display of "American Negro art" was, in part, meant to open people's eyes to black artistic talent and counter stereotypes about black cultural inferiority. "For many it will be a surprising revelation," he wrote, implying that this realization itself was at least as important as the messages the works carried. In addition to the conventional recognition given to African Americans' "achievements in music, dance and entertainment," Locke wanted to show the world their "quieter and more technically difficult achievements in the fine arts."[22] In fact, however, the technically more subtle visual arts packed a more powerful political punch than the "louder" theatrical productions at the exposition.

In his introduction to the art exhibit, Locke recognized African American artists' developing political attitudes, but he still emphasized the argument that even the more explicitly political art of the 1930s demonstrated black artists' virtuosity. Much of the art at the exposition was political only in the sense that it was evidence of the larger uplift of African Americans in American society. For example, Robert S. Duncanson's Blue Hole, Little Miami River (oil, 1851), the oldest painting in the exhibit, was politically significant more for its undeniably American style than for its subject matter. Like many of his contemporaries in the antebellum era, Duncanson portrayed American life in a romantic pastoral manner. Blue Hole and the other works in the exhibit's "memorial" section—by artists such as the exhibit's namesake Henry Ossawa Tanner and Edward Banister, William A. Harper, and Edwin Harleston—stood as proof that black artists had been connected to the major trends in American art since the middle of the nineteenth century. Even when discussing the exhibit's more recent works, completed during the 1930s, Locke emphasized the parity of talent among white and black artists: "Both the Negro and the white artist stand on common ground in their aim to document every phase of American life and experience."[23] Locke considered this an important step forward from the art of the 1920s and what he called the "Ghetto tradition."[24] By this he meant both that black artists had begun to break down the Jim Crow barriers to blacks' inclusion in white museums and galleries and that they were turning their eyes to subjects outside of the ghetto. For Locke, this was evidence that sophisticated black artists were doing their part to lead the way for the racial uplift.[25] Others in the African American art world agreed with Locke. For example, after seeing the Tanner Art Exhibit, Holger Cahill, the director of the Works Progress Administration's art program, wrote, "I think the art show of the American Negro Exposition is very good indeed and that it indicates that the Negro has definite contributions to make in the visual arts as he has already made in music, writing, the theatre and the dance."[26]

The artists of the late 1930s were not satisfied with merely showing off their technical ability or being recognized as part of the larger art world. Unlike their predecessors in the nineteenth century and during the Harlem Renaissance, the painters of the late 1930s used their work to document explicitly the terrible realities of American race relations. Locke remarked on the trend:

> More and more you will notice in their canvasses the sober realism which goes beneath the jazzy, superficial show of things or the more picturesqueness of the Negro to the deeper truths of life, even the social problems of religion, labor, housing, lynching, unemployment, and the likes. For today's beauty must not be pretty with sentiment but solid and dignified with truth.[27]

The ways in which the exposition's various exhibits defined and wrestled with the "truths" of the challenges African Americans faced in 1940 distinguished the participants' wide-ranging political and ideological orientations.

With the artists at the vanguard, the exposition was a forum for what Harold Cruse called "cultural leadership and cultural democracy." According to Cruse, "[i]n advanced societies it is not the race politicians or the 'rights' leaders who create the new ideas and the new images of life and man. That role belongs to the artists and the intellectuals of each generation. Let the race politicians, if they will, create political, economic or organizational forms of leadership; but it is the artists and the creative minds who will, and must furnish the all important content."[28] The IWP authors of the *Cavalcade of the American Negro* and the artists in the art exhibit indeed contributed the most

forward-thinking content within the political space "race politicians" provided at the exposition.

The Politics of Planning the Exposition

Struggles for control of the fair between the local and national Republican and Democratic Parties and between the old guard of respectable racial uplift leaders and the vanguard of newer class-conscious organizations that flourished in Chicago during the 1930s determined the exposition's planning, location, audience, and content. A group of prominent African Americans in politics, the media, and business emerged who used their connections to white politicians and philanthropists to fund the exposition.[29] This meant that the exposition's two leading groups emphasized racial uplift. The federal government promoted its role in improving African Americans' lives, while the fair's managers sought to demonstrate to a large interracial audience that African Americans had created their own viable urban institutions and sophisticated culture.

Chicago was a crucial battleground in the 1940 presidential campaign, and the exposition became an important stop on the campaign trail. In July, the Democratic Party held its national convention in Chicago, nominating President Franklin D. Roosevelt to run for a third term against Republican nominee Wendell Willkie. Chicago was a core city in the growing northern Democratic Party and a principal battleground for black votes. The Republican Party worked hard to take back the black vote, which from Reconstruction until the mid-1930s it had traditionally received.[30] The American Negro Exposition promised to give the Democratic Party a conspicuous stage both in Chicago and in the national black press.

The exposition was also a key event in the developing struggle between traditional racial-uplift advocates and a newer, more militant attitude regarding the need to uncover the roots of racial and class inequality and to force change. Exposition leaders sought to show that African Americans were capable of creating vibrant political networks, businesses, religious institutions, and a sophisticated culture. In this way, the exposition echoed earlier efforts during the 1920s Harlem Renaissance, when black artists, intellectuals, and political activists, especially in New York City, sought to show that African Americans had emerged from the Great Migration and World War I to create their own refined urban communities. The more traditional racial-uplift advocates at the exposition wanted to demonstrate that African American progress had endured the Depression and to deny common racist assumptions that African Americans were both unsuited to urban life and incapable of creating organized communities. There was, however, a crucial difference between the political contexts of the Harlem Renaissance and the Chicago Renaissance, from which the exposition emerged. By the late 1930s, black artists, social scientists, intellectuals, and activists were generally less optimistic regarding the opportunities of urban life the Harlem Renaissance had celebrated. Disillusioned by the hardships of the Depression and emboldened by the grassroots activism of the 1930s, African Americans sought new ways to create racial progress.[31] The exposition reflected both a traditional uplift ideology that promoted individual self-help, cultural assimilation, and respectable self-presentation and more recent movements that steadfastly criticized ongoing racial inequality in the United States and posited that the black working classes would lead the main struggles for racial progress.

Initially, the impetus for the fair grew out of a widely shared anger in Chicago's African American community regarding the 1933–34 Century of Progress Exposition. That wildly successful Depression-era show virtually excluded African Americans from its exhibits, except in racist portrayals of African Americans, such as the Darkest Africa show, and except in a few exhibits that African American civic groups forced the exposition to accept.[32] In 1935, Chicago real-estate entrepreneur James W. Washington acted on residual bitterness over the Century of Progress fair and began to organize support for a "Negro World's Fair." Washington, who was a Republican, saw the seventy-fifth anniversary of the Thirteenth Amendment as a fitting event to celebrate both African Americans' achievements and the Grand Old Party's contributions to racial progress.[33]

By July 1939, Washington had convinced the Illinois General Assembly to allocate $75,000 for the event, and he took charge of the Afra-Merican Emancipation Exposition, an incorporated body the assembly set up to oversee the funds.[34] State Republicans dominated Illinois's Exposition Corporation but soon lost much of their influence over the planning for the fair.

In December 1939, Associated Negro Press President Claude A. Barnett upbraided Washington for the slow pace of preparations for the event. "What on earth is the hold up in the matter of the Afra-Merican Emancipation Exposition?" Barnett asked, concluding, "We have gone along with your program supporting and seeking to aid you, but I confess we are beginning to be a bit dubious. . . . You are on trial in this matter and so is the whole race, as well as the state administration."[35] In January 1940, during meetings to determine the event's location, the revitalized group created a new nonprofit corporation, the Diamond Jubilee Exposition Authority, which was officially bipartisan but quickly came under the control of Democrats and their allies—including Barnett, local attorney and real estate entrepreneur Truman K. Gibson, and Robert Bishop, administrative assistant to Democratic Illinois Governor Henry Horner.[36] The key moment came in March 1940 when Barnett and Bishop convinced Secretary of Agriculture Henry A. Wallace to back the exposition.[37] As the Exposition Authority wrote in its final report, "Mr. Wallace saw the proposed exhibit outline and then, with his characteristic foresight and energy, called a meeting of the Department of Agriculture. From this meeting really evolved the Exposition."[38] In the wake of that meeting, the exposition's managers secured $75,000 from the federal government, a $15,000 loan from the Julius Rosenwald Fund (a principal interracial, liberal philanthropic organization), and a $10,000 loan from the managers of the Chicago Coliseum. With the federal government's imprimatur, the authority also sold booths to dozens of private exhibitors, totaling $9,735.[39]

By the time the exposition opened, then, Democratic officials and their allies had prevailed in rancorous fights over who would run the fair. Republicans objected to the Democrats' coup. Charles Jenkins, a black Republican state representative and disgruntled member of the Afra-Merican Emancipation Exposition Commission, wrote an angry letter to the black press. "Of course I was informed that . . . I was 'persona non grata' since I was a Republican," Jenkins complained, claiming that the exposition had been "the brainchild of a Republican Representative of the General Assembly, Colonel William J. Warfield," who had brought James Washington's idea to the floor of the Illinois General Assembly. But, Jenkins bemoaned, the fair "had now become the tail-end of a kite of the New Deal and . . . active Republicans were being excluded as rapidly as possible."[40] On August 14, partisan bickering came to a head when Jenkins attempted to have "the Federal Government Exhibit removed and the picture of President Roosevelt taken down because . . . they 'impressed the vicious New Deal on the minds of Negroes.'" At the same time, Republicans sent one thousand workers into Chicago communities actively seeking to keep people from the Chicago Coliseum.[41] One Communist Party newspaper joined the Republicans in rejecting the exposition, denouncing the event as merely a Democratic Party attempt to convince African Americans to cooperate with the war machine.[42]

The Democratic Party gave their opposition reason to gripe; the exposition clearly had become a stop on the campaign trail.[43] With Wallace's support, Arthur W. Mitchell, U.S. Representative from Chicago and the first African American elected to the House as a Democrat, pushed a bill through Congress that allocated $75,000 in federal funds to the exposition. Wallace also ensured that each of the New Deal agencies would have an exhibit. New Deal exhibits overwhelmed the main hall. They included displays of the Department of Labor and its Women's Bureau; the Social Security Administration; the Federal Works Agency; the Civil Conservation Corps; the National Youth Administration; the Department of Education; the Civil Aeronautics Authority; the Public Health Service; and the Post Office (which included its brand new Booker T. Washington stamp, the first ever to feature an African American).[44] The Illinois branch of the Federal Writers Project produced both the historical dioramas and the pamphlet *Cavalcade of the American Negro*. President Roosevelt himself opened the exposition on the Fourth of July by pushing a ceremonial button in his home in Hyde Park, New York, and sending a greeting to be read during the opening festivities.[45]

Building on their success in winning the federal government's support, the event's supporters created a buzz in white and black media outlets. Prominent politicians, intellectuals, journalists, authors, and artists publicized the exposition. Langston Hughes and Arna Bontemps, for example, gave multiple interviews to newspapers and radio shows.[46] Exposition Authority representative W. J. Alimono traveled to Cleveland, New York, Baltimore, Washington, Philadelphia, Richmond, and Jacksonville to promote the event.[47] And from May 16 to June 21, 1940, James Washington, who remained part of the Exposition Authority, traveled through ten southern states, visiting historically black colleges, offices of the United

States Extension Service, and local administrators of the Agricultural Adjustment Administration and the Farm Security Administration.[48] Barnett used his position as the head of the most important African American newswire service to spread word of the exposition in 164 black newspapers with a combined readership of approximately 1,406,800.[49] In addition, network radio broadcasts publicized the fair in June and brought the event to hundreds of thousands of Americans who did not make it to the Coliseum.[50] Barnett also arranged for special fares with railroads originating in New Orleans, Phoenix, Los Angeles, New York City, and Buffalo.[51] The white-run media also took notice. *Newsweek* mentioned opening day and in a September issue commented on the art exhibit's success and printed a photograph of Elizabeth Catlett's prize-winning sculpture, *Mother and Child*.[52] Even the archconservative *Chicago Daily Tribune* covered the organization of the fair and its events throughout the summer.

Despite all the organizers' efforts and the media attention they gained, the exposition drew just over one-tenth of the two million people they had expected. The Exposition Authority estimated an audience of 2,000,000, extrapolating from the 247,000 people who attended a similar celebration of the emancipation anniversary in 1925. Over a quarter million people attended what was a less-extensive fair only ten days long when Chicago's African American population barely exceeded 50,000. So, in 1940, when the city's black population had increased from about 50,000 to almost 300,000, the organizers suggested, it was reasonable to expect a greater audience.[53] Arguably, 250,000 visitors could be seen as a "success," but, in any case, that number seriously disappointed the organizers and made them targets of much criticism.

It is impossible to know why the Exposition Authority so dramatically overestimated its audience. Perhaps the organizers were overly optimistic or using the claim to create a buzz around the event. What is clear is that the organizers, and their critics, interpreted attendance figures as a failure. In its final report, the Exposition Authority defensively explained the relatively small crowds as a result of several factors, including the late start on publicity, and that the exposition competed for crowds with the New York World's Fair and San Francisco World's Fair, which were in their second year. More important, the authority claimed, "[T]hose who had been interested in having the celebration held elsewhere, together with those disgruntled individuals who felt they should have held key positions on the staff, worked hand in hand for the purpose of making the Exposition a failure." Moreover, "[t]he Exposition Authority . . . realized that it would be far more difficult to get mass approval and support of a cultural and artistic celebration than of an Exposition put on like a circus."[54]

The Exposition Authority focused on making the event, in Henry Wallace's words, "100 percent Exposition instead of 50 percent Exposition and 50 percent hokum."[55] Upon entering the Coliseum, visitors encountered a large replica of the Lincoln Memorial, representing the origins of black freedom. Renowned African American painter William Eduoard Scott and Persian-born portrait artist Salvatore Salla, who immigrated to Chicago in 1927, contributed portraits of approximately twenty prominent African Americans, as well as murals of important scenes in African American history.[56] The IWP's dioramas detailed eighteen moments in African American history, including life in Africa; the slave trade in Africa and Virginia; the loyalty of African Americans during the American Revolution, the Civil War, and the Spanish-American War; the difficulties of Reconstruction; and African Americans' "humble beginnings in business."[57] Each of the major New Deal agencies portrayed the federal government's benefits for African Americans. And numerous displays marked the success of African American businesses, churches, newspapers, fraternities, and sororities.[58] Prizes for the best poem, painting, drawing, song, and sculpture highlighted African American artistic achievement, while the "Miss Bronze America" pageant sought to display African American beauty. The exposition also included self-consciously respectable entertainments at the Tropical Gardens nightclub, constructed in the Coliseum specifically for the fair, which hosted a number of dance troupes, comedians, and nightly performances of a "swing version" of Gilbert and Sullivan's *Mikado*, the *Chimes of Normandy*, a "jazzed up Negro version of the famous old French opera," and a play by Langston Hughes and Arna Bontemps, "Tropics after Dark."[59]

Whether or not the exposition's "high" tone kept larger crowds away, it is clear that the organizers perceived the turnout in these terms. When Truman Gibson looked back on the exposition, he reported, "We have done what we set out to do and the result

has been such that no one need be ashamed. We have attempted to bring the race up and have consequently avoided the types of appeal that would bring in masses."[60] Nonetheless, Gibson refused to listen when an outside publicity consultant encouraged him to include some flash with the exhibits' educational materials.

> I wish to repeat the futility [*sic*] of attempting to secure a large volume attendance with a feature that is solely artistic and cultural. The mass of the public wants a 'side show'; a spectacle with deft touches of showmanship. . . . The public will absorb the education offered by your exposition (this being the primary object of it) if they are first 'lured' to the building then exposed to the culture. . . . Art but LIFE![61]

The Exposition Authority wanted more than anything else to show that African Americans had progressed to the point of deserving serious, high-minded consideration.

The exposition organizers' efforts to impress white audiences drew fire from Chicago's black community. In particular, arguments over where the exposition ought to be held reflected differences among African Americans regarding the event's relationship to the white community. The organizers considered sites throughout the city, including some locations in black neighborhoods, such as the Savoy Ballroom at South Parkway and Forty-Seventh Street, and the Giles Armory, which was home to Chicago's celebrated all-black Eighth Regiment and had hosted important gatherings such as the 1936 founding convention of the National Negro Congress.[62] By holding the exposition outside the city's South Side African American neighborhoods, the organizers not only made the event inconvenient for black audiences but they also reinforced the perception that the event was an accommodationist sell-out. Indeed, the Southside Merchants Association objected, "It is the consensus of opinion of many civic leaders of the community," that the Coliseum location was "a grave mistake."[63] In addition, at least some black unions used their position to punish the Exposition Authority. Claude Barnett complained, "The unions have pummeled us terribly. They had us at their mercy since the Coliseum is a union house. . . . [T]he carpenters' union took $35,000 from us in installation after we had most of our exhibits built; [and] the musicians made us pay $1,600 a week for a band we could have had for $600 ordinarily, by scaling the exposition as a class B house because it is downtown."[64] Consequently, the Exposition Authority could not afford to have black musicians—a great potential draw—play regularly at the fair.[65] Other critics, including Roy Wilkins of the National Association for the Advancement of Colored People (NAACP), wrote letters to the editors of black newspapers and to members of the Exposition Authority, bristling at the fact that the organizers hired a white-owned printing company to produce posters for the event and sold ice cream from a vendor that did not hire African American workers.[66] A columnist from the city's main black newspaper, the *Chicago Defender*, wrote, "The people who are running the exposition know what they want and whom they want to handle the various exhibits. . . . Let me make it plain! Have we become so educated that we CAN NOT see our own except through the white man's eyes?"[67]

The charges that the exposition was a "sell-out" hit hard because, to an extent, they were true; the organizers included exhibits planned by whites and intended to accommodate white audiences. Yet, it is important to note that the critics who dwelled on the fair's accommodationism often felt slighted by the event's planning and did not comment on the array of perspectives in the exhibits. In fact, the exposition offered not just white-biased platitudes on race relations but also competing visions of African American rural and urban history and heated debates over the best paths to improve life for black Americans in the country and the city.

"The Negro on the Land"

In 1940, almost one half of all African Americans lived in cities, and by 1945, for the first time, a majority lived in urban areas. At the same time, rural life still defined the vast majority of African American history. It should not be surprising, then, that a significant part of the exposition described African Americans' rural experiences. What is more interesting is that the exhibits showcased a now largely forgotten debate over African Americans' future in southern agriculture. The New Deal agriculture exhibit argued that African Americans in the city should move back to the farm, while those who had remained in the south should stay put. In retrospect, perhaps, this back-to-the-farm message is surprising. Yet, Henry Wallace and Arthur Mitchell shaped the agriculture display to promote an optimistic vision of rural life. Their anti-urban perspective, how-

ever, was out of step not only with the later course of history but also with at least two other views on display in the Coliseum. While Wallace and Mitchell celebrated the federal government as the best hope for black farmers, the *Cavalcade of the American Negro* and many artists in the art exhibit explicitly pointed to the failure of traditional attempts to overcome the hardships African Americans faced on the farm.

Described as "the most imposing exhibit in the exposition," the Department of Agriculture's display, "The Negro on the Land," included its own auditorium for film screenings and demonstrations and cost the department $40,000.[68] Visitors passed through three sections detailing "the story of how the obstacles to rural progress in the South are being met under a broad agricultural program."[69] The booths included descriptions of scientific progress in agriculture, a 4-H Club home demonstration, and explanations of the New Deal's efforts to improve rural life.[70] The exhibit celebrated black farmers' steady improvement, telling with "photographic enlargements of heroic size the story . . . of seventy-five years of struggle of the Negro toward a better rural life." The federal government starred in this story, helping black farmers to build new homes, improve soil conservation, and increase yields.[71] Despite the fact that local New Deal administrators in the south were notoriously biased against African American farmers and the fact that black farmers arguably benefited less than anyone from the New Deal, the agricultural displays presented not only a glowing description of the benefits of federal programs but also an explicit argument for African Americans' future on the farm.

Individually, Wallace and Mitchell had long celebrated the prospects for rural progress. Wallace, as President Roosevelt's secretary of agriculture, was possibly the foremost proponent of the use of science and public policy to improve rural life.[72] Mitchell, who had been Booker T. Washington's assistant, held onto a Washington-style accommodationism, despite the fact that he was the most prominent black member of Roosevelt's New Deal urban coalition. Mitchell actually deflected attention away from urban centers like Chicago. He did not pressure Congress or President Roosevelt to create better housing, ensure fair employment practices, or improve health facilities in Chicago. Instead, this native of rural Alabama, who retired at the end of his term in 1943 to a rural estate in Petersburg, Virginia, spent virtually all of his time in the House concentrating on the problems of the rural south.[73] In 1937, Mitchell traveled throughout the region, visiting black farmers and the rural communities already receiving the most federal support. Also, Mitchell met regularly with Roosevelt, Wallace, and local agricultural extension agents throughout the south regarding potential federal programs that he hoped would improve conditions for black farmers.[74]

For Mitchell especially, the American Negro Exposition represented a grand opportunity to continue to promote African Americans' rural prospects. Introducing the bill for a $75,000 appropriation to the exposition, Mitchell told the House of Representatives:

> It is hoped that, showing the possibilities for advancement of the Negro in returning to the land, an interest in such may help relieve the unemployment situation, especially in the urban centers. It has become evident that there are at least 50,000 Negroes who are technologically unemployed in and near Chicago alone, who are dependent upon relief. They in all likelihood never will get jobs. . . . To show these Negroes, whom industry cannot absorb, what has been done on the land in raising the value of the holdings of Negro families, as well as the increase in the standard of living, may tend to attract them away from the city back to the rural life, to which they are best adapted.[75]

Mitchell repeated similar statements in many of his letters and speeches from the late 1930s and early 1940s. Again and again, he assured his counterparts in Washington, "I can see no hope for the Negro in America ultimately except through the extension of Agricultural opportunity and development," and counseled his "superconstituency of 12,000,000" African Americans to look to the farm for their salvation.[76]

Mitchell's and Wallace's back-to-the-farm message took the notion that African Americans were culturally suited to rural life to its extreme.[77] It was an argument that was anything but threatening to the dominant white political establishment. On the contrary, Mitchell reinforced the New Deal's claims that it improved conditions for all Americans and at the same time appeased southern white Democrats who knew that black farmers posed no real threat to the status quo in the rural south. Wallace and Mitchell promoted a rural future for African Americans not only to appease southern white Democrats but also because they sincerely believed that African Americans were unsuited to life in the city. Despite the fact that a back-to-the-farm argument would be untenable just a few years later, they maintained faith in the potential for a rural future because they thought the obstacles blocking a mass return to agricultural life paled in comparison to the problems African Americans faced in urban areas. "I, having been directly connected with rural life," Mitchell told Congress, "know the great evil that attends this migration."[78] Thus, they sought the prevention of "colored people from the Southern States rushing from the rural districts and crowding into the cities, both in the South and in the North" and sought mass resettlement of African Americans from cities to farms.[79] What neither Wallace nor Mitchell acknowledged was that the oppressive sharecropping system, combined with prevalent extralegal violence and the legalized segregation of Jim Crow, ensured that millions of African Americans would continue to look to the city and industry for hope.

At least two artists at the exposition contradicted Wallace and Mitchell's idealistic, perhaps myopic, view of life for African Americans in the rural south. Hale Woodruff's *By Parties Unknown* (block print, 1938) indicted the south for the moral depravity of lynching, and Charles White's *There Were No Crops This Year* (crayon drawing, 1940) graphically portrayed the grinding oppression of the sharecropping system.[80] In Woodruff's dark scene, a lynching victim has been pulled down after his death and laid on the steps of a crumbling church, the central institution of respectable black and white societies. Here Woodruff not only decried the injustice of lynching; he implicitly reproached "respectable" society for failing to protect this victim while also warning the viewer that such acts were destructive for the society as a whole. While Woodruff portrays the acute physical violence that marked racial oppression in the south, White dramatized the effects of the chronic racial inequality in a sharecropper's life. White's *There Were No Crops This Year* was the most celebrated piece in the art exhibit. The drawing won first prize for the best black-and-white drawing at the fair and was on the cover of the art exhibit's catalog. White portrays a despairing man and woman holding an empty grain bag. Their unimaginably strong figures break the drawing's borders, and the close perspective draws the viewer intimately into a portrayal of African American farmers who were neither rising happily from the depths of slavery nor entirely broken by the oppression of the rural south.

It was not only in the art exhibit that the exposition's audiences encountered critical appraisals of oppression in the rural south. The *Cavalcade of the American Negro* echoed Woodruff and White:

> The destitution of most of the Negro tenants and owners [on southern farms] is incredible. The exhaustion of the soil through the one-crop system, the unequal fight against the boll weevil, illiteracy, the absences of money, lack of modern machinery and equipment, inability of the backward workers to apply scientific methods, difficulties of the individual farmer in getting credit, high prices and exorbitant interest rates paid for supplies, inadequate diet causing disease and abnormal death rates—these are the evils of the dispensation under which the Negro famer lives. The sum total of these circumstances has been to create a slave atmosphere in which reliance on the white landlords seems imperative.[81]

For this IWP author, the federal government was not the farmer's best hope; rather, "the most promising move is the effort being made by the beleagured sharecroppers themselves to work out their own salvation," through farmer-led organizations such as the Southern Tenant Farmers Union and the Delta Cooperative Farm.[82]

For those unsure that rural black folk could mount a successful movement against oppression, eminent African American painter Jacob Lawrence pointed to a historical example. Lawrence's contribution to the exposition, *The Life of Toussaint L'Ouverture* (oil, 1938), a series of fifteen oil paintings on the history of the Haitian Revolution, celebrated a revolutionary past.[83] Lawrence sought to portray something other than the mythologized, safe African American figures in the exposition's murals of Crispus Attucks, Benjamin Banneker, and the Tenth Cavalry on San Juan Hill. Instead of historical characters already relatively widely accepted as important contributors to U.S. history, Lawrence chronicled one of the most radical challenges to white supremacy in the Americas.[84] L'Ouverture led the only successful slave revolution in the Western Hemisphere, and his image haunted whites in the United States for years after the revolution. In 1940, L'Ouverture stood as a historical example for African Americans in the rural south fighting to improve their lives.[85] Moreover, in the context of the exposition, the portrayals of oppression, violence, and potentially revolutionary struggles in the rural south effectively countered the New Dealers' obtuse idealism and, not incidentally, more accurately foreshadowed the south's postwar civil rights battles.

In the City of Destruction and Rebirth

Alongside the debate about the prospects of a life for African Americans in the rural south, the exposition showcased a related and even more heated argument over the fate of African Americans in the city. By 1940, most interested observers—sociologists, politicians, activists, and much of the public—realized that African Americans as a whole could not escape an urban industrial future. They disagreed sharply, however, about the best ways to ameliorate economic hardship in the city. Three different perspectives stood out. There was a traditional middle-class uplift message that best complemented the exposition organizers' emphasis on the gradual improvement of African American life. The social science exhibit presented an alternative view of adjustment to urban life, based on Frazier's *Negro Family in the United States* (1939), which called on black men to forge a place for themselves in the urban industrial economy and save the African American family from its ostensibly pathological maternal structure. The young, militant artists and writers at the exposition also looked to the black working classes for leadership in the fight for racial progress. Individually, however, they also challenged the predominant depictions of black rural folk, African American motherhood, and African Americans' relationship to American history as a whole. In these works, the black artists at the exposition reached the heights of their cultural leadership.

The first prominent theme in the debate about African Americans in the city was the potential for black middle-class race leaders to lift the race by creating jobs, entrepreneurial networks, and cultural outlets for the African American masses. Exhibits from African American–run urban institutions—such as insurance companies, newspapers, the Negro Chamber of Commerce, and churches—celebrated both the past and future of African Americans' entrepreneurial achievements, claiming that the leaders of the Black Metropolis endured through the Depression, and were positioned to lead urban black communities toward renewed economic prosperity. Here was the core message of urban middle-class uplift ideology; by assimilating into the world of competitive capitalism, black entrepreneurs built the resources of public culture that allowed African Americans to articulate their views in the press, issue their own insurance, build their own homes, and buy goods at black-owned businesses.

The social science exhibits promoted racial uplift of a different kind, one that placed the burden not on the leadership of middle-class and elite African Americans but on black working men. Black sociologist Frazier suggested that African Americans' best hope was neither a return to the rural south, as Wallace and Mitchell would have it, nor the entrepreneurial vision of an unproblematic assimilation into urban life. Rather, Frazier focused on what he portrayed as the long-term destruction of African American culture and family structure. He argued that working-class African Americans in the city needed to adapt to urban life; black men needed to find industrial jobs and use their newfound economic and political opportunity to reconstitute the patriarchal family and rise into solid working-class status. In order to take part in the prosperity cities offered, Frazier argued, African Americans first needed to resolve their own social problems. He described these problems as the unemployment, "broken" families, juvenile delinquency, and drunkenness caused in large part by matriarchal family structure. His arguments appeared in both the *Cavalcade of the American Negro* and the exposition's social science exhibit. Frazier was acutely aware of the problems of rural life and sought a way for African Americans to rise above the hardships of southern oppression, migration, and urban life. His path out of rural "backwardness" and up from urban pathology comprised physical migration from the sharecropper's plot and a social move to economic stability.

For Frazier, the family was the core institution on which all other social organization depended. Rural to urban migration, according to Frazier, exacerbated the problems of the already high number of "maternal households" in both the country and the city.[86] Since Emancipation, Frazier asserted, "the Negro family" had evolved through four stages, and with the transformations in family structure also came broader social changes. Frazier's "patterns of the Negro family" fell into four categories, portrayed in the Hall of Dioramas: *In the House of the Mother, In the House of the Father, In the City of Destruction,* and *In the City of Rebirth.*[87] Frazier argued that slavery utterly destroyed the African American family, but during Reconstruction newly emancipated communities began to reconstitute a matriarchal family. As Frazier put it, the freed slave was a "refugee from a hostile world [and] was provided [for] in the family circle

of kinsmen and orphans under the guardianship of mother or grandmother." Without a patriarchal figure, Frazier warned, the family was inherently incomplete, and only when men began to return to their patriarchal responsibilities was it possible for former slaves to build the institutions of a successful community: "Upon the pioneer efforts of the freed men who first accepted the challenge of manhood responsibilities, were built the family, the church, the school, and industry." This initial success, however, began to fray during the "flight from feudalism." As the caption to the *City of Destruction* diorama put it, "To man the mills and factories of northern industry, a million black folk fled from feudal America to modern civilization. In the city many simple folkways of the South were lost." Migration, in this argument, was an ambiguous process. Families headed by men who could not meet the economic challenges of the city and maternal migrant households brought a barrage of urban difficulties onto "disorganized" families, a phenomenon that, Frazier argued, caused high crime rates and the persistence of backward rural religious and medical superstitions. On the other hand, for those men who migrated with their families and found industrial jobs, the city offered opportunity for social mobility and a reconstruction of African American families and social institutions. Still, even those who took advantage of the opportunities in "the City of Rebirth" needed to fight "color caste" and endure "the travail of civilization."[88]

Frazier was clear about the implications of African American families' failure to adjust to urban life. One of the most important, he suggested, was the disproportionately high crime rate in urban black communities. Although he suggested that relatively high crime rates were caused, in part, by "unjust arrests" and "deplorable economic and housing conditions," he also attributed crime to the "Negro's racial background," "slow adaptations to the white man's rule of conduct," "feeble-mindedness among the more backward," and, finally, "too rapid migration from country to city."[89] The message seems clear: migrants who were slow to adapt (often the result of family disorganization) ostensibly suffered excessively from urban poverty and therefore turned to crime. At best, this explanation contradicted the "superficial . . . impression that Negroes are criminally inclined." At worst, it still placed the blame for crime on the black population itself. In this version of migrant adjustment, the transition from rural to urban life engendered criminality in the black community. Crime could only be fought with "additional measures . . . to curb permanently both the irresponsible Negroes and the whites who exploit them."[90]

However stridently Frazier criticized black workers and their families, his work was attractive to his antiracist contemporaries because it seemed to offer a hopeful path to rise above the poverty, crime, and poor healthcare that afflicted urban black ghettos. By creating two-parent families in which the husband worked and the wife managed the household, Frazier promised, African Americans could lift themselves up to the middle class and show their poorer neighbors the way to do the same. For Frazier, the exposition offered a popular venue in which to counter racist descriptions of African American culture and to promote his vision of middle-class uplift.

As powerful as Frazier's argument might have been, it also explicitly blamed single parents, especially women, for the African American community's "pathologies." It placed the source of family disorganization in black sharecroppers' post-emancipation rural environment. Migrants, Frazier suggested, could carry their "family disorganization" with them on their "flight from feudal America."[91] The city's economic opportunities represented tenuous hope, according to Frazier, but only if the masses of African Americans reconstituted the patriarchal family and countered the pathologies of matriarchal social organization.

Frazier's criticism of the African American family structure is not entirely shocking, of course; it represents just one instance of one of the most prominent, and problematic, themes in modern American racial discourse. More surprising are the efforts at the exposition to counter derogatory stereotypes of black mothers and families. The best example is Elizabeth Catlett's sculpture *Mother and Child* (marble, 1940), which won the exposition's sculpture prize and wide acclaim in the art world. James Porter, who could be an incisive critic, praised Catlett's work for its sophisticated, realistic portrayal of a specifically African American mother and daughter in loving embrace.

> The simple, rotund massiveness of the work exemplifies good taste and soberly thoughtful execution. It avoids those pitfalls of sentimentality and over-elaboration into which have fallen so many academic bores who pumice the marble until it resembles a pin cushion more than a work of art. The [N]egroid

quality in "Mother and Child" is undeniable, and the work has poise and a profound structure.[92]

More to the point, Catlett's *Mother and Child* depicts the mother-child relationship with an unmistakable sense of solidity and wholeness. As an alternative to the images of the black matriarchy as a source of pathology, Catlett's sculpture shows a mother caring for her child with strength, not pathos.[93]

While Catlett implicitly countered Frazier's depiction of African American mothers, the *Cavalcade of the American Negro* questioned Frazier's emphasis on black workers' failure to take advantage of economic opportunities in the city. By fighting for access to industrial unions, the *Cavalcade* argued, black workers had advanced the fight against "the combination of lower wages, industrial and union color bans, discrimination in lay-offs and re-employments, [and] displacement of Negro workers by white workers in the cheap labor market . . . [which] have been too much to lick."[94] Yet, the *Cavalcade* did not end on this depressing note. Instead, it pointed out, "[t]oday, due to the increased political powers of labor unions and the hard lessons of the depression, Negro union membership is well beyond the 300,000 mark," a fact that augured progress. "It is reasonable to suppose," the *Cavalcade* concluded, "that the Negro will be more than a spectator in the significant economic and social surges of the next generation."[95]

Representatives of the more militant, class-based perspectives on racial politics—such as the IWP writers and the Marxist-influenced artists—took full advantage of the space opened by white racial liberals and black racial-uplift leaders. In some cases, however, they were pushed to the margins of the event. Renowned poet and novelist Margaret Walker, for example, captured the exposition's most militant spirit, but visitors to the exposition did not hear her voice.[96] Walker, who was a member of the Illinois Writers' Project in Chicago and Elizabeth Catlett's contemporary at the University of Iowa, wrote a 375-line poem specifically for the exposition, "Epic for the Jubilee Year of the Negro." Her "Epic," however, did not win the contest and was not, therefore, presented at the exposition. In fact, "Epic" has never been published. Yet, the poem presents a powerful summary of a radical version of the exposition's messages. Walker articulates pride in African Americans' achievements, along the lines of the main exhibits' messages of uplift and progress, but she goes beyond that story to call on America to remember the sins of slavery and racial oppression and to demand the fulfillment of freedom's promises. After recalling African Americans' forced removal from Africa—"from a free country that was our country /. . . . have we come wailing in your wilderness"—she spends much of the poem describing African Americans' contributions to the making of America: as farmers, workers, soldiers, preachers, teachers, and artists. This is, however, no safe version of African American history. For those who still demanded segregation, Walker admitted no separation between African Americans and America as a whole: "We have made you what you are, America, / we have made you what we are." For those who would elide the sins of the past, she wrote, "I will make you know the meaning / of my working and my living / and my dying on your shores."[97]

For Walker, white Americans' approval was not necessary for integration and assimilation. Black Americans had created America and needed only to claim what was already theirs. The key notion in Walker's poem is that African Americans were inseparable from America—"I tell you America, you too are a Negro"—and that African Americans were specially positioned to cut to the core of the false premises upon which American racial segregation depended.

> Come now my brothers and citizens of America
> and hear the strange singing of me, your brother,
> and see the strange dancing of me, your daughter,
> and know that I am you and you are me
> and the two are as one in danger and in peace,
> in plenty and in poverty,
> in freedom forever,
> in power, and glory, and triumph.
> I ask you, America,
> is this not a singing witness in your soul?

Walker's poem reflects the urgency for racial change—the demands of African American workers, farmers, soldiers, mothers, and fathers—that characterized the politics and culture of the Black Chicago Renaissance.

> Who are you to deny me the right
> to cast my vote in the streets of America;
> in the Senate halls of America?

> Who are you to deny me the right to speak?
> I who am myself also America.
> I who cleared your forests
> and laid your thoroughfares.
> Who are you to be presumptuous
> to tell me where to ride,
> and where to stand,
> and where to sit?
> Who are you to lynch the flesh of your flesh?
> Who are you to say who shall live
> and who shall die?
> Who are you to tell me where to eat
> and where to sleep?
> Who are you America but Me?

Conclusion

The exposition's organizers sought to bring recognition to the race as a whole, and the art exhibit attempted to bring attention to black artists, but at the same time they created a place to debate the many different perspectives on racial politics in 1940.[98] The exposition presented a stage not only for New Deal politicians and leaders of urban black-run institutions but also for the African American sociologists, artists, and writers who emerged from the thriving Marxist-inspired intellectual world in black Chicago in the 1930s. Together, they presented competing perspectives on race relations, migration, and the prospects for African American farmers and industrial workers.

The exhibits might best be seen as attempts to describe African Americans' history and the prospects for life in a modern America divided along lines of race, region, gender, and class. Democratic Party politicians sought to assume the mantle the Republican Party had long held as the party of liberation and progress, while appeasing their conservative southern counterparts and promoting their own (soon-to-be-outmoded) optimistic vision of rural life. Leaders of African American business, media, and religious organizations in the city took their own successful adjustment to urban life as evidence of black progress and celebrated the social mobility promised by entrepreneurialism and national networks of respectable society. The other main group of black professionals at the exposition, the social scientists, bemoaned the destructive effects of slavery and Jim Crow and staked the future of the race on the ability of the masses of African Americans to revive the patriarchal family by adjusting to urban industrial life. Most striking were the black writers' and artists' efforts to capture the working-class-inspired view of black history and visions for the future. Individually, they indicted middle-class society (as represented in the church) for its failure to face up to racial oppression in the south; recaptured examples in black history of revolutionary leaders who arose from the ranks of the black folk; denied the ubiquitous demeaning portrayals of black maternal relationships; and insisted on the need for black workers and farmers to lead movements for racial progress.

Most important was the fact that the exposition's liberal organizers did not attempt to exclude the black writers' and artists' versions of African American history and visions of black progress. Instead, the organizers wrapped all the exhibits, no matter their political messages, in an appeal for a white audience's respect for African Americans' entrepreneurial achievements, religious institutions, active and loyal citizenship, and cultural sophistication. However galling this attention to white opinions may have been to more race- and class-conscious black Chicagoans, there was an important similarity between the liberal and radical images of black history and the goals of racial politics. In different ways, all of the exhibits described African Americans' past and future as a story of progress toward full inclusion in American political, economic, and social structures. In this sense, the exposition truly was a grand display of progress and integration. The IWP writers and young black artists, however, articulated a new kind of radical integrationism that focused on the struggles of the rural and urban working classes and demanded that whites and middle-class blacks recognize the contributions of all African Americans—rural folk, proletariat, soldiers, and artists—to the spread of freedom and the creation of America.

Notes

1. Harold Cruse, *The Crisis of the Negro Intellectual: A Historical Analysis of the Failure of Black Leadership* (1967; repr., New York: Quill, 1984), 564.

2. Robert Bone, *The Negro Novel in America* (New Haven: Yale University Press, 1958), and "Richard Wright and the Chicago Renaissance," *Callaloo* 9, no. 3 (1986): 446–68; Carla Cappetti, *Writing Chicago: Modernism, Ethnography, and the Novel* (New York: Columbia University Press, 1993); Bill V. Mullen, *Popular Fronts: Chicago and African-American Cultural Politics, 1935–46* (Urbana: University of Illinois

Press, 1999), 75, 80; Craig Hansen Werner, *Playing the Changes: From Afro-Modernism to the Jazz Impulse* (Urbana: University of Illinois Press, 1994); Adam Paul Green, "Selling the Race: Cultural Production and Notions of Community in Black Chicago, 1940–1955" (PhD dissertation, Northwestern University, 1998).

3. The current chapter builds on the work of literary scholar Bill V. Mullen, who identified the exposition as a central Chicago renaissance event, and of Adam Green, who sees in the exposition an early example of the "cultural apparatus" black Chicagoans developed in the postwar period.

4. Cruse, *Crisis of the Negro Intellectual*, 3.

5. Beth Tompkins Bates, *Pullman Porters and the Rise of Protest Politics in Black America, 1925–1945* (Chapel Hill: University of North Carolina Press, 2001); Beth Tompkins Bates, "A New Crowd Challenges the Old Guard in the NAACP, 1933–1941," *American Historical Review* 102, no. 2. (April 1997): 340–77; Erik S. Gellman, "'Carthage Must Be Destroyed': Race, City Politics, and the Campaign to Integrate Chicago Transportation Work, 1929–1943," *Labor: Studies in Working-Class History of the Americas* 2, no. 2 (2005): 81–114; Lizabeth Cohen, *Making a New Deal: Industrial Workers in Chicago, 1919–1939* (New York: Cambridge University Press, 1990), esp. 323–60.

6. Adam Green traces the development of the media, political, and economic institutions within Chicago's black neighborhoods between 1940 and 1955. See also St. Clair Drake and Horace R. Cayton, *Black Metropolis: A Study of Negro Life in a Northern City* (New York: Harcourt, Brace, 1945).

7. The Coliseum at Fifteenth Street and Wabash Avenue no longer stands. Although just a few blocks from the edge of Chicago's black neighborhoods, the distance was significant. As discussed later, the location in a majority white neighborhood was symbolically important.

8. Horace R. Cayton to Claude A. Barnett, memo, March 9, 1940, frame 418, reel 1, series 1, part 3, microfilm, Claude A. Barnett Papers, Chicago History Museum (hereafter cited as Barnett Papers). In this memo, Cayton informed Barnett what the Exposition Authority had decided would be the language to describe the event's aims in letters to solicit support for the event.

9. The literature on labor civil rights movements and civil rights unionism is large and growing. For examples centered on the labor civil rights movements in Chicago during the 1930s and 1940s, see the works by Bates and Cohen, and Eric Arnesen, *Brotherhoods of Color: Black Railroad Workers and the Struggle for Equality* (Cambridge, Mass.: Harvard University Press, 2001). For an example that traces a similar narrative in Winston-Salem, North Carolina, see Robert Rodgers Korstad, *Civil Rights Unionism: Tobacco Workers and the Struggle for Democracy in the Mid-Twentieth-Century South* (Chapel Hill: University of North Carolina Press, 2003). For a comprehensive overview of the civil rights idealism that grew out of the war and developed into the twentieth century's grand "rights revolution," see James T. Patterson, *Grand Expectations: The United States, 1945–1974* (1997; repr.; New York: Oxford University Press, 1997). For a dramatic example of the

radicalizing effects of military service, see Timothy B. Tyson's *Radio Free Dixie: Robert F. Williams and the Roots of Black Power* (Chapel Hill: University of North Carolina Press, 2001). For a broad description of the ways World War II changed American liberalism, see Alan Brinkley, *The End of Reform: New Deal Liberalism in Recession and War* (1995; repr., New York: Vintage Books, 1996).

10. The majority of the work on the exposition consists of art historians' descriptions of the art exhibit, but these are generally cursory and often inaccurate accounts. Most descriptions of the Henry Ossawa Tanner art exhibit appear in biographies of major African American artists or in broad histories of African American arts in the 1930s and 1940s. For example, in a biography of Arna Bontemps, Kirkland C. Jones writes that the exposition took place in 1938, not 1940, and claims that "Langston [Hughes] and Arna, chaired the Exposition, with one of its stars, Etta Moten, assisting with music." Jones seems unaware of the fact that the "Cavalcade of the Negro Theatre," in which Hughes, Bontemps, and Moten did collaborate, was just part of Bontemps's contribution to the exposition and was never actually staged at the exposition. Kirkland C. Jones, *Renaissance Man from Louisiana: A Biography of Arna Wendell Bontemps* (Westport, Conn.: Greenwood Press, 1992), 90. In another example, a biographical sketch of Elizabeth Catlett, art historian Lowery Stokes Sims confuses the American Negro Exposition with another famous fair held in Chicago in 1893: "Catlett sent *Mother and Child* to Chicago to be exhibited at the 1940 Columbian Exposition, a national exhibition of African-American artists, where it won first prize in sculpture." Although mistaken nomenclature might be a minor point, Sims's essay points to the real problem that arises when art history is done without a close attention to context. Sims writes, "The context for Catlett's work at this time has been described in Charles S. Johnson's 1925 essay, 'Black Workers and the City,'" a landmark sociological description of black workers' struggle against the color line in northern industries. Without denying the significance of Johnson's essay, it seems more relevant to place Catlett's work in 1939 and 1940 in conversation with the sociological and artistic work of the late 1930s. The current chapter, for instance, argues that Catlett responded to the widespread denigration of the "pathology" of African American matriarchal family structure—most famously in black sociologist E. Franklin Frazier's work. Lowery Stokes Sims, "Elizabeth Catlett: A Life in Art and Politics," in *Elizabeth Catlett Sculpture: A Fifty-Year Retrospective*, ed. Lucinda H. Gedeon (Seattle: University of Washington Press, 1998), 13.

11. Rydell's book, *World of Fairs: The Century-of-Progress Expositions* (Chicago: University of Chicago Press, 1993), is one of a large literature on the racist portrayals of African Americans, Africans, Native Americans, Asians, and South Americans in expositions during the late nineteenth and twentieth centuries. See also Rydell, *All the World's a Fair: Visions of Empire at America's International Expositions, 1876–1916* (Chicago: University of Chicago Press, 1984), and Christopher Robert Reed, *"All the World Is Here!": The Black Presence at the White City* (2000; repr., Bloomington: Indiana University Press, 2002).

12. Rydell, *World of Fairs*, 191.

13. Green, "Selling the Race," 13–14. Green makes much of the concept of a "cultural apparatus," by which he means the media, entrepreneurial, and expressive culture resources a given community has at its disposal to debate ideas and project its ideas and values.

14. Mullen, *Popular Fronts*, 80. Mullen focuses on the art exhibit and on the exposition's radicalism because he is reacting against what he sees as an overly conservative historiography on Chicago's black cultural politics that, he suggests, overemphasizes the roles of Richard Wright and his break with communism. He contends, "[T]he critical gaps and historical inconsistencies in accounts of Chicago's South Side cultural and political scene of the late 1930s and 1940s are largely attributable to the successful erasure of the nature, influence, and practice of racial political thought and culture there." 24.

15. Curtis McDougal, preface, *The Cavalcade of the American Negro*, comp. Illinois Writers' Program (Chicago: Diamond Jubilee Exposition Authority, 1940; New York: AMS, 1975), 9. IWP members who wrote essays for the exposition include Henry Bacon, Alvin Cannon, Herman Clayton, Fenton Johnson, Edward Joseph, and George Lewis. *Cavalcade of the American Negro*, 7. Drafts of many of these writers' works are in the Illinois Writers' Project Collection in the Vivian G. Harsh Collection, Carter G. Woodson Public Library, Chicago.

16. Green, "Selling the Race," 4.

17. *Cavalcade of the American Negro*, 95.

18. Alain Locke, "Advance on the Art Front," *Opportunity: Journal of Negro Life* 17, no. 5 (May 1939): 132.

19. Andrea D. Barnwell, *Charles White* (San Francisco: Pomegranate Communications, 2002), 17–18.

20. Melanie Anne Herzog, *Elizabeth Catlett: An Artist in Mexico* (Seattle: University of Washington Press, 2000), 16.

21. Richard J. Powell, *Black Art and Culture in the 20th Century (World of Art)* (New York: Thames and Hudson, 1997), 102.

22. Alain Locke, "Introducing the American Negro Exposition's Showing of the Works of Negro Artists," Barnett Papers, 3:1:4:002–3; Alain Locke, ed., *The New Negro: Voices of the Harlem Renaissance* (repr., New York: Touchstone, 1992).

23. Locke, "Introducing the American Negro Exposition's Showing," Barnett Papers, 3:1:4:002–3.

24. Alain Locke, *The Negro in Art* (1940; repr., New York: Hacker Art Books, 1968), 3.

25. Locke's perspective on the role of "high art" in racial uplift was especially significant given the influence he had over how black art in general appeared in the popular black press. Locke's annual reviews of African American art and literature in the National Urban League's *Opportunity: Journal of Negro Life* were widely read, influential assessments of the most important trends in black culture during the late 1930s and early 1940s. In 1939, Locke wrote, "[W]e may justifiably say that Negro art has inaugurated a new phase of public influence and service." This new influence, according to Locke, could best be promoted by supporting the education and exhibition of a wide range of black artists because "our art . . . is, after all, the most persuasive

and incontrovertible type of group propaganda, our best cultural line of defense." Locke, "Advance on the Art Front," 136, 132.

26. Holger Cahill to Claude A. Barnett, July 11, 1940, Barnett Papers, 3:1:3:002.

27. Locke, "Introducing the American Negro Exposition's Showing," Barnett Papers, 3:1:4:002–3.

28. Harold Cruse, "Cultural Leadership and Cultural Democracy," in *The Essential Harold Cruse*, ed. William Jelani Cobb (New York: Palgrave, 2002), 57.

29. Those directly involved in financing, planning, and carrying out the event included political and media figures like U.S. Representative from Chicago Arthur W. Mitchell and Associated Negro Press President Claude A. Barnett; dozens of black artists, such as Elizabeth Catlett, Jacob Lawrence, Charles White, Margaret Walker, Arna Bontemps, and Langston Hughes; sociologists and intellectuals, including Horace Cayton, E. Franklin Frazier, Alain Locke, and Tuskegee President F. D. Patterson; as well as religious leaders from every major Christian denomination. Members of the white political establishment supporting the exposition included Illinois Governor Henry Horner, Chicago Mayor Edward J. Kelly, U.S. Senators James M. Slattery and Scott W. Lucas, Secretary of Agriculture Henry A. Wallace, and Secretary of Labor Frances Perkins.

30. William J. Grimshaw, *Bitter Fruit: Black Politics and the Chicago Machine, 1931–1991* (Chicago: University of Chicago Press, 1992); Drake and Cayton, *Black Metropolis*, esp. 342–77; and Elmer W. Henderson, "Political Changes among Negroes in Chicago during the Depression," *Social Forces* 19 (October–May, 1941), 538–46.

31. As historians such as Kevin Gaines and Victoria Wolcott have shown, racial-uplift ideology changed over time. In general, its advocates began with the notion that an individual who improved his or her life had a responsibility to further collective racial uplift. Individuals who acquired middle-class status were responsible for helping others lift themselves and for convincing whites that blacks deserved equal opportunity. Gaines, *Uplifting the Race: Black Leadership, Politics, and Culture in the Twentieth Century* (Chapel Hill: University of North Carolina Press, 1997). Evelyn Brooks Higginbotham in *Righteous Discontent: The Women's Movement in the Black Baptist Church 1880–1920* (1993) discusses the connections between racial uplift ideology and church-centered reform movements before 1920. Stephanie J. Shaw in *What a Woman Ought to Be and Do: Black Professional Women Workers during the Jim Crow Era* (1996) examines the lives of black professional women between the 1870s and 1950s and how they carved out models of womanhood that valued community-minded individual progress. Victoria Wolcott in *Remaking Respectability: African American Women in Interwar Detroit* (2001) explores the influence of uplift ideology on black social movements in Detroit between the world wars.

32. For a description of the community's anger regarding the Century of Progress Exposition, see Rydell, *World of Fairs*. For a description of the events at the 1933–34 fair, see Rydell, "Century of Progress Exposition," in *The Encyclopedia of Chicago*, ed. James R. Grossman,

Ann Durkin Keating, and Janice L. Reiff (Chicago: University of Chicago Press, 2004), 124–26. For descriptions of African Americans' movement for inclusion at the Progress Exposition, see Rydell, "Century of Progress Exposition," 126, and Cheryl Ganz, "A New Deal for Progress: The 1933 Chicago World's Fair" (PhD dissertation, University of Illinois at Chicago, 2005).

33. Rydell emphasizes the fact that Washington reacted against the racist depictions of Africans and the almost complete exclusion of African Americans from the 1933 Century of Progress Exposition in Chicago. Rydell, *World of Fairs*, 187–88. During the second half of the 1930s, the shift in electoral allegiances by African Americans who began to vote en masse further politicized the long-standing connection between black voters and the Republican Party.

34. Diamond Jubilee Exposition Authority, "American Negro Exposition: Report by Diamond Jubilee Exposition Authority to Afra-Merican Emancipation Exposition Commissions of the State of Illinois and of the Federal Government" (Chicago: Diamond Jubilee Exposition Authority, 1940), 6.

35. Claude A. Barnett to James W. Washington, December 27, 1939, Barnett Papers, 3:1:1:391.

36. The Exposition Authority consisted of A. W. Williams as secretary treasurer; Truman K. Gibson Jr., chair of the board of directors; and Claude A. Barnett, L. L. Ferguson, and Robert Bishop. Williams was president-treasurer of Unity Mutual Life Insurance Company in Chicago, and Ferguson was the general manager of Chicago's Jackson Funeral System. Diamond Jubilee Exposition Authority, "American Negro Exposition," 7–8.

37. Ibid., 4.

38. Ibid., 9–10.

39. Diamond Jubilee Exposition Authority, "Statement of Receipts, February 23 through November 30, 1940," folder 65, box 164, Julius Rosenwald Fund Collection, Fisk University Archives.

40. A description of Jenkins's letter is included in George W. Lawrence, chairman, Citizens Committee, Afra-Merican Emancipation Exposition Inc., to the members of the committee, June 12, 1940, Barnett Papers, 3:1:2:556–57.

41. Truman K. Gibson Jr. to Arthur W. Mitchell, August 14, 1940, folder 6, box 54, Arthur W. Mitchell Papers, Chicago History Museum (hereafter Mitchell Papers). The Democrats' dominance at the exposition apparently came back to haunt the Exposition Authority, however, when the exposition ended in the red. When Barnett attempted to secure additional funds from the Illinois General Assembly to help pay off the debt, he was rebuffed by Republicans, who made significant gains in Illinois during the 1940 elections. Incidentally, this added to Bontemps's and Hughes's disappointment regarding their part in the fair, as they were counting on the allocation of additional funds in order to be paid for their part in the theater productions. Bontemps wrote Hughes that a friend of his "saw in the paper that the state legislature, now strongly [R]epublican, was kicking about footing the EXPO shortage which they said was entered into by a [D]emocratic majority and used for the

advantage of that party." Arna Bontemps to Langston Hughes, March 28, 1941, in *Arna Bontemps–Langston Hughes Letters, 1925–1967*, ed. Charles H. Nichols (1980; repr., New York: Dodd, Mead, 1990), 79.

42. Rydell records the contention of the *Fighting Worker* that "[t]he Exposition was arranged and financed by the New Deal and its Negro henchmen precisely in order to make palatable the War." Rydell, *World of Fairs*, 190–91.

43. Whether or not the New Deal actually benefited African Americans equally was not, of course, the point. Indeed, the critical point is that the exposition showed how many different ways political calculations entered into the Democrats' messages about racial progress. African American voters were especially important to both the Republicans and Democrats in 1940. Roosevelt attempted to reinvigorate the African American labor urban coalition that had begun to fray in the late 1930s largely because the problems of the Depression were far from resolved, especially for African Americans. Bitter battles with Republicans over the New Deal and Roosevelt's hesitating support for the anti-Nazi war effort also chipped away at his electoral base.

44. *Cavalcade of the American Negro*, 92–94. The Federal Works Agency included exhibits from the Works Progress Administration, the Public Works Administration, the Public Roads Administration, and the Public Buildings Administration. Memo, unsigned, n.d., with descriptions of murals, dioramas, and exhibits, Barnett Papers, 3:1:1:715–28.

45. Stephen Early, secretary to the president, to Claude A. Barnett, telegram, 1:05 A.M., July 2, 1940, Barnett Papers, 3:1:2:982. Roosevelt's telegram was a rather bland blessing for the exposition. Most interesting is that Roosevelt subtly invoked the pressing war in Europe. He wrote, "The steady progress of our Negro citizens during the three quarters of a century that have elapsed since their emancipation emphasize what can be accomplished by free men in a free country. Moreover, their achievements in art, letters, science and public service possible during a brief seventy-five years of freedom should give all Americans renewed determination to marshal all of our strength to maintain and defend and perpetuate our priceless heritage of free institution[s]." Although Roosevelt was likely using this event to build support for potential military actions, he inadvertently points to the most substantive legacy of the war as a racial uplift event. Namely, African Americans' actions in the war itself became the basis for increasingly insistent demands for legal and social equality after the war.

46. Langston Hughes and Arna Bontemps to Claude A. Barnett, July 22, 1940, Barnett Papers, 3:1:3:146.

47. W. J. Alimono to Truman K. Gibson Jr., [n.d.], Barnett Papers, 3:1:3:969–71.

48. For Washington's itinerary, see Barnett Papers, 3:1:1:1061. Regarding cooperation among federal administrators in the south, see J. B. Pierce, field agent, Hampton Institute, to T. M. Campbell, field agent, Tuskegee Institute, May 13, 1940, Barnett Papers, 3:1:2:045.

49. "Circulation of Negro Papers," Barnett Papers, 3:1:3:1023–25.

50. "All three of Chicago's network stations, WBBM, CBS; WGN, MBS; and WENR, NBC, have been generous in allotting time for broadcasts commemorating the exposition," and broadcasts included descriptions of the exposition and the "Chimes of Normandy." "Exposition Airs Various Groups," *Baltimore Afro-American*, August 27, 1940, 8.

51. Exposition organizers arranged for special fares with the Illinois Central Railroad, the Southern Pacific Lines, the Missouri Pacific Lines, and the Lackawanna and Nickel Plate Lines out of upstate New York. Walter Lee and W. J. Alimono to Truman K. Gibson Jr., memo, April 26, 1940 Barnett Papers, 3:1:1:934; Southern Pacific Lines Passenger Traffic Manager J. T. Monroe to Texas & Louisiana Representatives, May 13, 1940, Barnett Papers, 3:1:2:047; and W. J. Alimono, Harlem Branch of the Negro Business Council, to Claude A. Barnett, July 11, 1940, Barnett Papers, 3:1:3:011–12.

52. "Negro World's Fair," *Newsweek* 16, no. 3, July 15, 1940, 19. "Negro World's Fair," *Newsweek* 16, no. 11, September 9, 1940, 20.

53. As Truman Gibson wrote to Claude Barnett, "On the basis of the 247,000 admission at the similar occasion held in Chicago 25 years ago to celebrate the 50th anniversary of Emancipation, when there were about 50,000 Negroes in Chicago and this year's far greater show with 300,000 Negro population and the entire country to draw from, it seems apparent that our goal of 2,000,000 visitors is not much overdrawn." Truman K. Gibson Jr. to Claude A. Barnett, memo, [n.d.], Barnett Papers, 3:1:1:562–69. "More than 2,000,000 persons are expected to see the exposition. . . . It will be similar in purpose but larger in scope to the fair held in Chicago 25 years ago celebrating 50 years of emancipation. At that time there were 247,000 admission to the smaller 15 day show." Associated Negro Press, National News Service, deadline release, attached to Claude A. Barnett to Arthur W. Mitchell, March 11, 1940, folder 4, box 51, Mitchell Papers.

54. Diamond Jubilee Exposition Authority, "American Negro Exposition," 37.

55. Ibid., 15.

56. Salvatore Salla was born in Kosrowa, Persia, and before World War I painted portraits for the Turkish sultan. In 1927, Salla came to Chicago and settled in Oak Park. He exhibited at the Art Institute of Chicago in 1929 and 1933 and was the official portrait artist for the Chicago Grand Opera during the 1930s. In 1935, Salla completed portraits of Illinois Governor Edward F. Dunne and Attorney General Otto Kerner. He remained a celebrated portraitist in Chicago into the 1960s. See *Chicago Daily Tribune*, September 27, 1931, E4; Eleanor Jewett, "Wealth of Exhibits for the Art Lover: Town and Suburbs Are Blossoming Forth with Paintings by Salla, Stacey, Grigware, and Others," *Chicago Daily Tribune*, April 17, 1932, G4; and *Chicago Daily Tribune*, December 29, 1935, E4. Murals included "The Debate" between Frederick Douglass and Stephen A. Douglas; "Entertaining Royalty," which showed the Fisk Jubilee Singers performing for Queen Victoria; "Music at Lincoln Shrine," showing Marian Anderson's controversial performance; "Interruption," depicting African Americans attempting to educate themselves despite the harassment of Ku Klux Klansmen; "One Way Out," showing Booker T. Washington, George Washington Carver, and Julius Rosenwald; "Athletics"; "Haiti"; "Negro Congressmen"; "Aid to

Ethiopia"; "DuSable Trading with the Indians"; "Thanks for Freedom," with ex-slaves thanking Lincoln; "The Sharecropper"; "New Church"; "Old Church"; and "War Scenes." Diamond Jubilee Exposition Authority, "American Negro Exposition," 17–18.

57. Diamond Jubilee Exposition Authority, "American Negro Exposition," 17.

58. Among the many exposition organizers, Associated Negro Press President Claude A. Barnett and Secretary of Agriculture Henry A. Wallace likely held the most sway over who would participate in the fair. Wallace led the federal government's participation, while Barnett spearheaded the letter-writing campaign to secure the participation of the governors of all forty-eight states (not all responded positively), the leaders of each of each Christian denomination, black sororities and fraternities, the leaders of numerous African nations, historically black colleges, and black businesses throughout the country. In addition, his connections with the many black newspapers across the nation placed him at the head of the publicity effort. The list of organizations Barnett contacted is much too long to detail here, but it is clear that he was biased in favor of liberals as opposed to radicals. In some instances, these choices were overtly political. Margaret Sanger's Birth Control Federation of America, for example, initially purchased space for an exhibit, but the Exposition Authority ultimately barred it largely because representatives from the Catholic Church objected to its pro-choice message. Barnett and others at first expressed great interest in Sanger's participation but abruptly canceled the exhibit in "an abiding spirit to create good-will toward all people." Margaret Sanger herself responded, "If . . . the action taken by representatives of the Roman Catholic Church is considered by you and your Commission an act of 'good-will,' there is little hope of unity and cooperation among the great majority of the citizens of this country toward those few in the Catholic Church who seek to impose their views upon the non-Catholic majority of our population." Margaret Sanger to Wendell E. Green, vice chairman, Afra-Merican Emancipation Exposition Commission, July 23, 1940, Barnett Papers, 3:1:3:157.

59. On the "Chimes of Normandy," see Diamond Jubilee Exposition Authority, "American Negro Exposition," 28; "Race Achievements," *Cleveland Gazette*, July 13, 1940, 1; "Jam Opening of 'Tropics after Dark' at Exposition," *Chicago Defender*, July 20, 1940, 3; and "Theater: North Hall," official program, "Diamond Jubilee of Negro Progress: 75 Years of Negro Achievement," (Chicago: Exposition Authority, 1940), 28. Arna Bontemps and Langston Hughes wrote "Jubilee: A Cavalcade of the Negro Theatre," a history of African Americans on the stage, that they meant to be staged at the Tropical Gardens, but it was never staged. This became a sore point for Hughes and Bontemps, who were not paid for writing "Jubilee." The Exposition Authority claimed, "Chimes became such a hit it was thought inadvisable to go to the expense of producing the other show." Diamond Jubilee Exposition Authority, "American Negro Exposition," 28. For a copy of "Jubilee: A Cavalcade of the Negro Theater," see folder 6, box 164, Julius Rosenwald Fund Collection, Fisk University Archives.

60. Truman K. Gibson Jr. to Arthur W. Mitchell, 14 August 1940, folder 6, box 54, Mitchell Papers.

61. Arthur M. Holland to Truman K. Gibson Jr., July 23, 1940, Barnett Papers, 3:1:3:155–56.

62. Union Amusement Company President Robert W. Mackie to the Afra-Merican Emancipation Commission, January 26, 1940, folder 1, box 164, Julius Rosenwald Fund Collection, Fisk University Archives. The organizers rejected these sites only "after heated and prolonged discussions," which opened wounds that almost certainly played a part in the antagonism some displayed toward the fair. Diamond Jubilee Exposition Authority, "American Negro Exposition," 7.

63. A. Lincoln Wisler to Dr. Midian O. Bousfield, telegram, January 24, 1940, folder 1, box 164, Julius Rosenwald Fund Collection, Fisk University Archives.

64. Claude A. Barnett to Mary Beattie Brady, July 31, 1940, Barnett Papers, 3:1:3:215.

65. Duke Ellington did play the exposition but only as a special appearance during the finals of the "Miss Bronze America" contest. Until the 1960s, the Chicago Musicians' Federation was segregated, with the African Americans in Local 208. Local 208 pulled its musicians out of the "Chimes of Normandy" show because the exposition had allowed the non-union Catholic Youth Organization band to play at the fair. Unidentified document, possibly a press release, [n.d.], Barnett Papers, 3:1:3:239–40. Truman Gibson wrote disappointed to Ellington, "Sincerely regret inability to advise you sooner. Musicians union has held us up at every turn, defeating efforts to get show or Tropics Room going due to their demands." Truman K. Gibson Jr. to Duke Ellington, telegram, July 10, 1940, Barnett Papers, 3:1:2:1090. In another instance, WPA Community Service Chief Robert I. McKeague wrote Barnett, "The following telegram was received. . . . 'Due to gross irregularities existing at the American Negro Exposition permission to use WPA musicians has been withdrawn. Likewise members of Local 208 will not render their services. This action takes effect immediately. Signed H. W. Gray, President Local 208, AFM." Robert I. McKeague to Claude A. Barnett, telegram, July 30, 1940, Barnett Papers, 3:1:3:207. Barnett commented to Mitchell, "The unions, even though they are part and parcel of our racial group, have treated us even more shamefully in proportion than the labor unions did the Chicago, New York and San Francisco fairs." Claude A. Barnett to Arthur W. Mitchell, August 7, 1940, folder 5, box 54, Mitchell Papers.

66. In a letter to Roy Wilkins of the National Association for the Advancement of Colored People, African American journalist Frank Marshall Davis, member of the exposition's publicity team, defended the Exposition Authority's hiring decisions. He wrote, "The Exposition had more trouble with and threats from the Negro Musicians Unions than from any white union. . . . [A]round 30,000 posters were printed at a commercial firm. . . . This commercial firm was white as were the printers of the 'direct mail publicity folders' because, frankly, no Negro firm was capable of doing the job. . . . As a matter of fact, the *Crisis* is also printed in a white shop. Why?" And, finally, "Speaking of 'the ice cream

and hot dogs being made in white plants,' it should be remembered that this concession was sold to the Young Drug Stores, largest Negro chain drug store in existence, and this firm knows precisely whose products it cares to handle." Frank Marshall Davis to Roy Wilkins, in *Crisis Magazine*, January 7, 1941, Barnett Papers, 3:1:3:793.

67. Fay Young, "The Stuff Is Here. Past-Present-Future," *Chicago Defender*, July 13, 1940, 24. Making matters worse, the Exposition Authority fired 141 workers in response to low attendance figures and drew a great deal of criticism when the Exposition ended in the red. "President Roosevelt Opens Exposition," *Chicago Defender*, July 13, 1940, 1.

68. "Exposition at Chicago Opens on July 4th," *Chicago Defender*, June 29, 1940, 2. Regarding final costs, see Diamond Jubilee Exposition Authority, "American Negro Exposition," 16.

69. Memo, unsigned, n.d., Description of the Department of Agriculture Exhibit, Barnett Papers, 3:1:3:1011–14.

70. *Cavalcade of the American Negro*, 92.

71. Joseph W. Hiscox, chief of agricultural exhibits, Department of Agriculture, to Claude A. Barnett, May 21, 1940, Barnett Papers, 3:1:2:153–6.

72. John C. Culver and John Hyde, *American Dreamer: The Life and Times of Henry A. Wallace* (New York: Norton, 2000), 19.

73. For a friendly retrospective on Mitchell's career, see "Ex-Congressman Still Active after 20 Years Retirement," *Ebony* 18, no. 10, August 1963, 40–46. The author thanks Dr. Perry Duis for providing this reference and for allowing him to use his MA thesis, *Arthur W. Mitchell: New Deal Negro in Congress* (University of Chicago, 1966).

74. When Mitchell argued that "Negro families" were "best adapted" to rural life, he echoed an old theme in racial thought according to which the rural south was "the Negro's natural home." As James Grossman argues in his classic history of the World War I–era Great Migration, this idea, which grew out of slave owners' justifications for slavery, eventually was part of Booker T. Washington's rural accommodationist ideology and served government officials' consistent interests in stabilizing the black labor force. Mitchell's commitment to African Americans' rural future was strikingly similar to Emmett J. Scott's efforts to convince blacks to stay in the south during World War I. Scott, special adjutant to the Secretary of War, was "Woodrow Wilson's wartime ambassador to black Americans and former secretary to Booker T. Washington." He attempted to help the Wilson administration diminish the migration's "unsettling effects on both northern cities and the southern labor market." James R. Grossman, *Land of Hope: Chicago, Black Southerners, and the Great Migration* (Chicago: University of Chicago Press, 1989), 15. Like Scott, Mitchell employed a romantic notion of African Americans as peasants tied naturally to the land. In his youth, Mitchell was also Washington's personal secretary, and Roosevelt viewed Mitchell as "his best known African American defender." Dennis Nordin, *The New Deal's Black Congressman: A Life of Arthur Wergs Mitchell* (Columbia: University of Missouri Press, 1997), 140.

75. Arthur W. Mitchell, speech to the Committee on the Library, quoted in Printed Report No. 1979, Committee on the Library, submit-

ted to the Committee of the Whole House by Mr. Keller, to accompany HR8826, April 18, 1940, folder 4, box 52, Mitchell Papers.

76. Arthur W. Mitchell to Henry Wallace, February 27, 1940, folder 11, box 50, Mitchell Papers; "The Cause of Negro Migration from the South—The Effect and Remedy," speech of Hon. Arthur W. Mitchell, 76th Cong., 1st sess., *Cong. Rec.*, February 9, 1939; Dr. Kelly Miller to Arthur W. Mitchell, copy, January 25, 1939; Arthur W. Mitchell to Dr. Kelly Miller, Howard University, copy February 7, 1939, folder 7, box 42, Mitchell Papers.

77. It should be noted that Wallace and Mitchell did not hold that African Americans ought to remain on the farm because biological differences made them unsuited to city life and industrial progress. Instead, the argument here is that biological explanations of race difference remained politically potent enough in 1940 to give a political imperative to a newer cultural explanation of race difference and African Americans' connection to rural life. Kelly Miller to Arthur W. Mitchell, January 25, 1939, quoted in "Cause of Negro Migration from the South."

78. Arthur W. Mitchell to Kelly Miller, February 7, 1939, quoted in "Cause of Negro Migration from the South."

79. "Cause of Negro Migration from the South."

80. Hale Woodruff began his explicitly political work as a cartoonist for the *Indianapolis Ledger* and continued to hone his political artistic vision while working among the many black American artists in Paris in the late 1920s and early 1930s and while studying with Diego Rivera in Mexico City in the mid-1930s. Woodruff took up a teaching position in Atlanta University's art department after four years in Paris and became one of the key figures in the growing national community of black artists in the 1930s and 1940s. Woodruff drew on his background in the synthesis of art and politics as an artist and teacher until his death in 1980. Al Murray, Oral History Interview with Hale Woodruff, November 18, 1968, Archives of American Art, Smithsonian Institution, http://www.aaa.si.edu/collections/interviews/oral-history-interview-hale-woodruff-11463 (accessed December 13, 2011). The exposition marked a significant professional turning point for White, who was only twenty-one years old in 1940. A native of Chicago, White had worked for the WPA and became part of the burgeoning local black arts scene, but he did not jump to the national stage until the years immediately after the Exposition. Barnwell, *Charles White*, 6–11.

81. *Cavalcade of the American Negro*, 63.

82. Ibid.

83. Lawrence's work at the exposition was part of a prolific period in his career between 1938 and 1941, when he completed two hundred paintings on African American history. During this time, he became the first black artist to be represented by a major commercial gallery. Lawrence painted "poignant social commentary on the effects of racism and bigotry in American culture." Peter T. Nesbett and Michelle DuBois, *Over the Line: The Art and Life of Jacob Lawrence* (Seattle: University of Washington Press, 2000), 11. *The Life of Toussaint L'Ouverture* anticipated Lawrence's 1941 series, *The Migration of the Negro*, in its

pedagogical purpose, its dramatic portrayals of black history, and in the liberating potential Lawrence saw in the actions of black southerners. Lawrence's work exemplified the way in which the exposition marked a transition in the role of black history. Before the late 1930s and early 1940s, black history, as practiced by Carter G. Woodson, Charles Wesley, and others, documented African Americans' past achievements in order to contradict the argument—dominant in white intellectual circles and popular understanding—that African Americans were somehow strangers within the nation. Lawrence's paintings represent the move to do more with black history than to just demonstrate African Americans' contributions to world history by highlighting liberation history.

84. *Cavalcade of the American Negro*, 91. Artist William Edouard Scott directed the painting of these murals. There were eighteen murals of African American achievement, including "Building of the Sphinx," "Discovery of Iron in Africa," as well as contributions to farming and science, thirty-two portraits of famous African Americans and depictions of dramatic moments in African American history, such as ex-slaves thanking Abraham Lincoln for their freedom. The murals also portrayed the evils of slavery, the slave trade, and the Ku Klux Klan. For a description of their themes, see Diamond Jubilee Exposition Authority, "American Negro Exposition," 17–18.

85. Significantly, Arna Bontemps's *Drums at Dusk* (1939) also took up the implications of the Haitian Revolution.

86. In a version of the book updated in 1948, Frazier argued, "The 1940 census showed a larger proportion of families with women heads among Negroes than among whites in both rural and urban areas of the South. Moreover, it also appeared that in the Southern cities a larger proportion of families were under the authority of a woman than in the rural areas. In the urban areas of southern states 31.1 per cent of the Negro families were without male heads while the proportion for rural-nonfarm areas was 22.5 per cent and for rural-farm areas 11.7 per cent." E. Franklin Frazier, *The Negro Family in the United States: Revised and Abridged Edition* (Chicago: University of Chicago Press, 1968), 103.

87. The following description of Frazier's contribution to the social science exhibit derives from the program distributed to the exposition's audience. Diamond Jubilee Exposition Authority, "American Negro Exposition," 12. This is, of course, just a summary of Frazier's arguments that does not capture the complexity of his thesis in *The Negro Family in the United States*. This version, however, suits the purposes of this paper because it is a close approximation of the message the exposition's visitors saw.

88. Diamond Jubilee Exposition Authority, "American Negro Exposition," 12.

89. *Cavalcade of the American Negro*, 17.

90. Diamond Jubilee Exposition Authority, "American Negro Exposition," 12. It is impossible to discuss fully the implications and history of Frazier's arguments in the space allotted here. The literature on the causes of social disorganization, "broken" families, and poverty is immense. A good starting place is Anthony M. Platt, *E. Franklin Frazier Reconsidered* (New Brunswick, N.J.: Rutgers University Press, 1991).

91. Frazier, *Negro Family in the United States*, 225–44.

92. James A. Porter, *Modern Negro Art* (1943; repr., Washington, D.C.: Howard University Press, 1992), 132.

93. This sculpture was just a hint of the monumental work Catlett continued to produce. After moving to Mexico in 1946, Catlett took advantage of the freedom of expression available there relative to the constrictions radical artists in the United States faced during the McCarthy years.

94. The *Cavalcade* reflected the hope in the late 1930s and 1940 that the Congress of Industrial Organizations, which was then creating interracial unions, would provide a new source of economic and political power, one not provided by the exclusionary American Federation of Labor. "The outlook for the Negro laborer depends mainly on the future attitude of the American Federation of Labor, the Congress of Industrial Organizations, and fair administration of the Wagner Labor Relations Act. John L. Lewis has not been blind to the rights and welfare of black workers. . . . On the other hand, William Green and the American Federation of Labor evade the real issue of discrimination" with empty rhetoric. *Cavalcade of the American Negro*, 58.

95. *Cavalcade of the American Negro*, 59.

96. Walker's later works, including the collection of poems *For My People* (1942) and the novel *Jubilee* (1966), explore African Americans' history and revolutionary potential in the United States.

97. Margaret Walker, "Epic for the Jubilee Year of Negro Freedom," Barnett Papers, 3:1:2:523–32.

98. Arthur Mitchell wrote Chicago Mayor Edward Kelley, "The exhibits which you are showing the American public will do much in bringing about this recognition which up to this time has been so unjustly withheld from him." Arthur W. Mitchell to Mayor Edward J. Kelly and the Members of the Commission of the American Negro Exposition, telegram, July 3, 1940, ,folder 8, box 53, Mitchell Papers.

Chapter 9

Chicago's Native Son

Charles White and the Laboring of the Black Renaissance

ERIK S. GELLMAN

Charles White applied his art as a weapon in Chicago. In 1935, he asked his teacher at Chicago's Englewood High School why their history textbook only mentioned African Americans once. The teacher told him to "Sit down and shut up." In response, White staged his first sit-down strike. As a self-described "very shy" young man, White felt that he "wasn't articulate enough to explain" his own interpretation of American history. Instead, he "sat down hard . . . for the whole year without participation." He remained silent the whole term and handed in a blank sheet of paper for his final assignment, thus failing the course. "I became a joke in the class," he concluded, "everybody treated me as a delinquent." With no other outlet for expression, White became secretly interested in art. He would soon become the youngest member of the Arts Craft Guild, an informal group of self-taught African American artists, and would win a scholarship to the Art Institute in 1937. For White, his development as an artist in Chicago had a direct connection to his feeling of isolation in school and

elsewhere. "I had no other tools to fight with," he concluded, "so the only way I had to fight was with my brushes."[1]

Charles White's artistic and political development provides a window into Chicago's cultural politics during the 1930s. White, an artist who emerged as a leading figure on the South Side during this turbulent yet prolific time, helped forge the social and ideological networks that connected a cadre of African American artists and black activists in Chicago. Scholars who have studied this era have concluded it represented a Chicago renaissance in the arts. Bill V. Mullen and Robert Bone have placed black artists within the radical political currents of the Popular Front (roughly from 1935 to 1947) by analyzing Communist Party activities and the influence of Marxism on cultural production. They both argue that this arts movement diverged from the Harlem Renaissance of the 1920s because of its participants' commitment to the working class. They show how these artists sought to break away from the somewhat solipsistic writers of Harlem and why they found the industrial metropolis of Chicago to be a particularly fertile ground.[2] Meanwhile, art historians describe these artists' politics as part of a stylistic change.[3] By focusing on the experiences of Chicago-born Charles White—both during his Chicago years in the 1930s and on his later artistic and political trajectory—this essay builds upon these works by asking how these African Americans transformed notions of history and racial protest and how these cultural politics change our understanding of the artistic movement in Chicago between the 1930s and 1960s.

As a young man, Charles White discovered African American history not in his high school class but at the Chicago Public Library. While at work as a domestic, White's mother, Ethel Gary, often had to leave her young son under the librarian's supervision. The library became a refuge for White as he systematically browsed all of its collection. "I [read] through everything in the children's section," White recalled, "and then, at the age of twelve, begged the librarian for a card that would permit me to enter the section where there were more advanced books." Despite being two years below the required age, one of the staff members gave in to White's persistence and issued him an adult-reader card. Authorized to explore these previously forbidden books, White devoured them. Then, as a fourteen-year-old, White witnessed the opening of the George Cleveland Hall branch of the public library that became a crucial institution for Chicago's South Side black community; during its first five years of operation, the library loaned an annual average of two hundred thousand books. As one *Chicago Defender* article explained, the library's establishment was "a milestone of attainment for the community," and its head librarian, Vivian Harsh, "worked relentlessly toward supplying universal service on material concerning the Race." Harsh would become a pivotal figure in the promulgation of black culture in Chicago, and her efforts made a direct impression on Charles White and other black artists.[4]

During one of his marathon sessions at the library, White "quite accidentally" found *The New Negro*, a book that changed his life. Edited by Alain Locke in 1925, this volume represented the most significant anthology of the Harlem Renaissance. It featured the celebrated black voices of poets like Countee Cullen, Claude McKay, and Arna Bontemps, novelists like Zora Neale Hurston and Jean Toomer, and intellectuals like W. E. B. Du Bois, Langston Hughes,

and James Weldon Johnson. "This book opened my eyes," White recalled, because "I had never realized the Negro people had done so much for this world of culture, that they had contributed so much to the development of America." The book inspired White "to search for other books on Negroes, which led to the Negro historical figures, individuals that played a role in the abolition of slavery." White read about the slave revolts of Denmark Vesey and Nat Turner as well as figures like Harriet Tubman and Sojourner Truth in his own self-taught U.S. history course. Perhaps most important for White, *The New Negro* volume had illustrations by Aaron Douglass. The idea that "blacks painted" mattered because he had earlier experimented with art by using his mother's curtains as canvasses, only to be punished by her and told to concentrate on music lessons instead. *The New Negro* proved to him that blacks had a rich artistic tradition, including the visual arts.[5]

The influence of *The New Negro* on Charles White suggests a different relationship between the Harlem and Chicago movements. Scholars have noted that *The New Negro* excluded A. Philip Randolph's socialism and Marcus Garvey's black nationalism, both Harlem-based 1920s political movements of largely working-class African Americans. Historian David Levering Lewis considered this exclusion "irresponsibly delusional," and literary scholar Arnold Rampersad claimed that *The New Negro* gave license for these artists and their audiences to turn their backs on the social movements of their day. These scholars have responded to a facile glorification of the Harlem Renaissance. As the celebrated African American writer Sterling Brown wrote in the 1950s, it had become fashionable to "make the thirties a whipping boy, while pampering the glorious twenties."[6] Although recent scholars have shown how the Harlem movement actually had more diverse and deeper roots in the black cultural politics of the 1920s, many black artists had been dismissive of the Harlem movement in the 1930s and sought to break away from it.[7] Yet, when Charles White discovered *The New Negro* at the library, he had no knowledge of the debates that followed its publication. He read only the finished product and found it to be a radical declaration of the "blossoming of Negro culture." As Locke wrote to introduce the volume, these artists had grown tired of being depicted as "the sick man of American Democracy." White made *The New Negro* a foundation for his own artistic goals. If, as Locke suggested, the "pulse of the Negro world has begun to beat in Harlem," White hoped that its rhythm could be expanded upon in Chicago.[8]

Depression-era circumstances also modified the black artistic rhythm in Chicago. Not long after White discovered black history and culture at the Hall library, he read about an informal art group that met on Sundays called the Arts Craft Guild. A fifteen-year-old White "timidly took a few drawings to their meeting" and became a member of the group of impoverished but determined artists. They held community exhibitions in churches, the YMCA, settlement houses, and even in vacant lots when no other space was available. The young members of the guild—including Bernard Goss, Margaret Taylor (later Margaret Goss Burroughs), William Carter, and Eldzier Cortor—would become the core of artists who would make up the black Chicago scene.[9] Living in small studio apartments adjacent to alleyways and taking manual labor jobs to survive, these artists imagined the strivings of laborers in Chicago from a distinct, working-class perspective. Similar to his cohort, Charles White worked as a dishwasher, janitor, cook, and valet while forging his career as an artist. During the early Depression years, he managed to get some lucrative work as a sign painter until he realized his employment was an attempt by the company's owner to avoid union laborers. Too young to join the union, its members eventually convinced him to quit.[10] Putting his energy into painting canvasses rather than signs, White and other guild members developed a cooperative learning environment to teach each other professional skills. William McGill, a commercial sign painter, organized the guild, but its eldest and most experienced artist, George E. Neal, became its master teacher by 1934. Neal, originally from Tennessee, was a twenty-three-year-old painter with some training from the Art Institute of Chicago who taught others in the arts guild at the Ada McKinley settlement house on Thirty-Second Street, his studio at Thirty-Third and Michigan (that later burned down), and wherever else he found space. The guild also raised money to send other members to the Art Institute by throwing parties. After a member completed a formal course there, he or she would then return to the group and teach the other members of the guild.[11] Before any government program in the arts, the guild harnessed and expanded the activities of a concerted group of African Americans on Chicago's South Side.

The activities of the guild occurred alongside a larger political reorientation of black Chicagoans in the mid-1930s. In February 1936, 750 delegates from twenty-eight states registered their names at the Eighth Regiment Armory in South Chicago for the first conclave of National Negro Congress (NNC). Inside the armory, banners read, "Jobs and Adequate Relief for a Million Negro Destitute Families" and "Black America Demands an End to Lynching, Mob Violence." Outside, thousands huddled around loudspeakers to hear the speeches of what the *Defender* termed "IKN's" or "Internationally Known Negroes." Top black intellectuals, churchmen, labor leaders, and artists—including Ralph Bunche of Howard University, Reverend Adam Clayton Powell Jr., James W. Ford of the Communist Party, Lester Granger of the National Urban League, Roy Wilkins of the NAACP, Langston Hughes, Richard Wright, and Arna Bontemps—participated in sessions on trade unions, youth, women, churches, businesses, war and fascism, and interracial relations.[12]

The NNC proved important for black artists who made connections with labor delegates. Chicago migrant Richard Wright chaired the "Negro Culture and History" panel that featured writers Arna Bontemps and Langston Hughes as well as artists Augusta Savage and Frederick Douglass Allen. The specific presentation by Wright, titled "The Role of the Negro Artist and Writer in the Changing Social Order," indicated how these artists sought to place themselves into a social movement to ameliorate dire Depression-era conditions. They agreed that "in the past Negro institutions have exploited Negro artists and writers" and that "Negro cultural workers have generally been neglected and suppressed" by both white and black elites. The Depression had caused the artists to work "at almost starvation levels," and, like their labor brethren, they saw the "Writer's Union" as a means to solve their poverty and combat "caricature and subservient roles" in white culture. They hoped that the NNC would sponsor Negro culture magazines, conferences, and exhibits to depict black culture and, alongside the Federal Writers Project, put them to work. By viewing themselves at the NNC conference as the "cultural workers" in the struggle for a "new Bill of Rights for the Negro people," these artists realized, in the words of Wright, that "they are not alone."[13]

The NNC sought to remake urban black communities by convincing African Americans to embrace militant protest tactics against discrimination. Both the NNC and many of its white allies had links to communists and fellow travelers who shared goals concerning organizing workers across racial lines, demanding a greater responsibility of the government for social welfare, and making human rights a priority over property rights. Some of these activists had joined the Communist Party, while others had been members of Marcus Garvey's Universal Negro Improvement Association in its 1920s heyday, but these affiliations mattered less than their commitment to specific causes during the Popular Front era in America. Over the next decade, NNC members in Chicago and elsewhere reoriented black communities by organizing thousands of workers into unions, integrating employment fields, fostering a militant version of black culture based on the history of slavery and Reconstruction, pressuring the NAACP to adopt a labor agenda, registering voters in the south, and petitioning the newly founded United Nations to remedy U.S. human-rights violations.[14] Many of these young artists joined the black-led NNC movement and as "cultural workers" helped legitimize new understandings of African American protest, history, and humanity.

In Chicago, artists, intellectuals, and activists cross-pollinated to an unprecedented degree during the Popular Front. The NNC's Fine Arts Committee in Chicago, for example, sponsored a symposium in April 1936 to follow up on its founding convention. This event honored Bontemps, the author of *Black Thunder*, a historical novel that described Gabriel Prosser's 1800 slave conspiracy in Virginia. At the Abraham Lincoln Center, a public community center built by the Unitarian Church, the NNC organized a symposium to discuss Bontemps's novel that featured a wide representation of African American leaders. The reporter and aspiring poet, Frank Marshall Davis, Vivian Harsh of the Hall Library, a prominent black social worker, Thyra Edwards, and a representative of the Association for the Study of Negro Life and History, an organization created by the historian Carter G. Woodson in Chicago two decades earlier, all took part.[15] The South Side Writers' Group, another development out of the NNC conference, also feted Bontemps for the publication of *Black Thunder*. For Wright, the leading force in the new writers' group, Bontemps's work "filled a yawning gap" for "competent" black novels. Margaret Walker, a poet and writer from Chicago, recalled that this

novel "came closest in feeling and philosophy" to the militant strain of black historical memory that these writers sought to recover in the 1930s. As important, "well known Negro artists" held an accompanying exhibit to the NNC's literary symposium.[16] Like Bontemps and other African American writers, White and his fellow visual artists increasingly sought to depict black historical events in ways that reclaimed past generations of African Americans as active rather than passive participants and as central to American history rather than peripheral.

This pulsating cultural activity among black Chicagoans made White realize that he was "not alone" in his aspiration to combine his art with black history. Previously, White sought to "conceal" his interest in art because other teenagers in the neighborhood considered it "effeminate." This network of black artists legitimated White's clandestine black history sessions at the Hall library and his identity as an artist. He admired artists like Langston Hughes, whom he sketched on a visit to Chicago (see figure 9.1), and he also remembered attending a party in the mid-1930s at the home of the dancer and choreographer Katherine Dunham, where he met black writers like Richard Wright, Margaret Walker, and Gwendolyn Brooks, who discussed philosophical and political ideas about the "direction of American life" with white leftist writers like Nelson Algren. He later recalled that this "free play and exchange of ideas" at other Saturday-night parties helped him become more determined to become a professional artist.[17] During this same period, White also engaged with white progressive artists. He remembered visiting the studios of Mitchell Siporin and Edward Millman, whose murals he found inspiring. Morris Topchevsky, a Jewish refugee from Eastern Europe, often invited White and other artists over to his studio at the Abraham Lincoln Center to drink coffee, view his work, and discuss politics. Si Gordon, an important mentor to the black sculptor Marion Perkins, loaned books on black history to these artists.[18] These contacts across the color line, under the left's motto "Negro and White: Unite and Fight" not only brought industrial laborers together but also became a significant aspect of the artistic movement brewing in Chicago.

In addition to their informal interactions at social events, these artists would become linked as professionals through New Deal arts programs. Beginning in 1933 when President Franklin D. Roosevelt signed the Federal Emergency Relief Act, continuing with

9.1. *Sketchbook*, 1937–42, by Charles Wilbert White, American, 1918–79, charcoal, pastel, ink, graphite, pen and inks, and watercolor on ivory wove paper, 260 mm × 205 mm (overall). White drew Langston Hughes in his sketchbook while listening to him lecture on the spread of fascism in Spain on April 1, 1938, in Chicago. White appreciated the artists of the Harlem Renaissance and also admired Hughes for his leftist cultural politics. Purchase by Ada Turnbull Hertle Fund, Director's Fund, Olivia Shaler Swan Memorial Endowment Fun, and Hugh Leander and Mary Trumbull Adams Memorial Endowment Fund; funds provided by Mary P. Hines, Mr. and Mrs. Robert S. Hartman, Ruth Hartman through the Regenstein Foundation, Marshall Field, Denise and Gary Gardner, John Nichols, Sandra and Deven Rand, Amina J. Dickerson, Jean Rudd and Lionel E. Bolin, Esther Sparks Sprague, Lynn Evans in memory of Beatrice Barnett Evans and John W. Evans Jr., James T. Parker, Patricia Pratt in memory of Marion White Pratt Lindsay, Edwin T. White Jr., Daniel Schulman, Frederick G. and Joele Jones Michaud, 2006.259, The Art Institute of Chicago.

the Public Works of Arts Project through the Civil Works Administration, and escalating numerically into a division of the Workers Progress Administration (WPA) in 1935, the Illinois Art Project (IAP) hired many of these artists. These programs expanded and contracted between 1935 and 1943 based on government quotas. Initially, Charles White and those in the South Side Guild hardly noticed this new government involvement. Increase Robinson, the Chicago-born director of the project until 1938, had previously operated her own gallery in the Diana Court Building on North Michigan Avenue that favored a particular "elite" (and white) group of artists. Once in charge of the federal government's budget for Illinois, she continued to favor these artists and imposed her own standards concerning artistic talent. She dictated "no nudes, no dives, no social propaganda" as IAP stan-

dards and often purposely fell short in filling artists quotas based on federal mandates.[19]

For black artists, Robinson's leadership meant virtual exclusion. Charles White remembered only one black artist (the already famous Archibald Motley Jr.) on the IAP payroll in its early years. White instead won a scholarship to the Art Institute in 1937, and Peter Pollack, owner of a North Michigan gallery, provided White and other black artists with their "first opportunity to exhibit downtown." White considered himself fortunate to receive this support because two other art schools offered White scholarships and then, upon finding out he was African American, withdrew their offers, and black artists were also virtually excluded from showing their work in downtown Chicago. For the time being, nongovernmental programs inspired and fostered an art community on the South Side.[20]

In late 1934, several white artists in Chicago formed an Artists Union to organize their ranks as they entered into the new government programs. These artists initially affiliated with the American Federation of Labor (AFL), whose leaders organized workers on a craft basis and rarely ventured across racial lines. As a result, the AFL dismissed the suggestion to strike by more radical members of this Chicago local; the only demand the union seemed to agree upon was the need to remove Increase Robinson as director of the IAP for her tyrannical methods. By 1937, however, these radical-minded artists gained more control of the union by allying with the new interracial movement of industrial workers represented by John L. Lewis and the Congress of Industrial Organization (CIO). Chicago's union local severed ties with the AFL and affiliated instead with the United Office and Professional Workers of America (UOPWA), a decision that would greatly impact black artists. Beginning the previous year, the CIO, with NNC assistance, had begun to organize interracial unions, especially in the steel and meatpacking industries.[21] The Artists Union affiliation with the CIO showed their desire to become part of this larger, interracial, and more militant movement of the working class during the Second New Deal.[22]

As a new union member, Charles White remembered taking immediate action in 1937. He joined in the nationwide strike originally called by the Chicago local and recalled how the police "arrested [him] a few times," which resulted in him spending "some nights in jail."[23] The sit-down strikes and pickets at the Merchandise Mart and WPA offices on Erie Street succeeded in getting Increase Robinson removed; she was replaced with the George Thorp in 1938. During the transition of leadership, IAP quotas expanded, which allowed Thorp to hire many more artists. At least one hundred new artists became part of the IAP, including White and many other black artists in his cohort. In addition, Thorp now shared power with two white arts officials who had strong connections with these African American artists: Peter Pollack and Morris Topchevsky. Pollack would become the administrator of the government-sponsored IAP art centers; Topchevsky became one of two Artist Union grievance representatives to sit on the IAP credentials review board.[24] All of these changes resulted in a more democratic and interracial representation of artists under federal supervision in Chicago. For these South Side artists, the experience in fighting for

IAP inclusion made them even more determined as activists. "My first lesson on the [IAP] project," White remembered, "dealt not so much with paint as with the role of unions in fighting for the rights of working people."[25]

Experiences with unionism also affected White's artistic vision. White remembered taking part in "the League against War and Fascism, and the organization for support of the republican government of Spain" and also showed his work at an "An Exhibition in Defense of Peace and Democracy" in 1938. Moreover, White's art during this period fixated on issues around work and, more specifically, the plight of black laborers in America. One of his earliest charcoal drawings, *CCC Camp* (also titled *Laborers*), portrayed the physical rigor of black workers for Civilian Conservation Corps, an early New Deal program that paid unemployed workers to perform manual labor on rural public works projects (see figure 9.2). Once hired by the WPA, White expanded upon this theme to produce bold images like *Fatigue*, featuring a laborer whose body appears distraught yet his eyes show a complexity beyond his physical appearance. By 1939, White's *There Were No Crops This Year* and *Fellow Worker, Won't You March with Us?* evinced how racial discrimination relegated blacks to perform unremunerated jobs but also highlighted the importance of forming bonds between workers (see figure 10.20 in the current volume for *There Were No Crops*). Describing the charcoal drawing *There Were No Crops*, one art historian explained that the "posture and sorrowful demeanor" of these workers showed how "black laborers . . . carry the weight of economic and social distress." Meanwhile, *Fellow Worker* signified the importance of solidarity among workers, making reference to the Artists Union and other civil rights unionism during the late 1930s. In 1940, White explained these works sought to "depict the whole social scene" and use paint as a "weapon . . . to fight what I resent."[26]

White's approach to art was a departure from those in the previous generation of black artists in Chicago. Although Willard Motley wrote in 1940 that these younger artists followed a "trail blazed years ago" by his brother, Archibald Motley Jr., and other artists like William Edouard Scott and Charles C. Dawson, these younger artists made a clear break from those who had earlier earned acclaim in Chicago. One of the artists Motley featured in the article, Charles Sebree, exemplified the difference

9.2. *CCC Camp* (also, *Laborers*), [ca. 1930]. Charles White's earliest drawings depicted both the hard labor and dignity of African American workers. Courtesy of the Charles Wilbert White Papers, Archives of American Art, Smithsonian Institution.

between these 1930s artists and their predecessors. Motley remarked that because "his star rose early," he considered Sebree the "problem child" of the group, calling him "an escapist" and "disillusioned." Sebree told Motley, "I'm tired of Chicago," and had plans "to sell all my paintings and go to New York."[27] These comments echoed the perspective of the older generation of Chicago artists who had studied at the Art Institute in the early 1900s and exhibited with the Chicago Art League and *Negro in Art Week* at the Institute, women's clubs, and the Century of Progress Exhibition in 1933. While Scott (the president of the Art League) and Dawson saw these respectable events as a step forward for black artists, Archibald Motley found them unappealing. Having become internationally famous two decades earlier, Motley chose not to live in the South Side's Black Belt, did not identify himself as a "Negro artist," courted patrons like the

Armour family (unions organized against the family's meatpacking plants in the 1930s), and according to Dawson, "never associated with [other black artists] to any extent after [Art Institute] school hours."[28]

The generational and political distinctions among these artists also became apparent when considering the works of art they produced. Motley focused on scenes that often depicted black Chicagoans engaged in unproductive or illicit activities.[29] And while Dawson tended to avoid racially demeaning themes—he won a prize for his painting of a black veteran of World War I to "counteract the eternal stereotyping . . . of the Negro"—his depiction of a black woman for a Poro Beauty College advertisement showed the difference between him and the next generation. Dawson chose to feature a thin, light-skinned, straight-haired woman for this drawing, naming her after the Egyptian goddess Isis. To imagine Isis, the artist used models from advertisements for Hair Dressing Pomade and Slick-Black.[30] In sharp contrast to this image, Charles White's drawings and paintings of black women, such as "Gussie," featured women with darker complexions, varying body types, and different styles of hair. White's representation of black women would eventually be recognized as a significant divergence from what one progressive black journalist saw as the common image of a black woman "as a light-skinned wretched character 'passing for white.'" In viewing a 1951 solo New York exhibition by White called the *Negro Woman*, this same writer asked, "Is there now, or had there been, any other artist who had consistently striven to portray the Negro woman as child, adolescent, woman, mother, worker, leader, artist?"[31]

Other Chicago artists, along with White, also broke from their predecessors. In a Chicago-produced issue of *New Challenge* magazine, local black writers declared, "We are not attempting to re-stage the 'revolt' and 'renaissance' which grew unsteadily and upon false foundations ten years ago." Richard Wright insisted that every black writer should instead apply the ideology of Marxism, "unify his personality, organize his emotions, buttress him with a tense and obdurate will to change the world" and combine it with life experience to create a "full awareness" of "values by which the race is to struggle, live and die."[32] While the visual artists seldom clarified their vision in writing, they used their creativity to depict a similar "full awareness" on canvas and in stone. Marion Perkins, for example, carved figures from soap, wood, and rock while selling newspapers on Indiana Avenue and Thirty-Seventh Street on the South Side. He also attended meetings of the South Side Writers' Group, and after his sculptures attracted the attention of other artists by the late 1930s, he began to study under the white leftist sculptor Si Gordon. Perkins's "male subjects," one art historian concluded, "display spiritual intensity and anxiety, while his female figures symbolize refuge and tranquility."[33] More overtly political than Perkins, Bernard Goss painted works with titles like *Slave Rebellion* and *Always the Dirty Work*. Deeming himself a "revolutionary painter" in 1940, he said, "I'm not satisfied with social and economic conditions [and] my aim is to do something about them."[34] Like White, these black Chicago artists produced a new aesthetic that centered upon African Americans as dignified and hard-working Americans.

The convergence of the IAP, local black leaders, and the Artists Union in late 1930s also led to a campaign for an art center on the South Side. Beginning in 1938, Pollack discussed the idea of a center for black artists with the new IAP director George Thorp and a number of black community representatives. They concluded that the government had the ability to sponsor the renovation as well as the center's teachers and materials if the community would raise enough funds to buy a building to house these activities. During the Second New Deal, the government sponsored approximately one hundred such centers nationwide, but few of them were located in African American neighborhoods. This project, legitimated by government support, would make a larger point about the significance of black culture to American culture. A group of black community members (including businessmen, social workers, and union organizers) discovered a dilapidated mansion at 3831 South Michigan Avenue.[35] Once the location had been decided, artists like the twenty-one-year-old Margaret Goss became especially active in fund-raising by working out of a headquarters on East Garfield Park but more often standing on street corners in Bronzeville to collect for their "mile of dimes" campaign. In an effort to create community-wide support, the *Defender* printed favorable editorials, and merchants along Forty-Seventh Street (the nexus of Bronzeville during this era) displayed works by the artists in their windows. To tap the pocketbooks of the elite of Chicago's black community, these art advocates conceived of an Artists and Models Ball in 1939. With the help of Marva Louis, the wife of then heavyweight boxing champion Joe Louis, they sold tickets to what would become an annual charity event of theater, dance, and art to benefit the South Side Community Art Center (SSCAC). All of these events netted them about $8000, a large sum during the Depression, and they purchased the building for the new center.[36]

In the course of this Chicago New Deal artistic peak, two events stand out: the American Negro Exposition and the dedication of the South Side Community Art Center. Just before the art center had opened, many black artists displayed their work as part of a larger Diamond 1940 Jubilee Exposition, sponsored largely by the Democratic Party to secure black votes in that year's election. At the Chicago Coliseum, the exposition celebrated the progress of African Americans in the seventy-five years since emancipation. Among the more than two hundred pieces at the south hall of the exposition was White's *There Were No Crops This Year*, which graced the cover of the exhibit catalogue and won a first-prize award. Locke, who would become increasingly involved with Chicago artists in 1940 through this exhibit and others, declared that the exposition featured the "most comprehensive and representative collection of the Negro's art that has ever been presented for public view" and "put Negro art on the map."[37] Meanwhile, the art center opened in late 1940 and held four exhibitions and a dozen classes before First Lady Eleanor Roosevelt officially inaugurated it in May 1941. For this dedication event, the police cordoned off two blocks on South Michigan Avenue to accommodate the thousands of African Americans who flocked to the center. There, and later at the Parkway Ballroom, they heard Roosevelt endorse the center and call for a "democracy in art."[38]

Chicago's African American artists took this idea of democracy in art seriously. In its first year, the art center staff organized two-dozen exhibitions, which twenty-eight thousand people saw, and enrolled twelve thousand members of the community in classes. The center's artists also did not shy away from hosting political events. Despite the organization's harassment from the congressional committee of Martin Dies for being "red," the NNC held a "folk party" at the center in 1941 to raise money to support its civil rights work. The artists taught classes and worked in center's studio, and their centralized workspace fostered a greater cultural cohesion among them.[39] For White, the energy produced by the center made him more politically ambitious in his art. Gordon Parks, whose photography studio occupied the basement of the center, remembered touring Chicago's poorest areas of the South Side with White to get a better sense of the plight of the people there. Describing these areas as "wrecked and bombed out," Parks returned to the art center and observed White "strengthen an arm with a delicate brush stroke or give anguish to a face with mixtures of coloring" to depict what they had encountered in the neighborhood. Amazed by White's "powerful, black figures," Parks claimed that they "pointed to the kind of photography that I knew I should be doing."[40]

Charles White not only became increasingly bold in his subject matter but also in his choice of artistic medium. To reach a wider array of people with his art, he designed and completed three massive murals in Chi-

cago in 1939–40. For the first Artist and Models Ball at the Savoy in Chicago, White unveiled what would become his first mural, *Five Great Negroes*, which represented both his revisionist education in black history and use of art as a weapon. The mural featured Sojourner Truth and Frederick Douglass, former slaves who became ardent abolitionists; Booker T. Washington and George Washington Carver, educators and intellectuals from the early twentieth century; and Marian Anderson, the contemporary mezzo-soprano, who, in an act of cultural defiance, performed in front of the Lincoln Memorial when banned from Constitutional Hall by the lily-white Daughters of the American Revolution (see figure 10.19 in the current volume).[41] During the next two years in Chicago, White would produce a commissioned mural titled *The History of the Negro Press* for the Negro Exposition and a second one called *Chaos of the American Negro* to be installed at the Cleveland Hall public library, a fitting tribute to his early education in black history there (see figure 9.3). When asked about his decision to paint on such a large scale, White acknowledged his debt to Chicago muralists like Mitchell Siporin and Edward Millman but also claimed the medium as specifically important for "Negro history." "Easel paintings hang in museums and galleries where they are apt to be seen only by the privileged few," he told a reporter. "But art is not for artists and connoisseurs alone. It should be for the people."[42]

The national spotlight on these Chicago artists also exposed class tensions among Chicago's African Americans. Having contributed money to the center, the elite members of the Bronzeville community now tried to impose their own views of culture on these artists. Similar to the intellectual battles between artists and organizers of the 1940 exposition (discussed elsewhere in this volume), the center became a focal point for battles over notions of respectability.[43] In planning the dedication ceremony, the art center's board failed to invite the artists whose activism and work had spawned the center. Artists like Margaret Goss did not take this slight lightly. She and others demanded that the artists be included at the dedication and gave a short speech in which she dedicated the space to George Neal, their mentor, who had recently passed away. Referring to this self-directed period under Neal, Goss told the audience at the dedication, "We were not then and are not now complimented by the people who had the romantic idea we liked to live in garrets, wear cast-off clothes

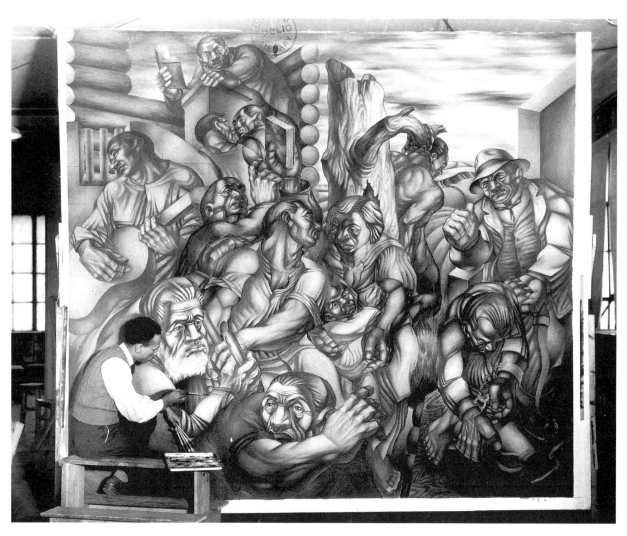

9.3 *Chaos of the American Negro*. Charles White sought out opportunities to paint public murals that depicted African American history, including *Chaos of the American Negro*, a WPA mural for the Cleveland Hall branch of the Chicago Public Library. Courtesy of Special Collections, Harold Washington Library Center, Chicago Public Library.

and go around with emaciated faces, painting for fun." Challenging the press accounts that romanticized their poverty as a source of their creativity, Goss instead claimed the center would provide "new hope and vistas" for the people in the neighborhood and serve as an important resource to "express our creativity and humanity."[44] Goss would later secure a position on the "elite board" of the center; with other progressive women like Pauline Kigh Reed and Thelma Kirkpatrick (of NNC affiliation), she fought to ensure the autonomy of the artists at the SSCAC.[45]

For these artists, political and artistic affiliations during the Popular Front sometimes crossed racial lines more easily than class lines. Parks, for example,

remembered with appreciation Pollack, the center's white director, who tried to protect the artists from the board: "A good deal of Peter's . . . time was spent assuaging the feelings of opinionated officers and trustees, all of whom had different ideas about running the place." Despite the feeling that "a revolt [by the board] was always at hand," Parks remembered the center as a "haven for striving painters, sculptors, dancers, writers and poets [and] always alive with some sort of activity."[46] Margaret Goss concurred. She remembered the "the days of 'black and white, unite and fight' [when] black and white people were together all the time." Her roommate during the summer of 1940, the renowned sculptor Elizabeth

Catlett, also asserted the "cultural needs" of the "working people of America." There was "greater collaboration between Negro and white," she wrote, "because of their common aim—economic security for the artist."[47] Rather than hampering their expression as African Americans, white leftist artists and IAP administrators encouraged it.

The onset of World War II dispersed some of the black artists from Chicago. In 1940, White married Catlett, moved to New Orleans for a short period, and then studied in New York. Thanks to two consecutive fellowships from the Chicago-based Julius Rosenwald Foundation, he worked in the south and New York before he enlisted in the army in 1944.[48] Soon thereafter, White and Catlett separated. After recovering from tuberculosis contracted in the army, White would eventually remarry and move to California. Gordon Parks also left Chicago for an international career as a photographer for *Life* magazine and, later, a filmmaker who would direct and produce milestone films like *The Learning Tree* and *Shaft*.[49] Pollack departed for the army and settled in New York after the war. As one teenage student of the art center, Gwendolyn Brooks, wrote to Pollack, "Foolishly, I had looked on you as a fixture here." Brooks wrote that Pollack "inspired [her] to start at the Art Center," and while she realized his departure was "for a noble reason," she nonetheless did not feel "joyous" about it.[50]

Those who remained in Chicago faced political and financial struggles when government and community support for artists dried up during and after the war. Increasingly after 1940, war production displaced arts programs. Before leaving for the army, Pollack, in an attempt to sustain the SSCAC, pitched the center as important to African American morale and convinced the WPA and later Office of Civilian Defense (OCD) to fund the production of war-related art.[51] Many artists put down their paints and instead created propaganda posters for government distribution. While these artists supported the war effort and the million black troops in uniform, the politics during the war nonetheless muted the artistic freedom that had existed for a time under the IAP. Once OCD funds diminished, the pressure to produce war-related art diminished, but it also put the center's future in jeopardy. Fortunately, a concerted group of women involved with the art center saved it from destruction. Pauline Kigh Reed formed a "Committee of 100" women, and they managed to

keep the center open, though at times its classes and resources were circumscribed compared to its first three years of operation.[52]

These artists also faced severe setbacks with the onset of McCarthyism after the war. The new political climate led the art center's board to evict communists and other progressives from the gallery and studios at the center. Although the board did not achieve its goal, the Cold War climate convinced artists like Margaret Goss Burroughs to take a long sojourn to Mexico in the early 1950s. Moreover, the new anti-communist repression in America severed many of the interracial ties between artists formed during the Popular Front era. As Burroughs explained, by the 1950s people believed that "certainly any white person who had a black friend was a Communist."[53]

The Cold War led these artists to form new alliances in Chicago and produced a stronger nationalist influence in their politics and artwork. After World War II, Margaret Goss, John Gray, and members of the Chicago Council of the National Negro Congress formed the National Negro Museum and Historical Foundation. This group published pamphlets, organized "Negro History Week" events, and held other cultural events that retained connections with labor at the Packinghouse Labor Center. At one of these NNC-sponsored events, White returned to Chicago to present "a report from the South," Goss performed "dramatic readings," and the audience sang "people's songs" and discussed the recent speech by W. E. B. Du Bois, "Behold the Land," that called for a southern civil rights movement in 1947.[54] This nonprofit group, according to the African American scholar St. Clair Drake, was the result of a backroom deal between prominent black leftists and the political head of the black Democratic submachine in Chicago, William Dawson. Drake recalled that Dawson offered to ensure the local "red squad" would not harass these artists for their past and present political affiliations if they would limit their protest to a "strict cultural nationalist line."[55] Although information on this deal between Dawson and black leftists does not appear in other sources, the documents of the early Historical Foundation do indicate a new level of cooperation between the Democratic machine and these activists. Their "Negro History Week" celebrations had the unprecedented endorsement of the mayor of Chicago and governor of Illinois, seemingly a concession secured by Dawson's black submachine. From the vantage point of these activists, they took this opportunity to continue to promulgate a revisionist version of black history that White and other artists had made central to their work during the Depression years. The members of the foundation demanded "Democracy in the South" and "Full Equality—Economic, Political, Cultural and Social—in the North" and made clear that "militancy and self-sacrifice for freedom is the tradition of American progress, and the Negro's struggle has strengthened it, kept it alive."[56] Moreover, Margaret Goss Burroughs and her new husband, Charles Burroughs (married in 1949), would start the Ebony Museum of black history across the street from the art center in 1961. A decade later, they convinced Mayor Richard J. Daley to donate a parks department building in Washington Park to found the DuSable Museum of African American History.[57] These accomplishments allowed this Popular Front generation of artists to remain culturally significant during a time of political repression. While many of the initial artists of Chicago's cultural renaissance dispersed during and after the war, those who remained sustained institutions like the South Side Community Art Center, organized new forums for African American culture, and would inspire a new generation of artists and activists in Chicago during the 1960s.

White left Chicago in 1940, but Chicago never left him. During the war years and into the 1950s, White's work became even more radical. White's earlier Chicago murals informed his most celebrated mural, *The Contribution of the Negro to Democracy in America*, a work he produced in 1943 at the Hampton Institute in Virginia. Like his *Five Great Negroes* mural, this one honored slave rebels like Vesey and Tubman and cultural figures like the blues singer Leadbelly but also contemporary political rebels like Max Yergan of the NNC and the internationally famous singer, actor, and activist Paul Robeson.[58] During the 1940s, White produced art in left-wing publications like the *Congress View*, the publication of the NNC during the war years, political pamphlets against lynching and other civil rights abuses, and communist-specific publications like *New Masses*.[59] For White, these causes were not peripheral to his art; they were the purpose of his art. He had heard stories about family members on his mother's side who had been lynched in Mississippi, and he barely escaped lethal beatings on two occasions when living in the south in the 1940s, once by a streetcar conductor in Hampton, Virginia, and a second time when

he entered an all-white tavern in New Orleans.[60] His portrayals of specific lynching cases helped publicize black, leftist civil rights causes but also became an intensely personal means of communicating his anguish over racial discrimination. Locke saw this work as art despite its specific political purpose. He wrote to White that a 1950 show of White's work in New York was a "joy to see, in spite of the heavy social criticism necessarily involved in your message." For Locke, White's use of art as a weapon had become overwhelming effective: "Though I grant the truth and urgency of the Trenton-Six and the Ingram case [two internationally publicized cases of racial brutality], I found myself at my age and stage too sensitive to take [these works] full blast except in staggered doses" (see figure 9.4).[61] Following this show and his *Negro Woman* show in New York, White traveled to Eastern Europe and the Soviet Union as part of a delegation for the Third World Festival for Youth and Students for Peace. Further radicalized, upon his return, he helped draft a press release against the increasing Cold War hostility in the United States. Declaring "We Will Not Be a Silent Generation," White and other youth leaders pledged to fight the "singling out of Negro youth among those of us subpoenaed [by the House of Un-American Activities]" and not be deterred by a "witch hunt . . . meant to create a 'silent generation' of youth, whose brains are dulled, whose mouths are closed."[62]

Though his travels and experiences would change his art, White remained resolute about depicting the "whole social scene" that concerned the pivotal place of African American culture in America. Upon seeing an exhibit of his work in 1961, Lorraine Hansberry, the black playwright and former neighbor of the White family in Chicago, believed that the "memories of that crucible, the Chicago Southside, must live deep within the breast of this artist. . . . For now what explodes from his boards, is a monumental essence of a people; with winged cheeks, the comforting and chastising eyes; the willful jaws set to book."[63] In oral histories and later writings, White always emphasized his years as a young man in Chicago: "I grew up in one of the poor sections of Chicago and have known hunger and misery. [M]y work is . . . dedicated with all the strength that I have to giving dignity to the lives of the people."[64]

By the late 1960s, White's emphasis on politically charged public art experienced a rebirth when black nationalists created installations on the South and

9.4. *Rosa Lee Ingram and Sons, Sammy and Wallace*, [ca. 1948]. Charles White's work increasingly depicted the civil rights struggles of African Americans during and after the Second World War, including Rosa Lee Ingram, a widowed tenant farmer in Georgia who in 1947 killed her white neighbor in self-defense but was nonetheless sentenced to death along with two of her sons. A campaign by the Civil Rights Congress, which Charles White supported, ultimately spared their lives. Courtesy of the Charles Wilbert White Papers, Archives of American Art, Smithsonian Institution.

West Sides of Chicago. In preparing a filmstrip on the progression of African American art for school children in the 1970s, White selected a chronology that originated in West Africa, continued despite repression during the slavery era, became modern and urban during the early twentieth century, revived a militant African American identity during the Popular Front era, and led to the 1960s generation with works like the *Wall of Respect*, a mural on Chicago's South Side (see figure 9.5). Conceived in 1967 as a tribute to "black heroes," this wall paralleled the Chicago murals of White. Yet, the two-dozen artists who originally created it took White's idea a step further by making it a collaborative, community-created mural. White approved of this new "mass art" and

hoped it would lead to the "full participation by all in the meaning of a new functional art." The *Wall* and other installations made Chicago a center for African American art once again, as black and Latino artists and activists would launch mural projects in a dozen other cities the following year.[65]

The trajectory from White's *Five Great American Negroes* to *Wall of Respect* bookend an African American renaissance in the arts of Chicago that congealed around black culture as intertwined with social justice. Before the federal government aided any of these artists, they formed their own classes under George Neal and learned from each other. The network created by the NNC also contributed to this black-led movement that went across racial lines but certainly

9.5. *Wall of Respect.* Charles White appreciated a new generation of artists who depicted militant African American history in public art exemplified by this mural at Forty-Third and Langley on Chicago's South Side. Photograph courtesy of Mark Rogovin.

did not seek to parrot white leftist politics. African Americans, these artists believed, had their own rich history and stood at the cultural vanguard of America, not its periphery. By the mid-1930s, progressive white members of the IAP and Artists Union witnessed the talent coming from the South Side and sought to join it. Although black "cultural workers" benefited from interactions with their white counterparts, scholars have assumed that too much of their radical politics was conveyed from white leftists to African Americans. The current chapter shows, however, that a black-led protest movement of the 1930s and 1940s inspired these artists as much as white leftists did. In fact, the members of IAP desired to join these black artists and activists as much as the black artists and activists wanted to join the IAP members.

At its early 1940s peak, the group of black artists that had labored in relative obscurity in Chicago became nationally known. Through the creation of the South Side Community Art Center, the Negro Exposition, and follow-up shows at the Library of Congress and Howard University, Chicago became the vibrant center of African American culture. Even Richard Wright, who had departed Chicago for New York in 1937, returned around 1940 to work on a book that would become *12 Million Black Voices.* "Voices are speaking," he concluded in this book, and African Americans are "with the new tide" that moves into the "sphere of conscious history."

This book, produced at the height of the black arts movement during the Popular Front era in Chicago, became one of Richard Wright's most optimistic assessments of black urban life and culture. By looking at the development of artists in Chicago, this essay helps explain this optimism. Parks remembered that Wright inscribed Parks's copy of *12 Million Black Voices*—that "became my bible"—as "to one who moves with the tide."[66] That Wright returned to witness and write about this tide is significant, however, because although Wright had been part of it in 1936, he had little to do with the high tide that crested four years later. The culture and protest politics of these African Americans became so intertwined in Chicago that, unlike the Harlem Renaissance, it is hard to separate them. This crossing of previously distinctive political and cultural spheres and class and racial lines informed the artistic development of Chicago's native son, Charles White, and he, in turn, left his mark on the city of his youth long after his departure from the South Side.

Although World War II and postwar McCarthyism severed many of these interracial alliances and deprived African American artists in Chicago of further national attention, the war and McCarthyism did not change the artists' mission to depict the humanity of working people and, specifically, the history of struggle by African Americans. The strong network of African American progressive "cultural workers" from the Depression era held together to inform the civil rights protests and black nationalism enacted by the next generation.

Notes

1. Dwight Casimere, "Charles White: Giant of American Art Portrays: The Original Man," *Muhammad Speaks*, Chicago, December 6 and December 20, 1968, copy, roll 3194, "printed materials," Charles White Papers, Smithsonian Archives of American Art, Washington, D.C. (hereafter White Papers); Charles White, interview by Betty Hoag, "Oral History Interview with Charles White, 1965 Mar. 9," March 9, 1965, 6–7, transcript at http://www.aaa.si.edu/collections/oralhistories/transcripts/white65.htm.

2. Bone focuses on Richard Wright and the South Side Writers' Group. Mullen's study looks less to Wright than to the "rapprochement between African-American and white members of the U.S. left." See Robert Bone, "Richard Wright and the Chicago Renaissance," *Callaloo* 28 (Summer 1986): 447–48; and Bill Mullen, *Popular Fronts: Chicago and African-American Cultural Politics, 1935–46* (Chicago: University of Illinois Press, 1999), 5, especially 75–105, which deals with Chicago's visual artists.

3. Daniel Schulman, "'White City' and 'Black Metropolis': African American Painters in Chicago, 1893–1945," in *Chicago Modern 1893–1945, Pursuit of the New*, ed. Elizabeth Kennedy (Chicago: Terra Museum and University of Chicago Press, 2004), 39–48; and Andrea D. Barnwell, *Charles White*, David C. Driskell Series of African American Art, vol. 1 (San Francisco: Pomegranate, 2002), 3–26. The most cogent account of 1930s artists and their politics focused primarily on New York. See Andrew Hemmingway, *Artists on the Left: American Artists and the Communist Movement, 1926–1956* (New Haven: Yale University Press, 2002).

4. White, interview by Betty Hoag, 6; Charles White, translation for an article after return to Europe, 4, n.d. [early 1950s], roll 3189, White Papers; "Miss Vivian Harsh Gets Library Post," *Chicago Defender*, July 11, 1931, 4; "Hall Branch Library Is 8 Years Old," Chicago *Defender*, January 20, 1940, 4; "George C. Hall Library Notes: 38th and Michigan," *Chicago Defender*, April 11, 1936, 30. White probably frequented the Ogden Park branch (in Englewood) of the public library, where Vivian Harsh worked as a librarian before her appointment as the head librarian of the Hall branch. White may have also spent time at the main public library in downtown Chicago.

5. White, translation for an article after return to Europe; Casimere, "Charles White"; White, interview by Betty Hoag, 6; and Alain Locke, ed., *The New Negro* (1925; repr., New York: Atheneum, 1992).

6. See Arnold Rampersad, introduction, in Locke, *New Negro*, xviii–xxi; David Levering Lewis, *When Harlem Was in Vogue*, (New York: Knopf, 1981); Sterling Brown, "The New Negro in Literature, 1925–1955," in *The New Negro Thirty Years Afterward: Papers Contributing to the Sixteenth Annual Spring Conference of the Division of Social Sciences*, ed. Rayford Logan, Eugene C. Holmes, and G. Franklin Edwards (Washington, D.C.: Howard University Press, 1955), 62.

7. See Michael Feith and Genevieve Fabre, eds., *Temples for Tomorrow: Looking Back at the Harlem Renaissance* (Bloomington: Indiana University Press, 2001); Venetria Patton and Maureen Honey, eds., *Double Take: A Revisionist Harlem Renaissance Anthology* (New Brunswick: Rutgers University Press, 2001).

8. White, interview by Betty Hoag, 6; Alain Locke, "The New Negro," in Locke, *New Negro*, 11, 14. White made a distinction between his memory of reading *The New Negro* as a young man and his criticism of the Harlem Renaissance in later years. During the peak of his political radicalism in the1950s, White told a reporter that the leap in maturity of black artists happened earlier than the 1920s and that the Harlem movement was more about the discovery of these artists by white patrons and critics. While White believed this discovery benefited artists by giving them exposure, he also claimed it led to an abandonment of their own people in favor of a "shallow cosmopolitanism." See Sidney Finkelstein, draft of an article, 1954, 13, roll 3194, White Papers.

9. Charles White, translation for an article after return to Europe, 5–7; Margaret Taylor Goss Burroughs, Chicago, interview by Anna M. Tyler, November 11 and December 5, 1988, transcript, 19–25, Afro-American Artists, Chicago Oral History Project, Smithsonian Archives of American Art, Washington, D.C.; Peter Clothier, "Charles White: A Critical Perspective," in *Images of Dignity: A Retrospective of the Works of Charles White* (New York: Studio Museum of Harlem, 1982), 12.

10. Willard F. Motley, "Negro Art in Chicago," *Opportunity* 18 (January, 1940): 21–22; Walter Christmas, "Artist Seeks Life of Man on Street," *Daily Compass*, n.d. [1951], subject files: *The Worker*, roll 3194, White Papers; and Charles White, translation for an article after return to Europe, 5; Barnwell, *Charles White*, 16.

11. Burroughs, interview by Anna M. Tyler, 19–22; Bernard Goss, "Art Chronicle: Ten Negro Artists on Chicago's South Side," *Midwest—A Review*, December, 1936, 17–19, clipping in scrapbook 1, roll 3195, White Papers; Leontine Collier and Violetta Harrigan to Charles White, January 8, 1979, subject files, George Edward Neal Art Committee, roll 3192, White Papers; White, interview by Betty Hoag, 4; and Clothier, "Charles White," 12.

12. *Chicago Defender*, February 22, 1936, natl. ed., 3. See also *1936 Delegates to the National Negro Congress*, comp. Lori Husband (Matteson, Ill.: Self-published, 1998). Nahum Brascher, a reporter for the *Defender*, wrote "Weather—Zero—cannot stop folks when they choose to know what it's all about." The same source quoted the banners and listed some of the "IKN's." "Race Congress Sidelights," *Chicago Defender*, February 22, 1936, 5.

13. "Race Congress Sidelights" and "Congress Opens: Delegates Crowd City for Sessions," *Chicago Defender*, February 15, 1936, 1, 2; Richard Wright, "Two Million Black Voices," *New Masses*, February 25, 1936, 15; "Outline of Program for 4-Day Session of Nat. Negro Congress," *Chicago Defender*, February 15, 1936, 2; National Negro Congress, *The Official Proceedings of the National Negro Congress*, (Washington, D.C.: NNC, 1936), 32–33; Hazel Rowley, *Richard Wright: The Life and Times* (New York: Holt, 2001), 115–16; Richard Wright,

"The Meaning of the NNC," n.d. [1936] item 882, box 79, Richard Wright Papers, Yale Collection of American Literature, Beinecke Rare Book Room and Manuscript Library, Yale University.

14. Erik S. Gellman, *Death Blow to Jim Crow: The National Negro Congress and the Rise of Militant Civil Rights* (Chapel Hill: University of North Carolina Press, 2012).

15. Fine Arts Committee, National Negro Congress, Chicago, "Reception in Honor of Arna Bontemps," flyer for April 26, 1936, event, "National Negro Congress" folder, box 21, Arna Bontemps Papers, Special Collections Department, Bird Library, Syracuse University. The advance for this novel paid for Bontemps's 1935 move to Chicago and got him a position on the Illinois Writers Project. Looking back on his novel in the late 1960s, Bontemps stressed that "the theme of self-assertion by black men whose endurance was strained to the breaking point was not one that readers of fiction were prepared to contemplate [in the 1930s]." Judging from the NNC reception and Bontemps's role in this artistic movement in Chicago, his recollection may have been obscured by the suppression of this cultural movement during the Cold War. Bontemps, introduction, *Black Thunder* (1936; repr., Boston: Beacon, 1968), xiv–xv.

16. "Reception in Honor of Arna Bontemps"; Richard Wright, "A Tale of Folk Courage," draft review of *Black Thunder*, item 1018, box 86, White Papers; Rowley, *Richard Wright*, 111; Margaret Walker, *Richard Wright, Daemonic Genius: A Portrait of the Man, A Critical Look at His Work* (New York: Amistad, 1988), 78.

17. Benjamin Horowitz, draft of essay for *Images of Dignity: The Drawings of Charles White* (Los Angeles: W. Ritchie Press, 1967), subject file: Howard University, roll 3192, White Papers.

18. White, interview by Betty Hoag, 8, 20; Burroughs, interview by Tyler, 45; and Barnwell, *Charles White*, 22.

19. George Mavigliano and Richard Lawson, *The Federal Art Project in Illinois: 1935–1943* (Carbondale: Southern Illinois University Press, 1990), 1–16, 24.

20. Article clipping [about November 1936 exhibit by White and Goss at Paragon studios, 3336 N. Michigan], scrapbook #1, roll 3195, White Papers; Margaret Taylor Goss Burroughs, essay in 50th Anniversary Advertising Book of the South Side Community Art Center (Chicago: South Side Community Art Center, 1991), copy in possession of the author (thanks to Dr. Burroughs); Horowitz, draft of essay, for *Images of Dignity*; and Charles White, translation for an article after return to Europe, 5, 7; and White, interview by Betty Hoag, 4.

21. Gellman, *Death Blow to Jim Crow*.

22. Mavigliano and Lawson, *Federal Art Project in Illinois*, 30–41.

23. White, translation for an article after return to Europe, 7.

24. Mavigliano and Lawson, *Federal Art Project in Illinois*, 25–46.

25. White, translation for an article after return to Europe, 7.

26. Goss, "Art Chronicle," 16–18; Barnwell, *Charles White*, 7; and Motley, "Negro Art in Chicago," 21–22.

27. Motley, "Negro Art in Chicago," 19, 29–31.

28. Charles Dawson, unpublished autobiography, 345, 358–59, roll 4191–92, Charles C. Dawson Papers, Smithsonian Archives of American Art, Washington, D.C. (hereafter Dawson Papers); Daniel Schulman, "'White City' and 'Black Metropolis': African American Painters in Chicago, 1893–1945," in *Chicago Modern, 1893–1945: Pursuit of the New* (Chicago: Terra Museum of American Art, 2004); Goss, "Art Chronicle," 17–18; and Bertrand Phillips, "William Edouard Scott (1884–1964)," *World Magazine*, November 3, 1973, "Material on other Artists," roll 3915, White Papers.

29. Amy Mooney, *Archibald J. Motley Jr.*, David C. Driskell Series of African American Art, vol. 4 (San Francisco: Pomegranate, 2004); Schulman, "'White City' and 'Black Metropolis,'" 48; and Amy Mooney, "Representing Race: Disjunctures in the Work of Archibald Motley Jr.," *Art Institute of Chicago: Museum Studies* 24, no. 2 (1999): 163–79.

30. Charles Dawson, "Famous Black Beauties in History and Mythology 2: Isis," advertisement for Poro Schools of Beauty Culture, Chicago, and advertisements for Hair Dressing Pomade and Slick-Black, roll 4191, Dawson Papers.

31. Clothier, "Charles White," 11; John Pittman, "Charles White's Exciting 'Negro Woman' Show at ACA," *Daily Worker*, February 26, 1951, and "Race Women Honored in Art Exhibit," *Pittsburgh Courier*, both in scrapbook 2, roll 3195, White Papers.

32. Richard Wright, "Editorial" and "Blueprint for Negro Writing," *New Challenge* 2, no. 2 (Fall 1937): 3–4, 36–49.

33. Toussaint Perkins, Eugene Perkins, and Fern Gayden, "Statement of Purpose: The Marion Perkins Memorial Foundation, Inc.," n.d. [post 1961], Material on Other Artists, roll 3195, White Papers; Rowley, *Richard Wright*, 117; Margaret G. Burroughs, "It Seems to Me," newspaper clipping, n.d. [1950s?], printed materials, roll 3194, White Papers; and especially, Daniel Schulman, "Marion Perkins: A Chicago Sculptor Rediscovered," *Art Institute of Chicago: Museum Studies* 24, no. 2 (1999): 221–43.

34. Motley, "Negro Art in Chicago," 19, 20–21; IAP, Bulletin Exhibition Division Month Ending December 31, 1940, printed material, exhibition announcements, roll 3194, White Papers.

35. Burroughs, essay in 50th Anniversary Advertising Book; Alain Locke, "Chicago's New South Side Art Center," *American Federation of Arts* 34 (August–September 1941), 370–74.

36. Locke, "Chicago's New South Side Art Center"; "Stars Prepare for Artists Models Ball," unidentified article clipping, October 1939, scrapbook 1, roll 3195, White Papers; Gordon Parks, *A Choice of Weapons* (1965; New York: Berkley Medallion, 1967), 170; "Chicago Active in Effort to Establish Community Art Center," *Chicago Defender*, May 20, 1939; "Howard Art Gallery Exhibits Works of Nationally Known Young Artists," unidentified newspaper clipping, April 29, 1939, scrapbook 1, roll 3195, White Papers; "The Community Art Center," editorial, *Chicago Defender*, March 1, 1941, 14; Robert Davis, "A Community Adventure," *Chicago Defender*, March 1, 1941, 13; "South Side Art Center Planned," *Chicago Sunday Times*, October 22, 1939, scrapbook, roll 4887, Peter Pollack Papers, Archives of American Art, Smithsonian, Washington, D.C. (hereafter Pollack Papers).

37. American Negro Exposition, "Exhibition of the Art of the American

Negro (1851 to 1940)," catalogue from Tanner Art Galleries show, Chicago, July 4–September 2, 1940, copy in materials on other artists, roll 3195, White Papers; Illinois Writers' Project, *Cavalcade of the American Negro* (Chicago: Diamond Jubilee Exposition Authority, 1940), 94–95.

38. Locke, "Chicago's New Southside Art Center," 374; "Editor Congratulates First Lady" and "So. Side Greets Mrs. Roosevelt," *Chicago Sunday Bee*, May 11, 1941, 1; and Chicago Park District Traffic and Engineering Section, Dedication of the South Side Community Art Center, 1941, and "Dedication by Mrs. Franklin D. Roosevelt, South Side Community Art Center," program for May 7, 1941 dedication, all roll 4887, scrapbook, Pollack Papers; and "First Lady Spends Busy Three Hours in Chicago," *Chicago Defender*, May 10, 1941.

39. Burroughs, "Saga of Chicago's South Side Community Art Center," 10; Locke, "Chicago's New Southside Art Center," 370–71; and Norman MacLeish in "Exhibition of Negro Artists of Chicago," catalogue, Washington, D.C., 1941, Material on Other Artists, roll 3195, White Papers.

40. Parks, *Choice of Weapons*, 171–72.

41. "Stars Prepare for Artists Models Ball"; Robert A. Davis, "The Art Notebook," *Chicago Sunday Bee*, October 6, 1940, scrapbook 1, roll 3195, White Papers; Motley, "Negro Art in Chicago," 21–22; Benjamin Horowitz, draft of essay for *Images of Dignity: The Drawings of Charles White*, 1967, subject files, Howard University, roll 3192, White Papers; Barnwell, *Charles White*, 4.

42. Barnwell, *Charles White*, 26; William Carter, "The Art Notebook," *Chicago Bee*, May 26 and May 27, 1940, scrapbook 1, roll 3195, White Papers; and "Art Today: Mural by a Talented Artist," *Daily Worker*, New York, August 28, 1943, scrapbook 1, roll 3195, White Papers.

43. For more on class divisions with respect to these African American artists in Chicago, see Jeff Helgeson, "Who Are You America but Me?" in the current volume.

44. Burroughs, "Saga of Chicago's South Side Community Art Center," 8, 9.

45. Another telling incident concerned J. Levirt Kelly, a local union organizer with ties to Chicago's underworld. Kelly had contributed a substantial amount of money to become a "life member" of the Art Center, but the other elite donors did not want him to attend the dedication ceremonies because of his connections to seedy enterprises and less-than-respectable behavior. To ensure his nonparticipation, the police brought Kelly to the station for "questioning" during the dedication. "Union Head Arrested Only 'For Questioning,'" *Chicago Defender*, May 11, 1941, scrapbook, roll 4887, Pollack Papers; and Burroughs, "Saga of Chicago's South Side Community Art Center," 8, 14.

46. Parks, *Choice of Weapons*, 166–69.

47. Elizabeth Catlett, "The Negro Artist in America," *American Contemporary Art*, April 1944, 1, 4–5,6, clipping in subject file "Catlett," roll 3191, White Papers; Locke in American Negro Exposition, "Exhibition of the Art of the American Negro (1851 to 1940)"; and Burroughs, interview by Tyler, 43–48.

48. Rosenwald fellowships proved crucial to artists like White and Parks when government-sponsored art funding dried up during the war. Unlike New York, Chicago had few rich benefactors willing to sponsor African American artists. The Rosenwald Fund, begun by Julius Rosenwald, the Jewish-born owner of Sears Department Store, and continued after his death, placed specific emphasis on funding African American cultural figures. See Benjamin Horowitz, draft of essay for *Images of Dignity*; White, interview by Betty Hoag; and William C. Haygood, director of fellowships, Rosenwald Fund, to Charles White, April 18, 1942, Mrs. William C. Haygood, acting director for fellowships, Julius Rosenwald Fund, Chicago, to Charles White, April 21, 1943, and Charles White, "Report of a Year's Progress and Plan for Renewal of a Julius Rosenwald Fellowship," all in subject files, Julius Rosenwald Fellowship, roll 3193, White Papers.

49. Parks, *Choice of Weapons*, 180. As his first assignment for *Life* magazine, Parks chose to photograph a gang in Harlem, a choice that paralleled his emphasis on working-class black life in Chicago. See Parks, "Harlem Gang Leader," *Life*, November 1, 1948, 96–106.

50. "Farewell Party for Mr. Peter Pollack," invitation, November 12, 1942, and Gwendolyn Brooks Blakely to Peter Pollack, November 13, 1942, Chicago, scrapbook, roll 4887, Pollack Papers.

51. The Lanham Act in 1942 allowed New Deal administrators to apply for funds if their activities related to national defense. See Peter Pollack, "Report to the Board of Directors," South Side Community Art Center, September 25, 1942, Daniel Catton Rich, "The Negro in the Art World," unidentified magazine article, n.d. [1942–1944], Peter Pollack, "Negro War Posters," unidentified magazine article, n.d. [1942–1944], all roll 4887, Pollack Papers; and Mavigliano and Lawson, *Federal Art Project in Illinois*, 17, 21, 46.

52. Burroughs, "Saga of Chicago's South Side Community Art Center," 15; South Side Community Art Center, "National Negro Art Exhibition: We Too Look at America: Exhibition of Paintings, Sculpture, Drawings," May 1941 exhibit catalogue, material on other artists, roll 3195, White Papers; South Side Community Art Center to Fellow Artist, n.d. [1965], and Fern Gayden to Charles White, March 9, 1966, both in subject files, SSCAC, roll 3193, White Papers.

53. Burroughs, "Saga of Chicago's South Side Community Art Center," 14; Burroughs, interview by Tyler, quote from 44, also 61. African Americans reacted differently to the Cold War repression of communism than their white counterparts in Chicago. Chicago poet and journalist Frank Marshall Davis claimed that during his stint as a reporter for the leftist *Chicago Star*, "Roughly a third of its subscribers were black, for South Siders independent of the dictates of the white power structure paid little attention to Red baiting. I personally knew of a sizeable number of lawyers, doctors, and schoolteachers who made cash contributions to the ghetto headquarters of the Communist party with the admonition, 'Keep my name out of it—but give 'em hell!'" Frank Marshall Davis, *Livin' the Blues: Memoirs of a Black Journalist and Poet* (Madison: University of Wisconsin Press, 1992), 282, quote from 298.

54. The Packinghouse Labor Center was located at Forty-Ninth and Wabash on the South Side of Chicago. The event discussed above took

place at the home of John Gray at 211 East Twenty-Sixth Street. "An Evening with the Executive Board of the National Negro Congress," March 30, 1947, Chicago, frame 440, reel 32, series 2, microfilm edition, Papers of the National Negro Congress, Schomburg Center for Research in Black Culture, New York Public Library, Harlem.

55. St. Clair Drake, interview by Robert E. Martin, July 28, 1969, number 462, transcript, 80, 118–21, Ralph J. Bunche Oral History Collection, Moorland-Spingarn Research Center, Howard University, Washington, D.C.

56. "Negro History Week Mass Meeting at DuSable Sunday," *Chicago Bee*, February 10, 1946, 6; Chicago NNC, "Negro History Week News," February 3, 1947, frame 454, National Negro Museum and Historical Foundation to Friend, January 13, 1947, frame 472, National Negro Museum and Historical Foundation, and Chicago NNC, "Negro History Folder," February 1947, frames 461–68, and National Negro Museum and Historical Foundation, "Win a People's Peace: Negro History Week," February 10–17, 1946, frames 353–60, all on reel 32, series 2, NNC papers. For the cultivation of this black-leftist network during the war years, see also "Rear Adm. Evers Is Speaker at Library Forum," *Chicago Tribune*, February 1, 1942, S7; and South Side Community Art Center, "Chicago Collectors Exhibit of Negro Art," April 8–May 3, 1945, Material on Other Artists, roll 3195, White Papers.

57. Eugene Pieter Feldman, *The Birth and the Building of the DuSable Museum* (Chicago: DuSable Press, 1981), 12–15, 61, 90.

58. "The Contribution of the Negro to Democracy in America," invitation to formal presentation of White's mural, Hampton Institute, Virginia, July 25, 1943, Subject Files, Hampton Institute, roll 3191, White Papers; White, interview by Hoag, 10.

59. See *New Masses*, April 23, 1946, May 7, 1946, December 12, 1946, and February 11, 1947, copies in Subject Files: New Masses, roll 3192, White Papers; Lou [Burnham] to Charles White, April 21, 1955, General Correspondence, roll 3189, White Papers. For examples of artwork in the *Congress View* (previously the *Congress Vue*), see November 1943, February 1944, and April 1945 issues; for examples of pamphlets, see Harry Raymond, "Dixie Comes to New York: The Story of the Freeport GI Slayings"; W. E. B. Du Bois, "Behold the Land" (Birmingham: Southern Negro Youth Congress, 1946); "We Demand Freedom! Two Addresses by William L. Patterson" (Civil Rights Congress, n.d.); and "An Appeal to Negro Youth: Join Hands to Free Walter Lee Irvin" (Washington, D.C.: N.p., 1952). Copies of White's artwork in these and many other illustrations for pamphlets are in printed materials, reproductions, roll 3194, White Papers.

60. White, interview by Hoag, 15; Christmas, "Artist Seeks Life of Man on Street," 24; and White, translation for an article after return to Europe, 9.

61. Locke wrote that although White's "Trenton Six" painting "was unsold" when he visited the gallery, he could not bring himself to buy it. See Alain Locke to Charles White, February 27, 1950, Subject Files: Alain Locke, roll 3192, White Papers; and Christmas, "Artist Seeks Life of Man on Street," 24.

62. Sidney Kramer, "It's About Time for PEACE!" *New Challenge* 1, no. 4 (December 1951), 4–5; White, translation for an article after return to Europe, 11–14; Charles White and Joy Silver, press release, January 15, 1942, New York, Charles White to Konstantien Nepomnyashe, "Charles White Tells a Story," n.d. [1952], and Charles White, Paul Robeson Jr., and other left youth leaders, "We Will Not Be a Silent Generation," signed statement, 1952, all in subject files, Third World Festival of Youth and Students for Peace, roll 3193, White Papers.

63. Lorraine Hansberry, quoted in Gallery 1199, New York, "An Exhibition of the Art of Charles White," September to December, 1980, Heritage Gallery, in Subject Files: Heritage Gallery, roll 3192, White Papers; Horowitz, *Images of Dignity*.

64. Charles White, "'Until the Day I Die, My Life Is Dedicated to My People'," *Freedom*, New York, n.d. [early 1950s], clipping found in Third World Festival for Youth and Students folder, subject files, roll 3193, White Papers.

65. Charles White, Black Art Filmstrip, n.d. [late 1960s or early 1970s], Subject Files: Scholastic Magazine, roll 3193, White Papers. William Walker headed the original "Wall of Respect" collaboration in 1967. *Ebony* magazine, based in Chicago, publicized the art project nationally. See "Wall of Respect," *Ebony* 23, no. 2 (December 1967): 48–50; "'Wall of Respect' Is Dedicated Here at Black Festival," *Chicago Defender*, October 2, 1967, 14–15; Jeff Donaldson, "The Rise, Fall and Legacy of the Wall of Respect Movement," *International Review of African American Art* 15, no. 1 (1998): 22–26; Jeff Huebner, "The Man behind the Wall," *Chicago Reader*, August 29, 1997, 1, 14–32; "Chicago Muralists Heralded," October 20, 2005, *Community Media Workshop*, http://www.newstips.org/?p=2758. The Block Museum at Northwestern University has created a website about the "Wall of Respect" at http://www.blockmuseum.northwestern.edu/wallofrespect/main.htm.

66. Richard Wright, *12 Million Black Voices*, photos by Edward Rosskam (1941; repr., New York: Basic Books, 2002), 146–47.

Part III

Visual Art and Artists in the
Black Chicago Renaissance

Chapter 10

Chicago's African American Visual Arts Renaissance

MURRY N. DePILLARS

The catalytic forces of the Great Depression made visible Chicago's African American arts renaissance, but decades of African American achievements in the arts prepared the ground for this emergence. Largely overlooked by art historians and other art mavens, Chicago's history of African American art has been preserved and articulated by a small core of ardent adherents who experienced this visual arts renaissance.

The most widely accepted theory among renaissance adherents places Chicago's visual arts renaissance from the beginning of the New Deal in 1932 to 1950, when postwar Chicagoans experienced newfound prosperity but also Cold War politics. For example, although it was not the intent of her research project, art historian Elizabeth Anne Herzog's research supported the flourishing of the black arts in Chicago. While gathering information on Elizabeth Catlett's brief 1940 and 1941 stays in Chicago, Herzog became acquainted with and impressed by the little-known achievements of some Works Progress Administration (WPA) era artists. Influenced by her

findings, Herzog wrote, "This was the period, of the Chicago Renaissance in the literary and visual arts, characterized by writers, playwrights, and visual artists who came together on Chicago's South Side to produce incisive, socially critical forms of cultural expression for a predominantly African American audience."[1]

According to this framework, the efflorescence was ignited by: (1) the inflow of black southerners into Chicago; (2) the creation of the WPA's Federal Art Project (FAP) administered by the Illinois Art Project (IAP); (3) the founding of the South Side Community Art Center (SSCAC); and (4) the artistic production and promotion of Chicago black arts scene by leading artists, such as Margaret Taylor Goss Burroughs, William Carter, Eldzier Cortor, Gordon Parks, Charles Sebree, and Charles White.

By contrast, other scholars have turned the chronology of this Chicago movement backward. In her essay about the Chicago African American artist Archibald J. Motley Jr. and the Art Institute, art historian Elaine D. Woodall noted that the artistic and literary momentum in Chicago "began during the early 1920s that sparked the city's 'Negro Renaissance.'"[2] Stretching the chronology and geography even further, music historian Samuel Floyd Jr. placed Chicago's artists as part of a global movement across a half century. Chicago's African American artists became part "of a worldwide movement that had its beginnings in the 1890s and continued into the middle of the twentieth century," according to Floyd, and "the Negro Renaissance embraced Washington, D.C., Atlanta, Paris, London, and other large cities around the world."[3] And writing specifically on the visual arts, in 2005, painter and curator Jonathan Liss marked the importance of the migration of blacks to Chicago as a catalyst for new forms of art. "Chicago played an important role in the history of African American visual art during the first half of the 20th century," he concluded. "As thousands of black families moved to the city after World War I, black artists found new opportunities to develop tight-knit communities."[4]

While the precision of these and other renaissance theories has not been tested through more thorough research, the explanations advanced to bolster the 1932–50 renaissance theory prove insufficient. Since the WPA began in 1935 and the SSCAC did not open its doors until late 1940, these institutions sustained more than sparked the visual-arts renaissance. In addition, the renaissance's vanguard artists had not attained the artistic maturity to represent an efflorescence that began in 1932. With an average 15.6 years of age, Margaret Burroughs, John Carlis Jr., Eldzier Cortor, Charles Sebree, and Charles White were high school students in 1932. While talented, these artists would have been the first to admit that they were not artistically mature so early. While a few others had finished high school, many had just arrived in Chicago to begin professional training. William Carter, a recent St. Louis high school graduate, arrived in Chicago in 1931 to attend classes at the School of the Art Institute. And artists like Gordon Parks did not relocate from St. Paul, Minnesota, to Chicago until 1940.

The late 1930s emergence of Chicago's younger generation of black artists became abundantly clear in the Hull House's 1939 *Negro in Art* exhibition. This exhibit of seventy-two paintings, drawings, and sculptures included works by Cortor, Sebree, White, Henry Avery, William Carter, Charles Davis, Ray-

mond "Ramon" Gabriel, Bernard Goss, Fred Hollingsworth, and Earl Walker. Persuaded by the quality of the seventy-two works included in this exhibition and subsequent interviews with a few of its most promising artists, Willard Motley wrote an article of praise. But Motley emphasized the potential of these artists rather than their current prominence: "This present generation hasn't found itself yet and realizes it. Some of the artists are still students. But one day they undoubtedly will have something powerful to say." Moreover, Motley noted, these young artists and students were "following the trail blazed years ago by William Scott, Archibald Motley, Charles Dawson, and William Farrow."[5]

In addition to the artists named above, at least a half-dozen others made up the early 1920s group of African American artists. A whole decade before the Depression, Henry Brown, Pauline Callis, Elmer Simms Campbell, Leroy Holmes, Leslie Rogers, and Vincent Saunders Jr. had spearheaded a period of unprecedented artistic momentum and vitality that contributed to Chicago being known by some as "one of the centers of Negro art" or "the center of Negro art." Scholars have begun to recognize the significance of this earlier group who migrated to Chicago as a place to express their art. "While Harlem has been heralded as the center," historian Davarian Baldwin notes, "when most migrants connected freedom with the urban North, 'the mecca was Chicago.'"[6]

As Baldwin and others have discovered, the achievements of Chicago's African American artists were not limited to painters. Filmmakers, for example, also contributed to the 1920s perception of Chicago representing the early-twentieth-century "mecca" of black expressive culture.[7] In 1910, William "Bill" Foster (1884–n.d.) launched America's black independent film movement when he founded Foster Photoplay Company in Chicago and produced *The Railroad Porter* two years later. This movement flourished during the next decade; between 1912 and 1920, black independent film companies sprang up in Chicago including the Ebony Motion Picture Corporation, Peter P. Jones Photoplay Company, Royal Gardens Motion Picture Company, Micheaux Book and Film Company, and Unique Film Company. In addition to newsreels, these companies produced more than fifty films by 1920.[8]

Visual artists during this earlier period served as role models, teachers, and mentors for this younger generation. Artists such as Dawson, Farrow, Motley, and Scott remained active through the post–World War II era.[9] This interaction with younger artists, coupled with their lengthy careers, made both their presence and works relevant to the later era. Rather than discrete and unrelated periods, the Negro renaissance and Chicago Renaissance felt adjoined and transgenerational.[10] By re-adjoining these periods, this chapter employs a wider lens to examine the productivity and innovations of black artists in Chicago.

Early Chicago and the Arts

The tragic Great Fire of 1871 led Chicago's leaders to remake the city with a greater attention to urban culture. A small group of prominent white Chicago leaders envisioned a new city as a world-class center of banking, commerce, and transportation, but they also promoted Chicago as a center for the arts. Included among the cultural and educational institutions established between 1871 and 1899 were the Auditorium Theatre, Chicago Symphony Orchestra, Orchestra Hall, Chicago Public Library, University of Chicago, Newberry Library, and Field Columbian Museum (the Field Museum of Natural History).

During this late-nineteenth-century period of rebuilding, a legion of Chicago organizations emerged to adapt vacant and underoccupied downtown office and factory buildings into artist and musician studios. These projects included Weber Music Hall, the conversion of loft studios in the Athenaeum Building (1885), and the conversion of the Studebaker brothers' former carriage factory and showroom into artist and musician studios.[11] By 1904, a feature article in the *New York Evening Post* deemed the Fine Arts Building's tenth-floor architect and artist studios as the "Chicago Parnassus."[12] Yet, perhaps the most significant new space for art came with the opening of Hull House on the Near West Side for immigrants and other working-class Chicagoans. Through its Butler Gallery, art school, and industrial arts department, the Hull House offered the most comprehensive art programs in the State of Illinois.[13]

Yet, these same institutions (with the exception of the Art Institute) practiced racial exclusion. For example, in her 1913 report, "The Colored People of Chicago," Hull House board of directors member and wealthy philanthropist Louise deKoven Bowen revealed that "though Hull House was not exactly segregated many of its residents felt that the presence of blacks might discourage other groups from

coming. The settlement seemed unwilling to come to grips with the 'black problem' in its own environs, yet Hull House was willing to be concerned with the same 'problem' elsewhere in the city."[14]

Chicago's Antecedent Years of Black Artists and Patrons, 1870–1923

The first art collector in Chicago dated to Chicago's first non–Native American settler: Jean Baptiste Point DuSable. In 1779, when the African American DuSable settled in Eschikagou (later renamed "Chicago"), DuSable became a wealthy landowner and trader, and his estate included a collection of twenty-three European paintings.[15] Yet, not until the late nineteenth century did institutions emerge among black Chicagoans to sustain support for the arts.

Blacks in Chicago suffered from the 1871 fire, but a fire three years later actually had a greater deleterious impact. This fire consumed 47 acres of land, 812 buildings valued at roughly $2,820,000, and roughly 85 percent of black-owned property.[16] Unlike the 1871 post-fire recovery, prominent white Chicagoans did not respond with philanthropic projects for these fringe areas of the city, but, nonetheless, black Chicago experienced a remarkable self-help recovery. By 1885, 200 black businesses existed in Chicago and would increase to 731 by the 1920s.[17]

In 1927, the Washington Intercollegiate Club of Chicago noted the paucity of black artists' work in public but did list significant private collections of some of black Chicago's most wealthy residents. "There is little record of the history of Negro artists in Chicago and vicinity," the report concludes, "except a few signed examples of their work still in the possession of some of the older settlers."[18] A leading abolitionist and one of America's wealthiest black men, John Jones, reportedly had a small but impressive collection of art, which included his portrait painted around 1865 by white portraitist Aaron E. Darling.[19] More surprising, Jack Johnson, the outspoken and brash boxing champion from 1908 to 1915, was also a discerning art collector. Johnson's palatial Cabaret de Champion, located on Chicago's Near South Side, featured Rembrandt and van Rijn paintings installed in the cabaret's foyer and a wall-size mural of Cleopatra depicted as a black woman in Johnson's cabaret.[20] The founder of Binga State Bank in 1908, Jesse Binga, commissioned a half-length portrait of himself by the South Carolina African

American painter Edwin Harleston as well as interior murals painted by Chicago artist William Edouard Scott. During the early 1920s, Binga also established the Jesse Binga Popularity Prize to provide funding for the Chicago Art League, the earliest black self-help artist organization.

The homes of Chicago's black elites became the principal location of early social life. As such, the homes of personages of their "element" necessitated at least a small library and collection of art. Harleston, who settled in Chicago for a brief period to study at the School of the Art Institute, remembered, "I played cards at one of the 'palaces' in which these [wealthy black] folks live. For miles the houses look like something in *Vanity Fair* or *Vogue*." Jesse and Eudora Johnson Binga's home, he continued, "is very nicely furnished, showing nice taste with a number of paintings, mostly landscapes."[21] (The Bingas' collection also included Harleston's painting *The Bible Student*, ca. 1924.) Writing on the homes of the black elite, the scholar Willard Gatewood similarly noted, "In the Chicago home of S. Laing and Fannie Barrier Williams 'the choices of pictures and an ample library' gave an air of refinement and culture."[22] And the achievement of "refinement" also included wealthy blacks who managed gambling establishments and policy wheels. The wives of these policy kings decorated their homes with art and would later become vital contributors to the 1930s black Chicago arts scene.[23]

Chicago's black arts movement traversed the walls of private homes after the turn of the century with the advent of galleries within Chicago's South Side institutions. Provident Hospital and Nursing School, Wabash YMCA, and the Arts and Letters Society provided space and early support of the visual arts. Established in 1891, Provident exhibited works by African American artists, including Lottie Wilson Moss's works in Provident's Esther Freer dormitory.[24]

Chicago's formative years of African American art also coincided with the artistic antecedence of the city's visual-arts renaissance. During an era when segregation became increasingly apparent in Chicago, this citywide arts movement included black participants. The School of the Art Institute of Chicago was one of America's few art schools that admitted black students. The Art Institute became a powerful magnet that attracted African American students from the Midwest, south, and to a lesser extent the east. In addition to well-trained resident and itinerant artists, minimally trained and self-taught artists also made significant contributions to Chicago's art scene during this early period. The next section of this chapter describes some of the achievements of this generation of African American artists in Chicago belonging to both categories.

Painting

Self-taught, **James Bolivar Needham** (1850–1931) was Chicago's earliest-known painter of African descent. Born in Chatham, Canada, Needham worked on lumber vessels as a teenager on Lake Huron and Lake Michigan. In 1867, Needham settled in Chicago and shortly thereafter began his career as a painter. Reclusive, prolific, and self-critical, he reportedly discarded three of five paintings completed for not being of a high quality. In spite of his self-effacing manner, Needham produced so many paintings that they covered his apartment's walls, filled up numerous boxes, and piled up three and four deep in the corners of his loft.[25]

Influenced by his work on schooners, Needham observed the interplay of light and the change of seasons upon the Midwest's waterway. He executed some of his finest paintings on the activities along the Chicago River and its environs, such as *Sailboat at Dusk* (1895–1915) (see figure 10.1). In this work, he convincingly captured light and shadows on the river, boat, buildings, and shore. By juxtaposing broad brush strokes loaded with color, he created a heavily textured canvas surface that conveyed a sense of movement, space, and atmosphere. This painting typified Needham's stylistic approach to painting.

In addition to his paintings of Chicago's waterways and harbors, Needham was also an accomplished painter of urban scenes and landscapes. *Footpath over Creek* (1899) and *River Bend-Summer* (1904) are excellent examples of Needham's facility as a landscapist.[26] Sixty-seven years after his death, these and other works were included in the *James Bolivar Needham* posthumous exhibition opened at the Robert Henry Adams Fine Art gallery, the first ever exhibition of his paintings.

During the late nineteenth century, when she relocated to Chicago from Niles, Michigan, to study at the Art Institute, **Lottie E. Wilson** (née Moss, n.d.) became the school's earliest-known African American student.[27] An able painter, many of her works have become lost except a reproduction of *Abraham Lincoln and Sojourner Truth* (n.d.) (see figure 10.2). This painting memorialized Lincoln and Truth's October 29, 1864, meeting at the White House, an important event in African American history that connected the abolitionist efforts of escaped slaves like Truth to the 1863 Emancipation Proclamation issued by Lincoln. Years later, William McKinley exhibited this portrait at the U.S. Executive Mansion in Washington. And in 1902, U.S. President Theodore Roosevelt accepted the portrait for the White House's permanent art collection, making Wilson the earliest-known African American painter to have a work exhibited and included in the White House's collection.[28]

With the exception of her Lincoln and Truth painting and an exhibition of her work at Chicago's Provident Hospital Esther Freer dormitory, the available information on Wilson's life and career remains obscure. After leaving Chicago, Wilson returned to Michigan for a brief period. From there, she relocated to Europe for further study in art and apparently branched out into sculpture.

In 1969, cultural anthropologist Cedric Dover concluded that expatiate Henry Ossawa Tanner was the first and **William A. Harper** (1873–1910) the last of "the significant Negro painters of the nineteenth century and its cultural intrusion into the twentieth."[29] Born on a farm near Cayuga, Canada, the Harper family relocated to Petersburg, Illinois, in 1885, and finally settled on a farm in Jacksonville, Illinois, in 1893. Shortly after earning his degree from Jacksonville's Brown Business College, Harper attended the Art Institute from 1895 to 1901. After briefly teaching in Texas, he studied in Paris from 1903 to 1905 and again in 1907 to 1908.

Upon his return from France, Harper's paintings The Hillside (ca. 1903), The Last Gleam (ca. 1903), The Gray Dawn (ca. 1903), and Landscape with Poplars (Afternoon at Montigny) (ca. 1905) were included in the Municipal Art League's 1905 Museum of the Art Institute exhibition (see figure 10.3). The curators selected Landscape with Poplars as the most outstanding landscape in the exhibition.[30] By emphasizing through the subtle tonal richness of warm and earth hues, Harper transformed this countryside location into a picturesque scene of atmospheric tranquility.

During his second period of study in Paris, Harper sought out the tutelage of Tanner. When Harper returned to Chicago and later settled in Cuernavaca, Mexico (to ease the effects of his tuberculosis), the impressionistic influence of Turner emerged in Harper's painting in works like Patio (1908). By

contrast with his earlier Barbizon-influenced works, this painting contains warm harmonious tones, a dense texture, and looser brush stokes that make the courtyard a colorful and bold scene.

Shortly after his death in Mexico, the Museum of the Art Institute installed the William A. Harper posthumous exhibition from July 26 to August 28, 1910. Alain Locke, Harvard University–educated philosopher and America's first African American Rhodes Scholar, observed in 1940 that Harper's "premature death was the major loss to Negro art in that generation, for critics judged him of great promise, and many thought him more creatively original than Tanner."[31] A generation later, James Porter, the painter and father of African American art history in the 1960s, wrote, "Harper's work, although strong and worthy of note in any chronicle of American art, has been neglected."[32]

Works left behind by several other painters in Chicago of African ancestry suggest a much-wider level of productivity despite their lack of historical records. Among these artists deserving of attention were Frederick Douglass Allen (1886–n.d.) and Augustus Dunbier (1888–n.d.). Allen migrated from Toledo, Ohio, to study at the Art Institute and was included in the 1916 exhibition there. Dunbier was born in Osceola, Nebraska, and later studied at the School of the Art Institute and the Royal Academy in Dusseldorf, Germany. A surviving portrait by Dunbier, Negro Woman (ca. 1934) indicates his adept style, but like that of Allen, few more biographical details have been discovered about him and other early Chicago black artists.[33]

Chicago's Renaissance of 1914–41

Before the creation of an official black arts center in Chicago, residents of the South Side knew that the "Wabash Y" frequently served as the hub for its artists. Founded in 1913, the Wabash YMCA held regular art exhibitions and provided space for artists to meet, which included the 1923 formation there of the Chicago Art League (see figure 10.4). Led by Charles Dawson and William Farrow through the Wabash YMCA's education department, the league formed because "art is fundamental to good citizenship." Its members promoted citizenship by highlighting works created by black artists, recruiting young persons to study art as an avocation, encouraging more black Chicagoans to attend exhibitions and lectures at the Art Institute of Chicago, and applying art to social problems by aesthetically enhancing the city's black communities.[34] As a labor of love for the Wabash Y, William Scott painted its interior murals; the Y's collection of art works included William Harper's landscape *An Autumn Day in France* (n.d.) and other works displayed in the Art League's annual "must attend" exhibition there.[35]

The Art League's accomplishments by the 1920s made black art a fixture among a new generation of Chicagoans. Members assisted public schools in establishing collections of original art, executed murals to enhance the interior environment of buildings, secured positions for artists, offered public art lectures and demonstrations on various art techniques, and provided exhibition opportunities for artists.[36] As an example of this art advocacy, league member Inez Brewer, head the art department at Roosevelt High School in Gary, Indiana, organized exhibitions and maintained a permanent collection of black Chicagoans' paintings as a "Negro Salon." By 1935, works executed by Charles Dawson, Arthur Diggs, William Farrow, and William Scott were among the paintings included in the Negro Salon's permanent art collection.[37]

While some early black artists left Chicago due to racial exclusion from the mainstream's venues of art commerce and its slow growth as an art marketplace, by the 1920s many more artists had arrived here to study and establish themselves as professionals. One of the unanticipated outcomes of population growth (spawned by the labor shortages of World War I) was an enlarged pool of resident and itinerant artists. This group included Scott, who was Chicago's earliest African American painter who attained international acclaim through his success in international juried exhibitions as early as 1914. Meanwhile, Chicago's School of the Art Institute continued to be an important magnet that attracted talented black art students. Outside the Art Institute's classrooms, the expansion of Chicago's black self-help art organizations and programs provided a base of support for African American artists. But perhaps most important, a group of able and committed artists formed the early agglutinate (including Farrow, Motley, and Scott) who anchored Chicago's visual arts community of the next decades.

The "Negro in Art Week," November 18–25, 1927, sponsored by a host of black civic and fraternal organizations, showed the self-help and uplift efforts of African Americans. As part of a larger program to educate the masses, the Women's Club indicated the "Negro in Art Week" would lead to "decreasing friction existing between white and colored people by placing before the public an exhibition of the best work produced by Negroes in Fine and Applied Arts, Music and Literature, in combination with an exhibition of primitive African sculpture."[38] Concurrent with this festival, the Art Institute of Chicago's exhibition committee juried and accepted works for the national juried "Negro in Art Exhibition." Out-of-town artists in this exhibition complemented and legitimized the Chicago artists. In his review of this exhibition, Frederic Robb wrote, "Outside of [Henry O.] Tanner the best of the artists are in the West, principally in Chicago and not in the East, as is erroneously believed by those who are not properly informed."[39]

These artists seemed distinct because their work appeared to be largely unaffected by Europe's modern art movement. According to art historian Susan Weininger, the stylistic approaches and thematic direction of Chicago's artists found inspiration in the Midwest School of Painting of 1910–40. These artists, Weininger noted, "regarded the post-Renaissance European tradition as superficial and crassly materialistic; and they viewed the culture of Native Americans or of their own ethnic, racial or even regional groups as suitable catalysts for artistic creation."[40] Artists, according to Weininger, tolerated and even respected ethnic, racial, and gender distinctions and "were able to retain and celebrate their identities without separating themselves from the mainstream.[41] Outside of these personal relationships among artists, African American artists had to contend with racism and increased discrimination in Chicago's cultural marketplace. "As artists," art historian Daniel Schulman wrote, "their works and aspirations were judged through a filter of conflicting expectations and agendas." Thus, "black artists found training, opportunity, and an audience in Chicago" in spite of adversaries who sought to marginalize their expression and limit their opportunities.[42]

The most common misinformed interpretation of African American artists stemmed from long-standing theories on "black primitivism" and the unfitness of black people to appreciate or produce art. French statesman Count Joseph Arthur de Gobineau was the earliest theorist to write on these subjects. In 1853, de Gobineau held "blacks were imbued with a vegetative sensibility" that was "an inferior quality" and whites with the "Apollonian rationality," which was "a superior quality." The "absence of intellectual aptitudes," he continued, "renders [blacks] completely unfit for the culture of the arts, even for the appreciation of what this noble application of the human intelligence can produce of significance."[43] Rather than reason and beauty, de Gobineau held, the creative expressions of black people were infused with "outbursts of fire, flames, sparks, vivacity, and spontaneity intrinsic to its soul."[44]

From a different perspective yet similar in his conclusion, New York Marxist and *Modern Quarterly* (later, *Modern Monthly*) editor V. F. Calverton (aka George Goetz) observed in 1921 that blacks were better positioned than whites to create a unique American art. Blacks, according to Calverton, were not duty bound to the heritage of an ancient civilization. Free from the artistic encumbrances of a foreign land, Calverton concluded, though "simple," "unsophisticated," and "untutored," Negroes' "art is, as all art that springs from the people, an artless art, and in that sense is the most genuine art in the world."[45] Two decades later, the idea of black primitivism persisted. In his July 10, 1943, *Daily News* review, "Groping for a Real Negro Art," the dean of Chicago art critics, Clarence Bulliet, expressed disappointment that black artists did not explore their "jungle" roots. Bulliet's review of the Museum of the Art Institute's *Negro Artists of Chicago* exhibition smacked of ignorance of the African diaspora: "Nothing is evident, as yet, in the creations of American Negro artists, that show any kinship with the impulses that developed and were perfected in the jungles along the Congo."[46]

The earliest "new world" art movement that challenged this "accustomed" imagery took place in Haiti. Having begun shortly after Haiti's independence in 1804, the striking feature of Haitian postrevolution art, according to scholar Veerle Poupeye, "was . . . for the first time in Caribbean art, black and coloured people were routinely represented with the dignity and decorum until then reserved for the white colonial elite, instead of as subordinates, curiosities or victims."[47] This movement prefigured Chicago's paintings by Scott and Dawson during the early renaissance. These artists sought to gain proprietorship or the representation of the black image in art and popular visual culture. Especially during the renaissance's second wave, black Chicago artists began to devote much of the oeuvre to depicting black

people with dignity and decorum. Rather than simply a response to white-supremacist imagery of blackness, this movement centered on the reclamation, reconstruction, and reaffirmation of the rich history and culture of Africans and people of African descent.

Painting

Known as Chicago's "dean of African American art," **William Edouard Scott** (1884–1964) was the most prolific and celebrated African American painter of this period.[48] Rather than being viewed as the bellwether painter of the city's African Americanized art movement that situated blackness with dignity and decorum into American art, many critics opined that Scott had squandered his unique talent. For example, in the information provided by Beloit College's Theodore Lyman Wright Art Center on its 1970 posthumous retrospective exhibition, *William Edouard Scott: An Artist of the Negro Renaissance*, it was noted, "With his skills, he could have been absorbed into the mainstream and might have built a personal reputation; he chose, however, to commit himself to the establishment of pride, dignity and self-realization for all Negroes."[49]

Born in Indianapolis, Indiana, Scott had already attained some success as a painter there before moving to Chicago to attend the Art Institute from 1904 to 1907. After graduating, he continued to study at the Art Institute until 1909. Paris was the most preferred city to study art and to attain recognition as an artist, and Scott, like his cohorts, sought out an overseas education, eventually studying at the Academie Julian in 1909–11 and Academie Colarossi in 1912–13. Before completing the first year of study abroad, Scott nearly exhausted his funds, but Tanner came to the rescue and invited Scott to stay at his summer home at Trepied-par-Etaples. There he not only benefited from critiques of his works by Tanner but Scott also had an opportunity to observe this master painter at work. The influence of Tanner on Scott's painting technique and palette is evident in *Etaples, France* (1911) (see figure 10.5). This painting showed his further development from his pre-Parisian paintings.

In 1912, Scott's painting *La Pauvre Voisine* (The poor neighbor) was accepted by the Salon de la Societe des Artistes Francais. For an artist to have a work accepted by a Paris salon was considered a major career boost. This achievement marked Scott as the second painter of African descent to have a work accepted by a Paris salon (in 1894, Tanner was the first).[50]

In addition to being reproduced on postcards, the painting received favorable comment in local newspapers. When *La Pauvre Voisine* was purchased by the Argentine Republic, Scott became the earliest known African American painter to have a work included in Argentina's national art collection.

In 1913, paintings by Tanner and Scott were accepted by the Salon de la Societe Artistique de Picardie Le Touquet at Paris-Plage. This was the first occasion that two black artists had works accepted by a Paris salon. When awarded the salon's Tanqueray Prize of 125 francs for his painting, *La Misere* (Poverty), Scott became Chicago's earliest known African American painter so honored. In 1913, his painting *Le Connoisseur* was accepted by Paris's salon at La Loque, and *Silver Sun at Boulogne* was included in London's Royal Academy of Art's juried exhibition. After returning to Chicago, Scott's success with Paris salons continued: he had paintings accepted for the Autumn Salon de Paris and Salon la Tourquet in 1931 and Salon des Beaux-Arts, Toquet in 1935.[51]

Prior to being awarded the William Elmer Harmon Foundation's special gold medal in 1928 for "high character" and "excellence" as an artist, Scott was well underway to becoming one of America's most prolific muralists. Three of his earliest Chicago murals were *Canterbury Pilgrims* (1908) at Highland Park School, *Landing of the Northmen* (1909) at Felsenthal School, and *Commerce* (also known as *Dock Scene*) (1909) for Lane Technical High School. Installed at John Daniel Shoop Elementary School, *DuSable Trading with Indians at Fort Dearborn* (ca. 1920) provided a pictorial narrative that challenged the widely held belief of John Kinzie, a white man, having been Eschikagou's (later known as Chicago) earliest non–Native American settler (see figure 10.6). (Kinzie settled in Eschikagou in 1804, five years after Jean Baptiste Pointe DuSable.)[52]

In his mural, Scott employs spatial distancing to contrast the relationship between Native Americans and white settlers with that of DuSable and Native Americans. In the extreme right and left sections of the mural is a lack of direct interaction between Native and white Americans. This suggests a comity of coexistence without trust and interaction. However, in the mural's center foreground, DuSable dressed in buckskin engages in conversation with the chief. Two Native Americans inspect items available for trade, while a mother and child are nearby. This center clustering of personages suggest a relationship of mutual respect and friendship.

Between the mid-1930s and 1950s, Scott painted thirty murals for the Chicago Park District and forty different churches.[53] Of his religious murals, *The Crucifixion*, *Resurrection*, and *Ascension*, painted in Chicago's historic Pilgrim Baptist Church in 1943, became some of his most famous.[54] Yet, by World War II, Scott also increasingly gained national attention as a muralist. In 1942–43, a national competition was held to identify seven American artists to paint murals for the U.S. government's Recorder of Deeds' new building. Of the painters selected from over four hundred applicants, Scott was the only African American artist. Each artist was commissioned to paint a mural portraying an important event in African American history. In his mural *Frederick Douglass Appeals to President Lincoln* (1943), Scott portrayed Douglass meeting with President Lincoln and two cabinet members. In this meeting, Douglass petitioned Lincoln to permit more African Americans to fight in the Civil War, to enforce equal pay for black soldiers already in the Union forces, and to address the poor treatment of black soldiers. Federal employees selected Scott's mural as their favorite, which resulted in his being commissioned to paint a scene of the new building's opening ceremony.

As a genre painter, Scott was the earliest African American painter to devote a substantial portion of his oeuvre to depicting ordinary rural southern black people. He depicted these people with unrelenting dignity. For example, paintings such as *It's Going to Come* (1916) and *Traveling (Lead Kindly Light)* (1918) typify his thematic interest in this subject matter and stylistic figurative (see figure 10.7).

His painting *Traveling (Lead Kindly Light)* may have been influenced by the experience of Scott's grandparents; in 1847, they traveled with all their possessions in an oxen-drawn wagon from North Carolina to Indiana. The ambiance of this painting is somber. However, through subtle compositional devices, Scott evokes a sense of hope: the male and female figures form an earth-tone pyramidal conformation, which denotes strength and determination, while the wagon's lantern that illuminates the path in the painting signifies divine guidance.

In 1931, Scott was awarded a Julius Rosenwald Fellowship to study and paint in Haiti, where he would complete 144 paintings in a single year. Prior

10.1. James Bolivar Needham, *Sailboat at Dusk* (ca. 1895–1915), oil on board. Courtesy of Chicago History Museum.

10.2. Lottie E. Wilson (née Moss), *Abraham Lincoln and Sojourner Truth* (n.d.), oil on canvas. Courtesy of Library of Congress Rights and Reproductions.

10.3. William A. Harper, *Landscape with Poplars (Afternoon at Montigny)* (ca. 1905), oil on canvas, 23" × 28". Courtesy of Howard University Gallery of Art.

10.15. Archibald J. Motley Jr., *The First One Hundred Years: He amongst You Who Is without Sin Shall Cast the First Stone: Forgive Them For They Know Not What They Do* (ca.1963–72), oil on canvas, 48½" × 40¾". Copyright Valerie Gerrard Browne, courtesy of Chicago History Museum.

10.16. William McKnight Farrow, *Peace* (1924), block print, 8.89 cm × 11.43 cm. Courtesy of William Farrow III/ Clark Atlanta University Art Collection.

10.17. Richmond Barthé, *Rugcutters* (1930). Courtesy of Moorland-Spingarn Research Center, Howard University.

10.18. Richmond Barthé, *Blackberry Woman* (modeled 1930, cast 1932), bronze, 35½" × 12¼" × 16¼". Courtesy of Smithsonian American Art Museum, Washington, D.C. / Art Resource, New York.

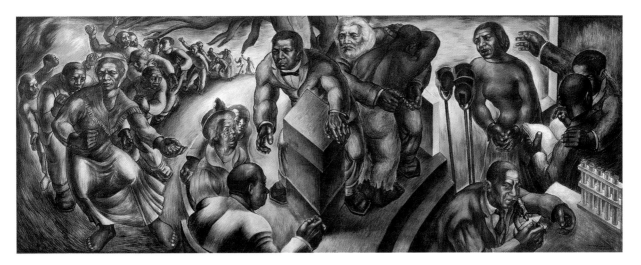

10.19. Charles White, *Five Great American Negroes* (1939–40), oil on canvas, 5' × 12'. Courtesy of the Charles White Archives.

10.20. Charles White, *There Were No Crops This Year* (1940), graphite on paper, 22¾" × 19¾". Courtesy of the Charles White Archives.

10.21. Charles White, *Wanted Poster Series #6* (1969), oil wash on illustration board, 58¾" × 26¾". Courtesy of the Charles White Archives.

10.22. Eldzier Cortor, *Southern Gate*
(1942–43), oil on canvas, 46½" × 22".
Courtesy of Smithsonian American Art
Museum, Washington, D.C./Art Resource,
New York.

10.23. Charles Sebree, *Head of a Woman* (1938). Courtesy of the Walter O. Evans Collection at the Savannah College of Art and Design.

10.24. Charles Sebree, *Saltimbanque in Moonlight* (ca. 1970). Courtesy of Eleanor W. Traylor.

10.25. Raymond "Ramon" Gabriel,
Seated Boy (ca. 1940), watercolor on
paper, 23¾" × 18¾". Courtesy of Patrick
L. Albano, Aaron Galleries.

10.26. William Carter, *The Card Game*
(1950), pen and ink and brush and
black ink and pen and blue and purple
inks on white gouache, with traces
of charcoal on wood-pulp laminate
board, 296 mm × 372 mm. Prints and
Drawings Collection, 1995.25, the Art
Institute of Chicago, courtesy of the
Mr. and Mrs. T. Stanton Armour Fund.

10.27. Charles V. Davis, *Newsboy* (1934), oil on canvas, 36" × 30". Courtesy of the Howard
University Gallery of Art.

10.28. Sylvester Britton, *Bondage* (n.d.), oil on canvas, 33" × 26". Courtesy of the Daniel Texidor Parker Collection.

10.29. Sylvester Britton, *Red Hat* (1954), colored inks on paper, 36" × 24". Courtesy of the Daniel Texidor Parker Collection.

10.30. Irene Clark, *Rolling Calf* (n.d.), oil on canvas. Courtesy of *African American Art and Artists* by Samella S. Lewis. Copyright 1994 in the format Textbook via Copyright Clearance Center.

10.31. Margaret T. G. Burroughs, *Face of Africa* (ca. 1965), linocut, $11\frac{13}{16}$" × 10". Courtesy of the Saint Louis Art Museum, Museum of Minority Artists Purchase Fund, 61:1998

10.32. Marion Perkins, *Man of Sorrows* (1950), marble, 17½" × 10" × 10". American Art Collection, 1951.129, the Art Institute of Chicago, courtesy of the Pauline Palmer Prize Fund.

10.33. Marion Perkins, *Dying Soldier* (1952), marble, dimensions and present location unknown. C21064, the Art Institute of Chicago. Photography © The Art Institute of Chicago.

to his departure, he had a one-man exhibition. Of the works exhibited, Haiti's President Stenio J. Vincent purchased twelve. For his contributions to Haitian art, in 1936 President Vincent conferred upon Scott the *Honneur et Merite*, which was the equivalent of the French Legion of Honor. He was the first American artist to be so honored by a Haitian president.[55]

One of Chicago's busiest portrait painters, in 1934 Scott executed fifteen commissioned portraits. Included among these works were portraits of Haiti's President Vincent and Chicago philanthropist Julius Rosenwald. Nineteen years later, Scott completed one of his most important portraits, *Pope Pius XII and Two Bishops* (ca. 1953), which memorialized the Pope's consecration of the Catholic Church's first two black bishops (see figure 10.8).

In 1955, Scott visited Mexico to study and paint. There he was diagnosed as having diabetes that would cost him his legs in the years that followed. Rather than being dispirited, he continued to paint until his death in 1964.

Having similar artistic convictions as Scott, **Charles Clarence Dawson** (1889–1981) stated, "Because my home town was comparatively liberal, I didn't feel different until I saw my people and myself almost totally stereotyped in illustrations. There was nothing about our contributions to Eastern and Western civilization."[56] Born in Brunswick, Georgia, Dawson studied at Tuskegee Institute (currently, Tuskegee University), 1905–12; New York City's Art Student League, 1907–12; and Chicago's Art Institute, 1912–17. Influenced by the nineteenth-century French painter Jean-Francois Millet, who portrayed peasant laborers with unyielding dignity, Dawson stated, "I wanted to paint as Millet did of the French peasants . . . the Negro in everyday life. They weren't running around as stereotypes, begging . . . or in patches."[57] This vision is evident in his large watercolor *The Crisis* (1933), which depicts black and white boys playing marbles (see figure 10.9).

Exhibited in the window of Chicago's downtown Findley Galleries, the painting sparked considerable disfavor. Recalling this rebuke, Dawson held,

The painting depicts a group of Negro and white boys playing marbles—in fact, they're down to the last one. That's why I called it "The Crisis." But the Negro boys aren't real black, and they don't look tough or have patches on their clothes. And they aren't playing craps, but marbles. White people didn't like that.

They wanted to hold onto the stereotype as to what constitutes a Negro. I've decided in all my years to undo that stereotype, to try—like Ignacio Zuloaga, the great Spanish painter who showed the beauty of his people—to show the beauty and the wide variety of my people.[58]

Similar to Millet's depiction of French peasants, Zuloaga's paintings of ordinary Spanish people, and Scott's of black people, Dawson's *The Bill Posters* depicted two blue-collar workers placing a holiday advertisement on an outdoor billboard. He depicted these workers with a dignity that was not customary in art and popular culture in America (see figure 10.10).

Dawson was a self-taught maven of African and African American history. During the early 1930s, he wrote and illustrated *A.B.C.'s of Great Negroes*, a children's book. The book consisted of twenty-six linoleum block prints of black leaders. The book, in alphabetical order by last name of each leader, comprised brief biographical sketches with portraits. The manuscript and illustrations were reviewed by three major white Chicago publishing houses. Rejected by two, the other offered to publish the book if Dawson removed illustrations depicting Akhenaton and Khufu as "Negroes," as well as all references to them as "Negroes" because, the publisher insisted, the pharaohs were Caucasian.[59] Rather than comply, Dawson founded the Dawson Publishing Company and published the book in 1933. Well received, the Tennessee Board of Education selected the publication as one of the best children's books on the Negro.[60]

As a commercial artist, Dawson was Chicago's earliest illustrator to introduce African motifs into his commissioned design projects. In the early 1920s, he introduced Egyptian motifs in design solutions for Madagasco, Noir-OI Hair and Skin Care Products, and O'Neall Chemical Company. Similarly, he incorporated Akan Adinkira symbols in his design solution for Chicago's Overton Hygienic Company's Aida Pomade. In 1940, Annie T. P. Malone, the founder and owner of PORO beauty school and products, retained Dawson as her marketing consultant and designer.[61] His earliest PORO promotional projects were "Black Beauties in History" and "The Evolution of the Negro Hairdress: from Isis to Present." In his Black Beauty illustrations, rather than Caucasianizing the facial features and hair, Dawson portrayed black women with facial features, skin coloration, and hair unique to Africans and African Americans. For the "Evolution of the Negro Hairdress," he depicted contemporary coiffures having been influenced by traditional African hair styles.

For the 1940 *American Negro Exposition*, with the aid of his assistants, Dawson constructed ten dioramas. This was his most ambitious project. The dioramas provided a visual snapshot of seven thousand years of African and African diasporic history, beginning with "the first great builders" of Ethiopia and Egypt and concluding with the world's four independent black nations. The dioramas included depictions of the discovery of iron and smelting in Central and West Africa, the slavery and reconstruction era, the history of black businesses in America, the first man to reach the North Pole in August 1909, and the heroism of black soldiers during World War I.[62] "Long before the phrase 'Black is beautiful' was born," journalist Barbara Parry observed in 1970, "artist Charles Clarence Dawson was proving this with his paintings. Admittedly obsessed with the black struggle for identity, he spent most of a lifetime mirroring the Negro in everyday life through paintings, sculptures and illustrations."[63]

Recurring themes in the oeuvre of **Walter Ellison** (1889–1977) were the South's race preference practices, the migration of blacks from the south to the north, and the urbanization of Chicago's black newcomers. Born in Eatonton, Georgia, Ellison settled in Chicago during the 1920s and studied briefly at the Art Institute in the 1930s. An able figurative painter, he adopted a naive stylistic, which gave the impression that he was a self-taught vernacular painter.

His paintings *Train Station* (1937) and *Leaving Macon Georgia* (1937) typify Ellison's stylistic approach to painting and thematic concerns (see figure 10.11). During the early twentieth century, the south's economy had been devastated by the boil weevil and floods. These plagues, combined with the south's racial intolerance and job openings in northern urban industrial centers, provided black southerners with powerful incentives to relocate. In some instances, African Americans desirous of relocating did not have the financial resources to purchase a bus or train ticket. Dangerous but free, "riding the cars" (boxcars) provided a mode of transportation to the north.

Affixed to the white post in the painting's background are directional signs to New Orleans, St. Louis, and Chicago. The two men ride atop an Illinois Central Railroad boxcar headed for Chicago.

The man to the painting's left has a letter in his back pocket. This letter recalls the practice of "testing." Under this practice, a relative or friend having previously relocated to Chicago or another northern city provided an assessment of job availability, racial climate, living accommodations, and educational opportunities in the form of a letter. This letter assisted the recipients in determining whether or not to migrate, and between 1910 and 1920, favorable letters resulted in migrants coming to Chicago in droves.[64]

On May 27, 1933, Chicago's Second World Fair, *A Century of Progress* (1933–34), opened. By contrast with the 1893 World's Columbian Exposition, this fair was not imitative of European culture; it celebrated America's technological supremacy and commemorated the one-hundred-year anniversary of Chicago having been incorporated as a village. The fair included a national invitational art exhibition and a national juried photography exhibition. Chicago photographer King Daniel Ganaway was the only African American included in the photography exhibition. Installed at the Museum of the Art Institute, the art exhibition included only three black artists: Henry Tanner, Richmond Barthé, and Archibald J. Motley Jr.

One of Chicago's most celebrated black painters, **Archibald J. Motley Jr.** (1891–1981), was born in New Orleans, but his family migrated to the north. Due to threats from white businessmen, his parents closed their general merchandise store and relocated, first to St. Louis and then to Buffalo, New York. By 1894, the Motleys settled in a predominately white neighborhood on Chicago's Southwest Side, but the family reconnected with their southern family by visiting New Orleans during the summers. Through these relatives, Motley became better acquainted with their African and Creole heritage. Later, these dual heritages influenced Motley's thematic concerns.

Between 1914 and 1918, Motley studied painting and illustration at the Art Institute of Chicago. Thereafter, Motley tried to establish himself as a portrait painter. Although he was unsuccessful in attracting sufficient portrait commissions when starting out, Motley remained determined to earn a living as an artist. In 1921 when his *Portrait of My Mother* (1919) was included in the Art Institute's annual juried exhibition, *Artists of Chicago and Vicinity*, Motley's career as a painter began to gain traction. For example, in 1925, he was awarded the Art Institute's Frank G. Logan prize for his painting *A Mulattress* (1924) and the Joseph N. Eisendrath prize for *Syncopation* (1924);

of the works included in the Newark Museum's 1927 exhibition, *Paintings and Water Colors by Living American Artists*, Motley's portrait *Mending Socks* (1924) was selected by the public as "the Best Liked Painting"; and in 1928, Motley was awarded the Harmon Foundation's Gold Medal for his portrait *Octoroon Girl* (1925) (see figure 10.12).

Motley took great care in this portrait to convey the elite persona of the sitter. Seated on a sofa against a rich earth-toned background, the sitter is the quintessence of composure and the black genteel tradition. A green hat covers much of her conservative yet stylish hair. She has a demure but self-confident gaze. Her high forehead, skin tone, thin lips, and tapered nose with small nostrils invite comparisons with the "pure Caucasian." Painted in muted tones, the *Octoroon Girl*'s necklace and engagement ring are tastefully executed and hardly noticeable. Motley employed this device to suggest a lady of the highest order. Her fashionably conservative velvet dress trimmed with a muted-red collar, cuffs, and cloth-covered sleeve buttons reflects this upper-class dignity. Her gloves held gently between long, tapered fingers are exquisitely rendered. The painting on the wall in the upper left corner, as well as the books and small statue on the cloth-covered table in the lower-right corner, convey the impression of a setting that caters to the elite, such as an exclusive private-membership club.

In 1929, at the request of Mary Beattie Brady, the director of the Harmon Foundation, Motley wrote "How I Solve My Painting Problems." About his portrait *Aline, an Octoroon* (ca. 1927), Motley noted, "In some cases, it is difficult to determine precisely whether or not a person is pure Caucasian or octoroon. I have seen octoroons with skin as white as people from northern Europe such as the Baltic countries; with straight blond hair, blue eyes, sharp *well*-proportioned features, and extremely thin lips." The octoroon's "head," he continued, "is normal and well-constructed and symmetrically balanced. The construction of the body—the elongation of the arms, a tendency toward a weak bone construction and large fat heels"—are "nonexistent" among octoroons; "[i]n fact," Motley held, "a very light octoroon could be compared favorably with a Swedish or Norwegian person. In this painting I have tried to show that delicate one-eighth strain of Negro blood. Therefore, I would say that this painting was not only an artistic venture but also a scientific problem."[65]

In 1928, when his one-man exhibit, *Exhibition of Paintings by Archibald J. Motley Jr.*, opened at New York City's New Gallery, Motley became the second black artist to have a solo exhibition in a private, white-owned New York City gallery (the first was Henry O. Tanner in 1908). The exhibition was reviewed favorably by art critics. For example, after devoting special attention to the African and voodoo-inspired paintings, art critic Edward Alden Jewell wrote in his *New York Times* review that Motley's works added substance to the New Negro construct.[66]

In 1929, Motley was awarded a John Simon Guggenheim Fellowship to study and paint in Paris. *Martinique Youth* (ca. 1929–30) and *Senegalese* (ca. 1929–30) were among the noteworthy portraits that he executed in Paris. He also completed some of his better-known genre paintings, such as *Blues* (1929). Rather than the panoramic view in some of his earlier works like *Black and Tan* (1921), *Syncopation* (1924), and *Stomp* (1927), the close-up view of a jazz dance band and couples dancing in *Blues* provided a far more intimate relationship between the viewer and subject matter. This painting served as a template for some of Motley's most successful post-Parisian paintings, such as *The Picnic* (1916) and, especially, *Hot Rhythm* (1961).

Executed in Paris, *Jockey Club* (1929) represents Motley's masterpiece (see figure 10.13). This painting exemplifies his modernistic approach to painting; successful experimentation with the harmonization of natural and artificial lighting into a unique warm and cool palette; and the mastery of compositional design, ambiance, and narrative. The stylization of form and gestural articulation are masterfully executed and evoke dynamism and energy.

Through the doorman, Motley introduced the social narrative of black otherness. The doorman leans casually against the Jockey Club's door frame with his legs crossed, and his tightly fitted red jacket with brass buttons and fitted neck collar draws attention to his face. The doorman's dark skin hue and processed black hair accentuated his wide grin with exposed white teeth encircled by swollen ruby-red lips.

Similarly, in *Lawd, Mah Man's Leavin'* (1940), Motley depicted the little girl as a disheartened pickaninny with dark skin, nappy hair, and exaggerated thick, red lips (see figure 10.14). The mother takes the form of the fictive stereotypic mammy: very dark complexion, bandanna on her head, swollen red lips, and a rotund body with huge balloon-like breasts. This treatment of the "dark purer Negroes" became a mainstay in Motley's genre paintings, which is at least traceable to his painting *Tongues (Holy Rollers)* (1929).

Writing on the iconography of such imagery, St. Clair Drake and Horace Cayton observed, "Kinky hair, thick lips, and dark skin become the esthetic antithesis of straight hair, small lips, white skin, and these physical traits are thought to be correlated with all of the unsavory characteristics" of blackness.[67] Seamlessly interwoven into art and popular visual culture, these iconographic markers become visual value in the definitional process. It is through this process that value becomes ascribed to what is being defined. By defining straight hair, small lips, white skin, and other physical traits of Europeans and people of European descent as "preferential," implicitly those persons not having these valued traits are automatically defined as "the other."

With the exception of his Mexico-inspired paintings of 1952–53 and 1957–58, *The First One Hundred Years: He amongst You Who Is without Sin Shall Cast the First Stone: Forgive Them Father For They Know Not What They Do* (ca. 1963–72) represents the most radical departure from Motley's subject matter concerns (see figure 10.15).

In this densely layered montage, Motley offered a critique on race relations in America, from slavery through the 1960s civil rights movement. The assassinations of John F. Kennedy, Martin Luther King Jr., and Abraham Lincoln become ghost-like portraits. Kennedy's portrait is in the upper left, King's is in the center, and Lincoln's is at the upper-right section of the mansion's facade. Through Kennedy, King, and Lincoln, Motley explored the theme of assassination as the ultimate silencer of influential leaders who attempted to dismantle racial privilege and white supremacy across a century in America.

Arthur Diggs (1888–1967) was an able landscape and figure painter who also explored modernist stylistic approaches. While he did not attain national distinction, Diggs anchored Chicago's black visual arts community. Having studied briefly at the Art Institute, by the late 1920s he began to attract attention as a promising landscapist. His mountainous scene painting *Oaks and Alders* (n.d.) suggests that Diggs was following in the tradition of nineteenth-century mountain panoramic painters. During the late 1930s, Diggs adopted an expressionistic style and explored subject matter bordering on black stereotypic im-

agery. This is discernible in *de Lawd and Moses* (n.d.), *de Lawd and Noah* (n.d.), and *The Green Pastures* (n.d.). This short-lived digression may have been influenced by the popularity and success attained by other artists of this style who had success in the marketplace.[68]

Having attended the School of the Art Institute, **Leslie Rogers** (1895–1935) attained national acclaim as a cartoonist and illustrator. In 1920, Rogers created the *Chicago Defender*'s comic strip *Bungleton Green*. Published regularly from 1920 until 1968, *Bungleton Green* became America's longest-published comic strip created by a black artist. The *Defender*'s millions of readers referred to it as "Bung," and the character's popularity stemmed from Rogers's synthesis of the popular trickster in black folklore and astute philosophical pragmatist of the modern age. Having an aversion to labor-intensive "heavy lifting" work and the eight-hour workday, Bung in top hat, bow tie, vest, tuxedo coat, and baggy pants lived by his wits. Rather than celebrating Bung's ill-conceived schemes to satiate his day-to-day comforts and to avoid legal obligations, the comic strip emphasized the moral and legal consequences Bung had to ultimately face.

Quite similar to Rogers, during the late 1920s, **Elmer Simms Campbell** (1906–71) received acclaim as an illustrator. Campbell was born in St. Louis, Missouri, and his family settled in Chicago in 1920. During his one-year stay at the University of Chicago, Campbell was on the staff of *Phoenix*, a publication devoted solely to humor. Shortly after enrolling at the Art Institute, he and a few other students created *College Comics*, a short-lived magazine. Mostly under a pseudonym, Campbell produced many of this publication's illustrations. After a stint at New York City's Art Student League in 1932, Campbell found employment at Triad, a St. Louis, Missouri, advertising agency.

At the encouragement of the National Urban League's (NUL) director of research and editor of *Opportunity* Charles Spurgeon Johnson and his assistant Ethel Nance, Campbell moved to New York City. There a friend and fellow Chicagoan Ed Graham assisted Campbell in obtaining freelance commissions and, later, a full-time advertising-agency position. Thereafter, he became the first African American to have his work appear regularly in white mainstream magazines, such as *Colliers*, *Cosmopolitan*, *Judge*, *Playboy*, *Life*, *Redbook*, *Saturday Evening Post*, and *The New Yorker*. His creation *Cuties* was carried by over a hundred newspapers in America and Latin America;

"Esky," the pop-eyed mascot, was featured on the cover of each issue of *Esquire* magazine; and between 1933 and 1958, his work also appeared in nearly every monthly issue of *Esquire*. Most of Campbell's fans never knew he was an African American "cross-over" artist over his forty-plus-year career. Similarly, few knew that Campbell was a prolific painter as well as an illustrator.

Ellis Wilson (1899–1977) and **Robert Savon Pious** (1908–83) trained and began their careers in Chicago but attained acclaim in New York City. Born in Mayfield, Kentucky, Wilson arrived in Chicago in 1919 to study at the Art Institute. After graduating, he remained in the city and worked as a commercial artist and assistant interior designer while also active with the Chicago Art League. Wilson concentrated on genre scenes, figure studies, and still life. Influenced by Alain Locke's 1927 Chicago speech and the available information on Harlem's New Negro Movement, Wilson moved to New York City in 1928, where he would attain recognition as a painter.

Similar to Wilson, Pious arrived in Chicago in 1921 from Meridian, Mississippi, to study at the Art Institute. After two years, he withdrew from classes to work full-time. An exceptionally talented draftsman and figure painter, Pious was awarded the 1931 Harmon Foundation's Arthur B. Spingarn Prize for his drawing *Portrait of Roland Hayes* (ca. 1930).[69] In addition to this prize, he accepted a scholarship to study at New York City's National Academy of Design.[70] Shortly thereafter, Pious became a highly regarded illustrator, portraitist, and figure painter.

Inspired by dreams and fantasies, there was a tendency to categorize the subject matter and stylistic approaches of self-taught intuitive painters as idiosyncratic or "childlike." **Samuel MacAlpine** and **Richard Milby Williams** were among the self-taught artists in Chicago during the early renaissance. Born in Alabama in 1892, MacAlpine earned an undergraduate degree in a nonvisual arts area from Morris Brown in 1918. After relocating to Chicago during the 1920s, MacAlpine worked as a framer and developed an interest in painting. Examples of his works were included in the 1928 and 1933 Harmon Foundation's annual exhibition and the 1933–34 *Century of Progress Exposition*'s art exhibition held in Chicago.[71] A native Chicagoan, Williams had only a primary school education. He enjoyed the support of a small but loyal group of patrons, including Mrs. S. D. Cowles, who bought his portrait of Charles Lindbergh (that was part of Williams's famous aviator series) to donate to Chicago's Lakeview High School. Examples of Williams's works were included in the 1931 Harmon Foundation's annual exhibition.[72]

Printmaking

The Chicago Art League's president **William M. Farrow** (1885–1967) was recognized as one of the "Negro Renaissance's" leading personages. Through his *Chicago Defender* column, "Art for the Home," Farrow expressed his unwavering support of African American artists. Born in Dayton, Ohio, Farrow studied at the Art Institute, 1908–17, where he also worked as an assistant to the curator. He later became the Art Institute's first known African American instructor. Etchings such as *Ringling House* (n.d.) and *The Messenger* (n.d.) typify Farrow's realistic approach and thematic interests. In 1933, the American Art Dealers Association selected Farrow's lithograph *Peace* (1924) as one of America's fifty best original prints (see figure 10.16).

Dox Thrash (1893–1965) was one of the twentieth century's foremost American printmakers. Between 1911 and 1923, Thrash lived in Chicago, where he befriended Farrow and Scott (whom he would refer to later as a mentor). Working as an elevator operator at American Bank Note Engraving Company in Chicago, he enrolled in evening classes at the Art Institute beginning in 1914 until he was drafted into the military. Wounded and then discharged in 1919, he returned to Chicago to resume his studies at the Art Institute, where he became an exceptionally gifted painter and printmaker. The figures in his charcoal and graphite drawings tended to emerge from densely dark backgrounds. The tonal variations achieved in these works encouraged him to explore the possibilities of producing similar qualities in prints.

After leaving Chicago in 1923, he had brief stays in Massachusetts, Connecticut, and New York before settling in Philadelphia. There he headed the WPA Graphic Arts division and created the carborundum print process, which provided the printmaker with enormous ranges in tonal qualities from the darkest darks to intermediate tint variations.[73] Because the subject matter in his prints emerged from the darkest darks, master printmaker and author Winston Kennedy characterized Thrash's technique as "out of the shadows."

Sculpture

Richmond Barthé (1901–89) from Bay St. Louis, Mississippi, first showed his talent in the south. Barthé's work caught the attention of Lyle Saxon of the *New Orleans Times Picayune*, who attempted to enroll him in the nearby White art school. In spite of Saxon's influence, Barthé was not admitted because of his race. As an alternative, a priest at New Orleans's Catholic Blessed Sacrament Church, Reverend Harry Kane, SSL, helped Barthé gain admittance to Chicago's School of the Art Institute, where he studied from 1924 to 1928.

Barthé's painting instructor, Charles Schroeder, recommended that Barthé enroll in a sculpture course to gain better command of rendering three-dimensional forms. A bust completed in his introductory sculpture class was included in the Art Institute's 1927 *The Negro in Art* juried exhibition. This entry led to commissions for Barthé to complete busts of artist Henry O. Tanner and Haitian revolutionary Toussaint L'Ouverture for Gary, Indiana's Lake County Children's Home. Exemplifying Barthé's extraordinary talent during this period are his busts of *Paul Laurence Dunbar* (1928) and *Booker T. Washington* (1928).[74]

The 1927 *Negro in Art Week* in Chicago marked the turning point in Barthé's career. Alain Locke spoke at the opening luncheon, and afterward he and Barthé met for the first time in what would become a long-standing friendship. In addition to playing a key role in convincing Barthé to move to New York City in 1931, Locke also became an effective promoter of his artwork.

Patrons also became interested in Barthé during the late 1920s. The Chicago Women's Club commissioned two sculptures for their Michigan Avenue headquarters. After viewing these works, Chicago attorney Frank Breckinridge offered to defray the costs of a Barthé one-man exhibition and became his unofficial agent. And Julius Rosenwald, chairman of Sears and Roebuck department stores, encouraged Barthé to apply for a Rosenwald Fund fellowship, which he subsequently won and used to fund his trip to New York to take up residence with the Student Art League.

When he returned to Chicago from his studies in New York, Barthé had practically abandoned painting for sculpture. In his 1930 exhibition, financed by Breckinridge and sponsored by the Chicago Women's Club, Barthé presented twenty-six sculptures, six paintings, and eight drawings, including *The Breakaway: Dance Figurine*.[75] In 1931, Barthé left Chicago for a permanent stay in New York, where he would gain national acclaim (see figures 10.17 and 10.18).[76]

The Spaces of the Black Renaissance

Despite the number of prolific and impressive artists in the first phase of Chicago's Black Renaissance, mainstream Chicago institutions continued their policies of race exclusion. As exceptions to this color line, the Art Institute and the School of Design were the only professional art schools that admitted black students.[77] For example, in 1937, Charles White was informed he was the winner of the Academy of Fine Arts and Mizer Academy of Art new-student scholarship competitions. When he arrived at the new-student scholarship recipient ceremony for each art school, White was informed that the jury had made a mistake in the selection process. Later, White obtained a copy of the catalog for each school and noticed the statement: "For Caucasians Only."[78]

It is widely accepted that the South Side Community Art Center was the WPA's gift to Chicago, and the artistic maturation of black artists came with its founding. Often overlooked, however, is the significant role played by the South Side Community Art Center Association (SSCACA). In 1939, the SSCACA conducted a successful fund-raising campaign and purchased a dilapidated, three-story mansion at 3831 South Michigan Avenue to serve as an art center.[79] The SSCACA obtained WPA Community Art Center (CAC) funding to renovate the building and staff art center. The refurbished building included a ballroom, meeting rooms, studios, gallery, and in the rear a carriage-house workshop.

Prior to the SSCAC's opening in late 1940, its board of directors issued a policy statement indicating that the art center would not practice or tolerate racial segregation. In keeping with this policy, the center's first director, Peter Pollack, was white. In addition, the SSCAC's board, staff, students, affiliated artists, and members were racially diverse. "In those days," Bernard Goss and Margaret T. G. Burroughs recalled, the SSCAC "was one of the few places that brought the Negroes and whites together on a cultural basis. The center was for everyone; a true symbol for an interracial tolerance."[80]

Nonetheless, and perhaps due to their long virtual exclusion from other venues, local black artists made up the SSCAC's December 1940 inaugural exhibition. However, the SSCAC's 1941 dedication exhibition, *We Too Look at America*, featured a racially diverse group of artists. Gertrude Abercrombie, Emil Armen, Margaret Brundage, and Sophie Wessel were among the local white artists included in this exhibition. In addition to the black artists included in the SSCAC's inaugural exhibition, examples of works by John Carlis Jr., Eldzier Cortor, and Charles Sebree were also included in the dedication exhibition.[81]

These exhibits led critics in Chicago to take notice of the quality of work at the SSCAC. In her May 1941 review of the Art Club's modern-art exhibition held at the Wrigley Building on Chicago's "Magnificent Mile," and the SSCAC's dedication exhibition, the *Chicago Sun's* art critic Dorothy Odenheimer observed that the quality of paintings by Negro artists in the SSCAC exhibition exceeded the works included in the Arts Club's exhibition. After devoting special attention to works by Avery, Carter, Carlis, Cortor, Kersey, Sebree, and White, Odenheimer wrote, "After visiting this exhibition we felt that the socialites at the Arts Club could profit by a visit down the street at their neighbors', the South Side Community Art Center."[82]

The May 1941 SSCAC's dedication address by America's First Lady, Eleanor Roosevelt, was aired live on radio. Later at the dedication dinner, the Chicago and African American artist Charles V. Davis presented Roosevelt with a portrait of her daughter, entitled *Holiday* (1941).[83] Subsequent to the dedication, in her 1941 nationally syndicated column, "My Day," the First Lady wrote, "Chicago has long been a center of Negro Art."[84] And in its May 19, 1941, edition, *Newsweek* magazine concurred, deeming the SSCAC a "Negro Temple of Art."[85]

The SSCAC not only served as a hub for visual artists but also for a young group of writers, dancers, and musicians. Poet Gwendolyn Brooks, singer and pianist Nat King Cole, poet and writer Frank Marshall Davis, dancer Katherine Dunham, novelists Willard Motley and Margaret Walker, and playwright Ted Ward were among the artists who congregated in the gallery, classrooms, and hallways of the center. Meanwhile, photographer Gordon Parks constructed a darkroom in the basement of the center, and other artists took up residence there, including William Scott, Elizabeth Catlett, Charles Davis, Raymond "Ramon" Gabriel, Marion Perkins, David Ross, and Hughie Lee-Smith.

The centrality of the SSCAC after 1940 should not, however, excise other spaces that predated it. Some

SSCAC artists, for example, continued to affiliate with the Abraham Lincoln Center (ALC). Founded in 1905 as a settlement house and put under the supervision of the All Souls Church after the stock-market crash of 1929, ALC evolved into the Near South Side's interracial center of progressive political, social, and cultural thought during the Depression years. Among the white visual artists affiliated with the ALC, Edward Millman, Mitchell Siporin, and Morris Topchevsky were recognized as leaders in the progressive art movement. Having studied and painted with Mexican muralists, such as Diego Rivera and Jose Orozco, Millman, Siporin, and Topchevsky developed an appreciation for New World artistic concerns of people of color. As such, they encouraged young black artists to draw upon the African American experience as a source of artistic inspiration, evidenced by its 1941 exhibition that included works by white artists like Siporin and Topchevsky but also their black allies and colleagues like Eldzier Cortor, Charles Davis, Bernard Goss, and Charles Sebree.

For some progressives, this exhibition exemplified "interracial cultural radicalism," as espoused by leftist organizations, which led to charges of communist influence of these artists, and these kinds of cultural events caught the attention of conservative politicians. The U.S. House of Representatives Sub-Committee to Investigate Un-American Activities chairman Martin Dies (D, Texas) gathered examples of art works executed by WPA and Federal Art Project (FAP) artists to prove that the federal government's arts programs had promoted communism. Dies led a movement that sought to terminate the WPA, and having aroused public disapprobation and unease within U.S. President Franklin Roosevelt's administration, Dies succeeded in having the WPA and its programs terminated in February 1943.

Actually, the loss of the WPA's funding of the Illinois Art Project (IAP) proved less severe than imagined because the program's administrators had discriminated against hiring black artists in Chicago. It was the IAP's general practice to refer black artists seeking employment under its art projects to nonvisual arts–related WPA jobs.[86] During its seven-year lifespan, IAP employed nearly 775 artists and administrators, but only "about five percent" (approximately 36 artists) were black.[87] Moreover, between 1935 and 1939, Sebree was the only black artist employed under a IAP premier-art job classification;[88] and prior to the SSCAC's founding, the few black artists employed by IAP were assigned to its art and craft projects or other less-visible roles, such as assisting (white) muralists.[89]

William Carter's story exemplified race discrimination in the IAP. Between 1935 and 1939, Carter regularly inquired about employment as an IAP artist but was informed no vacancies existed.[90] Yet, the official FAP/IAP employment data for the periods of November 1, 1935, through August 31, 1939, disclosed that IAP did not fill its federally allotted weekly employment quota.[91] In 1939, Carter was finally reassigned from his construction-laborer job to IAP's easel/mural project at a monthly salary of $92.00, a thirty percent raise over other black WPA employees.[92] Recalling his reassignment, Carter stated, "I guess I wore them out until they got tired of saying no." Later, he noted, at the time of his reassignment, "Three or four other black (artists) also got on the WPA about then," and together they gave the South Side "*its first black artistic set*" (emphasis added).[93]

The IAP appointment of "*its first black artistic set*" was influenced by the Chicago Artist Union's (CAU) successful campaign to relieve IAP's director Increase Robinson (Josephine Reichmann) of her duties for failing to fill federally allotted artist positions. IAP's racial preferment practices became a rider on CAU's written concerns. Robinson was succeeded by George Thorp, 1938–41, and he by Fred Biesel, 1941–43. Thorp and later Biesel addressed CAU's concerns and quelled perceptions of racial discrimination. Notwithstanding their contributions to the IAP, the major factors in IAP attaining its employment spike of roughly thirty-five black artists were the opening the SSCAC and subsequent need for full-time staff members there.

Faced with the loss of federal funds and innuendoes of having been a haven of communist activities, several influential personages severed their ties with the SSCAC after World War II. However, a group of determined women that included Pauline Kigh Reed, Wilhelmina Blanks, Fern Gayden, and Grace Thompson Learning stepped forward to ensure that the SSCAC remained a vital institution. Reed organized the Committee of 100 Women for the purpose of improving SSCAC's public image and to raise funds to defray the art center's scaled-back operational and program costs. Of the 110 FAP/CAC art centers opened during the WPA era, the SSCAC is the only one that remains open.

In addition to the ALC and SSCAC, there were small informal gatherings at locations, such as Katherine Dunham's apartment, Charles and Margaret Burroughs's carriage house, and the home of Marion and Eva Perkins. These informal gatherings contributed to the cross-fertilization of artistic and intellectual ideas. Anthropologist, dancer, and choreographer Dunham introduced Caribbean and African dance to the concert stage; Burroughs was rapidly becoming one of the leading figures in the visual arts, human rights, and civil rights movements; and Perkins was at the forefront of Chicago's African American modernist sculpture movement.

Chicago Renaissance: The Second Wave, 1941–60

Two important exhibitions announced the emergence of the renaissance's second wave of African American artists: the Chicago 1940 national juried exhibition, *The Art of the American Negro: 1852–1940*, and Howard University's 1941 *Exhibition of Negro Artists of Chicago*. The national juried exhibition was an integral part of the American Negro Exposition that commemorated the seventy-fifth anniversary of the Emancipation Proclamation. Alain Locke chaired the art exhibition committee, and Alonzo Aden, cofounder of Howard University's art gallery, acted as curator. The exposition opened on July 4, 1940, at the Chicago Coliseum in an area named the Henry O. Tanner Gallery.

In the spirit of Tanner, upon entering the Coliseum and exhibition hall, the transgenerational theme of Chicago's renaissance became visible. The Coliseum's main entryway had been transformed into "a Court of Honors" by Charles Dawson's ten dioramas depicting highlights of seven thousand years of African and African American history. Entering the Coliseum's exhibition hall, William Scott's twenty-four murals depicting the accomplishments of African Americans over the seventy-five-year period were prominently displayed. With the exception of Elizabeth Catlett winning the first prize in sculpture, the other first-place award recipients were Chicagoans: William Carter in watercolor, Charles White in drawing, and White for *There Were No Crops This Year* and his mural *A History of the Negro Press*, as well as an honorable mention for his watercolor *Fellow Worker, Won't You March with Us*. Evidently impressed by Chicago's artists, Aden brought their works to Washington, D.C., for Howard University's 1941 *Exhibition of Negro Artists of Chicago*. Washington was known as one of America's centers of black society and Howard University as its intellectual center. This exhibit, following on the heels of the national one in Chicago, put black Chicago on the map as the center of the arts movement in America.

Rather than being committed to a particular stylistic approach, second-wave painters worked with adeptness in two or three styles simultaneously. While the majority of these painters settled on a particular stylistic approach, others worked in styles ranging from naturalism to abstraction for much of their professional careers. Three painters in particular—Stan Williamson, William Carter, and Walter Sanford—embraced this range of styles and influences. Williamson (1911–n.d.), possibly influenced by the nineteenth-century French painter Paul Cezanne in his painting *Old Dwellings* (1958), explored the reduction of subject matter into geometric components painted in broad patches of color that delineated and defined the form of buildings. By contrast, his urban residential street scene *House in Chicago* (1959) exemplified his facility as a realistic painter.[94] Because of his tendency to work in various styles, Cedric Dover held, when Williamson settled on a particular style, "America will have another great painter."[95] Similarly, Carter's murals ranged from the cubist-influenced *Last Supper* (n.d.) at Reverend Johnnie Coleman's Christ Universal Temple Church to the expressionist *Cleopatra and Her Court* for a nightclub on the Near South Side to other realist portraits.[96] And while he was a proficient realistic and expressionistic painter, Sanford was clearly influenced by Pablo Picasso in his paintings *Susan and Friend* (n.d.), *Sun Ritual* (1958), and *Seated Nude* (1959).

Second-wave renaissance artists also extended beyond European and American traditions by taking inspiration from the Caribbean, Latin America, and, to a lesser extent, Africa. Short- to long-term study residencies in the Caribbean or Mexico were self-funded or sponsored by the John Simon Guggenheim Foundation or the Julius Rosenwald Fund. Among the artists who studied and produced art in the Caribbean and for Mexico were Sylvester Britton, Margaret Burroughs, Eldzier Cortor, William Harper, Frederick Jones, Lawrence Jones, Archibald Motley Jr., William Scott, and Charles White.

The artistic titans of the second period were Cortor, Sebree, and White. However, to delimit this period to these painters fails to explain how and why this period represented a further elaboration of Chicago's early renaissance and how it gained momentum when this trio of artists relocated to other cities. The pillars that provided stability and spurred this artistic momentum were artists such as Henry Avery, Margaret Burroughs, William Carter, Fitzhugh Dinkins, Bernard Goss, Frederick Jones, William McBride, and Leroy Winbush.

Painters

Born in Chicago, **George E. Neal** (1906–38) studied at the Art Institute. Works such as *The Hat* (1937), *The Red House* (n.d.), and *Still Life* (n.d.) reveal Neal to have been an able figurative painter. Although he did not attain national or regional acclaim as a painter, Neal's influence in shaping the renaissance's second wave was incalculable. Having died at the early age of thirty-two, Neal's imprint on art in black Chicago remained alive through the accomplishments of his students. Among his former students, Neal was revered as a master instructor and leader in Chicago's black self-help art movement.

Beginning with his South Side Settlement House's Saturday art classes, Neal taught some of Chicago's most important young artists during their fledging stages of artistic development. Among Neal's students were Henry Avery, Margaret Taylor (née Goss Burroughs), Eldzier Cortor, Charles Davis, Joseph Kersey, Mary Jackson McGee, and Charles White. Shortly after leaving the Settlement House, Neal offered classes and exhibitions at his carriage-house apartment-studio, known as Paragon Studio.[97]

In addition to the majority of his Settlement House students, Katherine Bell, William Carter, Bernard Goss, William McBride, and Charles Sebree took informal classes with Neal. The instruction offered and demands placed on his students were quite similar to those of a postsecondary professional art school. In addition to in-house instruction, Neal's students worked outdoors as well as visited galleries and museums. His open-door policy not only permitted community residents to view bimonthly student exhibitions but also to visit and observe classes. Neal encouraged these residents to ask questions of the students, and later these interactions influenced the thematic direction of Neal's students as well as fostered close relationships between professional artists and community residents.

In 1936, Paragon Studios caught fire and burned to the ground. Not deterred by this fire, Neal organized the Arts Craft Guild. In addition to many of his former students, the guild's members also included Fred Hollingsworth, Frank Phillips, Dan Terry Reed, David Ross, and Elsworth Terrance. Led by its president, William McGill, the guild met on Sunday afternoons to critique works, sketch, and offer mutual support. In 1939, when plans were underway to establish the SSCAC, its members dissolved the guild to become the SSCAC's Artist Committee.[98]

Native Chicagoan **Charles Wilbert White** (1918–79) was one of Neal's students who attained international acclaim. White studied at the School of the Art Institute in 1937–38. Despite working three part-time jobs, he completed the Art Institute's two-year certificate program in one year. In 1939, White was employed by IAP's easel/mural project and assigned to assist white muralists Edward Millman and Mitchell Siporin, and he took the opportunity to study how the compositional and technical demands of transitioning from small-easel to large-scale mural painting. Independent of his WPA job, White executed three important murals between 1939 and 1943: *Five Great American Negroes* (1939–40), *A History of the Negro Press* (1940), and *Contribution of the Negro to Democracy in America* (1943). Installed at the George Cleveland Hall Branch of the Chicago Public library at 4801 South Michigan Avenue, White's *Five Great American Negroes* mural accentuated the contributions of Sojourner Truth, Booker T. Washington, Frederick Douglass, Marian Anderson, George Washington Carver, and teachers of the black youth (see figure 10.19).

Shortly after the installation of this mural at the Cleveland Branch Library, White was commissioned by the Associated Negro Press (ANP) to execute a mural for its *American Negro Exposition*'s exhibit. In his mural *A History of the Negro Press*, White depicted the three pioneering figures in America's black newspaper industry: John B. Russwurm, Frederick Douglass, and Timothy Thomas Fortune. In 1827, Russwurm founded America's earliest black newspaper, *Freedom Journal*, which was circulated in eleven states, Washington, D.C., Canada, Europe, and Haiti. Douglass founded the *North Star* newspaper in 1847, and Fortune the *New York Freedman* in 1884. In 1887, Fortune changed the newspaper's name to the *New York Age*. The other figures in this mural are black linotype workers, pressman, staff reporter, cameraman, copy editor, and typesetter. Highly stylized, White's figures appeared to have been chiseled from large blocks of black jade, which conveyed a sense of monumentality, augustness, and figural power.

In 1942, while studying at New York City's Art Student League with instructor Harry Steinberg, White was encouraged to individualize through modeling his stylization of figures. Working in black-and-white media, he followed Steinberg's suggestion. At the same, time, he never abandoned the fundamental geometric construction of figures in his works. This was evinced in his 1943 *Contribution of the American Negro to Democracy* mural, which was installed at Hampton University's Wainwright Auditorium. The central personages in this mural are George Washington Carver, Frederick Douglass, Peter Still, Sojourner Truth, and Booker T. Washington.

Regarding the narrative elements in his work, White stated, "I use the Black image to make a very personal statement about how I view the world . . . my hopes, aspirations, and dreams about all people, And I say [to] the world, 'if you cannot relate to this Black image, that's your problem.' Black humanity has been thrust into history, has been catapulted into history as a universal thing about survival, a survival with dignity."[99] The black presence as universal archetypes permeates White's oeuvre from the 1930s until White's death in 1979.

For example, in *There Were No Crops This Year* (1940), White dramatically captured pathos of a farmer and his wife confronted by a season without a bountiful crop, and what this portends (see figure 10.20). Irrespective of race or ethnicity, through this black couple White evoked a universal response to a barren season, particularly among small farmers and sharecroppers. Hence, blackness was the filtering lens to illuminate the universal rather than the accustomed narrow lens of whiteness.

During the early 1940s, White's personal and professional life took him away from Chicago, though his influence on African American art in Chicago would continue to grow. White met fellow-artist Elizabeth Catlett and married her in 1941, and they lived for a short time together in Chicago. Later that year, Catlett became the head of Dillard College's art department, and White was awarded a $2,000 Julius Rosenwald Fellowship to study and produce art in the Deep South. After leaving Dillard in 1942, the Whites studied in New York City. The next year, Catlett accepted a teaching position at Hampton University, where White painted *Contribution of the*

Negro to Democracy in America, which the *New York Times* characterized as "a vigorous expression of protest against antidemocratic forces."[100]

Shortly thereafter, the U.S. Army drafted White to fight against those antidemocratic forces overseas. His engineering regiment was dispatched to sandbag dikes to avert further flood damage from the Mississippi and Ohio Rivers. Having become seriously ill from exposure to the weather (White had a preexisting acute respiratory condition), White was diagnosed with severe pleurisy. This resulted in a three-year stay at the Veteran's Administration Hospital in Beacon, New York. Never cured, he was plagued with this illness for the remainder of his life. For example, in 1945 White accepted an artist-in-residence position at Howard University but became ill again and had to be hospitalized. The toxicities of materials used in oil painting necessitated that White limit or abandon painting in oils. Accordingly, after being discharged from the hospital, White worked with much less toxic mediums, such as charcoal, conte crayon, prints, and pen and ink.

In 1947 Catlett and White traveled to Mexico and studied at Mexico City's Escuela de Pintura y Escultura de la Secretaria de Educación Pública (school of sculpture and painting) and the Talleres Gráficos de la Nación. Living with acclaimed muralist David Alfaro Siqueiros, the Whites met and worked with some of Mexico's leading artists, such as Pablo O'Higgins, Jose Clemente Orozco, Leopoldo Mendes, and Diego Rivera. Influenced by the social consciousness of Mexican artists and themes of *Mexicaness* in their murals, paintings, and prints, White indicated this period of study was a "milestone" that clarified his artistic direction.[101] He also acknowledged his indebtedness to fellow Arts Craft Guild member Lawrence Jones for having initially introduced him to the Mexican school of painting.[102]

After he and Catlett divorced, White married Frances Barrett and vacationed in Europe in 1950. Not only were Europeans familiar with his artistic output, White was received in Czechoslovakia, East Germany, France, Italy, Poland, the Soviet Union, and West Germany as a distinguished artist of international eminence. When the newlyweds returned to America, there was a dramatic increase among major art institutions in collecting and exhibiting White's works. For example, the Metropolitan Museum of Art included a work by White in its 1952 exhibition; in 1953, the Whitney Museum of American Art acquired for its permanent collection White's drawing *Preacher* (1952); the American Academy of Arts and Letters offered him a one-man exhibition; and he was the recipient of a John Jay Whitney Fellowship in 1956.

Socially conscious, White was enormously affected by the 1960s civil rights movement. Spurred by America's history of disregard of black life and rights, he executed some of his most powerful and penetrating works, such as *Wanted Poster Series* (1969). Influenced by slavery-era runaway reward posters for the return of runaway slaves, White created a wanted-poster series. The narrative element of this series explored the short distance between the treatment of slaves and the current state of black people in America. In the upper register of *Wanted Poster Series #6* (1969), the Confederate "stars and bars" form the background. The foreground is dominated by the image of a nude runaway black woman. The reward for her and a boy's return of $30,000.00 is stenciled behind the woman's head. A painted finger on each side of the female's shoulder suggests the reward for her body. Stenciled across the woman's abdominal area is "Article IV Section 2" of U.S. Constitution, which reads, "A person charged in any state with treason, felony, or crime, who shall flee from justice, and be found in another state, shall on demand of the executive authority of the state from which he fled, be delivered up, to be removed to the state having jurisdiction of the crime." A muted-toned American flag forms the lower register's background. In the foreground, an emaciated nude boy is seated on the ground. The seated position of the boy recalls the cramped conditions aboard the slave ships. The boy is also a symbol of abject poverty in late-twentieth-century America. Stenciled above and overlapping a portion of the boy's head and behind his back are portions of the September 18, 1859, Fugitive Slave Act. On a curvature under the seated boy's feet in capital letters is the word VALUABLE (see figure 10.21).

White's career—spanning the Depression years through the civil rights movement of the 1960s and 1970s—left a significant legacy on the history of American art and the importance of the Chicago movement. In his lifetime, White had more than fifty major one-man exhibitions, and his works are in the collections of over fifty museums in America, Mexico, and Europe.[103] In spite of his accomplishments, however, it is rare that White is mentioned in histories of American art.

In his 1947 novel *Kingblood Royal*, Nobel and Pulitzer Prize recipient Sinclair Lewis introduced his readers to **Eldzier Cortor** (born 1916). The novel's main character Neil Kingblood ruminates on what would distinguish the homes of middle-class Negroes from those of America's white middle class. Perhaps, the distinguishing factors, Neil conjectured, might be "signed photographs of Haile Selassie, Walter White and Pushkin?" Or, Neil continued, "an Eldzier Cortor painting."[104]

Corter was born in Richmond, Virginia. When he was about a year old, his family relocated to Chicago. He studied at the Art Institute from 1936 to 1941, where instructor Kathleen Blackshear had a profound and lasting influence on him. In her art history and composition classes, Blackshear acquainted students with Western and non-Western art, particularly Oceanic and African. Inspired by Blackshear's course and the Field Museum of Natural History's collection of African sculpture, Cortor's drawings, prints, and paintings began to introduce elongated female figures reminiscent of Senufo sculpture.

Through Horace Cayton, director of Chicago's Good Shepherd Community Center (renamed, Parkway Community House), Cortor was introduced to the Africanisms among South Carolina's Sea Island Gullah people, and when awarded a Julius Rosenwald Fellowship in 1940, Cortor used the funding to travel south and paint in the Sea Islands. Recalling this period of study, he stated, "As a Negro artist, I felt a special interest in painting Negroes whose cultural tradition had only been slightly influenced by whites. This series of pictures reflects the particular physical and racial characteristics of the Gullahs. I hope the assimilation of their background and mode of living has added not only to the authenticity of the paintings but also to their intrinsic value."[105]

In his Gullah-inspired paintings, Cortor explored the interplay of natural and artificial light on the dark skin of women. By elongating the face, neck, limbs, and torso, his paintings and prints evoke the serene, unspoiled, sensual, and natural beauty of black women.[106] This is evinced in his most widely known and reproduced work *Southern Gate* (ca. 1942–43) (see figure 10.22). His treatment of the semi-nude woman in the painting's foreground typifies Cortor's approach in portraying the augustness of black women. This work is densely layered with symbols of

decline, reclamation, and self-renewal. For example, in the lexicon of symbolism, the prime and secondary meanings of the sky, water, small bird, necklace, flowing garment, and nudity are rebirth, renewal, or regeneration. The small body of water in this work appears to be of minor significance. Yet, when the symbolic meaning of water is considered within the context of the significance Cortor ascribed to black women, it takes on increased importance. Symbolically, water represents "The Great Mother," the woman as "the carrier of water," which is the life force, and the woman represents a messenger to the water spirits. "The Black woman," Cortor held, "represents the Black race. She is the Black Spirit; she conveys a feeling of eternity and the continuance of life."[107]

Cortor was awarded a Guggenheim Fellowship in 1946 to produce works of art and to research Africanism in Cuba, Jamaica, and Haiti. Of these islands, he found Haiti to be the richest in Africanism (Haitians had developed the Caribbean's earliest indigenous art movement). Living among ordinary people, Cortor learned to speak patois, became acquainted with indigenous art forms and symbolism, sketched local scenes, and taught classes at Centre d'Art in Port-au-Prince. This experience expanded his awareness on New World Africanisms and provided confirmation of his artistic direction.[108]

Upon his return to Chicago in 1948, Cortor experienced the lingering residue of the WPA's and World War II's domestic surveillance programs. Under the hysteria created by "the Red Scare," Cortor recalled, WPA artists were labeled communist. Artists producing social-realist works influenced by civil rights or other problems confronting the masses were now characterized as "troublemakers," and the market for works having themes on blackness had been practically eliminated. "To survive," he recalled, "many artists eliminated black subject matter" in their work.[109]

In 1950, when *Life* magazine identified America's top "19 Young American Artists" under thirty-six years of age, the editors selected Cortor as the only African American. In addition to its lengthy featured article on the artists, *Life* magazine sponsored an exhibition at New York City's Metropolitan Museum of Art that featured selected works from its permanent art collection combined with works executed by the nineteen young artists.[110] In spite of having been selected as one of America's top young artists, art dealers continued to shy away from his works. This was one of the important factors that contributed to

Cortor's decision to relocate to New York City. Shortly after settling in New York, he was awarded a second Guggenheim Fellowship to study printmaking in Mexico. After returning to New York for a short period, Cortor resettled in Chicago but again felt stifled by the Chicago's mainstream art market there. After a brief stay, he once again moved to New York City.

Inducted in the U.S. Navy, **Hughie Lee-Smith** (1915–99) was stationed at the Great Lakes Naval Station, located in the northern suburban area of Chicago. Although the naval station was a tinder box of racial tension, the navy permitted Lee-Smith to paint a mural at the base, *The History of the Negro in the U.S. Navy* (ca. 1947). Until the completion of his mural, the contributions of black sailors were largely unknown. The proximity of the naval station to Chicago permitted Lee-Smith to frequently visit the SSCAC. During these visits, he and Cortor became close friends. Their friendship and similar artistic interests proved mutually beneficial.

Prior to being inducted into the U.S. Navy, Lee-Smith explored themes of dislocation and displacement. This is evinced in his lithographs *Artists Life: No.2* (1938) and *Dislocation* (1938). Cortor was also exploring similar themes in works, such as *Loneliness* (1940) and *Skin Deep* (1947). Mutual interest in exploring these aspects of the human condition resulted in the cross-fertilization of ideas and hastened their resolution in depicting such subject matter. After completing his navy tour of duty, Lee-Smith planned to settle in Chicago. Unable to gain full-time employment to support his family, the Lee-Smith family relocated to Detroit and later to New York City. There he later attained national acclaim.

The early works of **Frederick D. Jones** (1914–2004) were often mistaken for or compared with Cortor's. Like Cortor, Jones was among the few African American artists who treated semi-nude and nude black women as subject matter. For example, *Lady Godiva* (1950) and *The Violinist* (ca. 1952) are two of Jones's important works where the central figure is a black nude female. A modernist painting, the striking features in *The Violinist* are the simplicity of forms, design mastery, and highly sophisticated painterly technique.

Born in Raleigh, North Carolina, Jones studied at Clark University in Atlanta, Georgia, and later at Chicago's Art Institute (1941–43). Without much notice, he established a reputation as being one of Chicago's important artists, one of the important anchors of Chicago's African American visual-arts community,

and a highly regarded mentor to young artists who blossomed during the 1960s. A modernist figure painter, his works are included in collections such as the Walter O. Evans Collection of African American Art, IBM, U.S. Library of Congress, American embassies in Kabul, Afghanistan, and the Belgium embassy in Washington, D.C.

Prior to becoming the Museum of the Art Institute's first curator of modern painting and sculpture in 1954, Katherine Kuh owned a gallery under her name from 1935 to 1942. A modern art maven, Kuh exhibited works by leading European artists, such as Fernand Leger, Pablo Picasso, Marc Chagall, Paul Klee, and Joan Miro.[111] Of the few American artists that she represented, **Charles Sebree** (1914–85) was the only African American. In her 1936, 1939, and 1940 group exhibitions, Kuh included examples of Sebree's work. Each of these exhibitions was important; however, the 1940 exhibition was the most significant. It included works by leading modernists, such as Leger, Picasso, Henri Matisse, Carlos Merida, Amedeo Modigliani, and Diego Rivera. For Sebree to have had works in this exhibition suggests that Kuh considered Sebree to be an important young modernist painter.

Born in White City near Madisonville, Kentucky, Sebree studied briefly at the Art Institute and School of Design. Among his influences were Byzantine art, African art, Picasso, and the French painter Georges Rouault. Picasso's *Self-Portrait* (1905) provides a clue to Sebree's early treatment of the face, particularly the gaze of his jesters. This is discernible in Sebree's *Boy in Blue Jacket* (1938). Whether he patterned his life after Picasso is impossible to determine with certainty. However, there were similarities: Picasso was a painter, sculptor, graphic artist, and stage designer with an affinity for circus performers. Sebree was a painter, dancer, set designer, and playwright with a predilection for jesters.

Rouault's influence was evident in Sebree's early paintings, such as *Seated Woman* (1940) and *Pink Turban* (1939). Similar to Picasso, Rouault also had an affinity for clowns. This is evinced in Rouault's *Self-Portrait* (1925–26). Having apprenticed in stain glass, the strips of lead holding pieces of stained glass in place influenced Rouault's use of very dark, heavily painted outlines to accentuate the figure(s) in his paintings and at times to break up space within a figure's clothing to form smaller patterns of color. This is discernible in Rouault's *The Old King* (1916–37) painting. Similar to Rouault, Sebree experimented with stained glass and later mosaics. Rather than heavy, dark outlines, in his painting *Head of a Woman* (1938), the central figure is framed by burnt umber (see figure 10.23). The various brown tones in the background and the figure soften the heavy umber framing. While Rouault was influenced by the Fauves' intense impasto painting technique and warm colors, Sebree's palette more freely applied cool, translucent colors, which evolved a somber or mystic quality.

In spite of these discernible influences, Sebree was not imitative. Such influences represented points of departure paintings. He synthesized only these elements that were germane to his particular artistic concerns. Through this process, he developed his unique artistic voice. The jester, a recurring figure in his works, may have been a metaphor for Sebree's lifestyle, which was largely improvisational, economically and socially. Outwardly, the jester represents the unregenerate lower being without a past or future. Yet, having the abilities to anticipate and respond to the expectations of his audience, the jester controls the ritual of discourse to attain his desired ends.

Although he had developed a recognizable signature style, Sebree was engaged in an unrelenting and continuous program of experimentation with mediums and surface treatments to construct pictorial ambiance. As evidence in *Saltimbanque in Moonlight* (ca.1970) (see figure 10.24), the portrait is far more simplified than those in his early works; the use of beeswax provides the illusion of loosely woven fabric; and the figure's huge, penetrating eyes peering out at the viewer differs dramatically from his early works. In his stylistic approach to this work, here is almost a complete absence of clues linking it to Sebree.

Artists of entirely different temperaments, Sebree and **Raymond "Ramon" Gabriel** (1911–n.d.) had adjoining studios on the second floor of the Colored Lutheran Church on East Forty-Ninth Street. Born in the Virgin Islands, Gabriel was a talented painter as well as an accomplished violinist. He studied at the Art Institute and Hull House. Markedly different from his realistic tropical scenes, *Pool Room* (1937) and *Seated Boy* (ca. 1940) provide examples of Gabriel's modernist sensibilities (see figure 10.25). In August 1941, Gabriel was recognized in *American Magazine of Art* as "[o]ne of the lively and original groups of American artists anywhere to be found."[112]

Similar to Gabriel, native Chicagoan **John Carlis Jr.** (1917–2003) studied at the Art Institute and worked in a realistic and modernistic style simultaneously. Early in his career, Carlis demonstrated promise as a modernist painter, as evinced in *Two Women* (1940). In spite of being one of Chicago's talented young painters, he is probably best remembered for his greeting-card illustrations and book *How to Make Your Own Greeting Cards* (1968), published by Watson-Guptil, one of America's largest publishers of art instruction books.

Unless bedridden, after retiring as a Chicago public schoolteacher, **William Carter** (1909–96) painted from the early evening until dawn. His greeting to a fellow artist was, "Have you painted today?" Until his death at eighty-seven years of age, Carter maintained that he was "too young to have a (painting) style." As such, he was adept and equally comfortable working in a realistic or pure abstract style.

From at least the Great Depression era until his death, Carter produced many works priced to sell quickly. He referred to these works as his "breadwinners" to pay rent and purchase food. Over the years, these and other "breadwinner" works such as *Tete-a-Tete* (1938), *Study in Gray* (1939), and *Katherine Dunham* (n.d.) have unfortunately been used as yardsticks for measuring Carter's significance as a painter. One of Carter's early non–"breadwinner" paintings, *Ballerina* (1939), provides evidence of his adeptness as a figure painter.[113] A later work is *The Card Game* (1950) (see figure 10.26).

Born in St. Louis, Missouri, Carter studied at the Art Institute, 1930–31, and the University of Illinois at Urbana-Champaign, 1935–36. Carter recalled that at the University of Illinois, "[t]here wasn't any place on campus for Negroes to live."[114] Failing to find off-campus housing, Carter discovered that a janitor rented out cots to black students in the basement of one of the buildings where "ten of us lived . . . that year next to the coal and underneath the white boys."[115] Years later, he returned to the university and earned his degree in 1958.

Similar to Carter, **Henry Avery** (1906–82) was an able realist, abstract, and expressionist painter. Although he explored pure and figurative abstraction, his most accomplished works as a modernist were his expressionist paintings like his *Still Life* (1938). In this painting, Avery transformed a straightforward interior scene into a highly contemplative and dynamic painting.

Born in Margatan, North Carolina, Avery studied at the South Side Settlement House. During the late

1930s and 1940s, examples of his works were included in exhibitions, such as the forty-eighth annual Art Institute of Chicago exhibition *American Painters and Sculptors Annual Show* in 1939, Institute of Modern Art, Boston, Massachusetts, Library of Congress in 1940, and the American Negro Exposition's national juried exhibition in 1940.

Born in Evanston, Illinois, **Charles V. Davis** (1912–67) studied at the South Side Settlement House, Paragon Studio, and briefly at the Art Institute. Known for figurative works such as *Perhaps Tomorrow* (n.d.) and *Newsboy (The Negro Boy)* (1939), he was also an able modernist painter (see figure 10.27). In his cubistic painting *Tycoon Toys* (1938), he depicted a desolate industrial site in simplified geometric shapes.

This work may have been influenced by the controversial 1937 South Chicago Republic Steel strike. On May 30, 1937, approximately two hundred men, women, and a few children were having a picnic in the field in front of the steel plant when the police, hearing a shot fired, opened fire on the marchers. Ten marchers were killed, and roughly sixty injured or wounded. Forty policemen were injured. The title of this painting may have been a metaphor for the acrimonious relationship between management and workers that made Chicago's "Memorial Day Massacre" national news and led to greater sympathy for the union movement.

Native Chicagoan **Sylvester Britton** (1926–2009) studied at the Art Institute, Mexico's School of Painting and Sculpture, and Paris's Academie de la Grande Chaumiere. He attained success as both a designer and painter. Britton was one of the anchors, important mentors, and leading artist during the 1950s. His painting *Bondage* (n.d.) and drawing *Red Hat* (1954) provide examples of Britton's varied artistic concerns.

A powerful work, *Bondage* evokes helplessness and outrage. To be stripped of one's clothing is a source of humiliation and indignation. To be restrained with arms behind one's back adds to this indignation. On his knees, the nude man's head is bowed as he struggles to loosen the restraints holding his arms behind his back. This work recalls the treatment of some black men from the slavery era to present-day tactics employed to restrain "uncooperative" incarcerated prisoners (see figure 10.28).

Britton's *Red Hat* is a marked contrast with *Bondage*. Through his simplicity of form and sparing use of color in *Red Hat*, Britton infused the sitter in *Red Hat*

with a sense of dignity and unrehearsed stateliness (see figure 10.29).

Designer, painter, printmaker, and art collector **William McBride** (1913–2000) was born in Algiers, Louisiana. At the age of ten, McBride and his family relocated to Chicago. While he studied briefly at the Art Institute, McBride's stylistic direction was influenced by studying privately with painters and designers such as Ivan Albright and Leroy Winbush. McBride was highly regarded and a successful designer as well as an abstract and expressionistic painter, but he has become better known for his foresight to collect art and memorabilia. With over one thousand paintings, prints, and sculptures in his collection, McBride had one of the largest and most extensive collections of African and African American art; he also held the largest private collection of WPA-era works. Indeed, more than fifty percent of works by Chicago artists included in the 1978 *New York/Chicago: WPA and the Black Artist* exhibition came from McBride's collection.[116]

Born in Sedalia, Missouri, **Bernard Goss** (1913–66) graduated from the University of Iowa in 1935. After relocating to Chicago, he studied with George Neal and at the Art Institute. Goss was one of the most gifted painters of this period. An expressionist painter, in spite of having executed some exceptional works, he never realized the full extent of his talent. A watercolor, *Musicians* (1939), was one of Goss's early paintings. Through his treatment of form and use of color in this painting, Goss attempted to capture the melodic, harmonic, and rhythmic flow of a jazz quartet in a cabaret setting.[117]

In paintings such as *Always the Dirty Work* (n.d.), *Slave Revolt, Slave Rebellion* (n.d.), *Seven Generations* (n.d.), and *Oscar dePriest: Powerful Politician* (n.d.), Goss offered powerful sociopolitical comments on race particularism and black resistance to oppression in America.[118] Towards the end of his life, Goss produced some excellent prints, such as *Ethiopian Leader (Haile Selassie)* (ca. 1960s), *Sojourner Truth* (ca. 1960s), and *African Warrior* (ca. 1960s).

Designer, gallery director, and painter **Irene Clark** (1927–84) was born in Washington, D.C. She studied at the Art Institute Chicago's 414 Workshop and San Francisco Art Institute. An accomplished realistic painter, Clark adopted an expressionistic and later naive approach to painting. Her narrative influences evoke folklore heard and read as a child; her later works do the same for African and diasporic folklore.

Writing on the African influence, Clark noted, "Generation after generation of Africans have told stories among themselves, and whenever they moved they took their stories."[119]

Clark's painting *Rolling Calf* (n.d.) represents a Jamaican folktale about a restless spirit that reappears in the form of a sheep and undergoes four transfigurations (see figure 10.30). In this work, with the exception of the front-lower human foot, the spirit has been transfigured in the form of a sheep. The heads and portions of the bodies of the horse, dog, and cat are recognizable. However, the other parts of these animals' bodies remain in a transfiguring stage: the horse appears to be emerging from the sheep, the dog from the sheep, the cat from the dog, and the pig from the cat.[120]

Printmakers

Working in various printmaking techniques of woodblock, dry point, etching, lithographic, and silkscreen, several young painters became adept printmakers, including **Margaret Taylor Goss-Burroughs** (1917–2010), the only female artist to attain distinction.

Born in Rose, Louisiana, in 1917, she and her family relocated to Chicago in 1920. A poet, author, painter, printmaker, sculptor, musician, and art instructor, Burroughs was also the cofounder of the Ebony Museum of Negro History and Art, later known as the DuSable Museum of African American History.[121] In response to the pervasiveness of race exclusionary practices in the visual arts, Burroughs was a leader in developing opportunities for black artists to display their art. She was one of the cofounders of the SSCAC and National Conference of Negro Art Teachers in 1956 (currently known as the National Conference of Artists); in 1957, with the cooperation of the Lake Meadows' apartment management and shopping-mall merchants, Burroughs cofounded the Lake Meadows Outdoor Art Fair, which became one of Chicago's Near South Side's largest outdoor exhibitions. Skilled and effective at developing programs, institution building, fund-raising, teaching, and shepherding the careers of artists, Burroughs became a key link and generator of the 1960s black arts movement in Chicago that linked the 1930s and 1940s Black Renaissance to the next generation. Given this credit, however, Burroughs's artistic accomplishments have been often overlooked or minimized.

Working in different mediums, Burroughs prefers to be recognized as a printmaker, including her fine

Face of Africa (1965) and *Warsaw* (1965). The most striking features of her linocut print *Warsaw* are her sense of design, surface textural treatment, and the use of positive and negative space to animate and define spatial relationships between these buildings. By contrast with her modernist representational approach of buildings in *Warsaw*, Burroughs's *Face of Africa* woodcut print is naturalistic (see figure 10.31). Her mastery of technique gives the impression of this print being a drawing. The subject matter is a powerful statement on the augustness of black women. This is evident in Burroughs's treatment of the female figure's almond-shaped eyes, broad nose, thick lips, dark skin, short, kinky hair, and facial expression.

Because of her independence, conviction, and activities in support of human, civil, and women's rights, as well as her opposition to American and European imperialism, Burroughs was considered to be a threat to "national security." Among her alleged un-American activities was Burroughs's unwavering support of Paul Robeson. After the U.S. government declared Robeson unpatriotic, Burroughs raised funds to have him speak and perform in Chicago. This and other activities contributed to her being declared a communist sympathizer, but unlike many African Americans having been alleged to be unpatriotic during this period, Burroughs stood fast and defended herself against these allegations and blacklisting efforts.

Sculpture

With the introduction of new materials and techniques during the World War II era, sculpture became free from its naturalistic tradition. Sheet metal and advanced welding techniques encouraged experimentation and ushered in the modern period of sculpture, although many Americans continued to prefer naturalism as the appropriate sculptural form to memorialize significant historical events and highly accomplished personages. Largely unaffected by the modern abstract movement in sculpture, **Marion Perkins** (1908–61), **Joseph Kersey** (1908–), and **Clarence Lawson** (1909–88) emerged as Chicago's leading African American sculptors during the WPA and World War II periods.

Lawson was born in Beaumont, Texas, and Kersey in Chicago. Both studied at the Art Institute and became able sculptors. The striking feature of Lawson's naturalistic bronze bust *Head of a Negro Girl* (1932) is his sensitive treatment of the sitter's unique facial features, which evokes a charmful youthfulness. In addition to being a sculptor, Lawson also produced lyrical paintings such as *Malayan Village*, which recalls the Caribbean inspired scenes of Elmer Simms Campbell and Raymond Gabriel. Kersey's noncommissioned works tended to be more expressionistic, such as *St. Francis and the Bird* (n.d.) and *Anna* (1940); these works evoke a meditative calmness. By contrast, his marble-dust bust *Ellen* (1936) provides an example of Kersey's naturalistic stylistic approach.

Born in Charme, Arkansas, in 1916, Perkins left for Chicago after the death of his parents to be raised by his aunt Doris Padrone. Prior to studying with Si Gordon at the Wabash YMCA, Perkins had attained local acclaim as a self-taught sculptor. In 1940, he received his first major commission from Maurice and Bella Steuben, owners of Michigan's South Haven Biltmore Hotel, to create outdoor sculptures of Dutch children for the hotel's grounds. Perkins depicted the children with subtle African facial features.[122] His treatment of these children was informed by the early African presence in Scandinavia and the Netherlands. Bronze Age engravings and artifacts provide evidence of this presence, which include Africoid imagery of the sky deity Tyr, fertility figurines, and dancer-acrobat figurines.

By the late 1940s, Perkins's work had become highly stylized and reflected a mature figural modernist sensibility. In his bust *Man of Sorrows* (1950), Perkins depicts Christ with an elongated face framed by stylized long woolly hair, sideburns, and beard (see figure 10.32). Christ's crown consisted of adjoined stylized birds, which is symbolic of "mind of the divine healer." According to Perkins, "This is a piece that says what I want it to say. It shows the Negro peoples' conception of Christ as a Negro—which is as it should be."[123]

Perkins was deeply committed to the equal rights, human rights, and antiwar movements. As a U.S. Postal Service employee, it was alleged his involvement in these movements violated the 1947 Federal Employees Loyalty/Security Provision of Executive Order 9835. He was terminated as a postal employee in 1948. Executive Order 9835 and other government practices to silence dissent influenced Perkins's *Dying Soldier* (1952), a subtle but powerful antiwar statement (see figure 10.33).

The prone, stylized, nude male figure is reminiscent of small, pre-Columbian sculptural forms. With his head tilted backward, the figure appears to be in a deep sleep. Perkins's treatment of the highly textured hair of the figure's head conveys the impression of a stylized helmet. Starkly simplified, *Dying Soldier* is a haunting response to efforts undertaken to silence nonviolent protest against America's jingoism.

Conclusion: Waves of Black Renaissance

The achievements of black artists in the early twentieth century in Chicago led to the renaissance during the 1930s and 1940s, a second wave of national prominence from 1941 to 1960, and finally, the 1960s and 1970s Black Arts Movement, the Black Cultural Nationalist Movement, or "the African American renaissance." As the authors of the "Chicago Documentation Project" of the 1980s conclude, "Although African American artists have been a vital part of the art scene in Chicago for many years, the achievements of these artists and the activities of their organizations are relatively unknown to even informed audiences and are rarely documented in archival collections."[124] This chapter represents the shaking of trees to gather information that might stimulate further inquiries in reconstructing Chicago's history of African American art.

Notes

1. Melanie Anne Herzog, *Elizabeth Catlett: An American Artist in Mexico* (Seattle: University of Washington Press, 2005) 26.

2. Elaine D. Woodall, "Looking Backward, Archibald J. Motley and The Art Institute of Chicago: 1914–1930," *Chicago History* 8, no. 1 (Spring 1979): 55.

3. Samuel Floyd Jr., *The Power of Black Music* (New York: Oxford University Press, 1995), 131.

4. Jonathan Liss, "Historical Notes," in *African American Art by Modern Masters*, ed. Sandra Michels Adams (Chicago: Robert Henry Adams Fine Art, 2005), 31.

5. William F. Motley, "Negro Art in Chicago," *Opportunity* 28, no. 1 (January 1940): 19.

6. Davarian L. Baldwin, *Chicago's New Negroes* (Chapel Hill: University of North Carolina Press, 2007), 14.

7. Valencia H. Coar, *A Century of Black Photographers: 1840–1960* (Providence: Rhode Island School of Design, 1968), 11.

8. White J. Luther Pollard, a black man, was the public voice and representative of Ebony Motion Picture Company; all other aspects of the company were controlled by white persons. Although film scholars questioned this, in most books and articles on America's early history of black independent film, Ebony continues to be considered.

9. Archibald J. Motley Jr. offered classes at his home for talented young artists and promising students at $3.00 per lesson. Richmond Barthé was one of Motley's students.

10. These adjoined periods also fueled Chicago's 1960s art movement, known by some as the Black Arts Movement and Chicago's African American Cultural Renaissance.

11. Perry R. Duis, "Where Is Athens Now? The Fine Arts Building, 1898 to 1918," *Chicago History* 6, no. 2 (Summer 1977): 68–69.

12. Ibid., 69–71. Included among the art organizations that contributed to Chicago's artistic transformation were the Chicago Art Union, Chicago Art Guild, U. H. Cosby's Opera House, Chicago Art League, Swedish-American Art Association, Palette and Chisel Club, Bohemian Art Club, Illinois Art Association, Western Art Association, Central Art Association, Chicago Society of Artists, and the Cosmopolitan Club.

13. Jeff Lyon, "State of the Art: For 70 Years the Arts Club of Chicago Has Kept the City on the Cutting Edge of Culture," *Sunday, the Chicago Tribune Magazine*, October 12, 1986, 10–18.

14. Louise deKoven Bowen, "The Colored People of Chicago," in *100 Years at Hull-House*, ed. Mary Lynn McCree Bryan and Allen F. Davis (Bloomington: Indiana University Press,1990), 133.

15. Eric Bennett, "DuSable, Jean Baptiste Pointe," in *Africana: The Encyclopedia of the African and African American Experience*, ed. Kwame A. Appiah and Henry Louis Gates Jr. (New York: Basic Books, 1999), 643.

16. Dempsey J. Travis, *An Autobiography of Black Chicago* (Chicago: Urban Research Institute, 1983), 10.

17. Juliet Walker, *The History of Black Business in America* (New York: Macmillan Library Reference, 1998), 176; Walter Williams, "A 'Usable' History Emphasizes Successes," *Richmond (VA) Times Dispatch*, August 22, 2001, A11; W. E. B. DuBois, ed., *The Negro Artisan* (Atlanta: Atlanta University Press, 1902), 124.

18. Frederic H. Robb, *The Negro in Chicago, 1779–1929* (Chicago: Intercollegiate Washington Club of Chicago, 1929), 83.

19. See reproduction of this portrait in Allan R. Spear, *Black Chicago: The Making of a Negro Ghetto* (Chicago: University of Chicago Press, 1967), 46a.

20. Baldwin, *Chicago's New Negroes*, 199.

21. Edward Ball, *The Sweet Hell Inside: The Rise of an Elite Black Family in the Segregated South* (New York: HarperCollins, 2001), 242.

22. Willard B. Gatewood, *Aristocrats of Color, The Black Elite, 1880–1920* (Bloomington: Indiana University Press, 1990), 195.

23. Some of these entrepreneurs and their wives were also among the SSCAC's earliest supporters, such as Mrs. Edward Jones (unknown if she was the mother of the Jones brothers or the wife of Edward Jones) and Gonzella Motts (the wife of policy king Leon Motts, who was also the earliest black theater owner in Chicago). Policy kings Mack Jones, Ily Kelley, J. Levirt "St. Louis" Kelley, and Leon Motts, as well as some of their close associates were also early SSCAC supporters. See Nathan Thompson, *Kings: The True Story of Chicago's Policy Kings and Number Racketeers, An Informal History* (Chicago: Bronzeville, 2003), 148.

24. The permanent collection included works by William Harper and William Scott. See Robb, *Negro in Chicago*, 83.

25. Jerome Beam, "This Man Loved Chicago: Portrait of a Dreamer," in *James Bolivar Needham*, ed. Richard Norton (Chicago: Robert Henry Adams Fine Art Gallery, 1999), 3.

26. Ibid., 1. Remarkably, the first exhibition of his work occurred sixty-seven years after Needham's death. Had Chicago's Robert Henry Adams Fine Art Gallery not held the "James Bolivar Needham" posthumous exhibition in 1998, it is highly likely that Needham would have remained among many undiscovered Chicago African American painters. Well received, the works in this exhibition resulted in Needham being recognized as an important figure in Chicago's early history of painting.

27. Robb, *Negro in Chicago*, 83.

28. "Along the Color Line," *Crisis* 10, no. 5, September 1915, 215. Evidently forgotten, in 1996 when Hillary Clinton and U.S. President William Clinton unveiled *Sand Dunes at Sunset, Atlantic City* (1885) by expatriate painter Henry Ossawa Tanner, it was reported that this new acquisition marked the first painting by a black artist to be included in the White House's permanent art collection. Thirteen years after President Theodore Roosevelt accepted the portrait, it was reported in the September 1915 issue of *Crisis*, the National Association for the Advancement of Colored People's (NAACP) monthly publication: "We learn that the picture of Lincoln and So-journer [*sic*] Truth, reproduced on the cover of the August *Crisis*, is it reproduction of a painting by Lottie E. Wilson of Niles, Michigan, presented by her to President (Theodore) Roosevelt and now hanging in the permanent collection in the White House. Mrs. Moss is a colored woman." *Crisis* 10, no. 5, September 1915, 215.

29. Cedric Dover, *American Negro Art* (Little, Brown, 1960; repr., New York: New York Graphic Society, 1969), 29.

30. Guy C. McElroy, "The Foundations for Change, 1880–1920," in *African-American Artists, 1880–1987: Selections from the Evans-Tibbs Collection* (Washington, D.C.: Smithsonian, 1989), 32. *Landscape with Poplars* has been dated 1898 by some and 1905 by others. Perhaps, Harper executed a series on this particular scene, a practice not unusual for painters. If not, the accurate dating of this painting becomes an enormous source of confusion in documenting Harper's artistic progression. In addition, Benjamin Brawley indicated Harper's landscape *Tile Avenue of Poplars*, ca. 1903–5 was included in the Art Institute's 1905 exhibition. According to Brawley, this work was awarded the prize of $100.00. A painting by this title is not mentioned in the literature as having been included in the 1905 exhibition. It may have been one of the two Harper paintings included in the O'Brien Galleries' 1905 exhibition. However, since commercial galleries rarely awarded prizes, a collector may have purchased this painting at O'Brien Galleries for $100.00. Brawley, *The Negro in Literature and Arts in the United States* (New York: Duffield, 1930), 139.

31. Alain L. Locke, *The Negro in Art* (Washington, D.C.: Associate in Negro Folk Education, 1940), 132.

32. James A. Porter, *Modern Negro Art* (New York: Arno Press, 1969), 89.

33. This painting is reproduced in *The Barnett-Aden Collection*, ed.

John R. Kinard (Washington, D.C.: Smithsonian Institution Press, 1974), 74.

34. Renee Newman and Nancy Yousef, "Chicago Art League," in *Encyclopedia of African-American Culture and History*, ed. Jack Salzman, David Lionel Smith, and Cornel West, vol. 1 (New York: Thomson Gale, 1996), 533. This Chicago Art League should not be mistaken with the defunct Chicago Art League, which was a white organization that existed from 1880 to 1885. The founding members of the former organization were nine artists, five Chicago public school teachers, an architecture instructor, a Chicago Public Library employee, and a lawyer. William Scott served as the league's first president.

35. Before 1900, the downtown YMCA was integrated. Black men defeated a plan to segregate the YMCA, but by 1910 the plan was initiated with the understanding that wealthy white persons would donate a large share of the funding to build the Wabash YMCA. This YMCA, which opened in 1913, was considered as a symbol of "separate but equal" and became the preferred location for black society's meetings and social events.

36. By 1927, the league's members included Richmond Barthé, Mollie Brackett, Inez Brewster, Pauline Callis, Arthur Diggs, Elise Evans, Geraldine Glover, Claude Guess, Gas Ivory, Oscar Jordon, Nora Lee, Emma Lewis, J. D. Mayo, Mrs. John Patterson, F. W. Spann, William Webb, Carrie Williamson, Ellis Wilson, and Lawrence Wilson.

37. The Harmon Foundation, *Negro Artists, an Illustrated Review of Their Achievements* (New York: Harmon Foundation, 1935), 40.

38. Margaret Rose Vendryes, in Robb, *Negro in Chicago*, 48.

39. This exhibition included works of Edward Bannister (deceased), Aaron Douglas, John Hardrick, Edwin A. Harleston, Palmer Hayden, May Howard Jackson, Edmonia Lewis, Richard Reid, Augusta Savage, Albert Smith, Henry Tanner, Meta Warrick, and Hale Woodruff. Works by Chicago residents and itinerant artists in this exhibition were Richmond Barthé, Arthur Diggs, Elmer Simms Campbell, Charles Dawson, William Farrow, King Daniel Ganaway (photographer), William Harper (deceased), Archibald Motley, Leslie Rogers, and William Scott. See Robb, *Negro in Chicago*, 83, 233.

40. Susan Weininger, *Thinking Modern Painting in Chicago: 1910–1940* (Chicago: Block Gallery, 1992), 3.

41. Ibid., 3.

42. Daniel Schulman, "White City" and "Black Metropolis," in *Chicago Modern 1893–1945: Pursuit of the New*, ed. Elizabeth Kennedy (Chicago: Terra Museum of American Art, 2004), 39.

43. Joseph Arthur de Gobineau, in *Civilization or Barbarism, an Authentic Anthropology*, ed. Cheikh Anta Diop (Brooklyn, N.Y.: Lawrence Hill Books, 1991), 216–17.

44. Joseph Arthur de Gobineau, in *The Aryan Myth: A History of Racist and Nationalist Ideas in Europe*, by Leon Poliakov (New York: Basic Books, 1974), 234–35.

45. V. F. Calverton, "The Growth of Negro Literature," in *Negro: An Anthology*, ed. Nancy Cunard (New York: Frederick Ungar, 1910), 79.

46. C. J. Bulliet, cited in Daniel Schulman, "Marion Perkins: A Chicago Sculptor Rediscovered," *Selections from the Art Institute of Chicago, African American in Art* 24, no.2 (1999): 269.

47. Veerle Poupeye, *Caribbean Art* (New York: Thames and Hudson, 1998), 35–36.

48. Margaret T. G. Burroughs, "The Four Artists," in *Shared Heritage: Art by Four African Americans*, ed. William E. Taylor and Harriet G. Warkel (Indianapolis, Ind.: Indianapolis Museum of Art, 1996), 13.

49. Ibid., 166.

50. In the literature, most writers on Scott indicate the Salon d'Automne accepted this work. However, the most authoritative scholar on Scott's career, William B. Taylor, indicated the Salon de La Societe des Artistes Francais in Paris accepted the work.

51. See Taylor and Warkel, *Shared Heritage*, 160–66.

52. Ironically, a white man, John Kinzie, purchased and settled on land previously owned by Frenchman Jean Lalime. Paradoxically, Lalime purchased the property from DuSable in 1800.

53. Harriet G. Warkel, "Image and Identity: The Art of William E. Scott, John W. Hardrick and Hal Woodruff," in Taylor and Warkel, *Shared Heritage*, 37.

54. These murals remained as originally painted until a 2006 fire destroyed the church. Prior to this fire, the murals served as the touchstone for religious mural painting.

55. Taylor and Warkel, *Shared Heritage*, 165.

56. Charles Dawson, quoted in Roberta Toas Blasenstein, "I've Decided to Undo the Stereotype," *Christian Science Monitor*, December 10, 1969, 29.

57. Barbara Parry, "Painter Charles C. Dawson Has Been Finding Beauty in Black Subjects for 81 Years," *Philadelphia Inquirer Magazine*, July 19, 1970, 8.

58. Charles Dawson, quoted in Blasenstein, "I've Decided," 29.

59. Charles C. Dawson, *Touching The Fringes of Greatness, an Autobiography*, unpublished manuscript, n.d., Archives of American Art, Charles C. Dawson Collection, DuSable Museum, Chicago, Illinois, 369–71.

60. Ibid., 377.

61. After developing a successful line of beauty products for African Americans, Annie T. Malone opened Poro College in St. Louis in 1917. In 1930, Malone relocated Poro to Chicago. She was one of the first black female millionaires. The name PORO was derived from that of a secret African society in Sierra Leone. Among black Americans, PORO was one of America's most popular hair-care products. In his 1997 book, *Black Art and Culture in the 20th Century*, Richard J. Powell is one of the earliest known art historians who mentioned Dawson's having introduced African symbols in his commissioned works. 63.

62. The dioramas were conceived and designed by Dawson. However, the execution of the design was under the supervision of diorama specialist and architect Erick Lundgren. WPA Illinois Art Project artists assisted in the actual construction of the dioramas. Deemed to be

a significant work, the federal government donated the dioramas to Tuskegee Institute (currently, Tuskegee University). Damaged en route to Tuskegee, in 1944 Dawson was contracted to restore and supervise the installation of the repaired dioramas on Tuskegee's campus. He was also contracted to establish Tuskegee's Museum of Negro Art and Culture. At this time, Tuskegee had the Blondiau art collection, which consisted of African, African American, and Mayan art.

63. Parry, "Painter Charles C. Dawson," 8.

64. While labor recruiters were a factor in stimulating the pre–World War I inflow of southern black Americans into Chicago, the most critical factors according to St. Clair Drake and Horace Cayton were "testing" and migrants letters to "folks back home about the wonderful North." St. Clair Drake and Horace R. Cayton, *Black Metropolis: A Study of Negro Life in a Northern City* (1945; repr., New York: Harper and Row, 1962), 58.

65. Archibald J. Motley, quoted in Jontyle Theresa Robinson, "The Art of Archibald J. Motley Jr.," in *The Art of Archibald J. Motley*, ed. Robinson and Wendy Greenhouse (Chicago: Chicago Historical Society, 1991), 9.

66. Edward Alden Jewell, "A Negro Artist Plumbs the Negro Soul," *New York Times Magazine*, March 25, 1928, sec. H, 8.

67. Drake and Cayton, *Black Metropolis*, 267.

68. Panoramic painters who may have influenced him include Albert Bierstadt, Frederick Edwin Church, and Chicago's Henry Arthur Elkins. The artists who had commercial success include Paul Colin, Miguel Covarrubias, and Winold Reiss.

69. Hayes and Pious were from the south and experienced extremely harsh conditions. Although Hayes had attained international acclaim as a tenor, Pious admired his uncompromising integrity and courage in challenging segregationist practices. These challenges could have easily ended Hayes's successful career. For example, in 1926 he was contracted to perform in concert at Baltimore's Lyric Theater. Because of the Lyric's segregated policy, Hayes refused to perform. Rather than canceling the concert, the Lyric's management suspended its seating policy for this sold-out concert.

70. While in New York, Pious illustrated publications by Charles Christopher Seifert, an African and African American historian who was known as "Professor." One of his illustrations for Seifert was *The Hall of Karnak*, n.d., in which Pious Africanized all the figures on the columns. These works recall those completed by Dawson.

71. Harmon Foundation, *Negro Artists*, 52.

72. Ibid., 58.

73. A trade product, Carborundum, is a rough granular product of carbon and silicone and is used for grinding and polishing. Thrash used the crystals to resurface used lithographic stones. Through the use of various grades of these crystals, a range of tints and tonal variations is possible to create a print. See Leslie King Hammond, "Black Printmakers and the WPA," in *Alone in a Crowd: Prints of the 1930s–40s by African American Artists,* ed. M. Stephen Doherty (New York: American Federation of Art, 1993), 13.

74. Later, his depiction of the L'Ouverture was used by the Haitian government as the frontispiece for a new book. In 2006, Barthé's busts

of *Paul Laurence Dunbar* (1928) and *Booker T. Washington* (1928) were discovered in a storage box in a Richmond, Virginia, high school.

75. Due either to an oversight or by the time *The Breakaway: Dance Figurine* (1929) was added to the works to be exhibited, the four-page exhibition catalog had gone to press. As a result, this work was not listed as having been included in the exhibition. However, the work was mentioned in the Associated Negro Press's June 11, 1930, release.

76. In 1931 and 1933, the first and second one-man exhibitions at New York City's Caz-Delbo Gallery received rave reviews from New York's art critics; for the period of 1933 to 1945, his works were included in four annual Whitney Museum of American Arts group exhibitions; and in 1940–41, he was awarded a Guggenheim Fellowship. Prior to being awarded these fellowships, Barthé had become the first African American artist to be represented in the Whitney Museum collection; between 1933 and 1936, the museum purchased three Barthé works: *Blackberry Woman*, *Comedian*, and *African Dancer*. Thereafter, his works were included in the permanent collections of other museums, such as the Metropolitan Museum of Art, Pennsylvania Museum of Art; Virginia Museum of Fine Arts, and the Museum of the Art Institute of Chicago.

For a brief period during World War II, Barthé was America's best-known sculptor. The U.S. government enlisted Barthé and other highly recognizable black American artists to counter Germany's and Japan's campaigns focusing on America's segregationist practices to dissuade black Americans from supporting the war effort. By profiling selected black Americans, the U.S. government attempted to convey the impression of America having made "dramatic progress" toward constructing a society without race preferment. As a part of this campaign, the U.S. Office of War Information produced a film on Barthé that was shown throughout this country and abroad. As a result, printed material was in great demand, as well as requests for numerous guest appearances.

77. The Academy of Fine Arts and Frederick Mizer Academy of Art continued to have admission policies that forbade the enrollment of black students. Not as aggressively as labor recruiters attempting to attract black southerners to relocate to Chicago where employment was plentiful, when the new Bauhaus school was founded in 1937, Hungarian-born Bauhaus theorist and practitioner Laszlo Moholy-Nagy sought to attract African American students. Founded in Weimer in 1919 and relocated to Dessau in 1925, the Bauhaus sought to apply cubism aesthetic concerns to architecture, interior design, and art. Under Adolph Hitler, the Bauhaus school was closed in 1933. Initially, Chicago's new Bauhaus school had a short life. Not dissuaded, Moholy-Nagy founded the School of Design in 1939. Reorganized, the school was incorporated in 1952 as the Illinois Institute of Technology (IIT). Prior to this reorganization and name change, Eldzier Cotor, Charles Sebree, and Charles White were among the earliest black students who studied at the School of Design.

78. Romare Bearden and Harry Henderson, *A History of African-American Artists: From 1792 to the Present* (New York: Pantheon, 1993), 407.

79. On October 25, 1938, the first formal committee to establish a center on Chicago's near South Side was held at the Chicago Urban

League. Chaired by businessman Golden B. Darby, the committee developed a fund-raising plan to acquire a building to serve as an art center. The fund-raising plan included corporate solicitations, concerts, lectures, card parties, exhibitions, and "A Mile of Dimes," which involved soliciting the general public for a ten-cent donation. In 1939, the committee held its first Annual Artists and Models Ball at the Savoy Ballroom. The event netted $5,000, which was used as the down payment to acquire the Charles Comiskey family's mansion at 3831 South Michigan Avenue.

80. Bernard Goss and Margaret T. G. Burroughs, quoted in George J. Mavigliano and Richard A. Lawson, *The Federal Art Project in Illinois, 1935–1943* (Carbondale: Southern Illinois University Press, 1990), 67.

81. Anna M. Tyler, "Planting and Maintaining a 'Perennial Garden' Chicago's South Side Community Art Center," *International Review of African American Art* 11, no. 4 (1994): 35.

82. Dorothy Odenheimer, "Art News from Chicago," *Chicago Sun*, May 1942.

83. "Negro Temple of Art," *Newsweek*, May 19, 1941, 67.

84. Anna Eleanor Roosevelt, quoted in Margaret T. G. Burroughs, "Saga of Chicago's South Side Community Art Center (1938–1943)," in *The South Side Community Art Center 50th Anniversary, 1941–1991*, ed. Burroughs (Chicago: South Side Community Art Center, 1991), 10.

85. "Negro Temple of Art," *Newsweek*, May 19, 1941, 67.

86. Ibid., 68.

87. Ibid., 7 and 110. This writer's inspection of the official WPA/FAP final employment list revealed only twenty-three black artists were employed by IAP.

88. Mavigliano and Lawson, *Federal Art Project in Illinois*, 68.

89. Ibid., 68.

90. William Carter, quoted in Ron Grossman, "A Black Artist's Roots Recalling the 'Renaissance' of the Depression," *Chicago Tribune*, Wednesday, April 2, 1986, sec. 5, 3.

91. Mavigliano and Lawson, *Federal Art Project in Illinois*, 199–201.

92. Ibid., 68. Under the job classification of professional and technical artist, the average monthly salary was $94.00 with a maximum of $103.40 to produce art unsupervised. The average monthly and maximum salaries for skilled artists were $85.00 and $93.50 respectively. Mavigliano and Lawson, *Federal Art Project in Illinois*, 203. For comparative purposes, the average monthly salary earned by black Chicagoans employed under WPA's non-arts work projects was $55.00.

93. Carter, quoted in Grossman, "Black Artist's Roots," sec. 5, 3.

94. Black and white reproductions of both paintings are in Dover, *American Negro Art*, 177, plate 45.

95. Ibid., 52.

96. Ibid., 1.

97. Located near Thirty-Fourth and Wabash Avenue, the Settlement House was opened in 1919 by Ada S. McKinley as a reentry, readjustment, and skills-training center for returning World War I black soldiers. Later, the Settlement House expanded its community outreach services as a response to many unmet social and cultural needs. Paragon Studio

was located at Thirty-Third and South Michigan Avenue. Under George Neal's leadership, it operated quite similar to an art academy.

98. Margaret T. G. Burroughs, "He Will Always Be a Chicago Artist to Me," *Freedomways* 20, no.3 (1980): 151; Tyler, "Planting and Maintaining," 31.

99. Charles White quoted in Mary Hewitt, "A Tribute to Charles White," *Black Arts, an International Quarterly* 4, no.1 (1980): 36.

100. Bearden and Henderson, *History of African-American Artists*, 410.

101. Charles White, cited in ibid.

102. Lizzette LeFalle-Coliins, "African-American Modernists and the Mexican Muralist School," in *In the Spirit of Resistance African-American Modernists and the Mexican Muralist School*, ed. LeFalle-Collins and Shifra M. Goldman (New York: American Federation of Art, 1996), 55.

103. Information on his life and works are included in over 224 books, portfolios, catalogs, and films; and the illustrated feature article in the 1962 silver anniversary *American Artists* issue was "The Remarkable Draughtsmanship of Charles White." Between 1960 and 1965, Syracuse University established the Charles White Collection; at the Leipzig, Germany, International Graphic Exhibition, he was awarded the Gold Medal recipient; *Ebony* magazine's August 1966 issue established a precedent by reproducing White's drawing *J'accuse! No.10* on its cover rather than a full-color photographic image, which had been the magazine's tradition; New York City's Metropolitan Museum of Art purchased White's available etchings; and the Whitney Museum of American Art acquired *Sarah and Maternity* from White's *Wanted Poster Series*.

104. Sinclair Lewis, *Kingsblood Royal* (New York: Random House, 1947), 107; also cited in Elton C. Fax, *17 Black Artists* (New York: Dodd, Mead, 1971), 94.

105. Ralph Pearson, *Critical Appreciation Courses II: The Renaissance in the USA* (Nyack, N.Y.: Ralph Pearson's Design Workshop, 1950), 147–48.

106. Bearden and Henderson, *History of African-American Artists*, 275–77.

107. Eldzier Cortor, quoted in "Eldzier Cortor: The Long Consistent Road," in *Three Masters: Eldzier Cortor, Hughie Lee Smith, Archibald J. Motley, Jr.*, ed. Corrine L. Jennings (New York: Kenkeleba Gallery, 1995), 15.

108. There Cortor became aware of Haitians' resentment of the occupying American forces. Reportedly, the invasion and occupation were necessary because Haiti posed a significant threat to America as a potential staging ground for a foreign power, such as Germany to invade America. In addition, anti-American sentiments among Haitians posed a potential danger of them disrupting the day-to-day operations of the newly opened Panama Canal.

109. Eldzier Cortor, quoted in Bearden and Henderson, *History of African-American Artists*, 277.

110. "19 Young American Artists," *Life*, March 29, 1950, 82.

111. Katharine Kuh, *My Love Affair with Modern Art: Behind the*

Scenes with a Legendary Curator, ed. and completed by Avis Berman (New York: Arcade, 2006), xxi.

112. Ruth A. Stewart, *WPA and the Black Artist* (New York: Studio Museum in Harlem, 1978), 6. A black and white reproduction of *Pool Room* is on page 16.

113. Aside from *Ballerina*, another fine example of his abstract paintings is *Musicians* (n.d). Unfortunately, the whereabouts of this painting is unknown. However, it can be viewed on the Visioncast video "William Carter Art."

114. William Carter quoted in Grossman, "Black Artist's Roots," 3.

115. Ibid., 3.

116. Because of the quality of his collection, museum curators and discerning private collectors, such as Bill Cosby and Quincy Jones, often consulted with and purchased works from McBride's collection. His entrepreneurial spirit possibly began with a verbal agreement between Al Capone and McBride. Capone offered to pay twenty-five cents for each empty glass bottle McBride could collect and deliver undamaged. McBride enlisted the help of friends at a per-bottle rate of a penny. Courtney Challos, "William McBride, Artist, Collector, Force for WPA," *Chicago Tribune*, August 17, 2000, n.p.

117. A black and white reproduction of this work is in Locke, *Negro in Art*, 171.

118. Known among Black Chicagoans as a "Race Man," in 1914 dePriest became Chicago's earliest black city council alderman, and in 1928 he was the first elected African American from the north to the U.S. Congress. Rather than as an obsequious and powerless politician appealing to the conscious of white colleagues, Goss portrayed the congressman vigorously making a point. Through his facial features and with arm raised to pound the podium to accentuate a particular point, dePriest appears to be a politician of unshakeable resolve in representing Chicago's first and second predominantly black wards.

119. Irene V. Clark, cited in *African Art, the Diaspora and Beyond* (Chicago: Daniel Texidor Parker, 2004), 72.

120. Samella Lewis, *Art: African American* (New York: Harcourt Brace Jovanovich, 1978), 162.

121. In 1903, John Griffin, a successful white contractor, built the Griffin family mansion and carriage house at 3806 South Michigan Avenue. During the 1930s, black Pullman porters acquired this property, and the mansion became the Quincy Club. While this private club provided lodging for black Pullman porters, it was also known for its social events and dances. The club's rear carriage house became the home of Charles and Margaret Burroughs. When the Quincy Club closed, the property was acquired by the Burroughs. In 1961, the mansion's first floor became the Ebony Museum of Negro History and Art. Because too many people presumed the museum was affiliated with Johnson Publishing Company's *Ebony* magazine, the Burroughs agreed to change the name of the museum. The new name is DuSable Museum of African

American History and Art, America's oldest museum devoted to African American history and culture.

The SSCAC was located diagonally across the street from the museum. The SSCAC's board of directors was of the opinion that by including "art" in the museum's name, it posed a conflict with the SSCAC's mission, objectives, and goals. The board requested and the Burroughs agreed to remove "art" from the museum's name. This notwithstanding, over the years, the Burroughs acquired a collection of art that provides a snapshot of the richness of black visual culture.

122. See examples in Daniel Schulman, "Marion Perkins: A Chicago Sculptor Rediscovered," *Selections from the Art Institute of Chicago, African American Art* 24, no. 2 (1999): 226–27.

123. Marion Perkins, quoted in ibid., 103.

124. In 1985, the Archives of American Art initiated the "Chicago Documentation Project." The purpose of this project was to gather information from original archival collections on Chicago's pre–World War II history of art. It was anticipated by renaissance adherents that the archives' research project would provide confirmation that Chicago had indeed experienced a pre–World War II renaissance. Presented in 1987 at "The Coming of Modernism to Chicago Symposium; the Archives," its findings revealed that Chicago had a rich but little known pre–World War II history of art. With the exception of a panel that included Margaret T. G. Burroughs, the symposium presentations conveyed the impression that African American artists were inconsequential in the formulation of Chicago's rich early history of art. Unconvinced by the archives' findings, Burroughs, Anna M. Tyler, and Sophie Wessel met with the Chicago Documentation Project coordinator Betty Blum. These meetings and other factors contributed to the archives initiating the "African American Artists in Chicago Interviews, 1988–1989" oral-history project. The aim of this project was to gather information on Chicago's black artists and their organizations by interviewing six personages: painter, printmaker, and cofounder of the DuSable Museum of African American History Burroughs; painter William Carter; artist and *Ebony* magazine art director Fitzhugh Dinkins; painter Frederick Jones; painter and collector of art and memorabilia William McBride; and designer, design-firm owner, and first black president of the Art Directors Club of Chicago Leroy Winbush. In their 1989 "Midwest" report, Blum and the Archives' Midwest regional director Judith Gustafson wrote, "The Chicago Documentation Project, which began in 1985, *has begun* gathering information on this [Chicago's pre–World War II history of African American art] through a series of six oral history interviews" (emphasis added).

The verb *has begun* suggests the Chicago Documentation Project's inquiry was not as exacting as previously purported; the term also added credence to the concerns of Burroughs, Tyler, and Wessel. See Judith A. Gustafson and Betty Blum, "Midwest," *Archives of American Art Journal* 29, nos. 3 and 4 (1989): 71.

Notes on Contributors

HILARY MAC AUSTIN is an independent scholar, writer, and photo researcher. She is coeditor with Kathleen Thompson of three books: *America's Children: Images of Childhood from Early America to the Present, Children of the Depression*, and *The Face of Our Past: Images of Black Women from Colonial America to the Present*. She has written entries for *Black Women in America: An Historical Encyclopedia*, 2nd edition, and *Encyclopedia of African American History, 1619–1895*, among others.

DAVID T. BAILEY has been a faculty member in the history department at Michigan State University for three decades, where he has won numerous awards for his teaching. He has also taught at the University of California, Berkeley, where he received his PhD in 1979. His book *Shadow on the Church* is a study of slavery and its reception in evangelical churches of the trans-Appalachian south. His forthcoming book, *The Mystery of Commitment*, a study of activists between the world wars, investigates the causes for their lifetime commitment to social justice. He has been active in a variety of online projects, including *South Africa: Overcoming Apartheid, Building Democracy*.

MURRY N. DePILLARS (1938–2008) was educated in the public schools of Chicago. He earned an AA in fine arts from Kennedy-King Community College and a BA in art education and an MA in urban studies from Roosevelt University, both in Chicago. He received his PhD in art education from the Pennsylvania State University. Both his master's thesis, "Housing, Environment and Children's Art," and his doctoral dissertation, "African-American Artists and Students: A Morphological Study in the Urban Black Aesthetic," address societal issues. From 1976 to 1995, he served as dean of Virginia Commonwealth University's School of the Arts, Richmond, Virginia. A leader in the black arts movement in Chicago, he was also a member of AfriCOBRA, which provided a demanding forum, beyond the academic setting, through which the members challenged each other's art as they confronted societal and cultural issues, not only in America but also in other parts of the world. His paintings have been exhibited at Whitney Museum of American Art, the Studio Museum of Harlem, Museum of Contemporary Art in Chicago, Virginia Museum of Fine Arts, Hampton University, and Dittmar Gallery at Northwestern University. In 1998, he chose to devote his full attention to his painting. His passing silenced an important advocate for educational and artistic growth and achievement.

SAMUEL A. FLOYD JR. is executive director emeritus of the Center for Black Music Research, which he founded at Columbia College Chicago in 1983. He is the author of *The Power of Black Music* and is writing a new manuscript currently titled "Music in the Black Diaspora: A World History of Black Music." He is editor-in-chief of the Music of the Black Diaspora book series, copublished by the Center for Black Music Research and the University of California Press, and was editor-in-chief of the *International Dictionary of Black Composers* (1999), which received the Choice Award for outstanding title for 1999 and the RUSA Award for outstanding reference sources for small- and medium-sized libraries from the Reference and Users Services Association committee of the American Library Association (2000) and was named by the New York Public Library one of the twenty best reference books for the year 1999. During 2003–4, he was the John Hope Franklin Senior Fellow at the National Center for the Humanities, Research Triangle Park, North Carolina. Floyd received, in 2006, the American Musicological Society Honorary Lifetime Membership Award and the Society for American Music Lifetime Achievement Award.

ERIK S. GELLMAN is an assistant professor of history at Roosevelt University and a scholar of postbellum American history, specializing in African American studies, labor, comparative social movements, and Chicago history. He serves on the national board of the Labor and Working-Class History Association, the Chicago Center for Working-Class Studies, Mansfield Institute for Social Justice and Transformation, and Worker's Rights Board of Jobs with Justice. He is the author of recent articles in the *Journal of Southern History* and *Labor* and is currently working on two forthcoming books, *The Gospel of the Working Class* (with Jarod Roll) and "Death Blow, Jim Crow!" that examine the convergence of labor and civil rights movements in the United States during the Great Depression and World War II era.

JEFFREY HELGESON is an assistant professor in the history department at Texas State University–San Marcos. He received his PhD in U.S. history from the University of Illinois at Chicago in 2008. His book

manuscript *Striving in Black Chicago: Ambition, Activism, and Accommodation from the New Deal to Harold Washington* is currently being reviewed, as is an article titled "Horace R. Cayton Jr.: Black Liberalism and Its Discontents in Chicago, 1931–1947." Jeffrey has published reviews in the *Chicago Tribune*, *Urban History*, and *International Labor and Working-Class History*. In addition, he is one of the directors of the Labor Trail, a collaborative project of the Chicago Center for Working Class Studies led by historian Leon Fink (http://technewsbriefs.com/labortrail/).

DARLENE CLARK HINE is board of trustees professor of African American studies, professor of history, and chair of the Department of African American Studies at Northwestern University, Evanston, Illinois. She helped found the field of black women's history and has been a leading scholar in the history of African American experience. Hine served as president of the Organization of American Historians and the Southern Historical Association and has earned numerous honors, awards, and fellowships from the Rockefeller Foundation, Ford Foundation, and National Endowment for the Humanities. She has authored and edited many books, including *Black Victory: The Rise and Fall of the Texas White Primary*, *Hine Sight: Black Women and the Re-Construction of American History*, and *Black Women in White: Racial Conflict and Cooperation in the Nursing Profession, 1890–1950*. Hine is working on a history of the black professional class before *Brown v. Board*.

JOHN McCLUSKEY JR. is professor emeritus of African American and African diaspora studies at Indiana University–Bloomington, where he has taught courses in literature and fiction writing. He served as director of the Committee on Institutional Cooperation (CIC) Minorities Fellowships Program (1983–88), the largest minorities' graduate fellowship program in the nation, as well as associate dean of the graduate school. McCluskey also served as department chairman, during whose term four master's degree programs (three of them joint) and the PhD program were initiated or established. He is cofounder with Darlene Clark Hine of the Blacks in the Diaspora series for Indiana University Press. He has published many short stories and is the author of two novels, *Look What They Done to My Song* and *Mr. America's Last Season Blues*. He edited two editions of *The City of Ref-*

uge: The Collected Stories of Rudolph Fisher and coedited with novelist Charles Johnson *Black Men Speaking*. He is currently working on a collection of short stories.

CHRISTOPHER ROBERT REED is professor emeritus of history at Roosevelt University. He is a native Chicagoan who has blended a love of place with scholarship exploring the meaning of life in Chicago from its earliest days of founding in the late eighteenth century to the present. Reed received his doctorate in American history at Kent State University and returned to his first academic home, Roosevelt University, in 1987; he retired from the teaching faculty as a tenured professor of history in 2006. His community and civic activities have served to enhance his knowledge of the topic on which he has published extensively, black Chicago history. His publications include *Black Chicago: The Emergence of a Black Metropolis, 1920–1929; Black Chicago's First Century, 1833–1900; "All the World Is Here!": The Black Presence at White City;* and *The Chicago NAACP and the Rise of Black Professional Leadership, 1910–1966,* as well as many essays.

ELIZABETH SCHLABACH is a visiting assistant professor of history and American studies at the College of William and Mary. She obtained a PhD in American Studies from Saint Louis University. Her book *Along the Streets of Bronzeville: Black Chicago's Renaissance* is forthcoming from the University of Illinois Press.

CLOVIS E. SEMMES is professor of black studies and sociology and director of black studies at the University of Missouri, Kansas City. He is also professor emeritus of African American studies at Eastern Michigan University. His scholarly works include numerous articles and four books, *The Regal Theater and Black Culture; Roots of Afrocentric Thought: A Reference Guide to Negro Digest/Black World, 1961–1976; Racism, Health and Post-Industrialism: A Theory of African-American Health;* and *Cultural Hegemony and African American Development,* which was selected by *Choice* as an outstanding academic book. Semmes has received awards for his contributions to the field of African American studies, teaching, and scholarship, including a National Endowment for the Humanities Fellowship. His current research involves a comparative and transdisciplinary examination of prominent movie-stage-show venues in historic African American communities.

Index

Baker, Houston A., 80

Balaban & Katz (B&K Corporation), 45, 46, 47

Baldwin, Davarian, xxii, 169

Bamboula, The (Coleridge-Taylor), 22

Bannister, Edward, 129

Baraka, Amiri, xxii

Barnett, Claude A., 58, 131

Barnett, Ferdinand L., 5, 6

Barrett, Frances, 185

Barthé, Richmond, 15, 180, 194n76

Benson, Al (Arthur B. Leaner), xxv

Bentley, Charles E., 14

Bentley, Edwin, 5

Bentley, Florence, 5

big-band jazz, 29–31

"Big Boy Leaves Home" (Wright), 103

Big Sea, The (Hughes), 101

Bill Posters, The (Dawson), 175, *196-10.10*

Binder, Carroll, 14

Binga, Eudora Johnson, 169

Binga, Jesse, xxiii, 14, 15, 169

Binga State Bank, 15, 169

Birth of a Race Photoplay Company, 11

Bishop, Robert, 131

Bispham, David, 25

"black and tan clubs," 12–13

Blackberry Woman (Barthé), *196-10.18*

Black Boy (Wright), 32

"Black Bugs, The" (Cayton), 111

black Chicago culture before the Black
 Chicago Renaissance. *See* pre–Black
 Chicago Renaissance culture in Chicago

Black Chicago Renaissance: apex, xx–xxi;
 artistic and cultural production, xxii–xxvii;
 artists, 167, 168; aspirations, 31; boogie
 woogie, 33–34; Brooks role, 79, 80, 88–94;
 business and institution development, xxi;
 Caribbean influence, 182; Chicago's black
 origins, xvi; choirs, 37; classical music
 composers and performers, 32–33; contexts
 and perspectives, xv–xxi; as distinguished
 from other cultural movements, 42n47;
 essay summaries, xxvi–xxix; film production, 169; Great Depression successes,
 16–17; Great Migration, xvi–xviii, xxii,
 xxx nn3–9, xxii n39; Harlem Renaissance
 comparisons, xv, xxxi n35, 31–32, 38–40,
 126–27; as including pre-Black Chicago
 Renaissance culture in Chicago, 168–69;
 labor, class and political struggles, xviii–xx;

leading figures, 17; Mexican influence, 182;
 modernism, 39–40; musical accomplishments, 39; musical-literary interaction,
 37–38; New Orleans music, 34; newspaper,
 xxii–xxiii; overview of music, 31–38;
 painters, 190; Pan-Africanism, 21–22;
 patrons of the arts, 31; performing arts,
 xxv–xxvii; performing venues, 44–54; racial
 exclusion, 180, 194n77; racial tolerance in
 Europe, 73–74; radio, xxv–xxvi, 17; related
 events, xvii–xix; southern influence, 32;
 themes, xvii; theories about, 167–69; time
 frame theories, 168; titles and theories,
 191; varying musical tastes, 32; Works
 Progress Administration (WPA) impact, 31;
 Wright role, 79–88; writers, xxiv–xxv. *See
 also entries for specific individuals, ideas,
 institutions, events, works*

Black Metropolis, 12. *See also* Bronzeville

*Black Metropolis: A Study of Negro Life in a
 Northern City* (Cayton, Drake), xxiii, 80,
 81–82, 119–20, 121, 123

black nationalism, 22, 41n15

Black Power (Wright), 103

black primitivism, 172–73

Black Reconstruction (Du Bois), 8

Black's Blue Book, 12

Black Star Line, xx

Black Student (L'Etudiant Noir), 105–6

Black Thunder (Bontemps), xxv, 150

Black Workers and the New Unions (Cayton,
 Mitchell), 115–16, 120

Black World (UNIA publication), 21, 22, 107–8

Blake, Eubie, 25

Blake, J. Herman, 122

Blue Hole, Little Miami River (Duncanson), 129

blues music, 25–26

Body and Soul (film), xxvi

Bohemian Girl (opera), 14

Bondage (Britton), 189, *196-10.28*

Bonds, Estelle, 31

Bonds, Margaret, 32–33

Bone, Robert, 31, 147

Bontemps, Arna, xvi, xxiv–xxv, 38, 128–29,
 132, 150

Book of American Negro Poetry, The, 98, 104

Book of Negro Spirituals (Johnson brothers), 25

"Born a Slave, She Recruits 5 Members for the
 Communist Party" (Wright), 99, 100

Boston Guardian, 9

Bowen, Louise de Koven, 169

Brewer, Inez, 172

"Bright and Morning Star" (Wright), 100

Britton, Sylvester, 189

Bronzeville, 79, 80–87. *See also* Black
 Metropolis; *12 Million Black Voices*

Bronzeville: Black Chicago in Pictures
 (Stange), 82–83

Brooks, Gwendolyn, 57, 80, 81, 88–94

Brooks, Shelton, 10

Brotherhood of Sleeping Car Porters, xix–xx

"Brotherly Love" (Hughes), xxvii

Brown, Hallie Q., 4

Brown, Nikki, xix

Brown, Sterling, 96–97

Bulliet, Clarence, 173

Bungleton Green (comic strip), xxi

Burleigh, Harry T., 4, 22, 23

Burroughs, Charles, 158

Burroughs, Margaret T. G.: Arts Crafts Guild,
 149; Black Chicago Renaissance role,
 xxiii; Chicago Art League, xxiii, xxiv; Ebony
 Museum, 158, 196n121; *Face of Africa*,
 190; Mexico sojourn, 157; overview, xxiv;
 on South Side Community Art Center, 180;
 South Side Community Art Center (SSCAC)
 work, 154, 155–56

Butler Gallery, 169

Buy, Edna, xxvi

By Parties Unknown (Woodruff), 135

Cahill, Holger, 130

"Call of Ethiopia" (Hughes), xvii

Calloway, Cab, 30–31

calls and cries, 30–31

Calverton, V. F., 172–73

Campbell, Elmer Simms, 178–79

Campbell, Floyd, 16

Cane (Toomer), 25

Card Game, The (Carter), *196-10.26*

Carey, Annabel, xxiii

Carey, Archibald J., 114

"Carolina Shout" (Johnson), 27

Carter, William, 149, 182, 188

Carver, George Washington, 4

"Castle House Rag" (Europe), 24

Catlett, Elizabeth, xxiii, xxiv, 129, 138, 157,
 184

Cavalcade of the American Negro (pamphlet),
 128–29

mobility poem, xxvii; "Negro Artist and the Racial Mountain," 98; overview, xvi; poem samples, xvi, xvii
Hull House, 169
Hurston, Zora Neale, 25, 98, 104

"If We Must Die" (McKay), xviii–xix
Illinois Art Project (IAP), 151–52, 167, 181–82, 194n77, 195n92
Illinois Writers Project (IWP), xxv, 128–29
Imperial Opera Company, 14
In Bandanna Land (Cook), 23
In Dahomey (Cook, Rogers), 23
Industrial Revolution in the South (Mitchell), The, 115
In Praise of Creoleness, 107–8
"Intellectual Progress of the Colored Women of the United States since the Emancipation Proclamation, The" (Williams), 5
Islam as a Factor in West Africa (Ellis), 7
I Tried to Be a Communist (Wright), 100

Jackson, A. L., 5
Jackson, Mahalia, xvi, xxv, 36
Jackson, Tony, 10
James, William, 116
James, Willis Lawrence, 30–31, 31–32
Jazz Age of 1920s, 3, 12
jazz dance, 24
jazz piano, 27
Jenkins, Charles, 131–32
"Jesse B. Semple" (comic strip), xx–xxi
Jet Magazine, xviii
Jewell, Edward Alden, 177
Jockey Club (Motley), 177, *196-10.13*
John Reed Club, 97–98
Johns, Elizabeth, 116
Johnson, Charles S., xix, 3, 5, 15, 17n3, 111, 114–15
Johnson, Fenton, 8, 15
Johnson, Jack, 169
Johnson, James P., 25, 26–27
Johnson, James Weldon, 8, 23, 101, 104
Johnson, J. Rosamond, 23
Jones, Clarence M., 10
Jones, Frederick D., 187
Jones, John, 169
Jones, Mary Richardson, 11
Joplin, Scott, 4, 23

Jubilee: A Cavalcade of the Negro Theater (Hughes), 38

Keep Shufflin' (Johnson, Waller), 25
Kennedy, Winston, 179
Kersey, Joseph, 190, 191
Kimball Hall, 10
Kingsley, Harold H., 118
Kinzie, John, 174, 193n52
Kirkpatrick, Thelma, 156
Knot in the Thread (Fowler), 105
Kuh, Katherine, 187

Ladies Orchestra, 10
Laing, S., 169
"La Jeune Litterature Haitien" (Sylvain), 104
Landscape with Poplars (Afternoon at Montigny) (Harper), *196-10.3*
Langston Hughes sketch (White), *151*
La Releve, 105
La Revue du Monde Noir, 105, 106–7
La Revue Indigene, 104
Lasswell, Harold, 114
Lawd, Mah Man's Leavin' (Motley), 177–78, *196-10.14*
Lawrence, Jacob, 136, 145–46n83
Lawson, Clarence, 190–91
Layton, John Turner, 22, 23
Leadbelly (Huddie Ledbetter), 98–99
Leaving Macon, Georgia (Ellison), *196-10.11*
Ledbetter, Huddie (Leadbelly), 98–99
Lee, Russell, 85–88
Lee, S. J., 9
Lee-Smith, Hughie, 186
Légitime Defense, 105, 106
Leopard's Claw, The (Ellis), 7
"Let's Call it Love" (Armstrong), ix–xi
Levee Land (Still), 22
Lewing, Fred W., xxv
Lewis, David Levering, 13
Liberia in the Political Psychology of West Africa (Ellis), 6
Life of Toussaint L'Ouverture, The (Lawrence), 136
Lift Every Voice and Sing (Johnson brothers), 23
Lincoln Jubilee and Exposition, 10
Lionel Hampton's Swing Book, 38
Little Dreaming, A (Johnson), 8

Locke, Alain, 12, 101, 129–30, 170, 180
Lomax, Alan, 98
Long Old Road (Cayton), 116
Lotz, Rainier, 21
Louis, Marva, 154
Love, Hortense, 33
Lyman Wright Art Center, 173
Lynch, John R., 6, 7

MacAlpine, Samuel, 179
MacAustin, Hilary, xxviii, 57–78, 197
Mahlum. J. M., ix–xi
Majors, S. A., 6
Malone, Annie, xxi, 175, 193n61
Man of Sorrows (Perkins), 191, *196-10.32*
Martin, Sallie, 36
Mason, Charlotte, 25
Masters of the Dew, The (Roumain), 105
Maud Martha (Brooks), 92–94
McBride, William, 189, 196n116
McCarthyism, 157, 181. *See also* Cold War
McCluskey, John Jr., xxviii, 96–109, 198–99
McGill, William, 149
McKay, Claude, xviii–xix
McKenzie, Roderick, 113
"Memphis Blues" (Handy), 26
Memphis/Nashville Students, The, 23
Merriam, Charles, 114
Messenger magazine, xix
Metropolitan Funeral Systems Association, xxv
Metropolitan Theater, 13
Micheaux, Oscar Devereau, xxvi, 11
Micheaux Book and Film Company, 11, 169
Middleton, Henry David, 6, 8
Midwest School of Painting of 1910–40, 172
Mississippi Valley Historical Review, 7
Mitchell, Arthur W., xx, 132, 134–36
Mitchell, George S., 115
Modern Monthly, 173
Moon, Bucklin, 120
Moore, W. H. A., 6
Morton, Ferdinand "Jelly Roll," 10, 11, 34
Moss, Lottie Wilson, 169
Moten, Etta, 33
"Mother, The" (Brooks), 89–90
Mother and Child (Catlett), 132, 138, 146n93
Motley, Archibald J. Jr.: biographical information, 176–78; Black Chicago Renaissance role, xxiv; *Chicago Defender* articles, 57;

The University of Illinois Press
is a founding member of the
Association of American University Presses.

Designed by Jim Proefrock
Composed in 10.75/14 Quadraat
with Trade Gothic display
at the University of Illinois Press
Manufactured by Sheridan Books, Inc.

University of Illinois Press
1325 South Oak Street
Champaign, IL 61820-6903
www.press.uillinois.edu